The GUARD AND RESERVE IN THE TOTAL FORCE

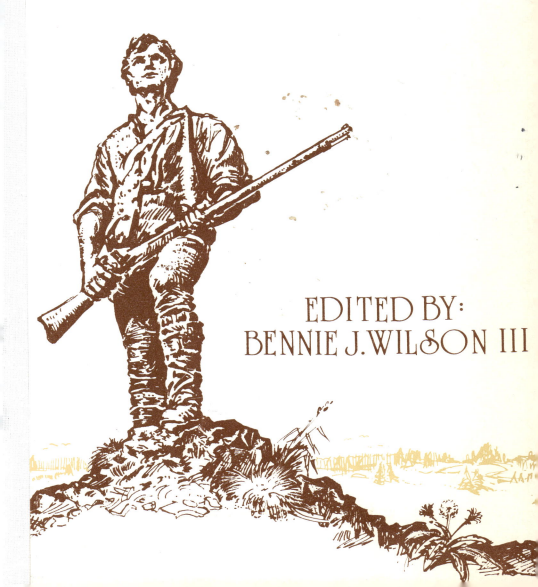

EDITED BY:
BENNIE J. WILSON III

THE GUARD AND RESERVE IN THE TOTAL FORCE

The First Decade
1973 - 1983

The GUARD AND RESERVE IN THE TOTAL FORCE

The First Decade
1973 - 1983

EDITED BY:
BENNIE J. WILSON III

1985

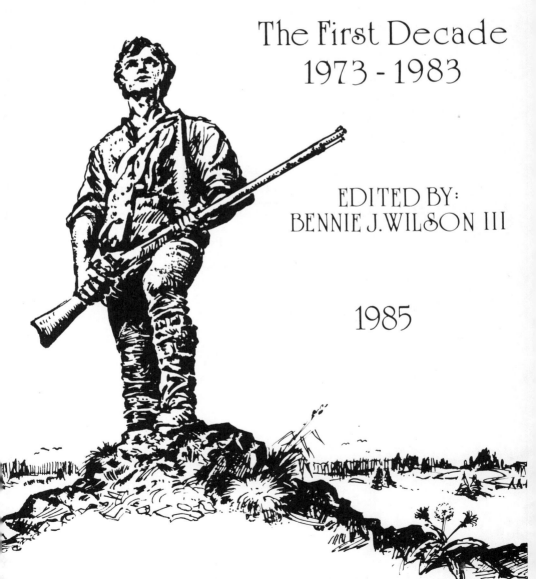

Opinions, conclusions, and recommendations expressed or implied within are solely those of the author, and do not necessarily represent the views of the National Defense University, the Department of Defense, or any other government agency. Cleared for public release; distribution unlimited.

Library of Congress Catalog Card Number: 84-601118.

SSR, Inc., of Washington, DC indexed this book under contract DAHC-32-85-M-1845.

First printing, May 1985.

NDU Press publications are sold by the US Government Printing Office. For ordering information, call (202) 783-3238 or write to: Superintendent of Documents, US Government Printing Office, Washington, DC 20402.

Contents

Figures and Tables

Figures

Tables

Foreword

In 1973, the United States inaugurated the Total Force by increasing the responsibilities of the National Guard and Reserve Forces as partners with the Active Forces in carrying out national security strategy. In the first book to examine how well Guard and Reserve Forces have met this challenge, Colonel Bennie J. Wilson III, US Air Force, has gathered a broad array of expert opinion about the first decade of the Total Force.

Although the idea of citizen-soldiers is as old as the nation itself, today the concept of responsive Guard and Reserve Forces is vital in new ways. Our national strategy of deterrence requires that the organization, training, and equipment modernization of the Guard and Reserve keep pace with improvements in our Regular Forces. As fully integrated members of the Total Force, Guard and Reserve units must continue to attract quality people and high-caliber leadership. Geopolitical conditions and economic constraints no longer permit us to think of the Guard and Reserve as merely forces of last resort; we must recognize them as indispensable to our ability to defend the nation.

Colonel Wilson's book will help us judge how well we are doing. The National Defense University is pleased to publish this wide-ranging anthology on the first decade of the Total Force.

Richard D. Lawrence
Lieutenant General, US Army
President, National Defense
University

Preface

It has been my experience that published materials regarding the National Guard and Reserve components of the total military force of the United States are often viewed with a skeptical, if not jaundiced, eye. My experiences have also shown that such skepticism is very often a well-founded reaction to what I would characterize as a superfluous, sometimes arrogant, and often reactionary approach to telling the Guard and Reserve story. The various Guard and Reserve components are not without some measure of responsibility for this situation, and, I might add, not without some justification.

Furthermore, I submit that a majority of the leaders and the followers in government today, both within and outside the Department of Defense, are largely ignorant of just how much our national security depends upon the men and women of the Guard and Reserve. Ironically, I believe those lacking the most knowledge in this area are those of us referred to as "regulars"—the men and women of the active military forces. This lack of knowledge has led to numerous misrepresentations and misperceptions on the part of active force members and others in government, and also on the part of Guardsmen and Reservists.

What are examples of the misperceptions of some of us outside the Guard and Reserve community? One of them is what I call the "weekend warrior syndrome," the view that it must be fun to play at fighting war during weekends, and even be paid for it, but we really will not be able to depend on the Guard and Reserve during a real war. This view was manifested in the remarks of one of my colleagues, who, while I was discussing with him my desire to prepare this anthology, remarked: "You just know that the Reservist who is a United Airlines pilot will not fly his

F-15 in a hostile environment." Such remarks are not uncommon and are often "supported" with the additional assertion that this is the reason there was no significant call-up of the Guard and Reserve during the Vietnam conflict. This belief, of course, suffers from little appreciation of history regarding Guard and Reserve contributions in *all* conflicts in which our nation has engaged, and lacks any appreciation of the political decisions made during the Vietnam era. More significantly, however, it represents a basic lack of knowledge about Guard and Reserve contributions to current military missions, both peacetime missions and those planned for wartime.

Another misrepresentation is the propensity of many of us to categorize members of the total force as either "part-timers" (Guardsmen and Reservists) or "full-time professionals" (active force members). Dichotomization is a common ruse in categorizing people, places, and things in an overly simplified way. But inventing a dichotomy of groups, the components of which are not mutually exclusive or contradictory, is a non sequitur. It is like categorizing all people as either "males" or "intellectuals." The point is, "part-timers" can also be "full-time professionals."

But what about the other side of the coin; that is, what about the misconceptions, or myths, contributed to by some members of the Guard and Reserve community? One, in my view, is the idea that the Guard and Reserve are equal, in a qualitative sense, to the active force. Think about that for a moment. Does that seem logical even on the face of it? Can a Reserve force—the members of which are not in twenty-four-hour, seven-days-a-week contact with their military environment—be "equal" to a regular military force?

This view is often "supported" by examples of Selected Reserve units that met or exceeded the performance of regular military units during military competitions, exercises, and inspections. Yet these accomplishments are very specific in nature in terms of time and space. Further, the Selected Reserve, while the most important and combat ready part of the Guard and Reserve, is still only a *part* of the total Reserve community. Is the Individual Ready Reserve the qualitative equal of the active force? What about the Standby Reserve? The point here is not to take away from the Reserve community the accomplishments and attributes it richly deserves, but to put these accomplishments and attributes in proper perspective relative to the total force.

A related misperception that I believe the Reserve community has, in part, brought upon itself is reflected in a remark of another colleague, a senior regular officer with impressive academic and professional military credentials and an individual not prone to overstatement. In giving me advice on obtaining articles for this anthology, this officer remarked: "And be careful of articles on the Reserve that are written by

Reservists." Part of the logic of this advice, of course, would admonish me to seek medical advice from someone other than a physician, or to learn mathematics from one unversed in basic arithmetic! Paradoxically, however, I both understood and appreciated the nature of his advice.

During the preparation of this anthology, my research served as an almost painful reminder of something I have long believed—published material on the Guard and Reserve appears primarily in magazines published by private and governmental organizations that are associated with the Guard and Reserve. Such articles, more often than not, simply extol the virtues of the Guard and Reserve community. I call these "gee-whiz" articles. Unfortunately, the education of the total-force community regarding the contributions and shortcomings of the Guard and Reserve within that community often is based solely on these periodicals.

The observations I have just reviewed represent my basic motivation for preparing this anthology and for contributing to it. My goal is to provide the national security community a tool for obtaining an appreciation for, and making an objective evaluation of, the status of the Guard and Reserve as elements of the US military establishment after ten years of total-force thinking. In this way, policymakers, military strategists, and operational specialists will be better equipped to manage *all* military assets within the total force in a coordinated, synchronous way.

I am deeply indebted to Dr. Ed Philbin, Wil Ebel, Jim Gould, and Jim Engelage for writing original pieces specifically for this book. In addition, General Stan Smith updated considerably a previously published article. Their unselfishness in taking time to insure the reader is provided up-to-date discussion on current Reserve issues means more to me than mere words could convey.

There are others, however, without whom this book would have no physical substance or discernable literary style, no matter how profound the material. My heartfelt thanks go to the staff at the National Defense University Research Directorate for assisting me in the preparation of this work. Special thanks go to Fred Kiley, a gentleman and a scholar in the truest sense and a man I am honored to claim as a mentor; to Evelyn Lakes, my editor and a person whose professionalism, charm, and unwavering patience constantly renewed my faith in this project during my "ordeal by pen"; and to Pat Williams, Laura Hall, and Carol Valentine, the editorial assistants who managed to retain their sanity in the face of my scribbled drafts, impatience, and unending meddling, and succeeded, nevertheless, in producing a manuscript of outstanding quality.

My love and appreciation go to my wife, Karen, and to my daughters, Benét and Claressa, for their unswerving loyalty and continued devotion to me—even during my need for solitude in the preparation of this book. Finally, to the two people in my life, without whom both this book and I would not have been possible: thanks Mom, thanks Dad.

Bennie J. Wilson III

The GUARD and RESERVE in the TOTAL FORCE

The First Decade
1973 - 1983

Introduction

The total-force policy was promulgated in 1973 by Secretary of Defense James Schlesinger. It was conceptualized, however, by his predecessor, Melvin Laird, three years earlier. Basically, the total-force policy integrated the National Guard and Reserve with the active force along several dimensions, including force structuring, mobilization planning, and operational evaluation. After ten years under this policy, there is much discussion and variation in viewpoints regarding its success. Most of the discussion revolves around the allocation of scarce resources.

Few would argue the value of the military as an instrument of national power; the same cannot be said regarding the nature of that instrument. In a world of limited resources and competing social, economic, and national security demands, valid arguments exist on all sides concerning how the resource pie should be sliced. There is nothing sinister about this; in fact, it is a natural and even desirable characteristic of the life of a nation-state.

Even with regard to the nature of the military as an instrument of national power, there is *some* general agreement concerning the desired effectiveness of the military establishment. In short, most Americans agree that our military should do what it is designed to do, and do it well. This includes having sufficient numbers of individuals appropriately trained and adequately equipped to respond in a timely way to a likely threat to our national interests. Americans disagree, however, on what is sufficient, adequate, timely, and likely.

It is not the purpose of this book to undertake the impossible task of resolving such disagreements. Rather, the purpose here is to present facts and varying viewpoints so that discussions on the status and characteristics of our total military force do not suffer from misinterpretations of relevant arguments.

Toward this goal, this volume focuses on five major areas that bear directly on the nature—the essence, if you will—of the roles, contributions, and potential of the National Guard and Reserve force within the total military force of the United States. Each of the five parts of the book addresses one of the following topics: history; image and attitudes; manpower; equipment and logistics; and mobilization readiness. This delineation into five discrete parts is merely an expedient to assist the reader in a logical review of the subject; for, in reality, each major topic is an inseparable variable within each of the other subject areas. For example, mobilization readiness is partly a function of equipment and manpower, and all the areas reflect historical considerations. Nevertheless, each major subject area has sufficient structural uniqueness to justify a separate focus of discussion.

Historical Perspective

Part 1 reviews the historical basis of our modern-day militia from colonial times to the present. The purpose of this discussion is to foster an appreciation of the cultural, philosophical, and constitutional background underlying our tradition of citizen-soldiers and forming the basis of our national perception of national defense as a moral responsibility of the individual citizen. Further, the readings in this part provide somewhat of a chronological progression of the people and events that affected the structure of today's Guard and Reserve forces.

In the first chapter, Robert L. Goldich, in his much acclaimed "Historical Continuity in the US Military Reserve System," traces the roots of the US military structure from its English antecedents to the post-World War II period. He asserts convincingly that if policymakers and military manpower analysts are to have a better grasp of the unpredictability, seeming irrationality, and always emotional basis of how a country raises and uses its armed forces, they must have an appreciation of the more tangible disciplines of history, philosophy, and politics. In his view, to do otherwise is, in effect, to reinvent the wheel in our attempts to maintain a healthy and effective military instrument.

This historical review is followed by Jonathan M. House's "John McAuley Palmer and the Reserve Components." In this chapter, House examines the professional thoughts, motivations, and actions of one of the architects of today's total force. The influence of one man, and how he was influenced by other great men, provide the structure for House's presentation of the social, political, and military variables that served as foundations for the rationale of a total force.

Image and Attitudes

Part 2 has the objective of providing the reader an appreciation of how the Guard and Reserve components of the total force, and its members, are perceived by insiders and outsiders emotionally, intellectually, and intuitively. There are also indications of why these perceptions exist and how they affect the viability of the total-force policy as an approach to the organization of our military forces.

In what could be described as the summary chapter regarding the whole range of issues affecting the Guard and Reserve in the total force, at least from the viewpoint of the Reserve community, Edward J. Philbin and James L. Gould provide a comprehensive picture of how the Reserve community views itself and how that community perceives it is viewed by others. It is primarily an elaboration of the recent pronouncement by the Secretary of Defense that Reserve forces can no longer be considered forces in reserve. Philbin and Gould also delineate the image problems the Guard and Reserve have experienced and discuss the need for improving the situation through tangible means.

Next, Gerald D. Ball and Frederick E. Bush, Jr., present the results of their study of "Active Force Perceptions of the Air Reserve." Their attitudinal survey addressed the capability and availability of the Air National Guard and the Air Force Reserve. They report findings of a generally positive attitude toward Air Reserve forces on the part of active Air Force officers, but also some doubts about the Reserve's availability during a real military emergency.

The chapter by James W. Browning II, et al., "The US Reserve System: Attitudes, Perceptions, and Realities," provides an additional basis for evaluating images and perceptions of the entire total-force community regarding the Guard and Reserve. Their study examines a wide range of factors impinging upon the perception issue, including the perceived success of the Air Guard and Reserve components, the shortcomings of the management and organization of the Naval Reserve, equipment problems, and historical, political, and psychological considerations. The chapter concludes with specific recommendations for improving the actual and perceptual problems the Guard and Reserve are experiencing in the total force.

Manpower

Each chapter in Part 3 provides a unique view of the Guard and Reserve portion of the total force from the perspective of manpower and related organizational issues. The lead chapter by Arthur L. Moxon, "US Reserve Forces: The Achilles' Heel of the All-Volunteer Force?" provides an overview of the growing pains the total force has experienced since the end of the military draft. He asserts that "the Reserves and the active forces have been deficient in their manpower proposals because they lack a total-force perspective in assessing their potential effectiveness." Moxon concludes with this observation: "It remains uncertain whether a total force can be achieved in an all-volunteer environment."

W. Stanford Smith takes issue with Moxon's rather pessimistic general evaluation of total-force manpower issues and, instead, addresses these issues relative to the separate military Services. Smith contends that generalizations lead to both overstatements and understatements that obscure the true nature of the manpower advances of the various Guard and Reserve components. He concludes that to fulfill the total-force responsibilities of the Reserves, the Department of Defense must cultivate increased public understanding and support. The Defense Department can best do this, according to Smith, by providing a realistic analysis of the needs, strengths, and shortcomings of the Reserve forces.

In the final chapter in Part 3, Bennie Wilson and James R. Engelage examine the strengths and shortcomings of the pretrained individual manpower resources of the total force. This little recognized, but highly significant, aspect of the total manpower pool has been the subject of many recent DOD and congressional initiatives. The authors discuss these initiatives in detail in an effort to correct many of the misconceptions surrounding the composition and capabilities of such Reserve manpower categories as the Individual Mobilization Augmentee Program, the Individual Ready Reserve, the Standby Reserve, and the Retired Reserve—categories representing a manpower force of almost two million men and women.

Equipment and Logistics

Part 4 is devoted to what many top DOD officials cite as the most significant problem in the total force today—equipment shortages. The seriousness of these shortages and their adverse effects on the combat readiness of the Guard and Reserve were vividly articulated in 1981 by W.D. McGlasson in a series of published articles. One of these articles, "Combat Readiness Suffers," is the lead chapter in Part 4. In it, McGlasson points out numerous examples of the poor state of equipment in the Guard and Reserve.

Largely as a result of the revelations of McGlasson and others, the Department of Defense initiated many studies in an effort to determine the extent of the total-force equipment and logistics problem and to seek solutions. The second chapter in Part 4 is one such study conducted by the Logistics Management Institute on behalf of the Department of Defense. The authors of the report, Edward D. Simms, Jr., Chris C. Demchak, and Joseph R. Wilk, point out in considerable detail the extent to which the active force depends on the logistical support of the Reserve components, both during peacetime and wartime. They conclude that the Reserve components must be fully interoperable with all the equipment, systems, and procedures of the active force; if not, "the total force will not be effective, [and] we will be unable to quickly project and sustain any significant military force."

In "Equipping the Total Force: The Continuing Dialog," Bennie Wilson and Wilfred L. Ebel remind the reader that the shortage of modern equipment in the Reserve is not a new phenomenon. What *is* new is the extent to which these equipment shortages degrade the nation's security. This results from increased dependence of our national security on the Reserve components as compared to the past. The authors assert that although the equipment problem might be alleviated through better distribution and management of spare parts, improved equipment life-cycle management, and more adequate equipment sharing and redistribution policies, the *real* problem is programmed equipment deficiencies.

Mobilization Readiness

Part 5 completes the volume with extensive discussions on the whole range of Guard and Reserve mobilization issues. The first chapter in this Part, "Mobilizing Guard and Reserve Forces," by Bennie Wilson and James J. Gould, describes the mobilization process and how it is designed to function during a military crisis. After a brief review of how the present mobilization process evolved, and a discussion of the governmental agencies involved in the process, the authors delineate the various principles around which mobilization plans are formulated. This is followed by a discussion of current Guard and Reserve mobilization issues.

The following chapter is Kenneth J. Coffey's critical analysis of the ability of the United States to mobilize rapidly and with sufficient ground forces to fulfill its commitment to defend Western Europe. He contends that the advent of the all-volunteer force had paradoxical effects that were at once supportive of and contrary to our ability to maintain our NATO obligations. On the one hand, volunteerism led to the adoption of the total-force policy, which, in turn, led to the upgrading of Guard and Reserve forces. On the other hand, the adoption of the total-force policy shifted a major portion of the Army's warfighting responsibilities to the Reserves, thus, Coffey asserts, weakening the Army's already questionable ability to sustain combat operations in Europe. Coffey offers several suggestions for reconciling the changing US military force structure with our NATO commitments.

The next chapter is another critical analysis of the potential for dysfunction in the mobilization of the Guard and Reserve during military crises. In this analysis, however, Jon P. Bruinooge discusses potential legal impediments to mobilization through such devices as applications for writ of habeas corpus, exemptions for conscientious objectors, breach of enlistment contracts, and other approaches that could effectively delay a timely mobilization. Bruinooge recommends several initiatives to preclude the disruption of this process, including the elimination of the discharge option for in-service conscientious objectors, and legislation that would temporarily suspend the privilege of the writ of habeas corpus.

The final chapter in this volume is Wilfred L. Ebel's candid discussion of where the United States has been and where it is going relative to the burning issue of mobilization readiness. Ebel not only provides a snapshot review of what has been discussed in detail earlier in the volume, but also offers some insights into the mobilization issues of the 1980s and beyond. He concludes with the dictum, "as long as the United States has neither the people nor the equipment to bring its Guard and Reserve units to full wartime capability, the total force cannot be fully ready."

Part 1

Historical Perspective

1
Historical Continuity in the US Military Reserve System

Robert L. Goldich

This chapter sketches the historical continuity of major aspects of the US military structure from its English antecedents to the present and seeks to relate this continuity to post-World War II policy proposals for a major restructuring of the Reserves. It is oriented toward Army Reserves and militia and makes no mention of Naval and Air Reserves; the personnel requirements of the manpower-intensive Army have always determined the overall military manpower policy of the United States. Reserve manpower *per se* is more important for armies than for navies and air forces, whose resources are measured primarily in terms of ships and aircraft and which are equipment-intensive rather than manpower-intensive.

The English Militia Tradition

American military Reserve policies and the attitudes that led to them are outgrowths of England's military tradition of manning its armies with contingents raised locally and commanded by the local nobility or

The author is indebted to Mark M. Lowenthal for his perceptive comments on a first draft of this article.

Originally published in *Armed Forces and Society* 7 (Fall 1980): 88–112, by the Inter-University Seminar on Armed Forces and Society. Reprinted by permission.—ED.

gentry. The nobility's leadership role was a direct result of feudal relationships and responsibilities. Under feudalism, nobles maintained their
own armed forces and theoretically were required to serve in royal military ventures as part of their obligations to the Crown (and to expand
and protect their own political and economic interests as well). The great
nobles' subordinate vassals, themselves nobles, were in turn subject to
service in their own right.[1]

Concurrent with this type of obligatory military service was the idea
of the feudal levy on all freemen for home defense purposes. This was a
militia (more and more bourgeois in nature as medieval gave way to
early modern times) led not so much by great nobles às by lesser members of the nobility and the bourgeois gentry classes. Its purpose was
home defense against invasion. In 1585 at Tilbury, Elizabeth I reviewed
such a militia brought together to resist an invasion of England threatened by the approach of the Spanish Armada. Some liability also existed
for expeditionary service abroad, depending on the temper of the times
(and consequent interpretation of statutes and responsibilities) and the
extent to which manpower was needed.[2] The compulsory service that
was irregularly levied on militia members and others—almost always
members of the lower classes and frequently those not gainfully employed or otherwise indigent—did not vitiate the basic principles of de
facto voluntarism and de jure localism in militia recruiting and service.[3]

These principles had the effect of providing both the "regular" and
"reserve" forces of England with a political and social base and structure
virtually independent of the central government. ("Regular" is used here
in the sense of those in active service for the purpose of prosecuting military ventures of the Crown.) Those forces on active duty in the service of
the Crown could be raised only with the cooperation of local civilian
leaders, who often filled all but the highest military offices as well. Reserve forces—the militia—were commanded, trained, and frequently
armed through the efforts of those same local elites.[4] Those elites in turn
secured their power more through their own status and achievements in
their communities, primarily through ownership of land, than through
the beneficence and patronage of the Crown. In an institutional sense,
therefore, military power flowed from individual communities to the
Crown, rather than from the Crown to the individual communities.

As the course of English military and political history resulted in a
militia whose power was independent of the central government, the
course of English constitutional and social history resulted in a civilian
population largely independent of, and often hostile to, even the constrained and community-based military institutions that had developed
in England. By the latter half of the sixteenth century, England already
had powerful traditions of local autonomy and civil and political liberty
underpinned by the incorporation of these traditions into the Crown's

own attitudes and political instruments. Tudor and early Stuart autocracy was greatly tempered and restrained by pluralistic institutions whose role in English society was not to become fully apparent until the English Civil War and later. England's island status guaranteed security from invasion. Thus the Crown, and the English people, were freed from the pressure of maintaining large standing forces backed up by large militias manned in part by compulsion, enabling the liberal-democratic tradition of voluntarism and localism in military affairs to flourish (although the *principle* of military service as an obligation of citizenship remained).[5] As many historians have noted, these feelings were exacerbated by Cromwell's military dictatorship. However, they were integral to English popular belief and conventional wisdom long before the Commonwealth and Protectorate of 1649–60.[6]

The effects of all this on the militia were mostly undesirable from a technical point of view. There was no structural integration of the militia and standing regular forces, which were first maintained—other than a few royal household troops and guards—after the Restoration, during the reign of Charles II. Recruiting, command, organization, and training (such as it was) were separate. The result of this separation for the militia included inadequate individual and unit training proficiency, incapacity of officers to lead and of men to follow, and casual attitudes toward discipline—among both officers and men—related directly to the popularity of the cause for which the militia were under arms, and the vigor and rigor of any regular commanders present. Particularly pernicious, from the point of view of military efficiency, was the entrusting of military command to civil leaders whose political qualifications included little military training and often involved corruption. Their adjudicatory, "get along by going along" attitudes, so appropriate for a (comparatively) liberal society, usually precluded the toughness and ruthlessness necessary in war, whether on the battlefield or behind a desk.[7]

The military inadequacy of the English militia system is not subject to much dispute. The period from Elizabeth I's ascent to the throne through the Restoration—that is, of first American colonization—is replete with examples of the inability of the English militia system to meet the military demands placed on it, and the enormous waste and inefficiency with which it met those demands. Examples can be drawn from English armies sent to Ireland or the Continent,[8] those raised to meet threats from Scotland,[9] or those assembled to repel possible seaborne invasion.[10] That this system survived and was not supplanted by the beginnings of a standing Army supplemented by a conscription-supported militia system was due mostly to the lack of sustained land-based military threats capable of direct assault on the independence and territorial integrity of the British Isles. Only the large manpower requirements for both standing and militia forces generated by such threats could have created a climate favorable to a reexamination of England's traditional belief in the local organization and the adequacy of mostly voluntary recruitment of military manpower.

The Colonial American Militia Tradition

English colonists came to North America with the concept of local militia recruitment firmly implanted in their minds. The initial military threats they faced, however, were far greater than those of the mother country. The initial increments of colonists were few in number, their ignorance of their new land profound, and their vulnerability to assault from native inhabitants great. The militia concept, actively implemented and rigidly enforced, was healthy and vigorous during the first decades of colonization after 1607. It may be that an effective militia ensured the survival of European colonization in North America during the early years, saving the tiny European communities from total annihilation in the most ferocious (in term of casualties as a percentage of total population) Indian wars in American history.[11]

The American colonial militias were structured in accordance with three major concepts: local recruiting, frequently including the election of officers; short periods of active duty for immediate threats only; and territorial restrictions on service when called to active duty. Militia units were theoretically composed of all able-bodied men in a particular settlement or jurisdiction. But the militia soon divided into two classes: the larger theoretical manpower pool, and those who, out of special interest, capacity, or ability, were able to spend more time on both military training and active duty. Officers were civil leaders occupying positions of trust, responsibility, and authority in the community.

The drastic social and economic consequences of mobilizing the militia—both the entire adult male population and the smaller pool of more vigorous volunteer militia—prevented its use in active service for long periods of time or for purposes other than meeting short-term threats to the immediate welfare of the community, with a few wartime exceptions. The profound attachments of the colonists to their local regions and individual colonies, plus their unwillingness to serve for a long period of time, resulted in considerable territorial restrictions on militia active duty. Militiamen generally were not subject to compulsory service outside their own colony (some colonial militia statutes made exceptions "for stipulated periods in special circumstances") and were frequently fractious when forced to venture far from their own jurisdictions within a colony.[12]

The colonial militia was thus strong during the first part of the seventeenth century because the immediacy of the threat made the militia's organizational shortcomings comparatively unimportant. As the frontier was pushed farther inland, the militia system atrophied in the major population centers of British North America. Compulsory military drill became less and less frequent. It finally became either a dead letter or a mostly social occasion in many settlements far behind the line of contact between white man and Indian. These same population centers were little inclined to provide military or financial assistance to people more frequently threatened on the edge of the westward expansion of European colonization, save when actual emergencies arose.

At the core of this popular attitude—and political leaders' willingness to abide by it—was the instinctive recognition that the Indians could no longer make English colonization as a whole untenable, despite the effects of their depredations on individual settlers and frontier communities. Even King Philip's War of 1675–77, called New England's "worst Indian war of the seventeenth century" by one historian, illustrates this.[13] Although "under the pressure of Indian attack the whole outer line of English settlement had crumbled," [14] the majority of New England colonists were inside this line and were never touched directly by the war. The balance of population shifted permanently and decisively in favor of the colonists very early in the colonial period—probably no later than 1650 and certainly no later than 1675.[15] The favorable population balance was supported by superior technology and organization, plus the comparative unity of the colonies when compared with the Indian tribes.

Similarly, the various Franco-British wars fought in North America during 1689–1763 in no way threatened the survival of British North America, although they brought great suffering to some British frontier settlements. Even the half-hearted and usually bungled colonial and joint expeditions againt Canada pressed the French to the utmost; the superior leadership, strategy, and organization of the French barely sufficing to check the lumbering and inefficient forces of Britian and its colonies. It was the British and their colonies who mounted efforts, no matter how inept, against New France, finally succeeding in 1763; no major French expeditions drove into the heart of British North America by land or assaulted the major cities of the eastern seaboard by sea. In failing to create a standing force and corollary militia system with more potential, therefore, the British colonists were in fact demonstrating a clear, if unconscious, grasp of the extent to which British North America was secure from serious threats to its survival.[16]

A further reason for the decline of the militia system was the colonies' social structure. Transplanted Englishmen and immigrants from other nations felt bound by few of the obligations and traditions of class felt by their predecessors in Britain and the Continent. America rapidly evolved a national social ethos under which the majority of the population defined itself as middle class and maintained the political and social attitudes of members of that class in Britain, regardless of the extent of social and economic stratification in American society. Americans exercised suffrage, enjoyed freedoms and options broader than those found anywhere else in the world, and fortified traditional British concepts of liberty with frontier exuberance and egalitarianism. Accordingly, they appropriated as the rights of all men the choices and privileges regarding military service that had belonged to only a minority of the British population; they lacked a class concept to support noblesse oblige, the basis of much military service performed by the British nobility and gentry.[17] The only obligation to perform military service that remained was necessity, and their strategic situation guaranteed that necessity would arise only infrequently after the mid-seventeenth century—and in the Continental European sense, it would arise hardly at all.

In opting for a military manpower system under which they sacrificed military efficiency (the American militia suffered from the same ills as its English predecessor) and the military security of some of their fellows (those on the edge of the frontier) for what they perceived as general liberty and freedom from unnecessary military coercion and military presence in society, the residents of British North America were blending their English heritage with colonial circumstances. The English heritage gave them belief in autonomous local militias and the adequacy of basically voluntary recruiting for both standing forces and regularly trained Reserves. The colonial circumstances—near absolute security from direct attack for most of the population and a militant egalitarianism—reinforced these traditions in a radical direction. The responsibility of citizens to perform compulsory military service in defense of the homeland remained part of American culture; however, practical strategic circumstances combined with social pressures to the contrary rendered it all but a dead letter. Almost all of these qualities and results, if not the geopolitical conditions, remain part of the American military tradition to the present day.

The Expulsion of European Power, 1775–1815

The legitimacy of the militia system described in the preceding section was enhanced by surviving the colonial wars of 1607–1763; it was burned into the military fiber of the new nation after surviving the tumultuous period from 1775 to 1815. It is instructive to enumerate the military actions of the United States during this latter period. They include the successful waging of the Revolutionary War during 1775–83; the civil disturbances that ultimately led to Shays' Rebellion in 1786–87; the Whiskey Rebellion of 1794; the quasi-war with France in 1798–1800; the War of 1812–15; and during this entire period, Indian wars and campaigns too numerous to list separately. When actual fighting or deployment preparatory to fighting was not taking place, the infant US government had to worry about the British presence in Canada and in the Mississippi and Ohio Valleys; the Spanish presence in the Southwest and Florida; and the Spanish (and briefly French) presence in what became the Louisiana Purchase territories. At the conclusion of the Revolution, we were surrounded by indifferent and often hostile powers. In 1815, we had not altered one iota our steadfast adherence to local militia, voluntary recruiting, and rigid restrictions in terms of time and geography on the militia's active service. We had won the Revolution; the War of 1812 had been a draw tactically, but strategically and geopolitically it had been a victory. There were no European powers left in positions of strategic importance in North America save the British in Canada and an impotent Spain (soon to lose Florida in 1819). We had subdued any Indian tribes east of the Mississippi capable of threatening the major patterns of European westward expansion.[18]

At the beginning of this formative period of American military history, the American militia system was codified in the militia-related clauses of the Constitution in 1789. It is worth quoting at length Russell F. Weigley's interpretive summary of these clauses:

> [Congress] might call the state militias into federal service "to execute the laws of the union, suppress insurrections and repel invasions." It might "provide for organizing, arming, and disciplining the militia, and for governing such part of them as may be employed in the service of the United States. . . . "
>
> [T]he Constitution also divided military power between the federal government and the states. The states retained their historic militias, with authority to appoint their officers and conduct their training (although Congress might prescribe the system under which training was to be conducted, and although no state might keep up troops without the consent of Congress). The militias might be called into federal service only for limited purposes, "to execute the laws of the union, suppress insurrections and repel invasions." The Second Amendment further guaranteed the status on the militia by declaring: "A well-regulated militia being necessary to the security of a free state, the right of the people to keep and bear arms shall not be infringed."
>
> [T]he Constitution . . . retained the dual military system bequeathed to the United States by its history: a citizen soldiery enrolled in the state militias, plus a professional Army of the type represented by the British Army or, more roughly, the Continental Army.[19]

The Militia Act of 1792 (1 Stat. 271, ch. 33; Act of 8 May 1792) provided implementing legislation for these constitutional provisions.

It provided that all free white, physically fit males between 18 and 45 were to be members of the militia; required militiamen to equip themselves with personal weapons and equipment; prescribed tactical units from company to division; stated that no militia members could be called to federal service by the President for more than three months in any one year; and required that all members must be called in "due rotation with every other able-bodied man of the same rank." [20] The strict interpretation of the limits of federal power in training the militia and time and geographical limitations on service ensured that the militia would be poorly disciplined, trained, and organized. The constitutional provision reserving appointment of officers to the states ensured that civil leadership and political connections—rather than any kind of proven military or executive capacity—would remain the primary qualifications for militia-officer status. Inevitably, the universality of militia obligations soon became a dead letter, and organized militia units were those that voluntarily trained and drilled. The volunteer militia units were better than nothing, but fell far short of even strict implementation of the loose provisions of the 1792 Act. [21]

"Judged by standards of military efficiency, the act indeed lacked much." Even if judged by standards of what was realistic in the American political and social context of the 1790s, it may have been all that was possible. [22] The central question, therefore, is how the United States managed to eliminate or neutralize the military threats it faced during 1775–1815 without altering its loosely organized, minimally effective militia system. It is not enough to note the powerful force of traditional Anglo-American military ideas; tradition bows to circumstance, if enough pressure is applied.

The pressure in this case would have been military pressure. That enough of it was not applied—that the Republic was never in enough danger to warrant creation of a more centralized and rigorous militia system—was due to circumstances having little to do with events and ideas within the United States. First was the overwhelming distance between North America and Europe and between points in North America. When all other factors are removed, it is hard to avoid the conclusion that if North America had been as close to Great Britain as the Continent, or North America as small as a European nation, the rebellious colonies (or, in 1812–15, the United States) would have been defeated regardless of domestic opposition within Britain, technological limitations of the era, or European cobelligerents of the Americans. [23]

Second was the preoccupation of Europe in general, and Great Britain in particular, with the wars of the French Revolution and Empire during much of the period in question. Had Great Britain been able to bring its full military power to bear against the United States during the entire War of 1812 instead of only its last few months (after the abdication of Napoleon and defeat of France in April 1814), a drawn conflict could easily have been a lost one. Furthermore, both France and Spain might have been inclined toward more involvement in North American affairs had they not been preoccupied with the wars of 1793–1815.

This lack of military pressure, combined with the above-mentioned traditions and beliefs, made both the Revolutionary War and the War of 1812 experiments with more systematic and compulsory use of the militia feeble indeed. The lack of effective central authority, the resurgence of antimilitary sentiment engendered by the events of 1763–75,[24] and probably the presence of sufficient neutralists, Tories, and practical apathetics prevented the effective imposition of systematic conscription of all available able-bodied men into the militia during the Revolution. Eventually, however, the pressures of war forced most states—at the request of the Continental Congress—to conscript men serving in the already existing state militias into the Continental Army, according to state quotas assigned by Congress, but through conscription machinery administered by the individual states. Response to this system was unenthusiastic and spotty, and it did not solve the never ending recruiting and strength problems of the Continental Army.[25] Revolutionary War conscription, what there was of it, represented a continuation of Anglo-American militia traditions, and their ineffectuality in time of major emergency, in the face of harsh realities, rather than a new and more forceful response to those realities.[26]

During the War of 1812, after the fall of Washington in 1813 and the realization later in that year that the impending defeat of Napoleon would free British forces for use in North America, the Madision administration proposed that the militia—defined by the Act of 1792 as all able-bodied white males ages 18–45—be classified according to age and condition and be subject to conscription for two years. Congress accepted different versions of Madison's legislative proposal, preserving and actually strengthening its basic thrust. It died in a House-Senate conference committee in late 1814, however, when the 1814 campaigning season was over and American forces had successfully muddled through owing to time, space, and luck. Peace, a few weeks later in early 1815, ended consideration of the matter. "The topic of conscription disappeared with it, for half a century." [27]

It is hard not to conclude that the United States barely avoided establishing more rigorous militia mobilization procedures and obligations during 1775–1815. By adopting the Constitution, the United States had certainly shown itself capable of adopting a more rigorous, powerful, and centralized civil authority than that which had existed before in British North America or during the first thirteen years of independence. In addition, although the United States showed little inclination to establish national military institutions before, during, and immediately after the Revolution, this attitude changed drastically during the late 1780s and 1790s. After the conclusion of peace with Great Britain, the Army was reduced to 80 men at one point, although it increased to 700 a day later. By 1803, in response to generally perceived national security requirements, the following military infrastructure had been established:

> [A] chain of forts along the northern and western frontier manned by an Army of 2,500-odd officers and men; frigates, navy yards, and a marine corps; arsenals at Springfield, Massachusetts, and Harpers Ferry, Virginia, as well as storehouses for supplies at various other locations; coast forts along the seaboard from Maine to Georgia; a newly formed military academy at West Point, New York; and a group of agencies in Washington to administer the whole.[28]

The extent to which this miniscule military establishment represented a radical departure from previous American conditions is indicative of North America's isolation from real military threats and of the preceding 180 years of US military history. Its formation represented a major adaptation to the circumstances of national independence by a newly formed nation. It can be posited, therefore, that had the times been more trying, more centralized control of the militia and compulsory military service (active or Reserve, depending on circumstances of peace or war) could very well have been established. The nation's political and military institutions and constitutional interpretations were inchoate enough that military pressure threatening the survival of the country could easily have enshrined compulsory military service in time of war, and a nationally uniform and centrally administered militia, as part of the American military tradition.[29]

By 1815, geographical isolation and a good deal of luck had provided the United States with forty years of history which appeared to validate the continuation of the local militia tradition and of voluntary military service. If the militia system worked in the face of numerous wars, smaller fights, and military-diplomatic conflicts with the great powers of Europe, why change it? The local militia tradition and the reality (if not the philosophy) of voluntarism had survived the formative years of the Republic. For almost a century, that tradition would not be bent even slightly to accommodate changing circumstances.

Strategic Isolation, 1815–98

If a better-organized militia less dependent on local and popular whims would have been useful during 1775–1815, a case can be made that such a militia was almost totally unnecessary during the rest of the nineteenth century. After the War of 1812, the subjugation and pacifica-

tion of major Indian tribes east of the Mississippi removed almost completely the need for military Reserves capable of rapid response to
immediate internal threats.[30] Militia were needed only on the frontier, if
at all; most of the population was well in the rear of the danger zone. The
major Indian tribes west of the Mississippi never seriously threatened settlement of the frontier; the floodtide of westward expansion had grown
too large by the mid-nineteenth century to do anything but overwhelm
the Plains, Northwest, Southwest, and Pacific tribes, regardless of the
hardships inflicted on individual settlers.[31] Furthermore, the regular
Army had grown in size and capacity—regardless of theoretical inade-
quacies in strength, training, and funds—and was much more capable of
assuming Indian policing duties than the tiny pre-1812 force.[32]

European military power either had been expelled or voluntarily
withdrawn. In addition, European ambitions in North America had been
effectively neutralized by 1812, even though the extent of this European
retreat was not yet fully apparent to Europeans, especially the British, at
the time. After 1812 there was increasing accommodation with
Britain/Canada, despite occasional war scares and periods of tension.
This accommodation resulted essentially from a progressive acceptance
by Great Britain of the strategic superiority of the United States on the
North American continent and its periphery. The growing population
and industrial power of the United States made potential American military power very substantial, given the geographical obstacles faced by
European powers in conducting effective military and naval operations
against the United States. The replacement of disunited provinces with a
cohesive central government also removed the basic organizational and
institutional obstacles that had prevented the colonies of British North
America from seizing Canada before and during the Revolution. No
more could Canada survive owing to the internal disunity of its intrinsi-
cally far more powerful southern neighbor.[33] Mexico never posed a real
threat to the United States and was reduced to total impotence by the
war of 1846–48.

In general, therefore, the overwhelmingly favorable effects of geographical isolation on the American strategic situation were less oper-
ative in the nineteenth century than they had been before. Effective
deployment of European expeditionary forces to North America was
still difficult, as the French incursion into Mexico in 1863–67 demonstrated. Shielded by the oceans, American military institutions continued in their established pattern after 1815, interrupted only by two
foreign wars against grossly inferior opponents, campaigns against
neolithic tribes, (the prosecution of which suffered as much from the
lack of real ruthlessness on the part of the government and the Army
as from Indian fighting skills), and one cataclysmic civil war whose
unique nature made it a poor model, in the eyes of the public, for military institutions.[34]

Accordingly, the United States had no pressing need for a large military establishment, including effectively mobilizable Reserves, during the nineteenth century. A quasi-police force to deal with the Indians and a small cadre for border control and retention of military-institutional memory was sufficient. Throughout the nineteenth century, the United States military mobilization system proved fully capable of meeting whatever military requirements the international or domestic situation levied on it—in the Indian wars, in the Mexican War, and in the Spanish-American War. The Civil War, by definition, was almost impossible to plan for in any way. The problems caused by the small size of the nation's regular forces and the ineffectuality and small size of its militia in 1816 would merely have been replaced by new ones had we possesed a larger standing Army and a centrally controlled militia. Both probably would have done little more than provide the Union and Confederacy with greater initial military capacity, as the standing Army disintegrated along regional lines and local militia contingents gave their allegiance to the active Union or Confederate forces, depending on their location.[35]

The United States, therefore, was occasionally hampered in its military efforts throughout the nineteenth century. This was due to the continued existence of the local militia tradition, the practical atrophy of the organized militia by the middle of the century, and the maintenance of an extremely small and voluntarily recruited regular force. It would be difficult to argue that the country was threatened by its lack of effective militia and its voluntary service tradition, or by its small standing force, as could have been argued for the 1775–1815 period. As far as coordinating military policy with geopolitical realities is concerned, the United States would be fortunate if its military policy always accorded so well with its strategic situation.

From 1898 to the Present

The Spanish-American War of 1898 and the colonial acquisitions that it engendered are often cited as providing the impetus for major reforms in US military organization and structure during the first two decades of the twentieth century. Actual impulses for such reform came earlier. During the latter part of the nineteenth century, the growth of American economic power and the increasing efficiency of transportation and communications led military analysts and other observers to realize that the United States would become more involved in international politics whether it chose to or not. Many such analysts and observers, as well as segments of the public, were caught up in prevailing ideologies of imperialism, social Darwinism as a model for international politics, and the racial/ethnic/national superiorities so prevalent among justifications for European military institutions. It was felt that without similar institutions, the United States could not be a true world power.[36]

In social terms,

> The era of insouciant wastefulness, planlessness, and *laissez faire* was about to die, and public reaction to the management of the Spanish War heralded the approach of muckraking and progressivism. A middle class that would soon grow intolerant of the wasting of human lives in slums, tenements, and anthracite fields was already unwilling to tolerate a waste of lives in which its own sons were involved, as they were in the regiments of the [Spanish-American War] volunteer Army.[37]

Specifically, the military reformers wanted to emulate the massive conscription systems and Reserve obligations the Continental European powers had developed, under Prussian tutelage, example, and involuntary pressure, in the post-1817 era. Under these systems, men were drafted into the active Army and involuntarily assigned to a specific Reserve mobilization billet upon release from active duty, with their Reserve training obligations varying according to the needs of the Army. This procedure ensured that the Reserves were filled exclusively by persons with prior active military service. It provided an orderly, manageable flow of trained personnel into the Reserves, generated large numbers of individual Reservists available for use upon mobilization, and fully integrated the active Army with the Reserves. To provide partial or complete American equivalent capabilities, suggestions were made by interested Americans during the pre-World War I period for universal military service and/or training; large-scale and possibly compulsory Reserve officer training of college men; and comprehensive unification of the state militias with the federal armed forces and/or the reduction in the importance of the former through the creation of large, purely federal Reserve forces.[38]

All these proposals came to naught for a variety of reasons. Perhaps the most important was that the United States faced few, if any, threats in North America requiring such massive Army Reserves and a concomitant radical restructuring of the militia system—possibly one with major constitutional problems. In addition, there was no indication before World War I that we would be called upon to deploy a truly massive military force overseas on short notice—one which could not be duly assembled and trained in the usual fashion of volunteerism perhaps supplemented by some form of conscription, all put into effect after the outbreak of war—and no survival-related strategic need at all for such a deployment.

The state militia, by now known as the National Guard, had an independent political and social base and was not about to be totally subsumed into, or completely bypassed by, the federal military structure. Although probably more analogous to the conscript forces raised by the

United States during both world wars, the Civil War state volunteer system had been appropriated by the National Guard as a validation of its organizational premise. The victories of the Spanish-American War (no matter how ineptly won) had done so more recently in the eyes of the Guard. Finally, the country's need for a force capable of suppressing civil disturbances was apparent, given the industrial violence of the late nineteenth and early twentieth centuries; also apparent was the continuing antipathy of the American people toward any kind of domestic paramilitary force maintained exclusively for such purposes.

Finally, the United States had not shed its intense distrust and dislike of a major military presence in American society and of compulsory military service, nor had its satisfaction with the dual state-federal nature of the National Guard abated.[39] The arrival of large numbers of immigrants from European countries where onerous conscription policies had existed reinforced these feelings.

Clearly, however, the colonial acquisitions of the post-1898 era and the greater American involvement in international politics, resulting from the nation's greater industrial potential and improvements in transportation and communications, required a larger and more effective military force and a somewhat more centralized and rigorous Reserve system than that of the pre-1898 Army and militia. Consequently, two decades of intermittent controversy after the Spanish-American War saw a compromise reached between the advocates of a Continental European system and those of the status quo. The basic framework was provided by three statutes enacted by Congress over a seventeen year period: the Dick Act of 1903 (33 Stat. 775, ch. 196; Public Law 33, 57th Congress; Act of 21 January, 1903); the National Defense Act of 1916 (39 Stat. 166, ch. 134; Public Law 85, 64th Congress; Act of 3 June, 1916), and the National Defense Act of 1920 (41 Stat. 759, ch. 227; Public Law 242, 66th Congress; Act of 4 June 1920). In broad terms, the results of these three public laws for the Reserve forces were the following.[40]

- A voluntarily recruited standing force, large in terms of proportion of the total population of the United States but smaller than those of Continental Europe

- The establishment of federal Reserve forces, primarily with support, specialist, and technical missions, while ground combat Reserve forces remained almost wholly the responsibility of the National Guard

- Increased federal control of, involvement in, and financial support for National Guard training, organization, and equipment, and increased Guard liability for federal service, without lessening the state militia responsibilities of the Guard

- Establishment of a Reserve Officers Training Corps program with a stated mission of producing Reserve commissioned officers, but not at all colleges and universities on a completely compulsory basis

When superficialities are stripped away, it can be seen that this system, firmly established by 1920, has survived to the present day. The United States has a large standing Army, but one much smaller than might be expected, given our role in international politics and the military strength of potential adversaries. We have a peacetime all-volunteer force. We have an Army Reserve composed overwhelmingly of combat support and combat service support units, and an Army National Guard composed of combat and front-line combat support units and containing almost all the combat units of brigade size or larger in the Army Reserve Components.[41] We have close federal control over the personnel management, organization, training, and equipment of the National Guard but no diminution of its availability and responsibility for state militia service.

The 1948–73 period of post-World War II "peacetime" conscription in the United States in no way fundamentally changed this system. The draft was superimposed on the traditional militia and volunteer system, not integrated into it. Volunteers continued to be recruited for both the active forces and the Reserves; all Services and components continued to compete in the marketplace for recruits. The draft was used only to make up a deficit of volunteers, rather than to systematically allot national manpower resources according to the needs of the armed forces. Consequently, neither the introduction nor the end of peacetime conscription in the United States materially affected the basic nature of the US Reserve structure.[42]

The system described above retained the same deficiencies that had plagued the militia system, albeit to a lesser degree. Reserve forces remained quantitatively and qualitatively inadequate in terms of training and equipment, particularly in the case of an adequate number of physically fit and professionally competent middle-grade and senior officers.[43] The survival of the system through both world wars was, once again, the result of time and space. Rapid, effective mobilization was not required for national survival and maintenance of US territorial integrity against ground invasion; the country faced no direct threat to the homeland. The United States also sustained light casualties during the initial stages of both world wars, obviating the need for a large pool of trained individual Reservists to replace casualties and support initial force expansion before enough draftees and volunteers could be made available.

The Post–1945 Anomaly in US Reserve Structure

After World War II, for the first time in American history the probability of the immediate engagement of massive US ground forces in the event of general war—a NATO/Warsaw Pact conflict in Europe and adjacent areas—became an integral part of US military doctrine as the result of US forward deployments in Europe. These deployments were deemed necessary to enable US and other NATO forces to defend Western Europe successfully without being forced to escalate to a strategic nuclear exchange. They were to prevent Soviet seizure of Western Europe and consequent dominance of the North Atlantic, with the major threat to North America that such Soviet acquisitions would pose.[44]

A corollary of this scenario is that a major war between NATO and the Warsaw Pact in Europe, the Mediterranean, and the North Atlantic, with ancillary air and naval action worldwide, would require massive and rapid manpower mobilization, principally to meet the Army's requirements for ground combat replacements and force expansion. Without such rapid mobilization, NATO would have insufficient theater-based war-fighting capability to hold Western Europe against a Soviet assault.[45]

There is little doubt that the traditional Continental European conscription-based Reserve system is much more suited to a rapid mobilization than the Anglo-American locally based, voluntarily recruited, and separately managed and structured Reserve system. The European systems have a proven capability of delivering immense numbers of trained Reservists to replacement depots and cadred units under desperate circumstances and at high speed. Thus, for the first time, an apparent contradiction exists between US military policy and the country's fundamental strategic situation. Given this contradiction, one might assume that the United States would have at least seriously considered shifting to some features of a Continental European conscription-based Reserve system, particularly during the 1948–73 period of conscription, and especially at the height of the Cold War.

The underlying reason the United States did not change its military Reserve policies in this manner, or ever come close to doing so, is the general unwillingness of nations to change their military manpower policies overnight just because their geopolitical situation changes, not without actual war to overcome centuries of habit and ingrained prejudices and ideals. This is particularly true in a democracy where interest-group politics and a free exchange of ideas are allowed to take place on national defense issues as well as all others. The United States has survived several major wars with a local militia system based wholly or substantially on voluntary recruitment in peacetime. Consequently, a national belief in a social contract expressed in the form of compulsory peacetime military service has not developed, and the independent political and social base of the Reserves has survived enormous social, economic, and technological change.[46] This might have changed somewhat during the 1775–1815 period or the Civil War, but it did not. The wars of those periods were won or drawn with variations of the militia system, and without a sustained threat in both peace and war requiring more rapid and extensive mobilization than the militia system could provide, any more rigorous Reserve mobilization system probably would have atrophied anyway once the immediate threat that engendered it had abated. It is not, as some have suggested, that the principle of compulsory military service as an obligation of citizenship in time of actual danger has been inoperative in America. Rather, the congenial strategic environment of the United States has enabled Americans to draw a narrow and restrictive definition of what constitutes "actual danger."

In any case, the current US Reserve system is by no means such a complete liability as some of its more extreme critics state. Even if many or most Reserve units cannot mobilize and deploy as quickly as current strategy requires, this does not mean the current Reserve force structure is useless. Reserves are a vital edge as a mobilization cadre for a long-term conflict; any trained military member is more useful than an untrained civilian. Planned short wars often, if not usually, become unplanned long ones. Furthermore, substantial incremental improvements in Reserve responsiveness have been made in recent years, within the broad framework of localism and voluntarism.[47]

In particular, the National Guard as a state militia meets a continuing requirement for powerful armed forces capable of coping with civil disturbance and disorders within the United States, such as the racial conflicts and political demonstrations since the 1950s. Such a force is essential in a geographically large, ethnically and racially diverse, and heavily privately armed country such as the United States. Equally essential, in the eyes of the American people, is avoidance of a national police or paramilitary force maintained solely for keeping domestic peace. Public attitudes favor the use of the National Guard for control of civil disorders; use of the active Army is a much more drastic measure and is viewed as such, although uniforms, procedures, weapons, and organizations are absolutely identical. Despite the transition of the United States from an agrarian ministate to an industrialized superpower, the Guard remains the local militia, and the active Army the force of the central government, as was the case 200 years ago. The blending of the two for national defense purposes, and their continued separation for domestic order purposes, represents a not often recognized triumph of American democracy.

Implications for Policy

This survey of the historical continuity of the US Reserve system from its English medieval roots to the present has illustrated one aspect of the fact that a nation's military manpower system reflects its entire history, culture, and especially its geographical and strategic circumstances.

Economists and quantitative analysis specialists, who dominate the ranks of military manpower analysts and policymakers in the United States (especially within the Department of Defense and particularly in the Office of the Secretary of Defense), repeatedly fail to take this into account in their work and policy proposals. This is especially true in the case of the Reserves, an area of military manpower policy where the military interacts closely with the civilian population and with civilian ideas. Thus, in the name of efficiency, there have been proposals within the past two decades to merge the National Guard and Reserves; [48] insert large numbers of active-duty military personnel into the Reserves as cadres; limit the higher echelons of Reserve leadership to active military officers detailed from the active force for that purpose; and in general reduce or abolish the local, autonomous nature of the Reserve components. [49]

These proposals generally have received short shrift because we have not had to adopt them in the past in order to survive and because the pressure to enact them is not compelling in the national consciousness. Implementing any of them, no matter how desirable from the point of view of technical efficiency and readiness for war, will continue to be possible only on the most painstakingly slow and incremental basis if at all. Yet, it is important to note that change does take place; there is a learning curve for American military policy. The US Reserve components today are infinitely more available for mobilization for war than the militia envisioned by the Act of 1792, or even the National Guard and Reserve troops called up for World War II in 1940–41. Change has taken place—but only to the extent that it has appeared absolutely necessary. It will doubtless continue to occur, as the United States continues to live in a demanding and violent world. To expect change to occur according to the demands of analysts rather than citizens, however, is unrealistic.

In many ways, it appears the United States has come full circle since its formative years, when it was menaced by strong foreign powers. Between 1775 and 1815, we were active participants in international politics, and our security was intimately involved with the general state of international relations. After 1815, a hiatus of almost a century occurred. Since 1898, our destiny and survival have once again become progressively involved with the survival of other nations. It is logical to assume, therefore, that the tensions and dangers of such active involvement in international politics since 1898, have been exerting pressure steadily on the US military Reserve system, driving it away from localism and voluntary recruitment and toward centralization and compulsion. The legislation of 1898–1920 was the first increment of this trend. The draft of 1948–1973 was another. Various administrative and managerial changes in the post-World War II era that have resulted in closer integration of the active armed forces and the Reserve components are a third. As long as these changes are not forced, it is likely they will continue.

It is imperative, therefore, that US military manpower analysts and policymakers keep their eyes on the more intangible disciplines of history, philosophy, and politics as well as the comparatively concrete ones of management, administration, and finance. They would thereby obtain a better grasp of the unpredictability, seeming irrationality, and always emotional roots of how a country raises and uses its armed forces.[50] Until then, numerous administrative measures and legislative proposals from a Pentagon ignorant of history will founder on the rocks of the American military tradition, using up much political capital and energy that policymakers can ill afford to lose.

2
John McAuley Palmer and the Reserve Components
Jonathan M. House

Americans have long believed that the part-time citizen-soldier is the best defender of a free society. They have traditionally seen a standing Army as expensive, undemocratic, poorly motivated and potentially dangerous to the nation that pays it. Only a minority have argued that the training and command of citizen-soldiers should be entrusted to professional officers as the people best equipped to conduct our defense.

The controversy over the merits of a citizen soldiery as opposed to a professional one was particularly strong at the beginning of this century, when the United States began to develop the institutions of a great power. One of the most influential participants in this debate was John McAuley Palmer (1870–1955). In sharp contrast to many other professional soldiers, Palmer believed strongly in the value of Reserve component forces organized, trained, and led by Reserve component officers. This unusual belief enabled Palmer to strongly influence the evolution of a compromise force structure that would include the regular Army, National Guard, and Army Reserve. Whether by conscious design or not,

The author wishes to thank Professor I.B. Holley, Jr., for his assistance on several points in this chapter.

Originally published in *Parameters—Journal of the US Army War College* 12 (September 1980): 11–18. Reprinted by permission.—ED.

our current force structure is in large measure a reflection of Palmer's ideas.

Any assessment of Palmer's role must begin by reviewing the debate in which he participated. This debate arose from the increased colonial and military responsibilities the United States acquired as a result of the Spanish-American War. To meet those responsibilities, many professional soldiers favored a large standing Army and national Reserve force on the model of the system used by the European powers. One version of the European model was a skeleton regular Army that was expansible by mobilizing federal Reservists or volunteers. Such Reservists or volunteers would be placed completely under the control of the regular Army, filling gaps in the regular ranks rather than forming their own units. This expansion concept had existed for centuries and had been pursued in America by as early an advocate as Alexander Hamilton. The bible of the expansible Army in this century, however, is *The Military Policy of the United States*, written in 1878 by Major General Emory Upton and belatedly published in 1903 by Secretary of War Elihu Root.[1]

This concept of a professional Army was bitterly opposed by advocates of America's citizen-soldier tradition. After the Spanish-American War, the Organized Militia units of the states, unofficially called the National Guard, rightly feared the expansible Army as a threat to their continued existence. As a result of his experiences in the Civil War, Emory Upton had seen little or no use for the militia, and in particular had distrusted citizen-soldier units commanded by "amateur" officers. Long after Upton's death in 1881, his disciples criticized the wide differences in organization, equipment, and training of the Guard units from one state to another. More important, most of the War Department General Staff believed that the militia was unsuitable for federal purposes because of the extreme constitutional limitations on that force. In 1912, the Attorney General, George Wickersham, would issue a formal opinion that fully confirmed these limitations. Wickersham would conclude that the power of Congress to use the militia was separate from the power to raise and support armies, and that under the Constitution the militia could only be employed for three purposes: to suppress insurrection, to repel invasion, and to execute the laws of the union. Under these restrictions, Congress could not deploy the militia beyond the borders of the nation except, perhaps, in hot pursuit of an invasion that had been repelled.[2] This strict interpretation of the Constitution would be consistent with a militia refusal to invade Canada during the War of 1812. Against this background, Secretaries of War such as Elihu Root and Henry Stimson sought a deployable, federal Army Reserve to replace the militia.

The National Guard Association attempted to counter these criticisms of the militia. Immediately after the Spanish-American War, the Chairman of the Senate Committee on Military Affairs, Senator Charles

Dick of Ohio, was also president of the National Guard Association. In a compromise with Secretary Root, Dick sponsored the 1903 Militia Act to provide federal equipment and tables of organization, as well as minimum training standards, for all Organized Militia units. The Dick Amendment of 1908 and the Volunteer Act of 1914 tried to circumvent the constitutional question by enabling the Organized Militia to volunteer and serve as deployable federal units in wartime, and by requiring the federal government to accept all such militia volunteers before opening enlistments to the general public.[3] But the War Department General Staff contended that mobilization plans could not be based on uncertain estimates of how many militiamen would volunteer—the country needed a reliable Reserve structure. In 1912, Chief of Staff Leonard Wood tried to implement the expansible Army concept by adding four years of unpaid "furlough" Reserve service to the obligation of regular Army enlistees. Since most regulars reenlisted at the end of their active-duty tours, however, Wood's efforts failed to produce a substantial Reserve.[4]

The education of John McAuley Palmer suggests that he should have been a typical advocate of the expansible Army concept. An 1892 graduate of the US Military Academy, he was one of the first products of Root's training system for General Staff officers at Fort Leavenworth and the Army War College. In all his military schooling, Palmer had been taught Emory Upton's beliefs about the expansible Army and the constitutional limitations of the militia. But Palmer had a respect for citizen-soldiers and a sense of political realities that were rare in the Army of his day. The reason for this was simple: Palmer was the grandson of a successful citizen-soldier and politician of the same name. The elder John McAuley Palmer had been a major general and corps commander of volunteers during the Civil War, and he later was elected Governor of Illinois and then a US senator. Soon after graduating from West Point, the regular Army grandson expounded the Uptonian gospel to the senator. The response was characteristic:

> Well, my boy, I am not an educated military expert as you are, but my worst enemies will admit that I am something of a political expert. And I can assure you, positively, that the American people will never accept that expansible standing Army scheme of yours. If that is your best solution, you had better forget it and work up a second best that will have some chance of getting through Congress.[5]

Under his grandfather's influence, Palmer began to think about ways to develop citizen-soldiers in peacetime, in order to avoid the chaos of mobilization and training in wartime.

It took years for Palmer to work out his final position on the citizen-soldier. Yet by the time he joined the War Department General Staff in

1911 as a captain, Palmer believed strongly in the desirability of some type of Reserve component Army, although he felt stymied by the militia provision of the Constitution. A willingness to take on such obstacles was nevertheless evident in his first major venture into the Reserve component question, the *Report on the Organization of the Land Forces of the United States of 1912*. Palmer wrote his staff study as a member of a committee to review the American defense structure. Secretary of War Stimson was so impressed with it that he had an edited version published as an annex to the secretary's annual report for 1912.

In the study, Palmer reviewed all the usual objections to the use of militia, but then, instead of dismissing militia forces from further consideration in the study, he suggested various means, including federal pay and a federal oath, for incorporating parts of the organized state militia into the national forces.[6] In fact, pending a solution to the constitutional issue, the 1912 report proceeded to plan for a full integration of a "National Guard," whether state or federal, in the mobilization of Army forces. Palmer wrote:

> It is the traditional policy of the United States that the military establishment in time of peace is to be a small regular Army and that the ultimate war force of the Nation is to be a great Army of citizen-soldiers. This fundamental theory of military organization is sound economically and politically.[7]

The force structure would therefore consist of three elements: the regular Army for minor contingencies and to act if necessary before the Reserve components could mobilize; an "Army of national citizen-soldiers" organized into their own peacetime units instead of filling out the skeleton regular Army; and an "Army of volunteers" to be organized and trained under prearranged plans once war began.

In time of war, Palmer insisted, the regular Army would supplement the Guard, rather than vice versa. He was quick to point out, however, that "reliance upon citizen-soldiers is subject to the limitation that they cannot meet a trained enemy until they, too, have been trained."[8] To assist the two nonregular components, Palmer therefore proposed the creation of sixteen geographic districts, each built around sufficient militia units to make up a division, and each staffed with regular Army "instructor inspectors."[9]

Although not all of these ideas originated with Palmer, his report would later provide ammunition to help enact such measures as the National Defense Act of 1916. Additionally, in his first published effort, Palmer had outlined the concept that he, himself, would even later write into law, a concept in which the regular Army would cooperate with Organized Militia units while developing a third line of skeleton, federal Reserve units. This construct differed greatly from that of individual Reservists sought by Emory Upton.

Having published this heretical theory, Captain Palmer was unseated by the provisions of the "Manchu Act" of 1912. This law prohibited General Staff service by any officer who had not spent two of the previous six years on troop duty, and thereby terminated the tours of many staff officers in the nation's capital just as the Manchu Dynasty had recently been terminated in China. In Palmer's case, there was added irony in that he was ordered to rejoin the 15th US Infantry Regiment in northern China!

While Palmer earned his major's leaves in China and the Philippines, his former comrades on the General Staff renewed their efforts to create an expansible Army. In 1915, under the impetus of the Great War in Europe, Secretary of War Lindley Garrison directed the General Staff to produce a concise proposal for national defense on the general lines of Palmer's 1912 *Report*. The result was neither concise nor in accordance with the views expressed by Palmer. After repeating verbatim the 1912 study on defense requirements and the regular Army's missions, the new *Statement of a Proper Military Policy for the United States* (1915) returned to the old arguments on what it badly described as the "Worthlessness of the Militia." This new study advocated instead a 379,000-man Reservist force, the "Continental Army," to be organized, trained, and commanded by regular officers. The militia was relegated to guarding coastlines, canal locks, and arsenals at home.[10]

The *Statement of a Proper Military Policy* caused such controversy that Secretary Garrison ultimately resigned. Despite public interest in "preparedness," a stalemate ensued in Congress, broken only when the US Mexican expedition of 1916 forced the hasty passage of a new law to strengthen both regulars and National Guardsmen. Among other provisions, the National Defense Act of 1916 provided federal drill pay for Guardsmen in specified units, while requiring such personnel to take a dual oath to the state and federal governments.[11] Yet, despite the excellent performance of the Guard on the Mexican border and during World War I, the basic argument between Uptonians and citizen-soldiers was unresolved.

In the interim, Palmer apparently decided that Congress could not or would not solve the problem of constitutionally imposed limitations on the state-operated National Guard. He therefore produced his first piece of writing designed to popularize his ideas. *An Army of the People*, published in early 1916, offered fictional examples of how a federal force of Reservists could ensure the national defense in a nonmilitaristic, inexpensive manner. Even though he temporarily turned his attention away from the state-operated National Guard, Major Palmer was still advocating an Army of volunteer Reservists, not an expansible regular Army.

Entire units were to be trained and commanded by citizen-soldiers, with only minimum technical advice from regular instructor-inspectors.[12] Upon his return to the General Staff in 1916, Palmer became an enthusiastic supporter of the Military Training Camps Association. Although the "Plattsburgh" camps, founded in 1915, eventually developed into officer candidate schools, in their origin they appeared similar in concept to Palmer's own beliefs.

World War I required mobilization on a scale beyond the numbers of the regular Army, the National Guard, and the infant Organized Reserve Corps. Sixteen of the eighteen National Guard divisions and an equal number of conscripted or volunteer National Army divisions were formed along the geographic lines advocated in Palmer's 1912 *Report*. The actual mobilization plan was produced in late 1916 by a staff committee that included Palmer. Many professional soldiers were again impressed with the need for a larger pool of trained Reserve component units to meet the demands of any future war.

Palmer himself went overseas as one of the first staff officers to accompany General Pershing. Palmer worked so hard, first as an assistant chief of staff and then as an instructor in the officer schools established in France, that his health broke down repeatedly. Finally, Pershing (in his own words) "was unwilling that he [Palmer] should return to the grind of staff work and assigned him to duty with troops." [13] It is a strange commentary that Pershing would consider service as an instructor more strenuous than command of a brigade in combat! In any event, Palmer ended the war as a temporary colonel commanding the 58th Infantry Brigade in the 29th ("Blue and Grey") Infantry Division. This group of National Guardsmen only reinforced Palmer's belief in the value of citizen-soldiers. Indeed, the outstanding performance of the National Guard and Organized Reserve in World War I provided strong proof that an expansible Army under regular guidance was unnecessary.

Soon after the armistice, Pershing sent Palmer home to the War Department to assist in planning a postwar military structure. According to Palmer, however, Pershing did not give any specific guidance about this structure, and Palmer never claimed to represent his former commander.[14]

Colonel Palmer arrived home to find that the War Department had already submitted its postwar plans to Congress. Not surprisingly, these plans called once again for an expansible Army. General Peyton March, the wartime Chief of Staff, had sold this idea to Secretary of War Newton Baker and President Woodrow Wilson. The March plan advocated a 509,000-man standing Army that would expand in wartime to more than one million troops by the recall of federal Reservists who had received compulsory military training. The National Guard was not even mentioned in March's proposal.[15]

If General March hoped to gain approval before the lessons of the war were forgotten, he was disappointed. To the usual complaints about the militarism and expense of a standing Army was added all the pent-up wartime dislike of regular officers in general and Peyton March in particular. Both houses of Congress delayed consideration of a permanent defense structure until August 1919. By October of that year, the Senate Committee on Military Affairs had decided to reject the March plan and was casting about for an alternative. The committee's chairman, Senator James W. Wadsworth, Jr., called upon Palmer to testify. Wadsworth later said that Palmer had been suggested as a witness by unidentified junior officers, but he may have been called simply as Chief of the War Plans Branch of the General Staff. In either case, Colonel Palmer had previously heard Senator Wadsworth ask the members of the Military Training Camps Association to give their honest opinions if called to testify. Palmer was more than willing to do the same.[16]

On 9 October 1919, Palmer appeared before a subcommittee chaired by Wadsworth. After expounding on the differences between the "militarism" of a standing Army and the democracy of an Army of citizen Reservists, Palmer roundly denounced the March plan:

> [The] proposal for an organized citizen Army in time of peace is merely a proposal for perfecting a traditional national institution to meet modern requirements which no longer permit extemporization after the outbreak of war. . . .
>
> In my opinion, the War Department bill proposes incomplete preparedness at excessive cost and under forms that are not in harmony with the genius of American institutions.[17]

After two days of such testimony on everything from universal military training to the powers of the Chief of Staff, Palmer seemed to be the indispensable expert the subcommittee needed. Senator Wadsworth asked for and received Palmer's assignment to assist in preparing new legislation. In the process, Secretary of War Baker carefully specified that Palmer did not represent the views of the War Department.[18] Colonel Palmer had clearly jeopardized his military career by his outspoken testimony. By the same token, however, he was now completely free to put his own ideas into the law.

During the next eight months, Palmer and a friend, Colonel John W. Gulick, labored to produce an integrated defense force comprised of the Reserve components and the smallest possible regular Army. At the same time, two other officers who represented the official War Department position advised the House of Representatives Committee on Military Affairs. This difference in advisors only exacerbated the differences between the various bills prepared by March, Wadsworth-Palmer, and the National Guard Association.

Palmer began his work with the opinion, stemming from his service with the 29th Division, that the National Guard should be reorganized as a federal force to end the duality of state and federal requirements.[19] In the course of drafting the new bill, however, he apparently became convinced that the National Guard could function in a dual role. On the other hand, Palmer was much less willing to change his mind on the question of universal military training. Together with March and many other soldiers, he considered some form of mandatory training essential to provide the trained manpower for whatever types of Reserves were finally chosen. Peacetime conscription was so unpopular, however, that the issue threatened to block any changes in defense organization. For that reason, Palmer agreed to sacrifice universal military training to get the Wadsworth bill past the full Senate.

Finally, his plans were again modified in a conference committee of both houses. The House members did not object to Palmer's plans, but they had been empowered to negotiate only an amendment to the 1916 National Defense Act, rather than a completely new law. The resulting Act of 4 June 1920 was a truncated version of Palmer's plan, but it included the essential provisions of that plan. The military establishment was defined as including the regular Army, National Guard, and Organized Reserve. The two Reserve components were to be formed in complete brigades and divisions within nine geographic corps areas. Most important, the detailed force structure was to be determined by a committee composed of equal numbers of regular and Reserve component officers. This provision alone ensured some measure of War Department cooperation in reorganizing the Reserve components after demobilization. Morever, the Civilian Military Training Camps were "regularized" and included in the law, and multiple provisions were introduced to provide regular Army support but not command of Guard units.[20]

Colonel Palmer was able to implement many of his other ideas as a member of the regular/Reserve-component officer board authorized by the 1920 Act. Essentially, this board planned to distribute the regular, Guard, and Reserve forces into the nine corps areas. Each corps was to have a combination of divisions from all three components. A regular Army corps commander, staff, and trainers, or inspectors, were responsible for training these divisions. Although the National Guard belonged to the states in peacetime, this system was intended to provide an even closer integration of the "total force" than that provided by the modern Army Readiness and Mobilization Regions.[21]

Two weaknesses limited the practical effectiveness of these plans. First, as already noted, the entire system depended on voluntary mapower, so that all three components had recruiting difficulties. These difficulties were compounded by a shortage of funds in the budget- and isolation-minded United States between the World Wars. The 1920 Act had authorized approximately 280,000 regular troops, the figure voiced by Palmer in his first day of testimony.[22] Army appropriations, however, never even approached the funding required to support this strength. As a result, the War Department shortchanged Reserve component support and skeletonized the regular divisions in a thoroughly Uptonian manner. Many regular soldiers, notably Major General Douglas MacArthur, gave citizen military training and the Reserve components their full support, but the results were uneven at best. Despite these difficulties, however, the mobilization structure of the World War I Army was preserved for its revival in 1940.

The combination of peacetime economies and his own notoriety stunted John McAuley Palmer's career, although he did retire as a brigadier general in 1926. When Pershing became Chief of Staff in 1921, Palmer requested and received a staff position that would allow him to write articles on national military policy. While working for Pershing, Colonel Palmer served on many advisory boards. In particular, he participated in the deliberations of the Harbord Board of 1921, which reorganized the General Staff to incorporate the lessons learned in France.[23]

After he retired, General Palmer continued his effort to influence public opinion by writing a series of books and articles about the use of the Reserve components. Like all good publicists, he repeated the same line of argument over and over. The only discernible change in his position was that once World War II loomed, he stopped trying to point out the wisdom of maintaining strong volunteer-manned Reserve components and began to reiterate his basic belief in universal military training.

Two of his works bear serious consideration because they illustrate his thought and long-term influence. The first of these, *Statesmanship or War* (1927) is a study of the Swiss militia system and its application to American defense. Here, Palmer described three functions for which the regular Army had to be retained. First, the regulars had to garrison strategic positions, such as Hawaii and the Panama Canal, where no Reservists were available. Second, within the United States a limited number of active-duty divisions had to be maintained at full rather than skeleton strength to handle minor emergencies and sudden deployments. Third, a minimum number of regular soldiers were required to provide administration and assistance for the Reserve components.[24] In the 1980s, Palmer's first function might be redefined to include divisions deployed in Korea and Europe, and his second function might be relabelled as the Army's contingency force within the United States. With these modifications, the clarity of Palmer's foresight is evident.

In the same book, Palmer distinguished between the three components of the Army. As already indicated, the regular Army would be a limited force, with the National Guard providing most of America's defense. In Palmer's view, Army Reserve units would be maintained only as cadres of commissioned and noncommissioned officers. In the event of war, these cadres would then train the volunteers or conscripts who had not entered the Reserve components in peacetime. This idea of a Reserve training cadre, when taken in conjunction with Palmer's belief that the Reserve components should run their own basic training on the Swiss model, is a clear forerunner of the Army Reserve training divisions formed 30 years later.

In 1930, General Palmer published his most serious work, *Washington, Lincoln, Wilson: Three War Statesmen*. While conducting research on the history of the American citizen-soldier, Palmer had discovered "Sentiments on a Peace Establishment," written by George Washington at the end of the Revolutionary War. In that essay, Washington had advocated both a small regular Army on the frontier and a well-trained Reserve divided into a general militia of all citizens and a select, highly organized force of the youngest adult men. Later historians, notably Richard Kohn, have argued that Washington's militia proposal was only a concession to the popular belief in citizen-soldiers. When Palmer first discovered "Sentiments on a Peace Establishment," however, he took it at its face value. Palmer concluded that Washington, Baron von Steuben, and Henry Knox had tried in vain to establish an organized militia similar to the modern National Guard. In *Washington, Lincoln, Wilson*, Palmer traced this militia concept from Washington forward. If nothing else, his study succeeded in damaging Emory Upton's historical case against the militia.[25]

During World War II, the ideas of John McAuley Palmer received an unexpected new lease on life because of Palmer's longtime friendship with the Chief of Staff, General George C. Marshall. The two men had known and corresponded with each other since 1910, when Marshall taught engineering while Palmer was a student at the General Staff College. Marshall later read and critiqued manuscript chapters from *Washington, Lincoln, Wilson*, and on several occasions tried to promote his friend's books and ideas.[26] Of *Statesmanship or War*, Marshall wrote:

> [The] ablest presentation ever put forth by an American Army or naval officer, in form, English, analysis, and conclusions. . . . I am strong for your views of the regular Army and the Citizen Army.[27]

When the United States entered World War II, General Marshall recalled Palmer to active duty to advise on manpower and on postwar defense structure. Palmer used all his well-polished arguments to further the argument for citizen-soldiers and universal military training in War Department Circular No. 347, which Marshall issued on 25 August 1944. The same case was made in a *Saturday Evening Post* article that Palmer wrote to publicize the circular.[28] The November 1945 *War Department Basic Plan for the Post-War Military Establishment* elaborated the circular's concepts into a complete scheme for use of the Reserve components.[29] Americans in 1945 were as tired of conscription as they had been in 1918, however, and universal military training was never really tested.

One can trace a significant continuity of thought from Palmer's 1912 *Report on the Organization of the Land Forces of the United States* through the National Defense Act of 1920 to our planning in World War II. Certainly it should be noted that George C. Marshall had much greater personal experience with the Reserve components than did Palmer, but Palmer's influence, whether through Marshall or by other means, was undeniably seminal.

It is always difficult to assess the effect of ideas, especially if, as in the case of John McAuley Palmer, those ideas were only partially implemented. Still, the fact that Palmer saw even some of his views incorporated into law while his Uptonian peers were thwarted should stand as a commentary on his success and his sense of political realities. Certainly the current total-force structure, with its National Guard and Army Reserve units run by citizen-soldiers and advised by the active Army's Readiness and Mobilization Regions, is too close an approximation of Palmer's ideas to be sheer coincidence.

Part 2

Image and Attitudes

3
The Guard and Reserve: In Pursuit of Full Integration

Edward J. Philbin
James L. Gould

Like almost every democratic nation wishing to maintain adequate military forces for peacetime deterrence and wartime defense, the United States is examining a variety of issues pertaining to the source and use of military manpower. These issues include a shrinking pool of seventeen to nineteen year-old males, conscription versus volunteerism, the role of women in the armed forces, and both the peacetime and wartime roles of Reserve forces* in national defense.

Historically, the combat and support missions assigned America's Guard and Reserve have steadily expanded. It is, therefore, not surprising that the United States is in the forefront of those nations which, challenging parochial and stilted views of the role Reserve forces can and should play, are seeking to derive maximum advantage from the employment of National Guard and other Reserve component assets.

---

*References to "Reserve forces," "Reserve components," and "the Reserve" include the National Guard.

This is an original study written especially for this book. It reflects the authors' insights into and extensive experience with total-force issues at the highest levels of our government. —ED.

This chapter examines America's Guard and Reserve components in some detail. After a brief historical review of the Reserves, it describes the nature of the total-force policy and its effect on America's armed forces. Next there is an examination of the recent extension of the total-force concept by Secretary of Defense Caspar Weinberger. There then follows a discussion of the substantial improvements being made in equipping Reserve forces and a summary of the steps being taken to refine the procedures for mobilizing those forces. This chapter concludes with a discussion of innovations, both in attitudes and management procedures, which can provide additional flexibility for making maximum use of the National Guard and Reserve in their expanded national defense roles.

Toward a Total-Force Policy

At the core of the steady evolution of National Guard and Reserve capabilities, and also of the almost inexorable increase in national defense responsibilities assigned to the Guard and Reserve, lies the citizen-soldier tradition, a tradition inherited from Great Britain. In the US colonial era, citizen-soldiers constituted the only military defense force. These citizen-soldiers organized themselves into a militia, and before the Revolutionary War, the militia provided the primary defense for colonial America. The organized militia eventually became known as the "National Guard," a name inspired by the French hero, the Marquis de Lafayette. In 1824, Lafayette referred to the New York State units constituting his honor guard as the "National Guard," a term derived from his previous command, the Garde Nationale de Paris. The name "National Guard" gained wide acceptance, and was soon adopted throughout the country.

In 1908, another organization of citizen-soldiers emerged. In April of that year, the forerunner of the modern-day Reserve came into being when the Medical Corps Reserve of the United States Army was created. Subsequently, each of the Military Services created a Reserve component. Today, America's Reserve forces comprise two National Guard components—Army and Air—and five Reserve components—the Army, Navy, Air Force, Marine Corps, and Coast Guard.

Until promulgation of the total-force policy in 1973, most military leaders regarded the citizen-soldier as primarily a citizen and only secondarily a soldier. This attitude produced several consequences that limited the contributions the Guard and Reserve were expected to, and, therefore, were allowed to make to national defense.

With few exceptions, members of the active establishment viewed the Guard and Reserve as forces to be held in the background, usually in a subordinate role and assigned secondary missions, until mobilized in the later and more desperate stages of the national military crisis. Because they were considered members of the second team, Guard and Reserve personnel were seldom consulted regarding ways in which Reserve forces could best support national defense programs. In particular, potential peacetime contributions to those programs were never adequately addressed.

Another detrimental consequence was consistent failure to adequately man, equip, and train Reserve forces. Defense dollars were allocated almost exclusively to the active component. The resources made available to the Guard and Reserve were extremely limited and were typically provided begrudgingly, at best. The notion prevailed that every dollar furnished the Reserve forces was a dollar unwisely—and unfairly—denied the active force.

Largely bereft of the equipment needed for training and combat, and with only limited opportunities for systematic training, members of the Guard and Reserve were all too frequently deprecated as "weekend-warriors," lacking dedication, military professionalism, and the commitment to report to duty if mobilized. The most prejudicial variant of this view held Guardsmen and Reservists to be amateurs who, having proven unable to measure up to active duty standards, continued on in a Reserve status to enjoy the best of two worlds: safe and undemanding military duty combined with a lucrative civilian career.

Because the total-force policy has enabled Guardsmen and Reservists to work side-by-side with their active-force colleagues, this bias has been largely replaced by the realization that citizen-soldiers are first-rate military professionals, as well as successful citizens. Where residual biases still exist, they are concentrated among individuals who have not had the opportunity to train or engage in military operations with the Guard and Reserve.

Negative views of Reserve capabilities frequently resulted in poor management and, in some instances, mismanagement. Many ineffectual structures, a few of which are still being eliminated or corrected, were created to manage and fund the Reserve components. Characteristic of those deficient structures was their failure to permit Reservists command authority over Reserve units and to accord Reservists responsible roles in managing the affairs of their components. In addition, opportunities to reform structures and procedures to improve the mobilization and combat readiness of the Guard and Reserve were frequently neglected or deliberately frustrated.

Fortunately, these impediments to effective use of the Guard and Reserves were overbalanced by several factors that led to the development of the total-force policy. That policy heralded a more realistic—and militarily sound—approach to the citizen-soldier equation, one that did not underestimate the significance of soldierly skills.

First, Americans maintained their traditional belief that, in a democracy, the major responsibility for the nation's wartime defense must be assigned to the citizen-soldier. The logical extension of this tradition is obvious: Missions assigned to the Guard and Reserve must keep pace with changes in military strategies and technology.

Second, prudent use of scarce national resources required that defense expenditures be held to the minimum consistent with military security. These two realities led to the demand that citizen-soldiers be permitted to contribute ever more of their civilian and military skills to national defense.

Third, the Congress sustained its commitment to adequately man and equip the Reserve components to carry out their missions, including the policy that they be trained and led by Reserve noncommissioned and commissioned officers.

Fourth, visionary active-component leaders, such as General George C. Marshall, recognized the importance of a combat-ready Guard and Reserve, and supported programs for improving Reserve-component capabilities. In his final World War II report as Army Chief of Staff, General Marshall wrote to the Secretary of War that "probably the most important mission of the regular Army is to provide the knowledge, the expert personnel, and the installations for training the citizen-soldier, upon whom, in my opinion, the future peace of the world largely depends."

Fifth, and perhaps most important, Americans, including leaders in Congress and other parts of government, never lost sight of the fact that when mobilized and committed to battle, citizen-soldiers have repeatedly acquitted themselves with distinction. The United States helped win World War II with 300,000 active-component military personnel and 13,500,000 Guardsmen, Reservists, and converted civilians. In the Korean War, some 900,000 members of the Guard and Reserve were called upon to fight. It should be noted that many Reserve-component personnel volunteered for duty during the Vietnam era. The fact that the Guard and Reserve were not mobilized in large numbers for the Vietnam conflict was a political, not a military, decision made by the President and his administration.

These factors contributed to the foundation of the total-force policy. Building on a concept first articulated by his predecessor, Melvin Laird, Secretary of Defense James Schlesinger promulgated that policy in 1973. The total-force approach to national defense is a fundamental milestone in the continuing evolution of the Guard and Reserve. The policy's basic tenet is that the Guard and Reserve constitute the primary augmentation for the active component in a military emergency. Fully trained, adequately equipped, and combat-ready Guardsmen and Reservists, not conscripts, have thus become the initial source of additional military manpower if US armed forces must deploy and fight.

The total-force policy brought to the fore several implicit features of the nation's defense posture. The most important of these was that the United States cannot successfully mount and sustain a significant military operation without the Guard and Reserve. It also acknowledged that constraints on military budgets require that an increasingly large portion of our military strength reside in the Guard and Reserve—forces that have proven exceptionally cost-effective when compared to active-component alternatives. And it recognized that members of the Guard and Reserve possess professional military skills comparable to those of their active-force counterparts.

Finally, the total-force policy provided a militarily sensible and practical response to a decisive feature of modern warfare: the rapidity with which military crises unfold necessitates that Reserve forces be maintained at combat-effectiveness and mobilization-readiness levels commensurate with those of the active forces they will augment. As a practical consequence, they must be integrated as fully as possible in peacetime with the units and staffs with which they will operate in wartime. Postponing integration of active and Reserve forces until a military crisis develops denies the nation deterrent and warfighting capabilities essential to its defense.

The total-force policy brought the National Guard and the other Reserve components into full partnership with active components for the purpose of deterring war, providing defense, and waging war. Full partnership meant a concerted effort to organize, train, equip, and employ both Reserve and active military assets in the most effective overall manner. Full partnership meant general equivalency for active and Reserve forces in training methods, performance standards, and readiness. For Guardsmen and Reservists, the total-force policy provided unprecedented opportunities for contributing to the national defense, particularly during peacetime.

Much more remains to be done, particularly in the equipment arena, if the Guard and Reserve are to be fully mission-capable. Nonetheless, in 1984, after a decade of strengthening the Guard and Reserve, there can be no doubt that the Reserve components are full and combat-ready partners on the nation's defense team.

Tangible Results of Total-Force Involvement

The total-force policy transformed the Guard and Reserve into one of the world's most powerful military forces. That force comprises military professionals, both men and women, whose strong sentiments of duty are reinforced by the self-confidence born of demonstrated ability.

It constitutes a significant portion of the total-force capabilities of all our combat arms and support units, and of key military staffs.

In the Army, the Guard and Reserve provide 38 percent of the divisional forces, 67 percent of the tactical support forces, and 100 percent of the training divisions and brigades. The Army Reserve contributes a critical number of engineer, ordinance, medical, transportation and other units to the US Central Command (CENTCOM), one of the nation's most deployment- and combat-ready fighting commands. Military plans provide that one-half of the deployable Army Reserve units will be committed within thirty days of mobilization, and that an additional 37 percent will deploy in the thirty days that follow. Practically all will be deployed within ninety days of mobilization.

Fourteen percent of the carrier air wings and 60 percent of the Navy's Military Sealift Command personnel are in the Naval Reserve. The air wings are equipped with fighter, attack, and reconnaissance aircraft. One of these wings is ready for carrier deployment at all times. Naval Reserve P-3 aircraft fly daily maritime patrol missions with their active-duty counterparts. In addition, the Marine Corps Reserve provides 25 percent of the Marine Corps' land and air capabilities, Aircraft of the Marine Corps Reserve routinely perform refueling missions for tactical squadrons flying across both the Atlantic and Pacific.

The Air Force Reserve provides about 50 percent of the strategic airlift crews for the C-141 and C-5 aircraft, and provides 40 percent of the maintenance capability for those aircraft. The Air Force Reserve will also furnish 50 percent of the crews for the new KC-10 aerial refueling tankers. In addition to this formidable mobilization force, a great number of daily missions are performed on a regular basis by units and individuals of the Air Guard and Reserve. For example, one-half of the air defense interceptor alert sites in the United States, and 65 percent of the Air Force air defense interceptors, are manned by crews of the Air National Guard. The Air National Guard is solely responsible for the air defense of the Hawaiian Islands. Additionally, the Air Force Reserve provides 70 percent of America's continental hurricane hunting capability. And, on a daily basis, Air Force Reserve and Air Guard crews are constantly on alert to provide emergency rescue service.

The Coast Guard Reserve would provide about one-third of the total Coast Guard manpower during a full mobilization. Approximately 80 percent of all Coast Guard Reservists hold mobilization orders for port safety and security duties, representing 90 percent of the Coast Guard's total available force in this critical mission area.

Individual Reservists also support daily operations of the active component. For example, members of the Air Force Intelligence Service, who are Individual Mobilization Augmentees (IMA), routinely staff Intelligence Indications and Warning Centers throughout the Air Force, including those in the Pentagon and at the Strategic Air Command.

In the event of full military reinforcement of NATO, approximately 50 percent of all Air Force augmentation would be Guard and Reserve. Similarly, one-third of the combat and two-thirds of the combat-support units in Europe would be provided by the Army Guard and Reserve. Between 10 and 20 percent of all Naval and Marine forces would be drawn from the Reserve.

The total-force policy, coupled with greatly expanded mission responsibilities, imposes very demanding requirements on Guardsmen and Reservists: Even though they are volunteers who serve during peacetime on a part-time basis, members of the Guard and Reserve must be prepared for immediate mobilization and rapid deployment into combat. This requires citizen-soldiers to achieve and maintain the high state of professional, mental, and physical readiness characteristic of active duty personnel.

The best way to maintain this preparedness is through integration of Reserve and active components in all aspects of military training and employment. This integration is referred to as the "One Army, One Navy, and One Air Force Concept," depending on the Service involved. The objective is to make Guard and Reserve forces virtually indistinguishable from the active components. This is being accomplished in a number of ways: First, and most important, is the emphasis within both the Reserve and active components on the military professionalism of Guard and Reserve personnel. The demands on, and contributions of, Guardsmen and Reservists are so extensive, and their performance has been so effective, that even though they serve part-time, they can no longer be regarded as anything but military professionals in the fullest sense of that term. Recognition of this professionalism has reinforced military elan and has contributed to a high state of combat readiness. And, it has fostered greater understanding and respect for Reserve forces on the part of active component personnel.

Second, the mobilization and mission readiness of the Guard and Reserve have been vastly improved through more rigorous and realistic field training, more frequent mobilization exercises, and testing to active-force performance standards. Active-component advisors are incorporated into the structure of an increasing number of Guard and Reserve units, thereby fully integrating active and Reserve personnel within the same military organization. A vital component of this integration is pre-assignment of Guard and Reserve units in peacetime to the active-force units with which they will fight in wartime.

No Longer Forces in Reserve

The Secretary of Defense recently acknowledged the evolution that has occurred under the total-force policy. In greeting the Congress of the Interallied Confederation of Reserve Officers in August 1982, Secretary Weinberger developed a theme that will stand as a major milestone in that evolution:

> We can no longer consider Reserve forces as merely forces in reserve. . . . Instead, they have to be an integral part of the total force, both within the United States and within NATO. They have to be, and in fact are, a blending of the professionalism of the full-time soldier with the professionalism of the citizen-soldier. Only in that way can we achieve the military strength that is necessary to defend our freedom.

This policy is a logical and timely extension of total-force thinking. It recognizes that the citizen is not secondarily a soldier, and reinforces the notion that citizen-soldiers should contribute an increasing measure of their civilian and military skills to the nation's peacetime and wartime defense.

Like all other major advances in military planning and operations, this expansion of total-force policy must be built on a sound theoretical foundation. Such a foundation must take into account several vivid military realities. First, constraints on the dollars available for defense require the nation to maximize contributions which can be derived from all sources of military manpower, both active and Reserve. Consequently, organizational structures and funding procedures that compel active and Reserve components to compete for the same scarce defense dollar can no longer be tolerated. Instead, more effective ways must be found for allocating resources to active and Reserve forces so both can contribute their full range of military capabilities.

Second, it is essential to expand upon the integration of active and Reserve forces that the total-force policy has begun. The total-force policy made it unacceptable to keep Reserve forces separate and apart from the active forces until both faced hostile fire. Its expansion, under the concept which regards Reserve forces as not merely forces in reserve, requires developing more innovative ways in which active and Reserve components can work together in peacetime. Consistent with sound fiscal and military planning, joint accomplishment of the widest possible array of missions, management tasks, and daily operations must become the routine way of doing business in the Department of Defense.

Third, the high-technology component of modern defense operations requires that we draw heavily on the talents of seasoned operational, technical, managerial, and analytical experts. Such experts are found not only in the active component, but in the Guard and Reserve as well. Using state-of-the-art tools and techniques, they also possess many of the skills required to manage effectively the complex operations of an increasingly complex organization like the Defense Department.

Several consequences flow from these realities. Guard and Reserve forces must be so well trained and equipped that citizen-soldiers are distinguishable from their active-force comrades solely by the fact that they serve part-time when not mobilized. As we have seen, much of that service encompasses daily military operations and results in extensive cost-savings. The Reserve-component aircrew members who routinely fly strategic airlift missions provide an essential capability at minimal cost, as their pay and entitlements are limited to the duration of the mission. The Reserve officer providing consultant support in a special field, such as operations research, does so at significantly less cost than a consultant retained from a commercial firm. Effective use of defense dollars requires that in both operations and staff duties, the potential for achieving cost savings be fully realized.

Equipment: The Continuing Total Force Deficiency

Recognition that Reserve forces are not merely forces in reserve should help overcome a major deficiency limiting the utility of Reserve forces as a source of defense manpower; namely, equipment obsolescence and shortfalls. Guard and Reserve forces that are not adequately equipped and that cannot be sustained in combat, can be neither credible nor effective in executing their wartime missions. Moreover, such forces can contribute only marginally to deterrence or to the military power created and projected by preparedness.

Although personnel shortfalls in the Guard and Reserve, principally in ground forces, hamper mobilization readiness, they are far less inimical to combat effectiveness than equipment shortages. Even in an extreme military emergency, manpower shortages can be mitigated far more quickly than can equipment shortages. In a crisis, however, an aircraft, a missile, or a tank not already in the hands of the troops cannot be promptly arrayed against a foe. It must be produced, and that requires time, the commodity least available in a military crisis.

The equipment problem has several facets. A particularly dangerous one is the impending obsolescence of entire generations and models of weapons systems. Because they have too long operated with outmoded equipment handed down by active units, many Guard and Reserve units find themselves with outdated weapons. This equipment is frequently nondeployable due to age and nonsustainable in combat due to replacement part shortages. It is also operationally incompatible with the more modern equipment possessed by the active force.

It is difficult to envision how incompatably equipped active and Reserve forces can acquit themselves well in battle. As for the Guard and Reserve, equipment problems create other deficiencies in their wake. They degrade training, cripple readiness and combat effectiveness, and increase maintenance costs. They undermine recruitment and retention. And, in the most extreme of circumstances, they subject Guardsmen and Reservists to unwarranted safety hazards—in training as well as in combat.

The strategy for solving equipment problems must be based on the integrated approach inherent in the total-force policy. Equipment distribution must reflect deployment schedules and missions assigned both active and Reserve units, so that forces which deploy and fight first are equipped first, irrespective of component. Procurement and distribution practices that force active and Reserve components to compete for equipment are unacceptable. On 21 June 1982, in a memorandum to the Chairman of the Joint Chiefs of Staff and to the Service Chiefs, Secretary Weinberger provided explicit direction on this issue when he wrote:

> Active and Reserve units deploying at the same time should have equal claim on modern equipment inventories. . . . Our defense program [must] produce compatible, responsible and sustainable combat, combat support, and combat service support forces throughout the active, Guard and Reserve force, and support structure.

Refining the Process for Mobilization

Recognition that Reserve forces are no longer merely forces in reserve adds further impetus to the work being done within the Defense Department to improve the process for bringing Reserve forces onto active duty. This is the process of mobilization.

To place Reserve-component mobilization in proper analytical context, it must be recognized that the transition from peacetime training in inactive-duty status to military employment in active-duty status involves numerous, extremely complex procedures. The procedures encompass many triggering events, decision points, execution actions, and organizational interfaces and responses. The complexity of mobilization is compounded by the fact that this extensive array of activities takes place within and among organizations which are themselves structurally complex, namely the Military Departments, the Joint Staff, and the Office of the Secretary of Defense. Moreover, mobilization of Reserve forces is not an autonomous activity. Rather, it is linked to the nation's overall mobilization effort, which is itself an option within the much broader context of crisis management.

It is the complexity of mobilization which is at once its most fundamental characteristic and the source of the most vexing challenges confronting mobilization planners. The complex features of Reserve-component mobilization have prompted research which, when completed, will portray the entire execution process in a reasonably comprehensive manner. It will provide a base line against which possible mobilization execution deficiencies can be identified, diagnosed, and remedied. Finally, it will provide a standard for ensuring that mobilization execution policies and procedures are complementary and mutually supportive, rather than contradictory and the source of systemic dysfunctions.

Complementary work is also underway on what can be termed the resource-mobilization equation. Presently, it is difficult to determine precisely how the expenditure, withdrawal, or denial of resources affect Reserve-component mobilization readiness and combat capabilities. Associated with this is the fact that planners and resource allocators cannot easily identify specific objectives, the pursuit of which can enhance military readiness and employment capabilities. The programs to which resource inputs are made can be identified; however, what those inputs purchase in terms of increases in Reserve-component readiness is sometimes not easily determinable.

The evolving techniques and tools will help determine how allocation of scarce dollars—which translate into human and other resources—can purchase maximum mobilization readiness and combat capabilities. They will also disclose how failure to allocate resources, or withdrawal of those already provided, degrade the capability to mobilize and employ the force. The information such tools generate will enable planners and budget officials to calculate relationships between dollars and mobilization enhancements, and therefore make optimal decisions regarding specific improvement objectives and alternatives. This adds a further dimension of objectivity to the resource allocation process, reducing possible competition for scarce resources among active and Reserve components.

This framework for more effectively relating resource investments to specific readiness improvements can buttress total-force approaches to the weapons and logistical system acquisition process, and perhaps even to weapons design. Weapons program managers have tended to overlook Reserve-component requirements during system acquisitions. These requirements may involve entire systems, operator or maintenance training, and training tools. Planning to meet these requirements in the acquisition cycle minimizes the risk that Guardsmen and Reservists, who serve in peacetime on a part-time basis, will not have adequate opportunities to acquire and maintain the expertise needed to operate new and complex systems.

The Department's remedial work in the mobilization arena has two important facets. First, Guard and Reserve mobilization is viewed increasingly within a systems context. This will result in development of a general systems theory of mobilization as a conceptual base for improving mobilization procedures and planning. Where the evolving interpretational model reveals further refinements to be necessary, existing procedures can be changed so they become part of an integrated mobilization system. Second, a more disciplined approach to mobilization has been achieved. A mobilization concept and process will thus emerge which provides sufficient flexibility to accommodate essential Service or mission-unique requirements, while assuring sufficient standardization to constitute an integrated whole.

Flexibility Through Innovative Thinking

The advances achieved by defense officials in equipping the Reserve forces, and in improving the process by which they are mobilized, have set the stage for making better use of Reserve assets. The responsibility for innovation rests heavily with active-force staff organizations and military commands. They establish procedures whereby the Department of Defense manages its daily business and its manpower resources. Those procedures, in turn, largely shape the options available to Guardsmen and Reservists for contributing their expertise to defense operations. A review of those procedures suggests that by making selected modifications, or by extending applications of existing practices, citizen-soldiers can more effectively support America's defense programs.

There are numerous options under study or actually being used. From the perspective of administrative procedures, greater flexibility in adjusting Reserve training requirements to the civilian career demands of Guardsmen and Reservists is a promising option. The overwhelming majority of these individuals can participate in accordance with standard training requirements. These typically comprise either a two-week tour coupled with six or twelve drill (training) weekends. However, some Reservists, such as physicians and highly specialized technical consultants, cannot readily meet these requirements. Procedures that permit, in certain critically essential skills, a lower or more flexible rate of participation will enable such individuals to remain in the Reserve force.

Individual Mobilization Augmentees (IMA), and selected unit personnel as well, can support a wide variety of pre-conflict missions and functions while in voluntary duty status. They can augment intelligence indications and warning and crisis management center operations, assist planning staffs to review and update mobilization and operations plans, and work with logistics planners whose workloads will increase significantly as premobilization readiness measures are taken in vital support areas.

Although missions must be carefully chosen, Guard and Reserve unit members can make important contributions to enhancing force readiness during periods of rising tension. They can, for example, perform accelerated maintenance, make last-minute reviews of transportation and deployment plans, and ready the personnel system to support rapid mobilization. Reserve forces can also assist the active component in enhancing its readiness. Typical are activities which prepare active installations for a rapid influx of mobilized Guard and Reserve units, or which enable active units to expedite deployment preparations. These employment options have application to both active and Reserve units and organizations. They can help defuse or stabilize a crisis in its early stage. And, most important, they can serve the dual purpose of helping to contain the crisis while laying the foundation for mobilization.

Other opportunities exist for expanding current practices so as to make better use of Reserve assets. Following the highly successful precedent established by the Air Force Reserve Associate Program, both staffs and units could develop a wider array of opportunities for Reservists to support daily staff work and mission operations. The activities identified should be of significance to mission accomplishment, draw fully on the individual's civilian and military expertise, and, in most instances, be related to his or her wartime job functions.

Considerable flexibility exists to structure tasks and work schedules so they accommodate active force business hours and citizen-soldier job responsibilities. In addition to annual active duty, an individual might also work with the active force four or eight hours during a normal work day since Reserve pay is based on four-hour increments. Another option available to the active force is to organize work schedules so that Guard and Reserve personnel can perform weekend training in active-force organizations that do not normally operate during weekends.

Enduring advantages would ensue from such innovative working arrangements: Reservists would obtain broader insight into ways of supporting defense programs; permanent staff and Reservists would establish collaborative professional and cordial personal relationships, thereby promoting the "One Force" concept, mentally as well as materially; defense officials would become acquainted with many highly qualified Reservists able to provide specialized support through active-duty tours, weekend work, and four- to eight-hour duty increments during normal work days; and both civilian employees and active-component officers would develop a better understanding of the extensive and varied professional talent available in the Reserve community.

The non-paid, voluntary training units existing in some of the Reserve components constitute another example of a resource that could be more productively used to the mutual advantage of both the active force and participating Reservists. Composed of citizen-soldiers who are highly seasoned civilian and military professionals, these units can produce staff studies, analyses, and reports which contribute to the Department's work. More flexible active-force management procedures, relatively inexpensive and easy to implement, could capitalize on this valuable resource.

In the total-force environment, and at a time when the Defense Department is placing more stress on cost-savings, it may be preferable to organize qualified Reservists, for whom staff or unit billets are not available, into specialized task forces that work on priority projects requiring their unique expertise. Some of these ideas may ultimately prove impractical. But given the nation's pressing defense needs, the requirement to meet those needs in a cost-effective manner, and the availability of talent residing in the Guard and Reserve, innovative approaches merit careful examination.

In addition to innovations that could be introduced by the active force to better utilize citizen-soldiers, ample opportunities for innovation also exist within the Reserve components. Indeed, if history is a reliable indicator, Guardsmen and Reservists will spearhead the effort to expand the ways in which they support active-force operations. Guardsmen and Reservists have traditionally played decisive roles in overcoming the prejudice, indifference, and restrictive management practices which for so long isolated them from the active force and prevented them from fully supporting active-force operations. They must continue to exercise leadership if the Defense Department is to make still better use of their talents.

The necessary leadership has several facets. It includes more effectively publicizing the fact that the work of the Guard and Reserve forces goes well beyond training. Training is, of course, essential for the acquisition, maintenance, and updating of military skills. But once trained, the citizen-soldier can—and does—apply professional civilian and military talents to accomplishing the Defense Department's daily missions.

Leadership also implies placing into proper perspective the contributions which can be realistically expected of professionals who serve on a part-time basis. Willingness to contribute more extensively to the nation's defense efforts is widespread among Guardsmen and Reservists. This desire to serve, however, must be carefully balanced against the time and availability constraints imposed by the part-time nature of Reserve duty. Some Guardsmen and Reservists have civilian careers which facilitate duty beyond that called for by standard participation requirements; many others cannot exceed these norms owing to the demands of their civilian careers. These limitations must be described in a forthright manner even as new ways for working with the active force are being developed. Not to do so would be misleading. It could also lead to situations in which Reserve forces accept missions which are so demanding that they undermine the cost-savings inherent in part-time duty.

Finally, leadership requires that the Reserve community devise new and more innovative ways to support the active component. For example, Guardsmen and Reservists who are foreign area specialists could sponsor seminars on the politico-military affairs of nations or regions of special interest to defense officials. Such seminars could be held at universities or at large military installations such as the Pentagon. They could be held on a one-time or continuing basis. And, they could be timed to coincide with recurring staff actions, such as the preparation of intelligence assessments, for which the subject matter has special applicability.

Reservists who are research scholars have the opportunity to pursue topics which meet the dual criteria of scholarly relevance and utility to the defense community. Manpower management, financial analysis, organizational and human resource development, science and engineering, area studies, medicine, and economics are but a few of the many fields in which scholars and defense officials share overlapping concerns.

The Guardsmen employed as a senior executive in a plant producing military equipment, such as missiles, could, with relatively little difficulty, develop orientation programs for active-force counterparts whose job performance would be enhanced by greater familiarity with missile production techniques. Missile crew members are obvious candidates for visits to missile production plants. But so are intelligence officers who monitor missile deployments of potentially hostile forces.

Many Reserve force members are teachers and university professors who can occasionally devote an entire summer or sabbatical leave to an extended tour of active duty, adequate time to make a significant contribution to important defense projects.

These are but a few examples of how the Reserve components, like their active-force counterparts, can make better use of Guard and Reserve personnel during this challenging period. The total-force policy, and the milestone in its evolution marked by the concept that Reserve forces are not merely forces in reserve, provide the opportunity to achieve optimum employment of Reserve forces during peacetime, during periods of military tension, and in wartime. The advances being made in equipping the total force, coupled with sustained improvements in mobilization plans and procedures, reinforce those opportunities. With full acceptance of the "One Force" concept, and skillful innovation within both the active and Reserve components, the Guard and Reserve can and will expand their contribution in support of national defense.

4

Active Force Perceptions
of the Air Reserve

Gerald D. Ball
Frederick E. Bush, Jr.

> The only probable means of preventing hostility for any length of time,
> from being exempted from the consequent calamities of war, is to put the
> National Militia in such a condition that they may appear respectable in
> the eyes of our friends and formidable to those who would otherwise be-
> come our enemies.[1]
> —George Washington

Belief in the citizen-soldier dates to the earliest days of nationhood. Although the concept served our country well through World War II, the
end of that war brought a new era. Technology ended the protection that
geography had afforded the nation since the 1700s. To meet the unprecedented demands of the Cold War, America opted for a large standing
peacetime military force. A major part of that standing force was a separate Air Force.

Ironically, even at a time when the nation was emphasizing air power, the Air National Guard and the Air Force Reserve entered a period
when national strategy all but excluded them from a meaningful defense
role. Air Reserve forces played only a follow-on role, augmenting an active force that was theoretically prepared to meet all immediate threats.

Originally published in *Defense Management Journal* 17 (Third Quarter
1981): 28–33. Reprinted by permission. —ED.

Unfortunately, the Air Reserve forces were also poorly trained, supplied with obsolete equipment, and assigned no real mission, contributing to the weekend warrior image that, to some extent, persists to this day.[2]

Active Air Force perceptions of Air Reserve forces are not just matters of academic interest. In the past decade, many factors, including economics, have spurred defense officials to integrate the Reserve components into the active force structure. Under the total-force concept, millions of dollars have been spent to improve the equipment and training of the Air Reserve forces. And by almost every static measure of readiness, the Air National Guard and the Air Force Reserve possess significant combat capability. Yet, inaccurate perceptions of the Air Reserve forces by the active force could mistakenly restrict the role played by those forces in future conflicts. To the extent the active force incorrectly evaluates the wartime value of Reserve resources, those resources might be misallocated, to the detriment of the nation's defense.

This chapter examines survey responses of two groups of actual or prospective Air Force leaders about the readiness of the Air Reserve force. Career line officers who attended the Air War College or the Air Command and Staff College in the resident classes of 1980 were asked to agree or disagree with eleven survey items directly related to Reserve readiness. Each officer was asked to use any available information, including intuition.

Survey items related both to the capability and the availability of Air Reserve forces. The first five items measured perceptions of capability. This discussion examines the basis for each statement and analyzes Air War College perceptions of its validity.

Air Reserve Capability

The first survey item dealing with Air Reserve capability stated:

Limited maintenance capability hinders the assignment of advanced aircraft to Air Reserve force units.

This statement was developed from major Rand Corporation research reports completed in 1967 [3] and 1977.[4] A person agreeing with this statement would probably do so because of concern that a part-time force cannot attain the proficiency required to maintain today's complex weapons systems. A person disagreeing might be aware of the work that full-time Air Reserve technicians do in support of Air Reserve force units and might also be aware that Reserve personnel frequently have prior active Air Force experience in their maintenance specialties that compensate somewhat for the part-time nature of Reserve participation. In fact, the 1977 Rand study found a maintenance-experience advantage for Reserve units over comparably equipped active Air Force units.

Of the 387 respondents, 69 percent generally disagreed with this perception of Reserve maintenance capability (21 percent strongly disagreed and 48 percent disagreed), while 20 percent were neutral and 11 percent generally agreed.

The second item dealing with capability stated:

All too often the Reserves have tended to be "social clubs" or a haven for retirement pay seekers, draft dodgers, and the like.

This item, taken from the landmark 1967 Rand study of the Air Reserve forces, reflects a perception of the Reserves that developed in the years following World War II. The perception may have been strengthened as a result of President Johnson's decision to induct much of the manpower needed to augment the active military forces in Vietnam rather than mobilize the Reserve.

Nearly two-thirds of the respondents disagreed with this perception; almost a quarter of the responses were neutral.

The statutory purpose of the Reserve components is "to provide trained units and qualified persons available for active duty in the armed forces, in time of war or national emergency and at such other time as the national security requires." [5] The active Air Force, Air Force Reserve, and Air National Guard share responsibility for assuring this readiness. Whether the statement is true—and there is substantial evidence that it is true at least for the Selected Reserve—the following item was intended to measure respondents' perception of how well prepared Reserve augmentation would be.

Almost three-quarters of the respondents agreed with the statement:

Reservists are, for the most part, adequately trained to make a positive contribution from the first day of recall.

Although only 14 percent strongly agreed, those who generally agreed outnumbered those who generally disagreed by a ratio of six to one.

Unlike other Reserve components, the Air Reserve forces have competed successfully in the no-draft environment. The Air National Guard and the Air Reserve forces exceeded their strengths from the last year that the draft was in effect. In *Air Force Magazine*, Bonner Day attributed that success to aggressive, active Air Force support of the total force policy; use of Reserve units for active-duty missions; work that is related to civilian occupations or is interesting in its own right; and Air Reserve technicians who provide day-to-day management and administrative continuity. [6] Although some technical specialties are critically manned, the Air Reserve forces as a whole are at or near peacetime strength ceilings.

The survey yielded different responses from the two schools concerning the statement:

One of the key problems facing the Air Reserve force today is under-manning of Reserve units.

The Air War College respondents generally agreed with this perception, but Air Command and Staff College students were evenly split between general agreement and general disagreement; only 14 percent gave neutral responses. It is interesting to speculate on reasons for this difference. Since recruiting and retention have been important problems for the active force during the past two years, senior officers may have extrapolated that difficulty to the Reserves. In contrast, officers in the intermediate school are closer in age and rank to many of the separating personnel, and they may have friends who stayed in the Reserves.

The final item on capability stated:

The Ready Reserve comprises manpower which could be useful primarily in a sustained conflict when a gradual build-up would occur since this would allow the time to train them for their specific assignments.

This item was constructed by substituting Ready for Standby in a description of the Standby Reserve.[7] The Ready Reserve comprises manpower that has received the training "required to maintain combat effectiveness"[8] prior to the initiation of a conflict, as opposed to during a sustained conflict. The Ready Reserve category includes all members who are obligated or who agree to report for active duty when called. Ready Reservists are required to respond when they are called by the President or the Congress, or whenever authorized by law.[9]

The combined Air War College and Air Command and Staff College reponses to this item were bimodal, with 43 percent generally agreeing and 38 percent generally disagreeing.

Air Reserve Availability

Air Reserve readiness also requires availability, which relates to the capacity of the Reserves to respond promptly. The first item related to availability stated:

I am confident that most [90 percent] Reservists will report for duty in response to a recall.

This item was developed in response to a perception noted in the 1977 Rand report: "Past mobilizations have shown that Air Reserve force units will fail to mobilize a significant number of people, because many claim medical and/or hardship deferments." The item asked only for the respondent's personal opinion on the reliability of Reservists during recall. The statement required no particular historical evidence to support the view.

In discussing their version of this perception, Rand researchers observed that because of medical or hardship deferments, both the Air National Guard and Air Force Reserve experienced dropout rates of approximately 20 percent during the Korean War and the Cuban and Berlin crises. As a result, the Reserves tightened entry and retention screening procedures. This action apparently had the desired result. During the limited Southeast Asia and Pueblo mobilization of 1968, less than one percent of the 10,511 Air National Guard personnel recalled received medical or hardship discharges. And some of those medical discharges resulted from duty injuries following mobilization.[10]

Although 72 percent of the survey respondents supported the statement, only one out of five of those agreeing indicated strong agreement, thus tending to dilute somewhat the significance of what appeared to be a large degree of support for the statement.

A second availability-related item measured the degree to which active Air Force officers believed a commercial pilot's occupation and mobilization obligation would conflict during a recall. Derived from one of the "common perceptions" identified by the 1977 Rand study,[11] the item asserted:

> Rapid mobilization of commercial airline pilots who fill Reserve crew positions is questionable (e.g., at the same time a mobilization occurs, an airline may be required to meet its commitment to the MAC Civil Reserve Air Fleet).

Rand researchers pointed out that, like other members of the Selected Reserve, Air Reserve pilots holding full-time jobs as commercial airline pilots must execute Ready Reserve service agreements. These agreements certify availability for active duty upon recall. Concerning a potential conflict with the Civil Reserve Air Fleet pilot needs, the Office of the Deputy Assistant Secretary of Defense (Reserve Affairs) reported in November 1979, that the ten top US commercial air carriers employed approximately 29,000 pilots. Of those, less than 2.5 percent are Reserve pilots.[12]

The responses to this item indicated that almost half of the population believed that commercial airline pilots in Reserve crew positions are questionable mobilization assets. Air War College officers held this perception more frequently that ACSC officers—55 percent of the AWC respondents and only 40 percent of the ACSC respondents generally agreed with the statement. Almost one-third of the officers indicated a neutral response.

The third item stated that:

> Legal constraints will probably delay the rapid mobilization of Air Reserve force units.

The legal bases for mobilizing the Reserves are clear. Despite these laws, slightly fewer than half of the officers surveyed believed that legal constraints would not delay a rapid mobilization; more than a quarter of the respondents gave a neutral response. These answers appear to reflect a serious concern over how quickly active-duty forces can expect help from the Reservists.

The ability of the Reserve components of all Services to be readily absorbed by the active forces is a recurrent theme in official investigations of the Reserves and was the subject of one of the survey items:

> *Reserve units are structured in a manner in which they may be rapidly integrated into the active force during a war or national crisis.*

In the past, the Air Reserve forces have scored well on this point. A 1975 Department of Defense report stated: "Air Reserve forces are ready to deploy earlier, are more thoroughly integrated into a single command structure, and operate equipment that is more modern than the Army or Navy Reserve components." [13] The General Accounting Office supported that position in a 1979 report. That report contained this finding:

> The Air Force gaining command concept and the Air Force Associate Program—in which Air Reserve units serve side-by-side with active Military Airlift Command units in flying and maintaining active Air Force equipment—have been particularly effective in integrating the Air Reserve force command structure with a minimal number of command layers and overhead personnel. [14]

Two-thirds of the surveyed officers generally agreed with the statement on rapid integration of the Reserves with the active forces. Of those officers not expressing agreement, more than half gave neutral responses.

Another survey item concerning Reserve availability stated that:

> *Political constraints will probably delay the rapid mobilization of Air Reserve force units.*

This statement reflects one of the commonly held perceptions of the Air Reserves identified in the 1977 Rand study. In the study, Rand noted that mobilizing Reserves has "significant national and international political consequences" requiring consultations with the State Department, congressional leaders, and others. Historically, such a process has averaged two weeks. Although consultations delay Reserve availability, the Rand report observed that "introduction of regular forces into hostilities or into an area of imminent hostilities is also preceded by extensive consultations." [15]

Whether consultations would delay mobilization is conjectural. The survey item sought to determine whether decisionmakers perceive a delay in their use of Reservists as they plan for mobilization and force deployment. Responses to the item produced a bimodal distribution, with more officers indicating agreement than disagreement—43 percent versus 36 percent. Air War College students felt more strongly than did Air

Command and Staff College students that political constraints would delay rapid mobilization—60 percent to 43 percent. The responses to this and the previous survey item reflect serious concern about the timeliness of Reserve mobilization and employment.

The final survey item dealing with perceptions of Reserve availability stated:

> Specific congressional approval is required for the nonvoluntary recall of Reservists during peacetime.

In fact, under certain circumstances the President may mobilize limited numbers of Reservists under existing laws without recourse to additional congressional action. He may authorize a limited expansion if he determines that the situation requires not more than 100,000 Selected Reservists, and the period of mobilization will not exceed ninety days. Or he may declare a national emergency which would enable him to mobilize Reservists for up to twenty-four months.

Of those responding to the item, 34 percent were neutral, 42 percent agreed with this perception, and 24 percent disagreed. Air War College respondents agreed with this item more often than did Air Command and Staff College officers—58 percent versus 38 percent. The Air Command and Staff College class was apparently better informed on this knowledge-based item.

Responses to the questionnaire suggest some general conclusions. The distributions of responses were similar for both senior officers and mid-career officers, and both officer groups showed substantial understanding and support of the Air Reserve forces. Yet, despite a generally positive attitude toward Reserve capability, a number of officers indicated a lukewarm acceptance of the total-force concept because of doubts about Reserve availability in a real contingency. Statistics indicate, and top-level defense leaders say, that the Air Reserve forces are ready. Nonetheless, the survey shows that many officers in the active force have questions and reservations about the availability and capability of the Reserves.

5
The US Reserve System:
Attitudes, Perceptions, and Realities

James W. Browning II, Kenneth C. Carlon,
Robert L. Goldich, Neal F. Herbert,
Theodore R. Mosch, Gordon R. Perkins,
Gerald W. Swartzbaugh

This chapter explores some of the less tangible and quantifiable aspects of issues currently facing the Reserve components of the Armed Forces. Numerous surveys, overviews, and programmatic reviews of the Reserve components of the total force have been conducted in recent years. Fewer discussions of *attitudes* and *perceptions* regarding the Reserves and National Guard, and how these attitudes and perceptions reflect and help shape Reserve policies and procedures, are extant. This chapter provides such a discussion. Our findings are based on the impressions received from numerous influential members of the Reserve and regular components, congressional staff members, interest groups, and on our own experiences as Reservists, National Guardsmen, regulars, or civilian analysts.

Published with the permission of the Commandant, the National War College. This is an abridged version of an unpublished research report submitted by the authors in 1982 in partial fulfillment of the National War College graduation requirements. References to "Reserve components" include the National Guard.—ED.

We identified six areas as being most worthy of comment as the Reserve components complete their first decade under the total-force policy:

- The comparative successes of the Air National Guard and the Air Force Reserve measured against the other Reserve components;

- The continuing problems faced by the Naval Reserve in its relationship with the active Navy;

- The surprising and welcome gains made by the Selected Reserve in recruiting and retaining personnel, and the sharp contrast provided by the unfavorable status of Individual Ready Reserve manpower;

- The absolute primacy of equipment as *the* major concern of senior Reserve and Guard personnel—in particular, equipment approaching block obsolescence which even enhanced DOD funding will not eliminate;

- The effects of changing military manpower policies and national strategy on the Reserve components; and

- The importance of historical, political, and psychological factors in regular-Reserve relationships.

Summarized here are the results of a survey of National War College and Industrial College of the Armed Forces students on their attitudes and perceptions of the Reserve components. These results from future leaders of the Armed Forces and from civilian national security agencies significantly—if not decisively—support and enhance our conclusions.

Success in the Air Reserve Components

There is a near unanimous belief within both the Reserve and active force communities that the Air National Guard and the Air Force Reserve are models of what Reserves can contribute to national security if they are given sufficient means and organizational support. This perception is all the more convincing because it is freely stated by uniformed personnel of other regular and Reserve components.

The transferability of successful Air Reserve Forces' policies to the other Reserve components will be addressed later. First, several reasons account for the high readiness, quick deployability, and thorough integration of the Air Guard and Air Force Reserve with the active Air Force. These include the following:

- Major active Air Force command emphasis, since about 1960, on the need to manage effectively the Air Reserve components and use them in accomplishing Air Force missions in both peace and war

- Close and formalized relationships between wartime gaining commands and Air Reserve component units in peacetime

- A low percentage of nonprior service personnel in Air Reserve component units and a corollary high level of experience among prior service personnel

- An active Air Force commitment to provide high levels of full-time personnel to Air Reserve components units

- An active Air Force willingness to support additional training for flying units of Air Reserve components well beyond once-a-month drills

- The Chief of the Air Force Reserve, himself a Reservist, actually commands the Air Force Reserve

- The effects of the technologically intensive nature of the Air Force in making it easier for the Air Reserve components to function at a high state of readiness

The Air Force requirement for high readiness also leads, almost automatically, to quick deployability if mobilized. Small flight, squadron, and wing headquarters, whose nature requires them to meet high peacetime standards, are much more easily mobilized and deployed than large ground units. The Air Force Reserve Associate Program also succeeds in large part owing to the unique nature of aircraft as machines, and because of the existence of large numbers of civilians—airline pilots—whose occupations are directly transferable to their Reserve component occupational specialties.

Finally, the success of the Air National Guard and the Air Force Reserve over the past twenty years has generated momentum for continued budgetary and political support. The active Air Force has a much more positive attitude toward its Reserve components than does any of the other active forces because it obtains so much value from them. The Congress has been similarly impressed by the Air Force's slow, steady record of Reserve-component support and integration. When the Air Force sought to deactivate some Air National Guard flying units, the Congress immediately required that ninety-one flying units of squadron size or equivalent be maintained in the Air Guard.[1] Congress has rarely been so concerned about force structures of similar size for the other Reserve components.

A close examination of the Air Reserve components reveals that their successes cannot easily be matched by the other Reserve components. The distinctiveness of air forces and aircraft is responsible for much of the high readiness and responsiveness of Air Guard and Air Force Reserve units. Nonetheless, some characteristics of the Air

Reserves would appear to be adaptable to the other components. These include:

- Long-term command emphasis on Reserve-component management, and on the necessity to use Reserve-component assets if for no other reason than "we need all the help we can get"

- Supervision and evaluation of Reserve-component organizations and personnel by wartime gaining commands

- Provision of high levels of full-time cadres and advisers in Guard and Reserve units, and budgeting for additional training time above the standard one weekend per month and two weeks per year as required by specific units and missions

The Naval Reserve: Is There Hope?

Although the Air Reserve components receive high praise from almost everybody, the Naval Reserve continues to be criticized, sometimes unfairly, as the least effective and most misused of the Reserve components.

It is vital to reaffirm that the Naval Reserve's deficiencies do not appear to result from substandard personnel, or obsolete equipment, or inadequate training per se. These may be contributing factors, but the most significant criticism of the Naval Reserve is directed against what has been viewed as the persistent unwillingness of the regular Navy to give more than nominal support to Reserve forces and acknowledge the utility of Reserves in performing naval missions in both peace and war. This apparent pro forma treatment of the Naval Reserve—in terms of command emphasis, budgeting, organization, and management—has in the past resulted in the poor use of available assets, missed opportunities for training and mission-oriented tasks, and, ultimately, lost combat power to the Navy.[2]

In the view of many senior officials, in and out of government, the following policies, practices, and attitudes support these criticisms:

- The apparent inability or perceived unwillingness of the Navy to produce valid requirements for the Naval Reserve, with resulting incoherence in defining Naval Reserve roles and missions; [3]

- The continued maintenance of the Chief of Naval Reserve's flag in New Orleans. As opposed to the other "Chiefs" of Reserve components, each of whom is located in Washington, DC, the Naval Reserve Chief is located a thousand miles from the Chief of Naval Operations and his staff, thus casting the appearance of exerting proportionately less influence;

- Until very recently, an apparent lack of detailed mobilization planning in both higher Navy staffs and gaining commands, compared with planning done by the Army and Air Force;

- Repeated comments on the part of regular Navy officers that the unique requirements and environment of the ship-at-sea and of naval deployments, as well as the inevitable concentration of naval bases and forces on the coastline, preclude effective use of Naval Reserve personnel in the surface forces;

- Evidence of the lack of confidence in full-time active duty Reservists as projected by the efforts of the active Navy during 1977–78 to replace them with regular Navy personnel; [4]

- The remnants of a less than optimum Reserve callup experience in 1968, the vivid memory of which still remains to taint the opinions and thinking of many regular officers in high positions today;

- Confusion about specific mission requirements; for example, CINCPAC's assignment of Naval Reserve Tactical Air (TACAIR) to an air defense mission, despite the associated logistic problems (Reserve TACAIR is not totally mobile—maintenance support is not in vans);

- The existing dilemma in the Surface Navy regarding the selection of the most operationally effective ships for the Naval Reserve, as well as who (the Fleet Commanders or CNAVRES) should have operational control of the ships of the Navy Reserve Force (NRF). Currently, operational control is under the Fleet Commander. Some members of Congress believe "that NRF ships should operate under the operational and administrative control of the Chief of Naval Reserve;" [5]

- The controversy about who should serve as the Chief of Naval Reserve. Currently, a regular Navy flag officer serves as Chief of Naval Reserve, unlike the National Guard and Reserve officers on statutory tours of active duty who serve as chiefs of their components in the Army and Air Force;

- Finally, most active duty Navy personnel do not seem to understand the Reserves or Reserve missions and capabilities. Major Navy educational institutions, such as the Naval War College and the US Naval Academy, provide little or no instruction on the Naval Reserve or on total-force policy.

Efforts to provide the United States with a responsive, combat-ready Naval Reserve began to gain credibility in 1979. Recognizing that the improvement of the Naval Reserve required concentrated attention, Admiral Thomas Hayward, the past Chief of Naval Operations, established the "sustained improvement of the Naval Reserve" as one of his specific objectives warranting personal attention by the Navy's uniformed leadership.[6] In addition, Admiral Hayward set forth the requirement for the direct involvement of gaining commands in the planning, development, and evaluation of the readiness training of Reserve units.[7] Likewise, Rear Admiral Frederick Palmer, Chief of Naval Reserve (CNAVRES), stated: "For fiscal year 1982, the continued improvement of mobilization readiness of the Naval Reserve is my top priority. This includes accurate unit reporting of training achieved, and an increased interaction between the gaining command and Selected Reserve units.[8]

In testimony before the House Armed Services Committee, both Secretary of the Navy John Lehman, Jr., and Admiral Hayward expressed their full intention of modernizing the Naval Reserve forces as early as possible.[9] Finally, the current Chief of Naval Operations, Admiral James Watkins, emphasized his commitment to the ongoing strengthening of the Navy Reserve through modernized equipment, improved training, and increased manpower, during his confirmation hearings before the Senate Armed Services Committee, 19 May 1982.

Some of the initiatives undertaken by the current Navy leadership include:

- Direct involvement of the gaining commands with their Reserve counterparts
- The introduction of new Frigates into the Reserve
- The transition of the first LAMPS I squadron to the Reserve in 1984
- Modernizing the Tactical Air Squadrons as early as possible by introducing the F/A-18 and the A-6E, as well as increasing the number of C-9 type aircraft
- Significant Reserve deployments in mutual support of the regular Navy; for example, the successful contribution of the Naval Air Reserve to the Navy's overall antisubmarine warfare effort
- USNR Training Program is now part of the regular Navy training—a recent change
- New proposed program of exchange officers with other Services, including the Army and Air National Guards

Secretary Lehman, himself a Navy Reservist, stressed the following:

> We in the Reserves have found year after year that talk is cheap. Always we find high hopes and rhetoric that we're going to modernize the Reserves, give them new equipment and new aircraft, new ships . . . but nothing ever happens. However, in the last 14 months, we have put forward a real program. . . . These are real programs, not rhetorical ones.[10]

In the course of this research project the question was asked why the regular Navy has been so reticent regarding the utility of the Naval

Reserve? The answer would appear to lie in fundamental characteristics of the Navy, some military and some social.

Navies have traditionally been national rather than locally based organizations. The Anglo-American tradition of armies as an outgrowth of locally based and recruited militia results in a comparatively greater understanding of and affinity for Reserves in the ground forces (and in the air forces, which are twentieth century organizational spinoffs from the ground forces). Navies, requiring massive capital investment in ships and shore facilities, and acting on behalf of the central government at sea rather than on behalf of local interests, do not have a tradition welling up from below. A "Naval National Guard," for example, is difficult to visualize for both technical and political reasons.

Massive and rapid mobilization has generally been, and continues to be, less important to navies than armies or air forces. The size of ships limits the rapidity with which any large number of Naval Reservists can be absorbed into a peacetime force structure in a quick mobilization—the Navy must fight with the ships it has on hand, although it can flesh out its crews and shore establishment with Reserves. This also requires more emphasis on individual Selected Reserve augmentees than on Selected Reserve units which mobilize and deploy as such, with consequent effects on peacetime Reserve unit cohesion and morale.

It appears that the Navy is moving to overcome its historically oriented attitudes about Reserves. The specialized and unique attributes of ships-at-sea, combined with naval forward deployments, do place some constraints on using Reserves. Such initiatives as the transfer of 1052-class frigates to the Naval Reserve and the FFG-7 program, however, suggest that attention is being paid to using the Naval Reserve up to the limit of these constraints. The expansion of the Navy's peacetime responsibilities into the Indian Ocean–Persian Gulf–Southwest Asia area has so stretched already over-committed active fleets that the Navy has become more disposed to obtain help from wherever it can get it, including the Naval Reserve.

By comparison, there is little controversy regarding the Coast Guard Reserve. Its mission is to provide a trained force of qualified personnel for active duty in time of war or domestic emergency (primarily in the field of port security) and, through augmentation training, support the active Coast Guard in normal peacetime operations. Although organized into units for training administration, most Coast Guard Reservists mobilize as teams or individuals to augment existing active commands. This places little demand on dedicated equipment for the Reserve, which trains mostly at active Coast Guard facilities, ships, and boats. This procedure correlates well with both the peacetime and wartime roles of the Coast Guard, and avoids the demographic problems facing the Naval Reserve.

Of greater concern today is the military readiness of the active Coast Guard and its interface with the Navy. With the Navy now emphasizing forward deployments and global preparedness, it has disestablished its former command structure for US littoral waters and cut back on its coastal zone posture. Yet, the threats to maritime economic activity within this area, ranging from direct attack to sabotage or terrorism, still exist. Recent discussions between the two Services under the aegis of the Navy/Coast Guard Board are concentrating on an increased Coast Guard role in wartime coordination and control in US littoral waters. Possible expanded Coast Guard responsibilities in this area would obviously affect the size and missions of the Coast Guard Reserve. Given the severe funding constraints in the non-DOD government sector, however, the Coast Guard (as part of the Department of Transportation) will be hard-pressed to do anything but maintain the Reserve at present levels at best.

The Coast Guard's many peacetime missions, its small size, and its unique relationship with the Navy obviously make the Coast Guard a highly imperfect model for the Naval Reserve or other Reserve components. Yet, its success in making peacetime use of Reserve assets and apparent lack of regular-Reserve friction certainly set at least a partial example for the Navy.

Manpower

One of the most surprising and least-noticed changes in the Reserve components since the late 1970s has been the major turnaround in overall Selected Reserve manning levels. From a low of 788,000 and 83 percent of wartime manning requirements at the end of fiscal year 1978, the Selected Reserve had a strength of 906,000 and 86 percent of much higher wartime requirements by the end of the first month of fiscal year 1982. Although skill shortages and mismatches between requirements and available skills remain a problem, the steady climb in overall Selected Reserve strength (which gives no sign of slackening at this writing) has almost erased one major problem from the minds of Reserve and mobilization planners.

The recruiting and retention successes of the Selected Reserve have resulted from command emphasis, political pressure from the Congress, and considerable doctrinal changes in broad national strategy. These changes include:

- A move away from the view that the principal manpower-intensive military emergency involving US forces—a major war with the Soviet Union and its Warsaw Pact allies in Europe, the Mediterranean, and the North Atlantic, with ancillary action worldwide—was bound to be short (60–180 days), quick, and decisive;

- The assertion by the Congress of its traditional interest and role as "protector" of the Reserve components by enacting Selected Reserve bonus and educational incentive legislation on its own initiative—not as the result of a DOD legislative proposal—in 1977 and 1978;

- Increased emphasis on Reserve recruiting organization and management within Service recruiting commands. An important part of this increased effort has been the large number of Guard and Reserve personnel called to active duty for recruiting service, and the mutual referral of likely recruits between active and Reserve component recruiters; [11]

- Recognition by National Guard and Reserve authorities that retention is as much of a problem in maintaining overall strength as is recruiting; and

- Belated recognition by the Services that a return to the draft, while not entirely unlikely, would require more pressure from either the international political situation or the status of recruiting than was likely to be forthcoming before the mid–1980s.

Evaluation of IRR strengths and requirements, on the other hand, is characterized by uncertainty. IRR requirements are based on the number of individual Reservists required to support and flesh out units in the current peacetime active force and Selected Reserve when mobilized for war. Expansion of the peacetime structure is not involved. The lack of regular training status for IRR personnel, and their existence as a pool of unorganized individuals, make their actual availability in time of war much more difficult to ascertain, monitor, and control than that of the active force or Selected Reserve. Moreover, the use of IRR personnel as casualty replacements makes IRR requirements dependent on casualty estimates for future wars—a further uncertain figure in the generally uncertain field of scenarios and projections.

Controversy over IRR requirements and shortfalls has revolved almost entirely around the Army Individual Ready Reserve. The Army requires by far the largest number of IRR personnel upon mobilization, primarily to flesh out active and Selected Reserve units and to replace losses. Estimates of Army IRR requirements and shortfalls have fluctuated drastically since DOD documents first discussed the issue openly in late 1975. These variations reflect the following problems and characteristics:

- Disagreements over availability rates and their predictability;

- A methodological distinction between (1) the number of unfilled spaces in the wartime force structure and (2) the size of the IRR pool that must be maintained to guarantee that those unfilled spaces are filled;

- A distinction between shortages in gross numbers and shortages in particular skills; and

- The responsiveness of the standby Selective Service System (of which the utility and presence of peacetime standby draft registration is a part).

Although the Office of the Secretary of Defense and the Army at one point apparently "resolved" the issue of the number of unfilled spaces—it was stated to be 270,000 in mid–1980—there is apparently no consensus on the actual number of IRR personnel required to eliminate the shortfall. The latter figure is held to be approximately 400,000 personnel by the Office of the Secretary of Defense, but appears to be closer to 600,000 if Army estimates are used.[12]

Assuming current, more pessimistic estimates of IRR requirements and show rates, the Individual Ready Reserve will still be several hundred thousand personnel short of requirements by fiscal year 1985. Therefore, the Army IRR strength increase required to prudently anticipate wartime requirements is apparently so great that incentives and policies adequate to make up merely marginal deficiencies would not be sufficient. Strength increases would have to be orders of magnitude greater than those attainable with currently envisioned plans. Unless the strength of the Selected Reserve is increased enormously—to compensate for a substantial proportion of the IRR shortfall—it is probable that some form of conscription will be needed if IRR requirements are to be met.[13]

Equipment: The Coming Shock of the Modernization Bow Wave

There is a universal perception in the Reserve community that the Reserve components are only a few years away from an absolute crisis in equipment. This shortage of modern equipment will result from a combination of block obsolescence of current equipment, exponentially escalating costs of replacement systems, and fiscal constraints on even the Reagan-projected defense budgets. As a result, by the late 1980s and early 1990s the Reserves and National Guard may simply not be worth maintaining, because of multiple generation gaps between their equipment on the one hand and that of both the active forces and the Soviet Union on the other.[14]

The reasons for the approaching shortfall in first-line equipment are related more to overall defense budget trends than to specific Reserve-component policies and practices. Dominating all other causes is the starvation of defense procurement budgets from the late 1960s through the late 1970s. Austere procurement budgets drove up unit costs of major weapons systems through smaller overall buys and slow production rates, making competition for resources within the Department of

Defense even more brutal. Current and programmed defense budget increases will only partially eliminate the enormous equipment shortfall created by a decade of neglect. At the same time, the Reserve-equipment inventory—composed largely of pre-Vietnam era stocks—is nearing the end of its useful life despite incremental modernization and improvement programs. Equipment one or two generations behind the most advanced systems can be used in time of war—not all Soviet equipment is state-of-the-art either. However, equipment that is three to five generations behind current first-line systems is logistically unsupportable and subject to battlefield massacre.

During the 1980s, the United States will implement the largest peacetime military equipment modernization program in its history. Major investment that was deferred during the Vietnam era and which limped through research and development and initial procurement during the middle and late 1970s will finally come to fruition. The limited resources and high unit costs seem destined, however, to preclude all but a fraction of this equipment from reaching the Reserve components. The Reserve budget projections of the Department of Defense confirm this impression.

This policy of allocating almost all first-line equipment to the active forces is anachronistic. Favoring the active forces for new equipment allocation might have made some sense, in the past, when political constraints on Reserve mobilization, a more favorable balance between US military power and potential threats, and a draft all existed. Today, this policy has been overtaken by events. Almost any military action, other than a minor show of force, will require the mobilization of Reserve-component units and individuals. Threat force levels and geographical areas of potential US military responsibility have expanded, while US force levels have declined. All these factors have made the initial use of Reserves absolutely essential in US war plans.

In those components where first-line equipment *has* been allotted without regard to active or Reserve status—the Air Reserve components and the Marine Corps Reserve ground forces, for example—doubts about the ability of properly supported Reserve units to maintain and use modern equipment have been shown to be wholly unfounded.[15] In no other area does active-force policy seem to be so tied to the past. Compared to a decade ago, most Services are well advanced in integrating their active and Reserve components in the areas of manpower, training, organization, and mobilization planning. A doctrine of separate but unequal seems to be in full force only in the field of equipment. This doctrine flies in the face of the missions that many Reserve units will have upon mobilization.

History, Politics, and Psychology

Individuals, civilians or military, who advance to substantial responsibility in the Reserve community, will be thoroughly acquainted with the politicized nature of Reserve-component policy issues. They will be just as aware of the important psychological factors involved in relations between the regular forces and the Reserve components, both at the national level and in everyday social interaction among individual military members.

These intangible qualities of the US Reserve system are deeply rooted in American and English history.[16] The Anglo-American Reserve tradition is based on local militias, whose primary ties are to localities and provinces and which are administered by local and provincial authorities with substantial independence from the central government. Derivative from this tradition are several distinguishing characteristics. These features include substantial ties to local and state political authorities and representative bodies at all levels of American government and a dual state-federal role as a law enforcement agency for the National Guard.

The point is, the Guardsman or Reservist *does* have a dual identity. He wants to be recognized by active duty personnel as a full-fledged soldier, sailor, airman, Marine, or Coast Guardsman, while maintaining his autonomy and local ties. Regulars who object to "catering" to this undeniable and understandable duality miss the point. Constructively accommodating this duality results in more, better, and increasingly satisfied contributors to the combat power of the armed forces.

The Reserve components also require more attention from military educational institutions. National Guard and Reserve forces are central to current war planning. Regular units will fight alongside, support, or be supported by Reserve-component units in any substantial future war. Regular personnel will serve with, command, or be commanded by Reserve-component members. Under these circumstances, the curricula of all echelons of professional military education (officer acquisition training, intermediate level schooling, and senior service colleges) should include major blocks of instruction on the National Guard and Reserve. If US regular officers were exposed to Reserve-component issues from their precommissioning training on through their entire careers, it seems likely that much of the misinformation, confusion, and occasional arrogance of ignorance would be at least partially dispelled.

The Effects of National Strategy and Policy Shifts

Three major changes in national strategy have had major effects on the Reserve components over the past decade. Their cumulative result has been to increase the dependence of the armed forces on Reserves should any military action beyond a minor show of force be required.

The first of these was the end of the draft in 1973, which had been approved as law in 1971. This change almost certainly resulted in the tacit acceptance of lower active force strengths than would have been considered prudent had a draft been available to fill the ranks. The Reserve components remained the sole available source of trained units and individuals to augment the active forces upon mobilization until such time as conscription could be reinstated. The net effect of the end of the draft, however, was to increase the responsibilities of the Reserve components, and hence the numerical strength requirements for Reserves, while simultaneously and drastically decreasing their ability to fill their ranks.

The second change in national strategy also evolved during the early 1970s. Battered by the Vietnam War, US defense planning once more fastened on familiar, comfortable terrain—war in Europe. Planning for global contingencies was sharply curtailed; force structuring was to center on how best to fight the Soviet Union and its Warsaw Pact allies in Europe, on the land flanks of Europe, and in waters and airspace adjacent to Europe. This redefinition of US strategy, by geographically constricting the potential area of US military responsibility, decreased the mobilization requirements of the armed forces, including requirements for Reserves (or at least was seen to do so by those responsible at the time).

During the mid-1970s the nature of a European war was further defined so as to reduce the need for Reserve components. Such a war, it was believed, would most likely be short, sharp, and decisive. The primary casualty of the short-war theoreticians was, therefore, Reserve-equipment modernization. Paradoxically, the belief of the short-war adherents that those Reserves which *were* needed had to be capable of rapid response resulted in 1976 legislation providing the Secretary of Defense with the authority to call up to 50,000 Selected Reservists (the number was raised to 100,000 in 1980) to active duty for up to ninety days without a declaration of war or national emergency.[17]

The third change in national strategy involved the collision of the second with the realities of international politics. Soviet and Soviet-proxy military involvement in the Third World, beginning in the mid-1970s, effectively precluded the United States from adhering to an exclusively European scenario, regardless of US wishes. A logical outcome of this conclusion was the need for a larger Reserve-component force structure and more emphasis on mobilization for a long-term conflict.

The Reserve components, therefore, are as important to the defense of the United States as their most ardent and allegedly parochial supporters say they are. As this section has shown, however, the Reserve components did not reach this position of importance by design or foresight—or as the result of the wisdom of the American people, their elected representatives, or their appointed officials.

Reserve Forces Survey Results

In an effort to develop quantifiable data to support or rebut attitudes expressed on a nonattrition basis by senior military and civilian personnel interviewed in the development of this study, a survey was administered to senior officer (0–5/6) and civilian (GS–14/15) students of the National War College (NWC) and the Industrial College of the Armed Forces (ICAF).

The National War College focuses on national security policy formulation and implementation. The school's mission is to prepare selected personnel of the armed forces, Department of State, and other US government agencies for exercise of joint and combined high-level policy, command, and staff responsibilities. The Industrial College of the Armed Forces focuses on the management of resources for national security preparedness and mobilization planning.

The survey questions concentrated on three general areas: (1) the role of the Reserve components in national security, (2) the relationship between the active forces and the Reserve components, and (3) particular problems, including equipment, training, manning, and mobilization. Of the total student body of each institution, the Industrial College had a 76 percent response, whereas the National War College had 67 percent.

Role of the Reserve Components in National Security

Both ICAF and NWC students viewed the Reserve components as important to the country's defense. Students, ICAF (94 percent) and NWC (86 percent), believed that the Reserve components contribute positively to the nation's security. In a national emergency, both ICAF (95 percent) and NWC (76 percent) viewed the National Guard and Reserve, rather than draftees, as the primary sources for augmenting the active forces. The vast majority of both schools considered Reserves dedicated (73 percent); reliable (70 percent); and not "too old" for combat (85 percent). They believed that at least 90 percent of the Selected Reserve personnel would report for duty upon recall (ICAF—61 percent; NWC—72 percent); and that Guard and Reserve forces have specific mobilization sites and missions in operations plans (ICAF—65 percent; NWC—58 percent).

The majority, however, were unaware of Reserve-component missions and roles. Significant numbers of students did not know that Reserve component units were part of CENTCOM (ICAF—77 percent;

NWC—76 percent). Although each Service expressed ignorance of Reserve-component roles and missions, Navy officers (ICAF—75 percent; NWC—64 percent) had the highest degree of such ignorance. In addition, a large number of respondents (ICAF—45 percent; NWC—50 percent) believed that Reserve-component forces are poorly and improperly utilized. The Air Force and Army responses were similar on this latter issue (45 percent); but an even larger number of Navy students (ICAF—61 percent; NWC—76 percent) believed Reserve-component forces are not being properly utilized. Despite the view of poor Reserve-component utilization, ICAF (95 percent) and NWC (85 percent) respondents considered Reserve-component personnel valuable assets.

Relationship Between the Active Forces and Reserve Components

Although were was general agreement that each Service has a written policy on the utilization and training of Reserve-component personnel (70 percent), there was significant difference between the Services concerning continued "lip service" to the total-force policy. The Navy generally agreed (44 percent) that only lip service is being offered, compared to the Air Force (58 percent disagreed) and Army (34 percent agreed). Furthermore, NWC Navy students agreed (52 percent) that a "we-they" conflict exists between Reserves and regular forces. Also, the Navy students (ICAF—67 percent, NWC—64 percent) indicated that the Navy had made little or no effort to educate them on Reserve capabilities, roles, and missions. In contrast, the Air Force and Army students indicated efforts by their Services to provide such education.

The students, ICAF (89 percent) and NWC (82 percent), agreed that Reserve components should be integrated with the active forces. A majority (ICAF—58 percent; NWC—56 percent) believed Reserve units can be structured to ensure rapid integration into the active force upon mobilization.

Army and Air Force personnel (40 percent) believed there is a close working relationship between Reserve-component units and the active units they augment upon mobilization. In contrast, the Navy (48 percent) did not see such a relationship in existence. The Air Force respondents ((ICAF—39 percent; and NWC—56 percent) as well as NWC Army respondents (49 percent) agreed that the inspection standards are less stringent in the Reserve.

The Air Force was identified as the Service with the best active-Reserve relationship ((ICAF—73 percent; and NWC—64 percent). This consensus was evident in each Service as well (Air Force—91 percent; Army—83 percent; Navy—53 percent). Although the Air Force was considered to have the best Reserve-component program, some problems do exist between active and Reserve-component forces even in this branch. For example, more Air Force respondents (22 percent) cited

Reserve integration with active units as a cause for retention problems than did the Army (8 percent) and the Navy (ICAF—6 percent; and NWC—20 percent). Although an overwhelming majority of respondents (92 percent) believed that working with Reserves has a real payoff, they viewed the allocation of resources as a possible source of friction. A majority of the respondents (77 percent) viewed the Reserve components and active forces as competing for resources; yet, most ((ICAF—80 percent; NWC—74 percent) believed that a redirection of the Reserve budget to the active forces is not in the best interests of the country. The written responses substantiated this opinion. Respondents believed that the enlargement of the active forces will be impossible due to resource limitations.

Challenges—Equipment, Training, Mobilization

Equipment shortages continue to be a subject presented to congressional committees by Reserve chiefs each year. Both ICAF (85 percent) and NWC (79 percent) believed Reserve-component personnel can use and maintain sophisticated equipment. Although agreeing generally that first-line equipment and weapons should be assigned to the Reserves, a significant difference in response existed according to Service (Air Force: (ICAF—85 percent, NWC—58 percent; Army: ICAF—62 percent, NWC—57 percent; Navy: ICAF—53 percent, NWC—only 24 percent agreed). Additionally, only 28 percent thought a limited maintenance capability in the Reserve components hinders assignment of advanced weapons systems to the Reserves.

Students, ICAF (60 percent) and NWC (48 percent), considered Reservists adequately trained to make a contribution. Although the Air Force (66 percent) and NWC Navy students (64 percent) agreed, the Army had only 44 percent who agreed; whereas the Navy NWC students (48 percent) disagreed.

Although the vast majority of the respondents (85 percent) were knowledgeable of Presidential powers relating to Reserve mobilization and believed the President and Congress will use Reservists in an emergency, a significant number ((ICAF—52 percent; NWC—48 percent) maintained that political and legal restraints would probably delay rapid mobilization of Reserve component units.

Seventy-three percent of the 158 ICAF students took time to write individual responses, many of which were extensive. The time these students devoted to the survey indicated the seriousness with which they viewed the subject of the Reserve components. The overwhelming majority saw the Reserve components as necessary for the defense of the nation; they believed the Reserves must be better integrated into defense plans, should be allocated modern equipment, and must be better trained. The ICAF students (both in their statistical and written responses) were extremely conscious of resource scarcity, emphasizing the need to use Reserve components to fill active force deficiencies. The majority of each Service cited the Air Force as providing the model for the ideal active-Reserve relationship.

Seventy-nine percent of the 116 NWC respondents took the time to write comments, which were less extensive than those of the ICAF students. Although some responses cited cost effectiveness as an important reason for Reserve support, NWC students did not emphasize resource allocation as did their ICAF colleagues. Ninety-two percent of the written responses endorsed the Reserve components as providing an essential part of national defense. Many recommended up-grading equipment and training to make the Reserve components more effective.

The following are examples of specific comments made by the students from the two senior service schools. They are presented by major subject areas.

Missions

Many ICAF students stressed the potential of the Reserve components and recommended they be better utilized; for example, "they must be given meaningful missions as the USAF has done with the USAFR and the ANG." A typical NWC student comment was that "Guard and Reserves should be confined to serving as fillers for active units."

Orientation

Several ICAF students urged more orientation of regular officers with regard to the Reserves. Some recommended tours of duty with Reserve-component units, noting that "generally, most 0–5s and 0–6s have little knowledge of the Reserves. To gain proper support, Reserve components must be integrated into the curriculum of all service schools." Several NWC participants noted the need for education on the Reserve components, stating that "most regular officers have not had any dealings with Reservists; therefore, they are not certain about their contributions."

Total Force

The ICAF respondents overwhelmingly supported the total-force concept and felt that the Reserve components needed better equipment and training. These ICAF officers see great potential cost-effectiveness in the Reserve components. Regarding the total force, a common NWC student comment was that the "total-force concept should become a reality." Several NWC officers felt that the Reserve components are not taken seriously by regular officers.

Readiness

The ICAF officers were more favorable toward the National Guard than the Reserve. Many cited combat readiness as the major reason. The Air Force Reserve and the Air National Guard were regarded as the best Reserve components. For instance, one respondent noted, "based on the Vietnam War, exercises such as Empire Glacier and being co-located with Reserve units, I'm convinced, at least in the Air Force, they are dedicated, competent, and ready to go—an invaluable component of the total force." Others, however, questioned Reserve-component readiness; for example, "it will take longer than expected to bring a Reserve unit into a combat status."

Concerning the subject of readiness, a representative NWC student comment was that "DOD should hold a bi- or tri-annual national mobilization exercise, involving civilian agencies as well as the military. This would test the readiness of all concerned with mobilization." Many NWC students noted the difficulty of getting Naval Reservists to sea for meaningful training.

Manning

Several ICAF students recommended use of bonuses to ensure proper manning. Some suggested a draft for the Selected Reserve and the Individual Ready Reserve. A recurrent NWC student comment was: "A draft for the Reserves." One NWC respondent justified a draft by noting: "A Reserve draft would provide good people to the Reserves, would be politically palatable, inexpensive, and would generate 'crossovers' to the regulars, and still emphasize the 'citizen-soldier' concept." Some ICAF and NWC personnel argued that the Individual Ready Reserve should never be relied upon.

Resources

On the subject of resources in general, a common ICAF student observation was: "If more funds are diverted to the Reserve components, the active components will suffer in readiness." Many NWC students, however, cited equipment, training, and manpower as being critical for effective Reserve roles, noting that the "Reserves should be funded to required mission capability consistent with deployment priority."

Although the survey results reflected a generally positive view of the Reserve components, it is interesting to note a few of the infrequently made negative comments. One ICAF student thought that members of the Reserve components are "personal opportunists who are taking advantage of a good deal (financial, personal) under the smokescreen of 'service to their country.' " Although some ICAF students thought the National Guard was the more dedicated of the Reserve components, others believed the Guard is too lax and cited "sloppy" appearance. In fact, one of the students stated "the National Guard is almost a joke. A small percentage of Reserve units may drill only 2–3 hours for a 'duty day' and then go home."

One NWC Naval officer noted: "Sir, I didn't know anything about the Reserves before I came here. I haven't learned anything about them here. My only experience with a Reserve officer was with a dope-smok-ing, Navy lieutenant commander who stated that he was in the Reserves only for the money and under no circumstances would he fight if called up. It was clear that he did not consider his attitude at all unusual. Thus, I can't answer your questionnaire."

Finally, a few NWC Air Force officers acknowledged the success of Air Force Reserve and Air National Guard programs but criticized al-leged preferential treatment given to Reservists returning to active duty. They were charged with obtaining better assignments, receiving faster promotions, and not having to deal with customary administrative and technical duties.

Two major assertions might be made as a result of this survey. First, the comments and recommendations made throughout this paper were, in general, endorsed by the overall survey results. Second, the future leadership of the national-security hierarchy in the United States has a generally favorable view of the Reserve components. Indeed, the favor-able reaction is so great and yet seems to conflict with current realities, one might additionally conclude that (1) even anonymously surveyed persons do not always tell their true feelings, (2) something happens to regular officers when they reach high rank, causing them to be less ac-commodating to Reserve-component interests, or (3) those who make Reserve-component policy for the Military Services are not, in fact, members of the national defense "elite" supposedly defined by the NWC and ICAF student bodies.

Conclusions and Recommendations

Despite efforts by Congress, the Department of Defense, and the Services to upgrade the National Guard and Reserves, questions persist about combat readiness, manpower shortages, mobilization timeframes, and obsolete or unavailable equipment. As a result of this study, it is clear that interest in these specific issues disguises a much larger prob-lem—the divergent attitudes and perceptions held by decisionmakers re-garding the entire Reserve system. Generally, one might conclude that official policies, plans, and pronouncements tend to support the National Guard and Reserve, while reality is different and less supportive. Specific conclusions might be the following:

- Strategy and policy shifts since the end of the draft in 1973 have actually placed greater reliance on the National Guard and Reserve as an integral part of the total force, yet appropriate levels of funding, equipment, and manpower have not been authorized to match the burden.

- Block obsolescence of equipment is of major concern to senior planners, but budgets contain little cure.

- Organizational effectiveness, preparedness, and mission identification vary significantly from component to component and within components.

- Regular personnel lack a generic understanding of the history, purpose, and nature of the Reserve components with whom they must work, train, and fight alongside upon mobilization.

- Reserve components suffer unnecessarily through ignorance and biased treatment on the part of regulars. Those who know and work with Reserves have very favorable impressions. Other regulars tend to view Reserves as "part-time" workers who do not belong in the military club, and they fail to understand the need of the Reservist to identify with both the military and civilian worlds.

In consideration of these conclusions, the following recommendations seem appropriate:

- Innovative thinking is required to define appropriate Reserve missions that reflect capabilities to meet wartime tasking. All Services can make use of Reserves if the circumstances are correct and the motivation sufficient. The Air Force Reserve and Air National Guard already have such clearly defined missions.

- Gaining commands should assume greater if not full responsibility for the training and readiness of Reserve components either on a unit or on an individual basis. Reserve organizations within each Service should be modified to integrate operations, training, and outfitting with the active forces. Personnel management, administration, and mobilization planning should remain under direct Reserve leadership.

- The Navy should consider a separate Naval Reserve organization similar to that of the Air Force Reserve. The Navy, in implementing the total-force policy, has developed the "One Navy" concept. In effect, action officers or program sponsors are required to evaluate their respective programs in light of both regular and Reserve issues—total Navy. Although the "One Navy" concept is persuasive, most of the personnel interviewed believe the concept is not working. The Naval Reserve needs a stronger, single voice, a voice considered equal in the planning and budgeting cycle.

- Each of the Reserve component chiefs should be in a three-star billet, similar to the Chief of the National Guard Bureau.

- Unless each Military Service, the Office of the Secretary of Defense, and the Congress undertake major efforts to modernize National Guard and Reserve equipment, the trend toward block obsolescence will become absolute. The "hand-me-down" philosophy is no longer practical or effective. The Reserves must be included in the initial buy of new weapons systems. The total Reserve-component equipment inventory must be reviewed and steps taken to reduce the risks associated with weapon obsolescence. Equipment allocation should be based on mobilization and deployment missions, not active versus Reserve status.

- Active units must continue efforts to increase their role in the quality control of Reserve-component readiness. Differences between Reserve component and active equipment create needs for additional methods that enhance combat training. Specific means are needed by which to evaluate Reserve-component capabilities.

- The Services must undertake a massive educational effort (for both active and Reserve-component personnel) to ensure that Reserve missions, roles, capabilities, and organization are understood by all. Included should be an introduction of the total-force policy at the Service academies and ROTC detachments, as well as at intermediate service schools and senior service colleges. Until the ignorance of National Guard and Reserve missions and capabilities is greatly reduced, short-sighted Reserve-component planning and budgeting is likely to continue.

- Clear policy concerning Reserve utilization and training must be expressed and implemented throughout each Service organization. Without such policy, negative attitudes and perceptions will persist—resulting in decisionmaking that could adversely affect the military's overall combat capability.

These recommendations would assist greatly in achieving a truly total force.

Part 3

Manpower

6

US Reserve Forces:
The Achilles' Heel of
the All-Volunteer Force?

Arthur L. Moxon

Since the adoption in 1973 of policies establishing the all-volunteer force and the total force, declining manpower levels have characterized the US armed forces. The all-volunteer force ended conscription and returned to an all-volunteer basis for raising and maintaining US military forces; the total force policy placed increased reliance on the Reserve forces as the primary means of augmenting the active forces in the event of mobilization. The rationale underlying the total-force policy is that the United States can achieve national security objectives more efficiently by maintaining smaller active forces and placing increased reliance on Reserve forces.

While many people have misgivings about the present and future effectiveness of the all-volunteer force (AVF), it has generally been judged a success because of its ability to meet the strength levels and recruiting goals of the active forces. However, the success of the total-force policy

This chapter is based on a paper Major Moxon presented to the conference "Changing Military Manpower Realities in the 1980s," held at Maxwell Air Force Base, Alabama, in 1979. A version of the paper appeared in *Changing US Military Manpower Realities*, Franklin D. Margiotta, James Brown, and Michael J. Collins, ed. (Boulder, Colo.: Westview Press, 1983), published in cooperation with the National Defense University.—ED.

is problematic. In 1976, the Defense Manpower Commission concluded:

> The Total Force Policy is still far from a reality, and the expectation of it may have been overstated. To assume that many National Guard or Reserve units will be operationally ready for deployment overseas 30 to 90 days after mobilization is not realistic; a more practical readiness time for most units would be from 120 to 180 days. There are some anomalies and some great differences among and within the Services as to the conditions of their Reserve components, and their support, readiness and what can realistically be expected of them.[1]

In his 1982 *Annual Report*, the Secretary of Defense stated that despite recent improvements in Reserve recruiting, emphasis on Reserve issues was still required because Reserve strength shortages and attrition continued to be a problem and the total-force concept depended heavily on Reserve mobilization and deployment.[2]

Total-force problems involve numerous issues and concerns. But this discussion focuses on the Reserve component, primarily because the problems of the active forces have been extensively studied and, in the near term, Reserve manpower shortages will be the salient problem of the total force.[3] Reserve manpower problems are critical to the total-force concept and closely related to the AVF concept in the sense that the total-force policy assigned increased roles and responsibilities to the Reserves, and the termination of the draft ended the major incentive for Reserve enlistment. The impact of these Reserve problems on the all-volunteer concept became apparent as individuals who had enlisted in the Reserves to avoid the draft, or had been drafted, completed their six-year military obligation. The rapid decline in Reserve strengths was the result of the departure of these individuals.[4] On the one hand, a number of unresolved issues have hampered proposals to resolve the Reserve strength problem; on the other hand, both the Reserves and the active forces have been deficient in their manpower proposals because they lack a total-force perspective in assessing their potential effectiveness.

This chapter seeks to identify some of these issues by addressing a number of questions related to the total-force and all-volunteer concepts. For example, what are the requirements and responsibilities of the Reserves in the total force? Are these requirements achievable in a volunteer environment? What are the implications of changing demographics in the 1980s and 1990s? What factors determine manpower requirements? Answers to these questions should provide some insight into the future of the all-volunteer and total-force concepts.

Manpower Requirements

Manpower requirements for the total force reflect existing US national security policy, international commitments, and general military strategy. Specific requirements derive from analyses of the wartime threat, essential combat and combat support structures, and peacetime support structures. These factors should interact to determine the total size of the armed forces and the mix of units among active and Reserve forces. Manpower levels depend heavily on the projected nature and duration of anticipated conflicts. In terms of required manpower, the most demanding conflict would be a sudden attack by Warsaw Pact forces against NATO forces. In that scenario, the US Army would have the manpower requirements shown in table 6.1. The Army requirement for 1.78 million individuals—which is 1 million beyond active strength (as of March 1981)—is the primary cause of concern about Reserve manpower shortages.[5]

A prolonged European conflict represents the greatest potential demand for manpower, but manpower must also be immediately available to match the capabilities of potential aggressors. The luxuries of early warning and time for lengthy development of a war-fighting capability are no longer available. The necessary levels of trained and available manpower are calculated and identified as mobilization day, or M-day, requirements. These individuals must be trained, and they must be capable of immediate deployment or deployment on short notice. As shown in table 6.2, the 1975 Department of Defense (DOD) total-force study provided estimates of M-day requirements for the various Services in fiscal year 1980.

Exclusive reliance on active forces to meet these requirements would, of course, yield the greatest assurance of quantity, quality, and timeliness of response, but the size and cost of the active force would be prohibitive. Thus, if the total-force policy can be effectively implemented, it is the least costly alternative for meeting wartime manpower requirements. The President's fiscal year 1982 budget request reflected the application of the total-force concept in providng military manpower. (Table 6.3 shows the President's requests for active duty and Reserve personnel.)

Table 6.1

US ARMY MANPOWER REQUIREMENTS IN A NATO/WARSAW PACT CONFLICT

Category	Time	
	Conflict Begins	120 Days Later
Combat-ready troops	660,000	1,525,000
Troops being trained	55,000	55,000
Casualty replacements		200,000
Total personnel	715,000	1,780,000

Source: Office of the US Secretary of Defense, *A Report to Congress on US Conventional Reinforcements for NATO* (Washington, DC: 1976), p. IX–3.

Table 6.2

FY 1980 M-DAY MILITARY MANPOWER REQUIREMENTS

(Thousands, estimated by DOD in 1975)

Service	Strength
Army	1,657
Navy	635
Marine Corps	262
Air Force	742
Total Requirements	3,296

Source: Defense Manpower Commission, Defense Manpower: The Keystone of National Security (Washington, DC: Government Printing Office, April 1976), p. 153.

Determining manpower requirements and the force structure necessary to meet these requirements is an extremely complex process; but general planning guidance provides some insight into methods of determining the responsibilities of the various total-force components. An examination of Reserve roles and missions in today's total force also confirms the importance of these components in our present military posture.

Table 6.3

ACTIVE DUTY AND RESERVE COMPONENT MILITARY PERSONNEL STRENGTH, FY 1982

(End year—in thousands)

Component	Strength
Active Duty Military	
Army	786
Navy	550
Marine Corps	188
Air Force	569
Total	2,094*
Reserve Components (Selected Reserve)	
Army National Guard	398
Army Reserve	237
Naval Reserve	88
Marine Corps Reserve	39
Air National Guard	98
Air Force Reserve	64
Total	923*

Source. US, Department of Defense, Annual Report Fiscal Year 1982 (January 1981), p. B-4.

*Numbers may not add to total due to rounding.

The Reserve Component:
Roles, Organization, and Availability

Total-force planning involves more than manpower resources; but the total-force policy recognizes that active-duty manpower will become increasingly expensive in all-volunteer environment and, therefore, places increased emphasis on the roles and responsibilities of the Reserve components. This transfer of responsibilities has permitted reductions in the required manpower strengths of the active forces. In respect to the general principle of transferring as many missions as possible to the Reserve forces, the *Manpower Requirements Report for FY 1982* describes the effect of the total-force policy on force structure planning.

> The force structure for FY 1982 continues to be based on DOD's Total Force Policy which recognizes that all units in the force structure contribute to our success in wartime. In structuring our forces, units are placed in the Selected Reserve whenever feasible to maintain as small a peacetime force as national security policy and our military strategy permit. Selected Reserve units are available upon mobilization to bring the total force to its required combat capability. These Reserve units must also be responsive to call-up for limited periods without a declaration of war or national emergency. Active units, on the other hand, are those forces needed for a contingency not involving mobilization for immediate deployment in a major war before Selected Reserve units can be deployed; and for forward deployment in peacetime as a deterrent against major conflict.[6]

Table 6.4 shows that this policy has led to reductions in active military strength and traces the decline in the active forces that is characteristic of the all-volunteer force.

The general purpose forces show the extent to which Reserve contributions have affected the 12 percent decline in active duty manpower since initiation of the AVF policy in 1973 and the 24 percent decline from pre-Vietnam levels. Approximately 85 percent of all Reserve manpower is allocated to the general purpose forces. More important is the fact that approximately 45 percent of all general purpose forces come from the Reserve components.[7] Reserve components provide approximately 33 percent of the Army's combat divisions, 50 percent of its artillery battalions, 60 percent of its armored cavalry regiments, and 67 percent of its tactical support forces. Air Force Reserve units possess approximately 34 percent of the tactical fighter aircraft, 57 percent of the tactical reconnaissance force, 65 percent of the air defense interceptors, 60 percent of the tactical airlift forces, and approximately 48 percent of the strategic airlift crews.[8] Obviously, the Reserve components play vital roles in the military capability of the United States, and their problems directly affect US military effectiveness.

Table 6.4

ACTIVE MILITARY STRENGTH

(End year—in thousands)

Fiscal Year	Strength
1964	2,687
1968	3,547
1972	2,322
1973	2,252
1974	2,161
1975	2,127
1976	2,081
1977	2,084
1978	2,049
1979	2,024
1980	2,050
1981	2,065
1982 (est.)	2,094

Source: US, Department of Defense, Assistant Secretary of Defense (Manpower, Reserve Affairs, and Logistics), America's Volunteers: A Report on the All-Volunteer Armed Forces (Washington, DC: December 1978), p. 366; US, Department of Defense, Annual Report Fiscal Year 1982 (January 1981), p. B-3.

Confusion about Reserve organization has been a major problem in assessing the impact of Reserve manpower deficiencies. The term *Reserve* is a source of confusion in itself. Members of the Reserve component range from full-time National Guardsmen and Reservists who are also full-time civilian employees of the federal government, to individuals who have retired from active duty after completing full military careers. Depending on the definition of the term, the number of individuals in the Reserve population in 1981 could vary from fewer than one million to over two million.

Organization and Recall of the Reserve Component

The Reserve forces consist of seven main components: the Department of Defense controls six; the Department of Transportation controls one, the US Coast Guard Reserve. The six Reserve components in the Department of Defense are the Army National Guard (ARNG), the Army Reserve (USAR), the Naval Reserve (USNR), the Marine Corps Reserve (USMCR), the Air National Guard (ANG), and the Air Force Reserve (USAFR). The Reserves and the National Guard differ in the sense that the Reserves operate under exclusive federal control for national defense purposes and National Guard components are organized by state and are under the control of state governors except when preempted by the President. The Reserve components are further divided into three categories: the Ready Reserve, the Standby Reserve, and the Retired Reserve.

The Ready Reserve. The Ready Reserve comprises the major portion of the manpower resource that can be used to augment the active forces and consists of the Selected Reserve and the Individual Ready Reserve (IRR). The Selected Reserve is largely made up of whole units that can be mobilized as integral groups, but the Individual Ready Reserve includes individuals who will serve primarily as fillers to augment deployed active and Reserve units. The Selected Reserve contains all the National Guard forces, all Reservists who are organized in Reserve units, and Individual Mobilization Augmentees. As the mainstay of the Reserve force, the Selected Reserve is the primary source for timely augmentation of the active force and is, therefore, the component that receives major DOD attention.

The Selected Reserve has the major mobilization mission and receives annual appropriations from Congress. Members of the Selected Reserve train with their units throughout the year and participate annually in active duty training (generally, two weeks in the summer and one weekend per month during the remainder of the year). Members of Selected Reserve units receive compensation for Reserve duty: the fiscal year 1982 budget requested $3.7 billion for this compensation and other Reserve and Guard personnel costs.[9] The Selected Reserves resemble the active forces in that they procure and retain their personnel directly. They enlist both non-prior service (NPS) recruits and prior service (PS) recruits (the latter are usually individuals who have separated from the active duty forces and subsequently decide to join the Selected Reserves).

Selected Reserve units are manned and equipped to reflect or mirror active units. They are programmed to deploy and fight independently of, or alongside, or are merged into, the active forces depending on the mobilization mission. The augmentation role for the Selected Reserve is programmed on a unit rather than an individual basis. For example, USAR brigades and battalions affiliate with active divisions for peace-time training and, when mobilized, deploy and fight as organic parts of those divisions.[10]

The Individual Ready Reserve (IRR) generally consists of personnel who have served recently in the active forces or in the Selected Reserve and have some additional period of obligation on their contract. The majority of IRR members do not participate in organized training, and they do not receive compensation. Individuals in the Individual Ready Reserve are also essential elements of the total force; however, this group has neither a force structure nor specific unit assignments.[11] Its importance lies in the members' potential availability to augment existing units or to increase manning levels.

The Standby Reserve. The Standby Reserve consists primarily of members who have completed their statutory six-year military obligation and have requested transfer to the Standby Reserve. Congressional action is necessary for mobilization of these Reserve members.

The Retired Reserve. The Retired Reserve consists of members who request to be transferred to the Retired Reserve or who are mandatorily retired because of age or years of service. These Reserve members are available for involuntary mobilization as authorized by Congress.

All three segments of the Reserve are subject to recall during war or during an emergency declared by Congress. As a result of various policy actions, Reservists may currently be recalled in the following order: Selected Reserve, Individual Ready Reserve, Standby Reserve, Retired Reserve. The Selected Reserve would be employed in a partial mobilization, and expanded mobilization would come from the Individual Ready Reserve on a selective basis. A European war or other major mobilization scenarios would require that all Reservists be mobilized and that there be a continuous flow of new volunteers or conscripts.[13]

Defense Department planners do not expect all individuals from each category of Reserves to be available in the event of a mobilization. Table 6.5 shows the estimated percentage of availability as determined by the 1975 DOD total-force study. The Defense Manpower Commission and others have criticized these figures as being overly optimistic, and their questioning results from the much lower yields experienced during the three Reserve mobilizations since World War II.[14] Shortfalls in the projected availability would further increase the manpower shortages already projected for a major mobilization.

Table 6.5

PROJECTED RESERVE COMPONENT M-DAY AVAILABILITY

(Percentage of assigned strength)

Component	Percent Availability
Selected Reserve	95
Individual Ready Reserve	70
Standby Reserve	50
Retired Reserve	10

Source: Defense Manpower Commission, *Defense Manpower: The Keystone of National Security* (Washington, DC: Government Printing Office, April 1976), p. 412.

The Reserves in the All-Volunteer Environment

As mentioned earlier, the initial effect on the Reserves of the AVF decision was the initiation of the total-force policy, which increased the responsibilities of the Reserve components and provided for reductions in active duty manpower to levels that presumably could be attained in an AVF environment. In addition, the decision to end the draft dramatically affected not only the Reserves' ability to acquire individuals but also the type of individual who enters the Reserve forces.

Declining Reserve Strength

Before 1973, long queues of draft-eligible men waited to join Reserve and Guard units because they recognized both the Reserves and the National Guard as a way to satisfy their military obligation and concurrently pursue their civilian careers. They also realized that the Reserve forces would not be activated en masse to fight in Vietnam. Estimates show that the draft motivated approximately 80 percent of the enlistments in the Air National Guard and the Air Force Reserve during this period.[15] When the draft ended, the lines of applicants disappeared, and Reserve recruiting difficulties and shortfalls began. For example, Reserve enlistments for NPS individuals decreased from approximately 180,000 in fiscal year 1970 to fewer than 50,000 in fiscal year 1974.[16] The Vietnam buildup was also a major influence on Reserve separations. Significant losses began in 1974 as large numbers of individuals who had joined the Reserves between 1968 and 1972 completed their military obligation. The net result was a continuing decline in Reserve strength through fiscal year 1980. Table 6.6 traces the trends in Selected Reserve strength through fiscal year 1980.

Table 6.6

SELECTED RESERVE STRENGTH

(End-year strength)

Fiscal Year	Strength
1964	953,256
1968	922,318
1972	924,557
1973	918,963
1974	924,568
1975	896,898
1976	822,992
1977	812,800
1978	788,000
1979	807,000
1980	850,000

Sources: US, Department of Defense, Office of the Assistant Secretary of Defense (Manpower, Reserve Affairs, and Logistics), *America's Volunteers: A Report on the All-Volunteer Armed Forces* (Washington, DC: December 1978), p. 373; *Defense 80* (July 1980): 24.

The programmed increases for fiscal years 1981 and 1982 anticipated further improved recruiting for and retention in the Selected Reserve. Indications are that these programs have been somewhat successful, but Selected Reserve strength is still short of peacetime objective strength.[17]

The most dramatic decline in manpower during the no-draft era has occurred in the Individual Ready Reserve. In 1973, more than 1,200,000 individuals were members of the IRR pool. By March 1981, the actual strength was 405,000.[18] Because the Individual Ready Reserve consists primarily of individuals who are completing the final years of their six-year military obligation, the major reasons for the decline are the smaller active-duty force levels that have been in effect since the early 1970s, the longer enlistment periods in the all-volunteer force, and the marked increase in the entry of PS individuals into the Selected Reserve. The Army is testing a program of direct entry into the Individual Ready Reserve as part of its MINUTEMEN Training Study, and in 1978, women enlisting in the armed forces began incurring the same six-year military obligation as males.[19] These programs have helped to reduce the decline in IRR strength, but as long as active force strength remains near its present level, significant increases in IRR strength will require bold initiatives.

Although congressionally authorized strengths have been reduced annually to reflect realistic estimates of the Reserves' ability to recruit and retain volunteers, the Reserve components still either fall short of these levels or achieve them with great difficulty.[20] The annual reductions in congressional authorizations lead to understatements of the size and seriousness of the Reserve manpower shortages. In his *Military Manpower and the All-Volunteer Force*, Richard V.L. Cooper, the director of defense manpower studies for the Rand Corporation, notes:

> For the Army Reserve and Marine Corps Reserve, simple comparisons of actual and authorized strengths probably underestimate the magnitude of the manpower shortage, since their "declining" authorized strengths may be less a measure of Reserve force requirements than they are an indicator of what the Services have felt could be sustained in the absence of the draft. Thus, whereas it is probably reasonable to review authorized strength of active duty forces as being more-or-less demand driven, the authorized strengths for the USAR and USMCR may have been much more supply-driven since the early 1970s.[21]

The inability of the Reserves to attain the authorized levels is certainly cause for concern. Of much greater significance, however, is to measure the shortages in Reserve strengths against the manpower requirements for a prolonged European conflict or other mobilization scenarios.

Estimates show that the Selected and Individual Ready Reserves can expect shortfalls of 400,000 to 850,000 individuals in the event of a prolonged European conflict.[22] Two issues hamper any effort to determine the seriousness of these projected shortfalls. In the first place, what should be the role of the Selective Service System in meeting manpower requirements? And second, what is the likely duration of a major European conflict?

The decision to end conscription placed the Selective Service System in what DOD officials described as a "deep standby" status. As a result, they estimated that the Selective Service could not begin to deliver manpower until mobilization plus 110 days (M+110) and it could deliver only 390,000 individuals after six months. This situation meant that the Reserve components were not merely the primary but the sole source of augmentation manpower for major conflict scenarios, and this probably implied an unreasonable and unrealistic situation. To correct the problem, the Selective Service System is being revitalized, a joint DOD-Selective Service System effort, and eighteen-year-old males are being registered for the draft. It is expected that these initiatives will enable the Selective Service to deliver the first inductee thirteen days after M-day and to deliver 100,000 inductees within thirty days after M-day. Inductees, however, become a meaningful source of mobilization manpower only after they have received the legally required minimum of twelve weeks of military training.[23]

The questions regarding the duration of a European conflict concern the probability of a prolonged conflict. In the event of an intense early conflict, a relative balance of opposing forces, and a potential escalation to nuclear conflict, many analysts perceive only a limited possibility that a conventional conflict between NATO and Warsaw Pact powers could last beyond thirty to ninety days.[24] However, a decision to provide manpower for a prolonged conflict (six months) would require a fully operational Selective Service System. The diminished IRR pool associated with the all-volunteer force and the difficulties in maintaining a Reserve force at full strength suggest that it is prudent to continue the initiatives undertaken to revitalize the Selective Service System and to register eighteen-year-old males.

Discussions of the Selective Service and Reserve roles and the probability of a prolonged conflict tend to divert attention from what may be the most critical Reserve manpower shortage, the shortage of mobilization manpower. The total-force policy has assigned Reserve forces increased roles and responsibilities immediately upon the outbreak of a conflict and mobilization. This action significantly extends the responsibilities of the Reserves beyond their traditional role as a backup and manpower pool for the active forces in the event of a prolonged conflict. Mobilization and deployment capabilities are no longer the sole responsibilit⁊ of the active forces; the Reserves now have a major part of this responsibility. Wartime structure requirements indentify M-day demands for the various force components; table 6.7 compares those wartime structure requirements with programmed Reserve strength in fiscal year 1982.

Table 6.7

FY 1982 SELECTED RESERVE WARTIME REQUIREMENTS AND PROGRAMMED STRENGTH

(In thousands)

Component	FY 1982 Wartime Requirement	FY 1982 Budget	Diff.
Army National Guard	446.1	397.7	− 48.4
Army Reserve	285.8	236.6	− 49.2
Naval Reserve	112.7	87.4	− 25.3
Marine Corps Reserve	42.0	38.5	− 3.5
Air National Guard	100.8	98.3	− 2.5
Air Force Reserve	67.8	64.0	− 3.8
Total	1,055.2	922.5	−132.7

Source: US, Department of Defense, Manpower Requirements Report for FY 1982 (1981), p. II–4.

If, in fiscal year 1982, the Selected Reserves attained their requested levels of 73,000 members above fiscal year 1980 levels, they still faced a gross shortage of about 132,000 individuals; the shortage increases to 179,000 individuals if we subtract the 5 percent of the Selected Reserves that would be unavailable on M-day. Furthermore, the shortage would be more severe should the Selected Reserve fail to increase from present levels to authorized strength and fail to retain the expected yield of 95 percent. The shortage becomes even more severe when one realizes that it is concentrated in the Army Reserve and the Army National Guard, which means a shortage of skilled enlisted combat personnel. These vacancies must be filled from the Individual Ready Reserve that must augment the land-force active and Reserve units and replace casualties during the early days of combat. At current manning levels in the regular Army and Selected Reserve, IRR mobilization manpower requirements are estimated to be between 200,000 and 500,000 (numbers vary depending on estimates of early combat casualties and projections of the number of IRR personnel who will show up when mobilized). Compounding the numbers problem is the skill mix. Only one-third of the Army's IRR members are trained in combat and medical skills, but over two-thirds of the augmented personnel and casualty replacements needed would have to have such skills.[25] This concentration of shortages further diminishes IRR capability to reduce them.

Changes in Composition and Quality of the Reserves

In addition to the problem of declining strength, the Reserves have made significant adjustments in the composition and quality of their accessions since the inception of the all-volunteer force. For example, the mix of NPS and PS recruits has changed dramatically since 1973. Historically, the Reserves relied on a mix of approximately 70/30 NPS and PS recruits during the draft era. The immediate postdraft period saw a switch to a mix of approximately 35/65.[26] In fiscal year 1970, 15 percent of those entering Guard and Reserve units were PS individuals; in fiscal year 1977, the figure was 65 percent. Objectives for Reserve accessions during the period 1978 to 1982 called for an NPS/PS mix of approximately 45/55. Although fiscal year 1981 recruiting objectives for Selected Reserve NPS and PS were achieved, one must question whether future goals can be attained without significant adjustments in Reserve compensation and recruiting budgets.[27]

In 1978, the Department of Defense undertook a number of initiatives to improve the ability of the Reserves to recruit NPS individuals. It conducted tests with full-time recruiters for the Guard and Reserves, examined reenlistment bonuses, and in June 1978, recommended significant changes in Reserve compensation. As a result of initiatives—enlistment bonuses, educational incentives, alternative enlistment options, joint-service advertising, and full-time recruiters—Selected Reserve strengths increased in 1980/81.[28] However, all indications are that the Reserve components will continue to depend heavily on PS accessions, and there is no consensus as to whether this heavy dependence on PS individuals is desirable. Some sources favor reliance on PS individuals because their experience and training allow the Reserves to maintain smaller, more effective manpower strengths and to reduce training costs.[29] Others argue that heavy reliance on PS individuals results in higher compensation costs, grade stagnation, and an aging force of questionable capability for mobilization.[30] Nevertheless, under current and forecast conditions, the Reserves do and will depend heavily on PS individuals to meet their annual accession requirements.

The other change resulting from the all-volunteer system has been the quality of the Reserve accessions. Two indicators are commonly used to judge enlisted recruit quality: level of education completed, high-school or non-high school graduate, and scores received on the DOD enlistment qualification test. Test scores are grouped into five categories: one and two, above average; three, average; four, below average; and five, markedly below average—and ineligible to enlist. In fiscal year 1981, Congress imposed ceilings on the number of category four recruits that each service could accept: 25 percent for fiscal years 1981 and 1982 and 20 percent thereafter.

The proportion of non-high school graduates increased from 6 percent of NPS male enlisted Reserve recruits in fiscal year 1970 to 58 percent in fiscal year 1980.[31] In terms of mental aptitude, category three individuals increased from 33 percent in fiscal year 1970 to 64 percent in fiscal year 1980, and category four figures increased from 5 to 13 percent. In January 1976, the Department of Defense introduced new tests for aptitude and trainability that were in effect through fiscal year 1980. During that period, tests were miscalibrated, which resulted in faulty score distributions. Recalibration of the scores—still ongoing for the Reserve components—has decreased the percentage of active force NPS accessions in category three and significantly increased the percentage in category four. For example, the DOD overall reported accessions in category four changed from 6 to 33 percent for fiscal year 1980. Therefore, the 89 percent NPS Reserve accessions in categories one, two, and three and the 11 percent in category four reported for fiscal year 1980 will be significantly different when revised to account for scoring error.[32]

The Future of the Total Force

The ultimate challenge to the AVF concept may lie in the years ahead. Two factors have contributed to the current relative success of the all-volunteer force. First, the pay for junior enlisted personnel is roughly comparable to wages in the private sector. Second, growth in the youth population and a decline in active duty strengths under the total-force policy have resulted in the military taking a smaller proportion of the available manpower pool. The eligible population more than doubled in the 1960s and 1970s, but the military is recruiting a smaller number of people for the active and Reserve forces.[33] Both of these factors, however, will change in the 1980s and 1990s. Legislation for pay comparability and initiatives in AVF compensation increased manpower costs from $24 billion in the last pre-Vietnam year, fiscal year 1964, to $83.2 billion in the President's budget for fiscal year 1982. As a percentage of total defense outlays, manpower costs climbed from 47 percent in fiscal year 1964 to a high of 61 percent in fiscal year 1976. These costs are projected at 42 percent in the proposed fiscal year 1982 budget. Efforts to hold down federal spending, the need to replenish war reserves, and the need to modernize weapon systems will impose severe constraints on increased military compensation to reduce manpower shortages.[34]

The 1980s and 1990s will also see a reversal in the availability of manpower. In 1978, the prime recruiting pool—males between seventeen and twenty-one years of age—reached its highest level, 10.8 million.[35] By 1990, that pool will have declined by 17 percent to approximately 9 million, which means the military will be competing with educational institutions and private employers for a dwindling number of young high-school graduates. Because enlistments are very much influenced by the state of the economy, it can be expected that recruiting trends during this period will fluctuate depending on employment opportunities in the private sector. Even in unfavorable economic times, however, the military must offer increasingly costly incentives to attract and retain quality people in the active and Reserve components.[36]

An Analysis of Prescriptions

Those dire projections have brought several proposals for policy changes and alternatives in defense manpower management. A principal deficiency in these proposals for both the active and the Reserve forces has been the absence of a broad viewpoint. Proposals for active force manpower management fail to consider the present relationship between the active and the Reserve forces. Thus, they fail to assess the impact of active force proposals on the Reserves and the total-force manpower situation. The same criticism holds true for various proposals to correct current deficiencies in Reserve manpower strength. Furthermore, only a few of the Reserve proposals do more than correct current deficiencies, and they fail to address the problem of further reduced manpower in the 1980s and 1990s.

The Reserve components are essentially part-time employers, but the active military is a full-time employer. The need to assess changes in the manpower policies of either type of force in terms of their effect on the other is, thus, not always readily apparent. However, three characteristics of today's Reserve forces make this assessment necessary. First, the Reserves currently depend primarily on PS individuals to meet their annual accession requirements. Changes in the size of and the rate of turnover in the active forces will directly affect the Reserves' access to these individuals. Second, enlistment in the Selected Reserve implies a six-to-twelve-month period of full-time initial training, and the Defense Manpower Commission has supported the assumption that the majority of NPS recruits will come from the same pool that provides manpower for the active forces.[37] Third, slightly more than 12 percent of the individuals undergoing military training and education are members of the Reserve components. Changes proposed for active military training will have a significant effect on the Reserve components, and correspondingly, changes in the number of NPS individuals recruited by the Selected Reserves will affect the training loads of the active forces, since more than 90 percent of all Reservists are enrolled in either basic or specialized skill training.[38]

Because of the primary role of the active forces in the total force and their budgetary predominance, most of the management alternatives have been directed toward the manpower problems of these forces. An examination of the force structure and budgetary adjustments that would be required of the Reserve forces if various proposals were adopted points to an obvious need to analyze proposals from the perspective of the total force. Although this viewpoint demonstrates that claimed budgetary savings and ability to meet manpower goals may be overstated in many cases, it also identifies a potential for testing and implementing proposed changes. The Rand Corporation, the Congressional Budget Office, and the Defense Manpower Commission have offered some proposals, and the Department of Defense has already implemented many of them.[39]

Reducing Attrition

The proportion of individuals who enlist in the active forces in a given year and do not complete their first three years of service has increased from approximately 25 percent to approximately 35 percent in the AVF environment. Department of Defense efforts to reduce first-term attrition rely primarily on improved leadership, training, compensation, quality of life programs, . . . and a more careful selection of persons taken into the armed forces.[40]

Reduction of first-term attrition is in the best interests of all the components of the total force since recruits come from the available manpower pool and, on attrition, are lost as manpower assets. Furthermore, one of the major costs of attrition is the loss of the training investment in individuals who do not complete their first enlistment. The Reserve components can be used to retain some of the training investment, and they can help to discourage attrition. All individuals who have completed training but do not complete their first enlistment should at least be placed in the Individual Ready Reserve if they have potential for service upon mobilization. The Army began following this procedure in 1979, and projections are that these additions will increase IRR strength by about 80,000 by 1985.[41] Certain individuals should also be considered for placement in the Selected Reserves. Both actions would reduce the loss of the training investment when people do not complete their first enlistment, and such actions may also reduce a person's tendency to void his or her enlistment contract.

Lower Enlistment Standards

On the one hand, the purpose of lowering the mental and physical standards for enlistment is to increase the number of eligible recruits. On the other hand, higher standards result in increased performance, and the current trend toward smaller forces with increasingly sophisticated weapons systems implies a need for more capable and flexible personnel. Lowering enlistment standards also does not help meet the objective of reducing attrition, since higher enlistment standards reduce attrition.

The Reserves already recruit a lower-quality NPS individual than the active forces. The success and capabilities of these individuals and units should be examined to determine the potential for reducing the quality goals of the active forces. Some analysts argue that the Reserves should actually seek a higher-quality individual than the active forces since Reserve personnel train only part-time and must retain skills over longer periods with less practice and supervision.[42]

One means of reducing quality standards and stemming the serious decline in IRR strength would be to enlist unqualified active duty volunteers directly into the Individual Ready Reserve. During their initial training, these individuals could be evaluated for possible entry into active duty units if their performance is acceptable. The training should also produce some positive benefits for society and for the individuals. This approach would resemble the approach in Project 100,000,[43] except that it would include a screening process.

Increased Recruitment of Women

Both the Reserves and the active forces have already greatly expanded the percentage of women among NPS recruits. In 1971, women composed only 0.4 percent of the total Selected Reserve strength. By 1981, women represented 7.8 percent of Selected Reserve strength and 17 percent of Selected Reserve NPS recruits.[44] However, the legal restrictions and societal questions regarding women in combat pose special problems for the Selected Reserves, who constitute a significant portion of the combat power of the armed forces. Most of the current shortages of personnel in the Selected Reserves are concentrated in the combat arms—infantry, armor, field artillery, and air defense artillery—of the Army National Guard and the US Army Reserve.[45] Current Army policy, as established by the Secretary of the Army, is to assign women to all units except battalion and smaller sized units of infantry, armor, cannon field artillery, combat engineers, and short-range air defense artillery.[46] Unless further changes regarding the role of women in combat are forthcoming, an increased recruitment of women into the Selected Reserves will not significantly affect the problem of the concentrated shortages in the combat arms.

The heavy reliance of the Selected Reserves on PS individuals and the shortages of PS individuals with combat skills means that Selected Reserve units must concentrate on male NPS accessions to fill vacancies in the combat arms. This, of course, places them in direct competition with the active forces who draw on the male NPS pool for similar reasons. The adoption of the six-year military obligation for both female and male enlistees in 1978 has helped to slow the decline in the IRR pool.

Increased Use of Civilians

Military manpower constraints have led the Defense Department to rely increasingly on federal civilian employees and private sector contractors for services not requiring military personnel. The majority of these civilians provide services directly related to the readiness of operational forces in such areas as logistics, communications, medicine, and maintenance of ships, aircraft, and weapons systems. If civilians are not available to perform these functions, military personnel must perform them. The size of the DOD civilian work force in 1981 was 135,000 less than what was required to support military peacetime and mobilization support needs. Increasing the size of the civilian force or an increased use of private sector contractors would free military personnel for combat units and thus reduce active force manpower requirements.[47]

Any proposal to reduce the number of active military billets would reduce both active annual accession requirements and departures from the military. Reductions in annual departures or active duty losses would also reduce the number of PS individuals available to the Reserves each year. This means that a part of the reduced annual active force requirement for NPS individuals would be balanced by increased Reserve requirements.

The current practice of organizing and equipping Reserve units to mirror active units also poses problems when large numbers of active military tasks are converted to civilian jobs. For example, if a contractor maintains an aircraft (T–43) for the active forces, what are the cost and manpower implications if the aircraft is transferred or added to the inventory of Reserve aircraft?

A major constraint on the conversion of active military billets to civilian jobs has been the matter of maintaining the capability to mobilize and deploy. A significantly different Reserve concept could help ease this constraint. In a national emergency, Reserve units and individuals could be programmed to perform mobilization or deployment functions normally performed by civilians or contract hires.

Capital/Labor Substitution

Proposals for an increased substitution of capital equipment for manpower are based on rapid increases in the relative price of military labor since 1971,[48] but the nature of Reserve duty limits the savings from this substitution. Essentially, the Reserves employ a part-time labor force in contrast to the full-time labor force in the active component, and capital goods are more difficult to employ on a part-time basis. Thus, Reserve units become more expensive as capital equipment is substituted for manpower—as in the active units.

Here again, a significantly different Reserve role could assist in implementing the substitution. Reserve personnel could function as individual fillers rather than serve in units that would augment active units in the event of mobilization. This would allow using a part-time, labor-intensive Reserve to augment a capital-intensive active force.

First-term/Career Mix

Proposals designed to lower the proportion of first-term individuals in order to reduce training costs and annual accession requirements would also have an adverse impact on the Reserve forces. These proposals would reduce the number of PS individuals, especially the relatively junior members, that are available to the Reserves. The resulting increase in Reserve NPS accession requirements would counterbalance some of the decrease in active accession requirements. More important, these NPS members would require individual and specialized training in contrast to Reserve PS accessions. The cost of this additional training would offset considerably the reduction in training costs that would result from a substitution of career for first-term personnel on active duty.

The Reserves also provide an excellent opportunity for examining a force whose members are predominantly career oriented as opposed to first-term personnel. The Reserve compensation system study found high compensation costs, grade stagnation, and an aging force of questionable mobilization capability to be the negative results of this type of force composition.[49]

Military Compensation/Retirement Changes

The total-force policy requires that proposals to change active duty compensation and retirement systems be considered in terms of their impact on the Reserve forces. Compensation for Reserve drill is directly linked to active duty compensation, and retirement credits are significant elements in Reserve compensation. Retirement credits for Reserve duty are especially important factors in the ability of the Reserves to attract PS individuals.[50] Most of the proposals for changing active duty compensation and retirement credits have failed to recognize the relationship between active and Reserve compensation. This neglect, in turn, has resulted in a failure to address the effect of the proposed changes on the Reserves' ability to recruit and maintain manpower strengths.

The Need for a Total-Force Viewpoint

Operating in a total-force environment requires assessing proposed manpower management alternatives for their effect on the total force rather than on one component of the force. The Selected Reserve and IRR manpower strengths inherited from the days of the draft have been depleted. Current and projected manpower shortages in the Reserve component can no longer be treated in isolation from the problems of the active component.

Under current total-force policy, the Reserve forces are organized, manned, and equipped to mirror active units and have similar roles and missions. Generally, Reserve units are not structured to embody some unique or special capability necessary only in the event of mobilization.

They are programmed to be used in the same manner as active units and have similar organizations and equipment. Therefore, any significant changes in active force structure and organization require similar adjustments in Reserve structure and organization.

Critics of annual accession requirements for the active forces frequently overlook the fact that the Reserves depend on PS individuals to meet their manpower requirements. Consequently, proposals to reduce the annual accession requirements of the active forces fail to address the effect of such reductions on Guard and Reserve accessions. Proposals to reduce the accession requirements of the active forces are actually programs designed to reduce losses of manpower in the active forces. That is, if overall strength is to remain constant, the annual accession requirements will directly correspond to losses for all causes (death, retirement, resignation, dismissal, and attrition). Overlooked is the fact that a large portion of the losses to the active forces are not actually losses to the total force. The Selected Reserves recruited 128,400 PS individuals in fiscal year 1980.[51] Furthermore, PS individuals bring valuable aptitudes, experience, and training into the Selected Reserves. Thus, although these individuals represent losses that must be replaced in the active forces, they continue to contribute to the total force.

Some critics of the accession requirements of the active forces have also used the NPS/PS mix of the Reserves to justify smaller Reserve forces. According to their logic, a reduction in the number of PS individuals available to, and recruited by, the Reserves should require more than a one-for-one replacement with NPS individuals. The use of a PS rather than an NPS individual also allows for considerable reductions in training costs.

Although the active forces will continue to draw the bulk of management attention and manpower initiatives, the total-force policy requires that proposed changes in the active forces be assessed in terms of their impact on the Reserves. Former Secretary of the Army Clifford Alexander perhaps best expressed the need for this perspective in these terms: "There are not specific Guard or Reserve topics; every important action taken by the Army concerns each of the partners who comprise the Total Army. We must continue to dispel the notion that there are 'active force issues' and 'Reserve force issues' because that concept does not square with our Total Army posture." [52]

Continuing Fundamental Reserve Issues

Reserve manpower problems represent the principal current challenge to the total force. These problems have been created in large part by what has been described as twenty-five years of neglect in the management of the Reserve forces. Although the volunteer environment increased their problems, the Reserves began the volunteer era with relatively few manpower problems, largely as a result of personnel acquired during the days of the draft. Therefore, proposals to correct Reserve deficiencies have only recently surfaced and are still in the test stage. Management practices and unresolved issues hamper the implementation of specific proposals to correct Reserve manpower shortages. For example, Reserve compensation will require significant adjustments to counter current and future manpower shortages.

The Gates Commission recognized the need for changes in Reserve compensation when the draft ended, and the Defense Manpower Commission reaffirmed the need for change when it recommended new incentives and compensation options for National Guard and Reserve programs.[53] However, continuing questions regarding Reserve requirements and desired force composition limit the design of specific compensation packages, recruiting programs, and other innovations. Improvements in the Selective Service System; the resolution of issues associated with Reserve requirements, availability, and composition; and increased congressional authorizations would significantly improve prospects for correcting deficiencies in the Reserves.

The Selective Service System

Relegation of the draft to its "deep standby" status made the Reserves both the primary and the sole source of manpower in the event of a prolonged conflict—this was unrealistic in a volunteer environment. The critical shortages in manpower for a prolonged conflict result from the tremendous decline in the Individual Ready Reserve since the end of the draft. The smaller active forces and the longer enlistment periods characteristic of the all-volunteer force make it unlikely that the Individual Ready Reserve will ever again attain sufficient strength to provide more than the augmentation manpower required for mobilization. This depletion of the Individual Ready Reserve underscores a critical need for a fully operational Selective Service System. That system should provide the additional manpower for a prolonged conflict, and the Reserves should maintain sufficient manpower to meet mobilization requirements.

Critical Manpower Issues

Three questions regarding actual mobilization manpower requirements, actual mobilization availability of various total-force components, and the optimum force structure and composition of Reserve units need to be answered before specific management actions can correct Reserve deficiencies. Disagreement over the answers to these questions has led to a lack of concern about Reserve shortfalls and has hampered developing specific corrective measures.

Mobilization requirements resulting from the 1975 DOD total-force study have been criticized as too high for a major European conflict. This criticism stems from questions regarding the length of a European conflict, present airlift and sealift capabilities, and casualty estimates.[54] Consequently, a former Assistant Secretary of Defense for Manpower and Reserve Affairs directed a detailed review of mobilization manpower requirements. Following determination of those requirements and a review of the Selective Service System, specific programs can be designed to ensure that the Reserve forces are capable of fulfilling their required roles.

The validity of assumptions regarding the availability of various total-force components has also been questioned. Three limited mobilizations since World War II support the contention that expectations of availability are much higher than the real capabilities of the Reserve forces.[55] Two simulated government-wide mobilization efforts, Nifty Nugget (1978) and Proud Spirit (1980), provided data for a realistic reassessment of these assumptions. Both exercises revealed huge shortfalls in IRR manpower —250,000 to 500,000 soldiers—and severe shortages of skilled technicians and medical personnel.[56]

Since the end of the draft, the Selected Reserves, largely as a matter of necessity rather than of design, have depended primarily on PS individuals to fill accession requirements. The objective calls for more NPS individuals than the number being recruited, and the study of the Reserve compensation system set out to design a package that would help to achieve this objective. But at the same time, the Reserves are commended and judged more capable because of their high number of PS recruits.[57] Obviously, management actions to increase Reserve strength depend on resolution of this issue.

After the required and desired levels of Reserve forces have been determined, Congress should discontinue its practice of reducing authorized strengths to levels that Reserve forces can realistically achieve each year. This practice creates the impression that the Reserves have no severe manpower shortages and no firm manpower requirements. Concerted action in this area should significantly improve the prospects for correcting Reserve manpower shortages and for making the total-force concept a reality.

Will the All-Volunteer and Total-Force Policies Survive?

The all-volunteer force clearly depends on the total-force policy for its success. If the nation had unlimited resources, it could best meet its security requirements with active forces, but it does not have unlimited resources. The smaller active duty forces realistically attainable in a volunteer environment require increased reliance on capable and effective Reserve forces. What do the Reserve manpower problems mean for the future of the all-volunteer force? The answer seems clear. Continuing manpower shortages in the Reserves prevent the total force from fulfilling assigned responsibilities. The Reserves simply do not have enough trained and available members to perform their mobilization missions and replacement functions, and since the all-volunteer force depends on the total force, the manpower problems of the Reserves directly threaten the volunteer concept. These problems are primarily a result of the volunteer experience and the removal of the draft incentive. The Reserves have adjusted to their manpower shortages by relying more heavily on PS individuals, and this adjustment has allowed them to function effectively with fewer individuals.

Recommended changes in the active force to meet demographic changes during the 1980s and 1990s portend more problems for the Reserves. Reductions in active military strength and less turnover will directly reduce the number of PS individuals available to the Reserves and will further increase Reserve manpower problems. Can the total force be made a reality? Does a successful total force ensure the success of the all-volunteer concept? The answer to the first question is yes, but it remains uncertain whether a total force can be achieved in an all-volunteer environment. The problems of the all-volunteer force involve much more than total-force and Reserve-manpower problems. Although correction of Reserve manpower problems is vital to the all-volunteer force, it is not enough to ensure the success of that force.

However, the total-force concept probably does represent the most rational use of national resources in providing defense and security for the nation. Some mixture of higher-cost active forces and lower-cost Reserve forces is the optimum combination of efforts and resources employed in the nation's defense.

7
Reserve Readiness: Proving the Total-Force Policy a Success

W. Stanford Smith

Ten years of experience provide the opportunity now to appraise the capability of the nation's Reserve forces under two major DOD manpower policies adopted in 1973—the all-volunteer force and the total-force policy. By any reasonable criteria, the Reserve forces must be given high marks. In training exercises and readiness inspections, units of all the Reserve components are constantly proving their capability to perform alongside their active-force counterparts.

Not all the manpower problems of these forces have been solved. But steady gains in Reserve strength since the end of fiscal year 1978 have proved the validity of research that indicated the need for incentives in an all-volunteer environment. And additional incentives may well be needed to meet serious problems in the future when business conditions improve both full-time and part-time job opportunities and the population of prime recruiting age declines.

Snapshot pictures of National Guard and Reserve strength trends in the first six years of these manpower policies caused many to pronounce

Adapted from W. Stanford Smith, "Reserve Readiness in a Changing Environment," *Defense Management Journal* 17 (Third Quarter 1981): 21–27.—ED.

the total-force policy a failure. These conclusions, however, failed to recognize that almost no initiatives to encourage recruiting and retention in the Reserve forces in an all-volunteer environment had been implemented while many incentives caused some recruiting successes in the active forces.

Although the citizen-soldier concept is as old as the Republic, the total-force policy and the all-volunteer force have placed even greater reliance on the National Guard and Reserve than ever before. Half of the nation's combat power and two-thirds of its support capability are maintained in the Reserve forces. Simply stated, deterring our potential adversaries depends significantly on maintaining the strength of these forces and providing a correct perception of this strength.

In his analysis of the Reserve (chapter 6), Moxon's pessimistic view that the total-force policy has not been successful suffers from an overemphasis on failures in its early years. Further, he relies on analyses undertaken before the Reserve manpower initiatives began to take effect. Pessimistic views of "show rates" (the percentage of Reservists who would answer a mobilization call) are not substantiated by analysis or comparable experience in past call-ups. Current policies are more likely to increase, not decrease, the "show rates." Furthermore, any assumption that large numbers of National Guard and Reserve personnel would not answer the call in a national emergency is contrary to the experiences of history and to the basic American spirit of voluntarism.

The greatly improving capability of the Selective Service System to provide draftees promptly in any future national emergency reduces the time during which active and Reserve forces in being must provide our total defense. Furthermore, Moxon is not correct when he asserts that manpower shortages are and will continue to be the "predominant problem facing the total force." All concerned now recognize that the enormous equipment shortages in the total force, particularly the Reserve ground forces, represent a far more serious problem.

But Moxon is on target when he says "confusion about Reserve organization has been a major problem in assessing the impact of Reserve manpower deficiencies." His chapter contributes to an understanding of this organizational structure.

Public discussion of the real capability of Reserve forces has been obscured by overstatements or understatements concerning their strength problems and by generalizations that fail to differentiate among the major components of the Reserve forces. Even within the Department of Defense, some midlevel management personnel have sometimes drawn erroneous inferences about the entire Ready Reserve based on the severe decline in strength of the Individual Ready Reserve. A realistic analysis of the strength of the Reserve forces must examine and evaluate the individual Reserve elements.

The Ready Reserve now has a strength of more than 1,350,000 personnel, with a personnel strength of units in the National Guard and Reserve of more than 850,000.[1] A fact often overlooked in public discussion is that these units train regularly and comprise a force larger than the active armies of France and West Germany combined.

The other major element of the Ready Reserve is the Individual Ready Reserve (IRR). Historically, the size of the Individual Ready Reserve has been a function of the size of the active force, since individuals released from active service must remain in the Individual Ready Reserve until the end of their statutory military service obligation. As large numbers of men were drafted during the Vietnam years, the IRR element reached a strength of 1.5 million. Because this sum exceeded any foreseeable mobilization requirement, serious management attention was not focused on the Individual Ready Reserve. Its greatly reduced strength remains a serious problem because it is the primary source of fillers for active and Reserve units and of replacements for early combat losses. However, care must be taken not to generalize about the IRR element. It also must be examined in relation to its separate role in the air, naval, and land Reserve forces.

Air Reserve

The Air Reserve forces present a textbook case of success for the total-force policy. Units of the Air National Guard and Air Force Reserve ended fiscal year 1982 at all-time high strengths of 100,700 and 64,400, respectively. A measure of this success is reflected in the fact that these units have repeatedly demonstrated their capability to mobilize and deploy within seventy-two hours. Using the standards applied to active Air Force units, operational readiness inspections confirm the readiness of these units. Furthermore, the Air Reserve forces maintain interceptors and crews on an around-the-clock, peacetime-alert status. Air Reserve tankers also refuel Strategic Air Command bombers on a regular basis and sustain a contingent of fighter aircraft on alert status. Units in an associate program within the Air Force Reserve use active Air Force aircraft such as C–141s to perform needed peacetime missions as a by-product of training. Reserve crews who regularly fly such aircraft are indistinguishable from active-force crews.

One reason for the outstanding success of the Air Reserve forces was early recognition by the Air Force of the essentiality of these units to the total-force concept. The decision to assign adequate numbers of full-time personnel to the units—usually as many as 20 percent of the total strength—and to provide mission-related training has enhanced morale and contributed significantly to strength maintenance.

The principal strength problem of the Air Reserve forces is similar to that of the active Air Force: retaining highly skilled middle-management officers and senior noncommissioned officers. Retention of these highly skilled personnel is essential to maintaining the high levels of readiness achieved by the Air Reserve forces. Increases in pay have helped, and planned future pay increases should assist in further reducing attrition.

The Individual Ready Reserve is a much less serious problem for the Air Force because of the strength and readiness of the Air Reserve forces. While the strength of the Air Force Individual Ready Reserve has declined in active Air Force strength, the IRR element remains at about 43,000, a level sufficient to augment the Air Forces by about 25 percent. Air Force tests have confirmed the ability of the Air Force to locate and issue recall orders to these personnel.

Strength of the Air Ready Reserve forces since the end of the draft is shown in table 7.1.

Naval Reserve

The Naval Reserve suffered for several years from indecision within the Department of Defense as to the required strength of its Selected Reserve. Since 1972, five studies have reached varying conclusions about the Naval Selected Reserve's required strength. None of the studies recommended less than a strength of 87,000. Nonetheless, for three consecutive years, the Department of Defense asked the Congress for a Naval Reserve strength of only 52,000. Congress, however, rejected these recommendations and continued authorizing a strength of 87,000 or more.

Despite the damage to the morale of the force, the Navy maintained fairly constant Selected Reserve strength throughout this period of indecision. The lowest end strength of 83,000 occurred at the end of fiscal year 1978, but this was rectified in succeeding years by a dedicated effort within the Naval Reserve. By the end of fiscal year 1980, the end strength reached 87,000, and it has continued to increase, ending fiscal year 1982 at 93,900. Further increases in the Naval Selected Reserve are programmed, and there is little doubt that the Navy can achieve this programmed strength.

An important element of the Naval Selected Reserve is its air arm. Like its Air Force counterpart, this Naval Reserve element has demonstrated a high level of combat readiness. The Naval Reserve's two carrier air wings have consistently proved this capability to the Navy and the Department of Defense. Similarly, Naval Reserve patrol units on both coasts have earned praise from their active Navy counterparts by consistently performing on a par with active fleet squadrons.

Admittedly, the Navy's Individual Ready Reserve has declined along with the decreasing strength of the active Navy. Today, that end strength stands at about 78,000, a level that is capable of providing fillers and replacements to meet the predraft needs of the Navy. This level will

Table 7.1
AIR READY RESERVE STRENGTH
(In thousands)

	FY 1974	FY 1976	FY 1978	FY 1980	FY 1982
Air National Guard	93.9	91.0	91.7	96.3	100.7
USAFR Selected Reserve	46.4	48.4	53.9	58.9	64.4
Total Selected Reserve	140.3	139.4	145.6	155.2	165.1
Individual Ready Reserve	121.0	82.9	46.0	46.7	43.4
Total Ready Reserve	261.3	222.3	191.6	201.9	208.5

allow the Selective Service System adequate time to draft inductees and provide the Navy with an opportunity to train them for additional fillers and replacements.

Like the other Services, the Navy faces the problem of retaining highy skilled personnel in both the active Navy and the Reserve. The market research indicates that the financial incentives—including the attraction of retirement under the Reserve retirement laws—will help solve this problem.

Strength trends of the Naval Ready Reserve forces are shown in table 7.2.

Land-forces Reserve

The land forces represent the most serious strength-maintenance problem in both the active and Reserve components. When the Department of Defense began implementing the all-volunteer force, it concentrated its energy and resources on manning the active force through financial incentives, more and better recruiters, and advertising. Only in the past four years has the Department of Defense made similar efforts to enhance recruitment and retention of personnel in the Reserve components. These steps were desperately needed by the Army to reverse its Selected Reserve losses of about 100,000 and its IRR's decline from a strength of more than a million to about 150,000 in fiscal year 1977. Fortunately, this picture is now changing significantly and favorably.

Table 7.2
NAVAL READY RESERVE STRENGTH
(In thousands)

	FY 1974	FY 1976	FY 1978	FY 1980	FY 1982
Selected Reserve	114.9	97.0	82.8	86.8	93.9
Individual Ready Reserve	178.9	106.4	93.2	97.0	77.7
Total Ready Reserve	293.8	203.4	176.0	183.8	171.6

Those unfamiliar with manpower management often ask why the Army has more serious recruiting problems than the other Services. It has always been more difficult to recruit for what is perceived to be the most dangerous form of combat. The other Services also offer far more military occupational specialties with skills that can be more readily transferred to civilian life.

Sheer size is another reason why recruitment for the Army Reserve appears difficult. The Army Selected Reserve constitutes approximately two-thirds of the total DOD Selected Reserve. If the Marine Corps Reserve is included, land Reserve forces total more than 70 percent of the entire DOD Selected Reserve.

During the Army Selected Reserve's precipitate decline in strength, it was necessary to set intermediate strength objectives each year. Congress authorized and appropriated funds only for whatever strength seemed reasonably achievable. Given these circumstances, the Army could achieve 100 percent of its goal in a given year and yet make no progress toward eliminating its shortfall. Many observers failed to perceive the consequences of this approach or the effect it had on the Army's Selected Reserve status when compared to the strength levels of the other Services.

Aware of the need to rectify this situation, the Department of Defense is now programming to achieve the goals it wants to achieve, not those it only thinks it can reach. This changeover recognizes significant improvements in the Army National Guard and Army Reserve strength during the past four fiscal years. In fiscal year 1979, the Army began the turnaround in the strength shortfall of its Selected Reserve by gaining nearly 9,000 over its fiscal year 1978 end strength. During succeeding years, the momentum increased when the Army Guard and Army Reserve strength increased annually to 407,600 for the Army National Guard and 256,700 for the Army Reserve at the end of fiscal year 1982. (See table 7.3.)

These gains are not attributable solely to financial incentives. To say that would be failing to recognize the enormous effort put forth by the Army Forces Command, the Army Recruiting Command, and the unit leadership throughout the Army National Guard and Army Reserve to reverse the negative recruitment and retention trends facing the Guard and Reserve. Employing challenging training, providing modern equipment, and recognizing the service of units and individuals also have contributed greatly toward heightening morale and increasing end strength.

Further gain in the number of drilling Reservists in the Army Selected Reserve is being helped by the increase of full-time personnel in Army units. These increases contribute significantly to improved training, recruiting, and administration. The Air Reserve forces have proven

Table 7.3
LAND-FORCES READY RESERVE
(In thousands)

	FY 1974	FY 1976	FY 1978	FY 1980	FY 1982
Army National Guard	403.4	362.3	341.0	366.6	407.6
Army Selected Reserve	234.9	194.6	185.8	205.7	256.7
Marine Corps Selected Reserve	31.2	29.6	32.7	35.4	40.5
Total Land Selected Reserve	669.5	586.5	559.5	607.7	704.8
Army IRR	532.6	226.4	168.6	205.3	219.0
Army Inactive National Guard	8.2	14.8	8.6	7.2	11.0
Marine Corps IRR	89.7	53.9	39.6	56.8	44.6
Total Land IRR/ING	630.5	295.1	216.8	269.3	274.6
Total Land Ready Reserve	1,300.0	881.6	776.3	877.0	979.4

beyond a doubt that full-time personnel help commanders provide an environment that supports and retains unit strength.

The Marine Corps Reserve is a significant element in the land Reserve forces that also has suffered strength problems. Like the Army, the Corps has exerted a major effort to correct its strength shortfalls. Since fiscal year 1976, the Marine Corps Selected Reserve has been gaining slowly while maintaining its high standards of acceptance. The Reserve units' able performances under those high standards are visible during unannounced mobilization tests with active Marine units.

The greatest manpower problem lies in rebuilding the pool of pretrained personnel to provide fillers for land-force active and Reserve units and to replace casualties in the early days of combat. The Army sets this requirement at 500,000. (Table 7.3 also shows the end strength of Individual Ready Reserve and Inactive National Guard land forces since 1974.) Analysts differ in their calculations of the gross size of this mobilization manpower shortage because of varying estimates of early combat casualties and differing projections of the show rate of IRR personnel at mobilization. When these factors are evaluated, the shortage appears to be in an unacceptably high range. Obviously, this shortfall in strength is extensive. It is further compounded because of military occupational specialty mismatches—a need for young combat-arms personnel versus an Individual Ready Reserve of older personnel trained in diverse specialties.

There are, however, other sources of mobilization manpower, including the option to recall Standby Reservists and military retirees. Use of these personnel is a short-term expedient until the Department of Defense can implement a long-range program to increase to required levels the other elements of the pretrained manpower pool. Since 1978, initiatives to improve the management and strength of the pretrained manpower resource have resulted in the maintenance of an excellent mobilization asset. New initiatives to build this pool require funding for enlistment and reenlistment bonuses. A test of direct enlistment into the Individual Ready Reserve for initial training and assignment to the mobilization pool was moderately encouraging as a new source of accessions for the Army.

Initiatives to improve the management of the Army's Individual Ready Reserve can also contribute to reducing the net shortage of personnel for mobilization. For example, keeping personnel records current and preassigning personnel to specific mobilization slots can assure that IRR personnel can be located with a minimum of delay and that they will report promptly. Any improvement in the predicted 70 percent IRR show rate contributes to reducing the projected shortage.

Public Support

Public understanding and support is the critical factor in achieving the strength goals of the Reserve forces. This is why the Department of Defense identified increasing public support for the Guard and Reserve as a major goal of the Deputy Assistant Secretary of Defense for Reserve Affairs.

An extensive program of DOD-supported research confirms that the Reserve components as a whole can reach required strength levels in the years ahead only with public support. Although recent public opinion polls show generally favorable attitudes toward the military, action must be taken to develop support and understanding for enlistment among groups that have traditionally exerted a negative influence. The research also confirms the importance of financial incentives and indicates that the educational assistance now offered should not only be cost-effective, but also be geared to higher quality prospects. Incentives for affiliation or reenlistment with a Selected Reserve unit have the best chance of enhancing retention. External factors, such as attitudes of spouse and employer, also are shown to exert an important effect on reenlistment decisions.

If the Reserve forces are to play a major part in deterring our potential adversaries, they will require the support of the general public. That support will be forthcoming if our defense planners can provide a realistic analysis and presentation of Reserve forces' needs, strengths, and shortcomings. An informed public understanding, combined with an appropriate investment and application of resources, can enable the Reserve components to achieve their required manpower levels and to fulfill their enhanced missions under the total-force policy.

8
Pretrained Individual Manpower: Albatross or Phoenix?

Bennie J. Wilson III
James R. Engelage

> God save thee, ancient Mariner!
> From the fiends, that plague thee thus!—
> Why look'st thou so?—With my cross-bow
> I shot the Albatross.
> —Coleridge, *The Rime of the Ancient Mariner*

With the emphasis on units, rather than individuals, in the management of military manpower, some within the Defense community would assert that, like the Ancient Mariner who killed the pious bird of good omen, the total force faces untold peril if it persists in denying sufficient resources in the management and administration of its pretrained individual manpower (PIM) assets. Others within the same community would claim just as eloquently that, after a period of considerable neglect, the past few years have seen a resurgence of resources devoted to these assets, reflecting an increased appreciation of the value of PIM resources within the all-volunteer force environment. They would liken the newly found status of these manpower resources to the rebirth of the phoenix rather than to the death of the Mariner's albatross.

The purpose here is to motivate students of national security to seek the information needed for an informed exchange of views on the merits

---

This is an original article written especially for this book.—ED.

and the shortcomings of a controversial source of total-force military manpower. This could be a difficult task. Experience has shown that few members of the total-force community fully appreciate the intricacies of what some have characterized as the more insipid side of the military manpower algorithm—pretrained individual manpower.

What, exactly is pretrained individual manpower and why should it be the subject of interest and discussion? Pretrained? As in prior to training or as in trained beforehand? Individual? As opposed to organized unit? Unfortunately, nomenclature can be confusing, particularly if it says what it means, yet one is conditioned to the "bureaupathic" [1] utterance from within the Department of Defense.

In fact, pretrained individual manpower is a resource of individuals, trained and experienced in military skills, and available to provide those skills during a national emergency. Their individualism derives from the fact that they are not members of military units in the traditional sense. [2] Generally, however, the members of the PIM resource are as experienced in the skills of war as many of their active force and Selected Reserve unit compatriots. Nearly all pretrained individuals are former members of active force and Selected Reserve units.

More technically, pretrained individual manpower refers to those prior service individuals who are no longer on active duty or in Selected Reserve units, who have received initial military training, and who are available during a mobilization to fill initial wartime manpower requirements until the draft can sustain such needs. The components comprising pretrained individual manpower include the Individual Ready Reserve (IRR), the Inactive National Guard (ING), Individual Mobilization Augmentees (IMA), the Standby Reserve, and retired military personnel.

At the present time, the supply of trained military manpower from all sources under the managerial control of the Department of Defense and planned for use during a mobilization falls woefully short of wartime requirements. For example, during fiscal year 1983 the aggregate manpower shortfall—not considering skills—was estimated to be 179,000 in the Army alone and affected significantly our ability to sustain a full mobilization. This situation continues today. During a full mobilization, European-based and early deploying units would have to fight at less than wartime required strength. Later deploying active and Reserve units and US-based units would have to provide trained personnel to replace casualties and to fill early deploying units. There would be severe shortages of combat and medical skills; the shortage of trained people would continue for more than six months. There simply could be no early expansion of the force beyond the current structure. [3]

This, therefore, is the primary motivation for Defense manpower managers at all levels to be knowledgeable of the issues bearing upon PIM assets, and forms the underlying thesis of this chapter. Having obtained such knowledge, it is for these managers to decide whether pretrained individual manpower is a dying albatross, a rising phoenix, or a hybrid, and to respond accordingly.

Before examining PIM assets in detail, it is useful to note that PIM issues are different from, although somewhat associated with, issues regarding the pros and cons of the all-volunteer force (AVF) relative to peacetime conscription. These latter issues, while pertinent to methods of military recruitment and manpower management in a peripheral sense, do not address the more comprehensive aspects of managing and efficiently allocating pretrained military manpower assets. Further, while the AVF versus draft debate may have certain academic utility, such esoteric discourse rarely meets the tests of today's political and economic realities.[4] The political realities opposing a return to the draft, plus the economic realities of allocating scarce resources, set immediate limits on implementing a form of conscription within either the active force or the Guard and Reserve forces.

Having said this, however, it should be noted that the subject of a restricted draft into one segment of the PIM resource will be addressed in some of the paragraphs that follow. Nevertheless, the issues involved in the total discussion of pretrained individual manpower as a mobilization asset have much more depth, substantively and intellectually, than that involved in a strictly AVF versus draft debate. Rather, this chapter focuses on the challenge of insuring, or at least approaching, equilibrium in the military manpower arena in terms of supply and requirements without the need for peacetime conscription.

Individual Ready Reserve

The Individual Ready Reserve (IRR) has been called the most important source of pretrained individual manpower.[5] Of all the PIM categories, IRR members are among the best trained and are readily available for mobilization during a national emergency.[6] They are primarily individuals who have served up to four years on active duty and are serving the remainder of their military service obligation in the IRR element.[7] About 24 percent of IRR members have elected to remain in the Individual Ready Reserve beyond their statutory obligation. About 90 percent of IRR members originally joined the military through the active force, while most of the remaining members originally joined through the Selected Reserve unit program.

From its peak strength of about 1.6 million members in fiscal year 1971, the Individual Ready Reserve declined to a low point of only 334,000 members in June, 1978 [8]—primarily as a result of the active force strength reductions after the Vietnam conflict. Largely owing to several strength initiatives, to be summarized later, the strength of the Individual Ready Reserve stood at about 406,000 at the end of fiscal year 1983.

The dynamics of IRR strength manifests itself in several ways. It is largely a function of the strength of the active force. As noted earlier, the vast majority of IRR members have been recently released from active duty and are serving the remaining portions of their military service obligations in the Individual Ready Reserve. But IRR strength is also a function of the amount of time initially served on active duty and of the number of IRR members who voluntarily remain in the Individual Ready Reserve beyond their military service obligation.

Among past initiatives to increase IRR strength was establishing a military service obligation for women and men over the age of twenty-six who entered the military, and eliminating the automatic transfer of IRR members to the Standby Reserve during the sixth year of their military service obligation. Shorter enlistment options for active duty—for example, two or three years—were also offered and, thus, increased the amount of time an individual served in the Individual Ready Reserve. Further, largely at the urging of Congress, the Army implemented the Transfer in Lieu of Discharge Program (TLDP) whereby selectively screened individuals who would otherwise be discharged before completing their active duty enlistments are transferred to the Individual Ready Reserve instead (examples are failure to complete initial military training, unsuitability, hardship, pregnancy, and sole survivor). In addition, during fiscal year 1981, Congress authorized a one-year test of an IRR reenlistment bonus. Finally, in fiscal year 1983 the Army introduced a program to permit direct enlistment into the Individual Ready Reserve.

These actions are credited with adding nearly 74,000 members to the IRR element at savings of over $500 million in replacement, recruiting, and training costs. These "savings," however, ignore certain ongoing "costs," or disadvantages, resulting from some of the initiatives. Further, not all the initiatives led to a net strength increase in the total force, although IRR strength was increased. For example, during the past few years the Army's Transfer in Lieu of Discharge Program has resulted in the transfer of approximately 32,000 soldiers to the Individual Ready Reserve. Although these individuals represent roughly a mere 8 percent of the total IRR membership in the Department of Defense, and only about 14 percent of the Army Individual Ready Reserve, they probably account for a high percentage, rightly or wrongly, of the misconceptions and misinformation regarding the IRR element. It is not unusual to hear members of the Congress, the media, and even officials of the Department of Defense, express the view that the Individual Ready Reserve might not be considered a viable mobilization force because it includes members who either have not finished their initial entry training or who receive uncharacterized discharges.

It is often claimed that the Army initiated the Transfer in Lieu of Discharge Program at the insistence of Congress—this is only partly true. In a 1978 report, the House Committee on Armed Services did urge the Army to transfer dischargees to the IRR element if they were to receive an honorable discharge or a discharge under honorable conditions, because "it does not make sense to summarily discharge these individuals of their statutory obligation." [9] However, the House went on to say in the same report that it is understandable if the Army does not transfer to the Individual Ready Reserve those individuals who are discharged for failure to complete training. Nevertheless, since December 1980, the Army has transferred to the Individual Ready Reserve more than 4,600 soldiers who failed to complete their initial training.

Although the General Accounting Office (GAO), an arm of the Congress, has questioned the appropriateness of a portion of the Army's Transfer in Lieu of Discharge Program, the Army wants to retain the program.[10] The Army's rationale is that, given the less-than-desired strength of the Individual Ready Reserve, transferees under the Transfer in Lieu of Discharge Program have mobilization potential, and the cost of the program is minimal.

Still another IRR measure must be considered with regard to "savings": the offer of shorter active duty enlistment options. Although this initiative extends the time members serve in the Individual Ready Reserve, it does not, *per se*, increase total-force manpower strength. More significantly, it might be argued that this initiative *reduces* the mobilization potential of the total force by putting manpower assets into the IRR element which might otherwise have remained in the active force under longer enlistment periods. It is argued legitimately, however, that had not the shorter enlistment options been offered, some of the individuals would not have joined the military in the first place. The point to remember is that programs to increase IRR strength—as important as they may be to the total force—nevertheless must be evaluated in relation to the manpower needs of the active forces and the Selected Reserve.

In any event, these actions have not been sufficient to maintain an increased IRR strength level. While they added nearly 74,000 members to the Individual Ready Reserve by fiscal year 1981, the *net* increase to the IRR element from the advent of these initiatives in 1978 to the end of fiscal year 1982 was only 50,000 members because IRR strength decreased in fiscal year 1982. Anticipating this downward trend, the Office of the Secretary of Defense recommended additional measures for increasing IRR strength levels.

Some of these relatively new initiatives were in the form of legislative changes proposed by the Military Manpower Task Force,[11] and have since been passed into law. They include authorization for the Secretary of Defense to extend the military service obligation (MSO) of future entrants into the military from the current six years to up to eight years (see note 7). This new variant of an old idea is viewed as a long-term, permanent solution to the problem of mobilization manpower shortfalls.[12] Still another recent legislative provision is the reinstatement and enhancement of the IRR reenlistment bonus program that the Army tested during fiscal year 1981. It also has been recommended, but not yet enacted into law, that eligibility for Servicemen's Group Life Insurance (SGLI) be extended to IRR members as an incentive to remain in the Individual Ready Reserve.

An initiative that has also been recommended by the Military Manpower Task Force and that can be implemented at the option of the Services is to impose an IRR obligation on active force members and Selected Reservists who reenlist. The Army has approved this program. It requires individuals to serve a two-year period in the Individual Ready Reserve after completing their reenlistments, even though the military service obligation may have expired.

Finally, a DOD initiative, which the Army implemented in fiscal year 1982, is the IRR Direct Enlistment Program. Under this program, an individual can undergo initial entry training and remain in the Individual Ready Reserve without having to serve either on active duty or in the Selected Reserve, other than to undergo periodic refresher training. This program was developed to apply to combat skills only; however, the Army has expanded it to include medical skills.

It was estimated that these IRR strength initiatives could add up to 280,000 members to the Army IRR force by the end of fiscal year 1992. This would mean that by 1993, for the first time in history, the aggregate mobilization manpower shortfall would be eliminated in peacetime without the need for a military draft.

The mobilization manpower shortage, however, is more than one of numbers—it is also one of skill mismatches. The aggregate shortfall distorts the skill-imbalance problem by combining the supply of all officers and enlisted skills.[13] The mobilization skill imbalances form the most serious manpower concerns within the total force. There is considerable disagreement, however, regarding how these imbalances should be resolved, at least insofar as they include the Individual Ready Reserve. The solutions offered can be summarized under three approaches: the shotgun approach, an IRR draft, and the skill selectivity approach.

The shotgun approach to increasing IRR strength merely involves having an excessively large IRR force, thereby increasing the likelihood of having sufficient numbers of appropriate military skills. For example, if the Army has an aggregate shortfall of about 150,000 people at mobilization, the skills imbalance may be 300,000 people: the shortfall under the shotgun approach is about 600,000. The advantage of this method is that it creates a larger IRR pool of replacement and reinforcement manpower, but it assumes the excess IRR members are flexible in the skills they possess.[14] The obvious disadvantage is that it is a very inefficient use of a resource. Unfortunately, many of the past IRR strength initiatives and some of the current proposals, to varying extents, are forms of the shotgun approach and share this shortcoming to some degree.

An IRR draft has been proposed as a way of resolving IRR skill shortages.[15] Without addressing the political and social implications inherent in such an approach, there are other considerations of equal import. One of these is cost. According to officials of the Selective Service System, the basic yearly cost of operating the draft machinery, even before the first draftee is notified, is approximately $90 million. As OSD studies show, at that cost an IRR draft would only be cost effective at induction levels exceeding 100,000 draftees a year. At these levels, however, the training of such large numbers of IRR draftees would require an extensive expansion of the training base at tremendous cost. Further, the result would be a large number of unmotivated soldiers forced into the Individual Ready Reserve, and who would have no unit-oriented combat training and experience. The IRR draft approach, therefore, while interesting in its simplicity, is economically, managerially, and, of course, politically and socially unattractive.

The third approach toward resolving mobilization skill imbalances involves selectively manning the Individual Ready Reserve with personnel who possess the most important and critically short military skills. It is the approach that requires the most innovative techniques in recruiting and retaining needed mobilization manpower resources and that focuses directly on the pertinent dimensions of the manpower problem and on the relevant means for resolving it. Examples of this approach include an IRR direct enlistment program and an IRR reenlistment bonus program limited to needed critical mobilization skills.[16]

This rather detailed discussion of the Individual Ready Reserve emphasizes the importance the Department of Defense places on it as an integral part of the total force. This sense of priority in providing for the peacetime management of the Individual Ready Reserve is shared, to some degree, by all elements of the defense community. The Army, with the largest shortfall, has been the most aggressive in working with the Office of the Secretary of Defense in developing and implementing IRR strength initiatives, followed closely by the Marine Corps, which has essentially solved its mobilization shortfall problem. The Navy, in the process of implementing a suitably flexible data automation program, has expressed a desire to improve the management of its Individual Ready Reserve. Finally, while the Air Force has not shown a propensity for expanding its current program for managing the Individual Ready Reserve, it has developed an extensive computerized data information network for monitoring the IRR force during peacetime and for activating it during a mobilization.

Inactive National Guard

Briefly, the Inactive National Guard (ING) is largely the National Guard's counterpart to the Individual Ready Reserve and is a part of the Ready Reserve. Established by law [17] to augment National Guard units, the ING element is composed of former members of National Guard units who are unable to continue unit participation and who remain attached to their former units of assignment. The major difference between the Inactive National Guard and the Individual Ready Reserve is that the ING member continues to be associated with a specific unit and, in many cases, to have a specific position within that unit. IRR members, on the other hand, are part of a general manpower bank.

Although both the Air National Guard and the Army National Guard may have an Inactive National Guard, only the Army National Guard currently has an ING program.[18] It is the policy of the Army National Guard that unit commanders make certain efforts to stay in contact with their ING members to insure the currency of the members' affiliation. Among the techniques for doing this is the requirement that each ING member attend annually a one-day meeting, or muster, with other members of the unit. As of the end of fiscal year 1983 there were approximately 10,000 Army ING members, and this is expected to increase to about 35,000 members within the next few years.

The ING program suffers from two major constraints that prevent it from achieving the level of mobilization vitality originally envisioned. The first defeats the very purpose for which the Inactive National Guard was established. National Guard units, as part of the Selected Reserve, may be mobilized under the President's 100,000 call-up authority, under which a national emergency need not be declared.[19] But, in order to mobilize the Inactive National Guard, the President must declare a national emergency (see note 6). As a result, National Guard units could be mobilized and deployed without benefit of augmentation by attached ING members. Even if the Inactive National Guard were subsequently mobilized, it would be too late for them to fill their augmentation roles for specified units, and they for all practical purposes would become part of a general mobilization manpower pool, much the same as the Individual Ready Reserve.

To remedy this situation, the Army has proposed legislation to expand the President's 100,000 call-up authority to include IRR and ING members. The Office of the Secretary of Defense opposed such legislation because it would undermine the various initiatives to increase the strength of the Ready Reserve, specifically the Individual Ready Reserve. This view was shared by the Departments of the Navy and the Air Force. As a result, the Army plans to modify its proposal to include a limit of

5,000 ING and IRR members who could be mobilized in a 100,000 call-up.

The other negative aspect of the ING program is that, despite being liable for the same high mobilization priority as IRR members, ING members are at a considerable disadvantage in comparison with their IRR counterparts. Because ING members are in what is referred to as an "inactive" status, current law prohibits them from receiving pay for training, being eligible for promotion, or earning points for retirement credit.[20] In comparison, IRR members are in an "active" status and are, therefore, eligible for all three of these benefits.

Maintaining that this inequity is a disincentive to persons who desire to retain their National Guard affiliation and continue to serve their country, the Office of the Secretary of Defense, at the urging of the Army, proposed legislation to correct the situation in 1981. The Army did not subsequently support this proposal on the grounds that it would not enhance the Army's overall mobilization capability, and on the incorrect assertion that ING members are protected from being mobilized except under circumstances resulting in the mobilization of their units.[21]

In any event, the Inactive National Guard can be an important part of the PIM pool that would be available to the total force in the event of a national emergency. Should the constraints discussed above be resolved, the Inactive National Guard as a mobilization asset would be enhanced even more.

Individual Mobilization Augmentees

In May 1980, the Assistant Secretary of Defense for Manpower, Reserve Affairs, and Logistics provided the Army, Navy, and Marine Corps policy guidance to establish Individual Mobilization Augmentee (IMA) programs by October 1981. The Air Force had long had such a program and, in effect, the policy directed the other Services to follow suit. Basically, the IMA program was recognition that Reservists could fill active force manpower authorizations that become effective during a mobilization. Because these requirements would activate immediately during a crisis, whoever fills them has to be able to report for duty and begin functioning without delay, orientation, or postmobilization training. The achieve this, Reservists have to be preassigned to these active force wartime positions and have to train in these jobs during peacetime.

Several aspects of the IMA program make it unique among the various categories of pretrained individual manpower. First, Individual Mobilization Augmentees are *individual* members of the Selected Reserve and are not members of Selected Reserve units. As Selected Reservists they may be ordered to active duty by the President under his 100,000 call-up authority (see note 19). As a result, IMA Reservists can rapidly fill active force positions in wartime.

The second key aspect of the IMA program is that these Reservists are assigned to, and actually train with, active force units during peacetime. The manpower authorizations they fill are a part of the manpower documents of their active force units—authorizations that become effective upon a mobilization. The procedure of assigning Individual Mobilization Augmentees to their units during peacetime to permit training precludes the necessity for postmobilization training. Thus, these Reservists "hit the ground running" when mobilized.

To insure the integrity of the IMA program as a means of augmenting the active force, the 1980 policy guidance emphasized that the program would not be used to augment Selected Reserve units. Further, the policy stressed the need to assign these Reservists to active force authorizations that become effective during mobilization, not to peacetime manpower positions. It is important to understand the rationales supporting these exclusionary provisions if one is to appreciate fully this vital PIM resource.

There have been proposals that Individual Mobilization Augmentees be used to fill critical skill shortages in Selected Reserve units. Such a procedure, however, would be contrary to what is known as the concept of Reserve unit training integrity. Basically, this concept holds that all manpower authorizations within a Selected Reserve unit require the incumbents to train as a team at the same maximum Reserve training level, even though some of the authorizations, if viewed individually, might require different levels of training.[22] The reasoning is that the essence of an effective, combat-ready unit is the ability of its individual members to respond as a cohesive, coordinated team rather than as a collection of separately trained individuals. Therefore, augmenting Selected Reserve units with Individual Mobilization Augmentees would dictate that such Reservists train at the maximum level regardless of the training requirements of their manpower positions and contrary to the underlying rationale for an IMA program. In such circumstances, the question arises as to why these individuals should not be unit members rather than IMA members. Otherwise, using Individual Mobilization Augmentees in lower training categories would degrade the readiness of the Reserve unit.

There have also been proposals to assign IMA Reservists to temporarily vacant active force peacetime authorizations. These proposals have been dismissed on the basis that they are contrary to the concepts underlying the IMA program and, more substantively, on the simple rationale that other mechanisms exist to ameliorate temporary skill shortages in the peacetime active force. These include delaying the reassignment of needed personnel, reassigning active duty personnel from less critical active force positions, and retraining active force personnel, either voluntarily or involuntarily, to fill more critical skill requirements.

Table 8.1 indicates the magnitude of the IMA program since its implementation throughout the Department of Defense in 1981, in terms of both numbers of personnel and program costs.

Table 8.1

IMA TRAINING CATEGORIES, FY 1983
Mobilization Augmentees

Service	A	B	C	D	Cost ($M)
Air Force	565	9,267	—	1,000	$32.3
Army	—	—	—	8,600	8.6
Navy	500	—	—	551	2.1
Marine Corps	436	100	300	100	2.3
Totals	1,501	9,367	300	10,251	$45.3

Source: Service Program Objective Memoranda, FY 83–FY 87.

The more than 21,000 individual mobilization augmentees programmed during fiscal year 1983 represent highly trained Reserve manpower assets that would be available immediately during a mobilization to "round-out" the wartime requirements of certain active force units. By fiscal year 1988, the total number of IMA Reservists within the Department of Defense is expected to be about 30,000. Of the three Services that did not formerly have IMA programs, the Army has been the most aggressive in instituting such a program. This process was simplified, however, by merely converting the Army's Mobilization Designee (MOBDES) program, established in 1948, to the IMA program. The primary difference between the MOBDES and IMA programs was that, prior to the 1980 guidance, mobilization designees were members of the Individual Ready Reserve, not the Selected Reserve.

Table 8.2 indicates the types of officer and enlisted skill requirements that as of March 1982 were filled by Army and Air Force Individual Mobilization Augmentees. The initially modest Navy IMA program includes requirements in the medical, dental, and intelligence fields. Marine Corps IMA members will serve primarily as staff assistants who will augment mobilization processing centers.

The versatility of the IMA concept is reflected not only in its use within each of the Military Services, but also in the assignment of IMA members to joint activities within and to agencies outside of the Department of Defense. Examples of the former include the Defense Logistics Agency (DLA) and the Central Command (CENTCOM), while examples

Table 8.2
IMAs BY DOD OCCUPATIONAL CATEGORIES

	Percent of Officer IMAs	
Officer Occupations	Army	Air Force
General Officers/Executives	*	3
Tactical Operations	18	2
Intelligence	10	16
Engineering/Maintenance	10	25
Scientists/Professionals	22	19
Medical	8	12
Admin/Comptrollers/Info/Security	17	13
Supply/Procurement	15	9
	Percent of Enlisted IMAs	
Enlisted Occupations	Army	Air Force
Combat Arms	12	1
Electronic Equipment Repair	14	4
Communications/Intelligence	23	15
Medical	7	11
Mapping/Photo	2	9
Admin/Personnel/Finance/Info	29	26
Electrical/Mechanical Repair	3	9
Craftsmen (Metal, Construction, Utilities)	2	8
Supply/Food/Transportation/Police	8	17

Source: Reserve Components Common Personnel Data System, Defense Manpower Data Center.
*Less than one percent, i.e., 26 positions.

of the latter include the Selective Service System and the Federal Emergency Management Agency (FEMA).

In 1982, the Army and the CENTCOM staff began an intensive effort to establish an IMA program within CENTCOM so that the mobilization augmentation needs of that organization would be met quickly and effectively. This new program will not only expand the Army's IMA program, but will provide Army Reserve personnel the experience of joint assignments and considerable expertise in developing and implementing joint strategy concepts.

The use of individual mobilization augmentees outside of the Department of Defense, but in capacities related to defense concerns, is best illustrated by the Federal Emergency Management Agency. In 1979, President Carter transferred the functions of the Defense Civil Preparedness Agency (DCPA) and the disaster preparedness functions of other agencies to FEMA.[23] This transfer had the very practical effect of removing the Department of Defense from the civil defense arena. Nevertheless, the President directed that:

> To the extent authorized by law and within available resources, the Secretary of Defense shall provide the Director of the Federal

Emergency Management Agency with support for civil defense programs in the areas of program development and administration, technical support, research, communications, transportation, intelligence, and emergency operations.[24]

This provision of the Executive Order forms the basis for the use of Individual Mobilization Augmentees by FEMA in much the same way they were used by the Defense Civil Preparedness Agency. To assist in the continuity of civil defense functions, the Military Services continued to fund temporarily the cost of the IMA Reservists they provided FEMA. Under a DOD-FEMA agreement, FEMA was to bear this cost, beginning in fiscal year 1983. The Individual Mobilization Augmentees, however, continue to be members of the Reserve forces of the various Military Services while retaining their assignments within the FEMA organization. There are currently only about 1,100 such Reservists in FEMA.

Although an integral part of the Reserve contribution to the total force, the IMA program is not without growing pains. Predictably, as with all programs that have implications across the Military Services, the difficulties of the IMA program are reflected primarily within the varying missions and organizational perceptions of the Services.

As noted earlier, the Army has made extensive strides toward implementing the IMA program. It has been observed, however, that possibly the greatest challenge currently facing the Army IMA program is filling the IMA positions authorized.[25] A significant portion of the vacant positions are for enlisted personnel and, historically, enlisted participation in the Mobilization Designee Program—the predecessor of the Army's IMA program—was not extensive. A probable partial explanation is that Army IMA positions carry the lowest training category and thus lead to the least remuneration, making participation in the IMA program financially unattractive. Perhaps a programmed expansion of the IMA program to include positions with higher training requirements and, therefore, increased potential income from increased participation, would ameliorate this situation. The Army is also considering the possibility of enhancing the grade structure of enlisted IMA positions to assist in resolving this issue.

Related to this problem, and illustrative of the value the Army places on the IMA program, is the continuing consideration of proposals to selectively transfer, involuntarily, IRR members to the Selected Reserve as Individual Mobilization Augmentees. The purpose of these proposals is to fill IMA requirements for critically short skills for which there are insufficient numbers of volunteers. In fact, the Army has undertaken such involuntary transfers in the past on a limited basis.[26] The Army, with the concurrence of the DOD General Counsel, has found that the involuntary transfer of individuals from the Individual Ready Reserve to the Selected Reserve is permitted by law.[27]

The original guidance issued in 1980 establishing a DOD-wide IMA program did not address the issue of voluntarism in the appointment to IMA status. It could be argued, however, that an involuntary transfer proposal would be inconsistent with the voluntary nature of the Selected Reserve.[28] Clearly, these and other arguments must be weighed in the light of fundamental considerations of the urgency for manpower skills that are not readily available.

Although supportive of the IMA concept, the Navy has maintained serious reservations regarding the categorization of IMA personnel. In a memorandum sent in February 1982 to the Assistant Secretary of Defense for Manpower, Reserve Affairs, and Logistics, the Navy asserted that classifying Individual Mobilization Augmentees, whose training categories are less than the maximum, as Selected Reservists was not only contrary to provisions of law, it was inconsistent with the wishes of Congress. The Office of the General Counsel of the Department of Defense, however, disagreed with the Navy's interpretation of the law and affirmed the view that IMA Reservists of all appropriate training categories could be classified as Selected Reservists.[29]

The hesitancy of the Navy to include Individual Mobilization Augmentees in the Selected Reserve has its roots in many areas. The primary basis for the Navy's concern rests in assuring the nature of the Selected Reserve *unit* program is not diluted by a Selected Reserve *individual* program. It is partly a desire, shared by all the Military Services, to ensure the Congress—as keeper of the purse—does not conclude that, because Individual Mobilization Augmentees train at varying levels, certain Selected Reserve units could retain their mobilization readiness through reduced training and associated costs. This concern on the part of the Military Services is an extremely valid one and impinges directly upon the basic concept of unit integrity.

As delineated in a February 1981 report of a study on behalf of the Deputy Assistant Secretary of Defense (Reserve Affairs), both the Navy and the Marine Corps favor extending the parameters of the IMA program beyond those contained in the 1980 policy.[30] In particular, the Sea Services have supported the augmentation of Selected Reserve units, in addition to active force organizations, by Individual Mobilization Augmentees. In fact, a hybrid form of IMA program has long existed within the Navy. This takes the form of what have been referred to as augmentation units.

It was noted in the Loome et al., study in 1981 that the organization of the Navy's Selected Reserve is heavily oriented toward augmenting active Navy units. These augmentation units would be disestablished upon mobilization, and their resources would become integral parts of the active force units they augment. The Navy has contended that these are in fact IMA units and are consistent with OSD guidance on establishing IMA programs; OSD officials disagree because the gaining active force units do not administer the units during peacetime and, it is argued, true integration of augmentation unit members with their active force comrades is not obtained. The Navy counters that a Reserve organization is more effective than active force units in undertaking the unique tasks of Reserve administration.[31]

It would be a mistake to characterize as conflict any perceptual differences between the Military Services and the Office of the Secretary of Defense regarding the IMA or any other PIM program. Rather such divergences of opinion should be seen as healthy signs of dynamic interaction leading to problem solving between the Services and the Office of the Secretary of Defense. Such interaction is the key to insuring that Defense programs are flexible enough to accommodate the varying missions, structures, and traditions of the separate Services.

Standby Reserve

The nature and purposes of the Standby Reserve are among the most difficult aspects of the Reserve programs to rationalize or explain. As a result, the Standby Reserve, among all the PIM categories, is the most affected by the varying OSD and Service interpretations of its roles and missions. Part of the reason for this situation has its basis in the law.

Federal statute stipulates that each Reservist shall be categorized as either a Ready, Standby, or Retired Reservist.[32] In establishing the Standby Reserve, however, the law referred only to an inactive status list of the Standby Reserve.[33] Since the existence of an inactive status implies at least the possibility of an active status, the Department of Defense established an active status list of the Standby Reserve as a matter of policy through regulatory procedures.[34] This combination of law and policy in the establishment of two categories of Standby Reservists has contributed to difficulties in the administration and management of this mobilization resource.

Generally, the Standby Reserve consists of individuals who no longer have a military service obligation, who desire not to maintain membership in the Ready Reserve, but who desire to retain an affiliation with the military community. Specifically, those in the inactive Standby Reserve are ineligible to earn Reserve retirement points, to receive pay, or to be promoted. They may, however, be ordered to active duty on an individual basis by their Service Secretary if Congress has declared war or national emergency, and if there are not sufficient numbers of Ready Reservists with the needed skills.[35]

Members on the active status list of the Standby Reserve face slightly different circumstances, both regarding reasons for being in the

Standby Reserve and regarding availability as mobilization assets. Basically, such members are *temporary* members of the Standby Reserve who, through no fault of their own, are unavailable for timely recall to active duty during a mobilization and therefore cannot serve in the Ready Reserve. Active Standby Reservists, by policy, are eligible for promotions up to, but not including, the flag and general officer grades, and may participate voluntarily in Reserve training without pay, but for retirement points. The temporary nature of their tenure has also been the basis of divergent views regarding the active Standby Reserve.

Before discussing these views, however, it is worth addressing the types of individuals who constitute the active Standby Reserve and the magnitude of the entire Standby Reserve asset.

Essentially, the active Standby Reserve is made up of former Ready Reservists who have been designated key civilian employees, who suffer a temporary physical disability, or who face a temporary hardship condition.[36] The expectation of the OSD policy regarding active Standby Reservists is that, upon termination of the key employee designation or other temporary condition, the individual will return to the Ready Reserve.

Table 8.3 provides a summary of the number of Standby Reservists from September 1980 to September 1983. The tremendous decline in the Standby Reserve in such a short period is attributed to several factors, the primary one being the Military Services' Standby Reserve screening programs. Under these programs, adopted as a result of OSD policies, the Services periodically identify those Standby Reservists who have valuable mobilization skills and encourage them to transfer to the Ready Reserve. Standby Reservists whose military skills are determined not to be needed for mobilization are discharged from the Reserve. Still others are continued in Standby Reserve status for additional evaluation in the future.

Table 8.3

STANDBY RESERVE STRENGTH LEVELS

(In thousands)

	Inactive Standby	Active Standby	Totals
September 1980	62.1	24.0	86.1
September 1982	41.6	10.5	52.1
September 1983	37.3	6.5	43.8

It would seem reasonable to expect a general decline in the number of Standby Reservists, given an aggressive screening program that more than offsets new entrants into the Standby Reserve. Indeed, the decline in the Standby Reserve strength is due almost entirely to the Army's conscientious efforts to streamline its Reserve structure relative to the efficient use of its Reserve manpower resources. From September 1980 through September 1982, the Army reduced its total Standby Reserve by 98 percent! On a DOD-wide basis, however, this reduction was ameliorated somewhat by much slower rates of reduction in the Standby Reserve strengths of the Navy, Marine Corps, and Air Force.

The importance of the Standby Reserve as a mobilization asset has been the subject of much debate. First, the active Standby may be viewed as not being a military mobilization asset at all, because most of its members would remain at their civilian occupations during an emergency. Second, because a significant number of members of the inactive Standby have not been on active duty or in the Ready Reserve for several years, the usefulness of their military skills could be questioned.[37] Third, it has been alleged that there exist some conflicting signs from the Office of the Secretary of Defense regarding the status of the Standby Reserve as a mobilization asset. Finally, some of the Services have pursued Standby Reserve policies that are not consistent with guidelines promulgated by the Office of the Secretary of Defense. These last two points deserve elaboration.

The Office of the Secretary of Defense issued the following, unclassified, guidance to the Services in 1979:

> The following [initiative] for the Standby Reserve will be implemented at all levels of fiscal guidance: . . . the [active status] Standby Reserve will not be considered a source of pretrained manpower for full mobilization after FY 1981, [and] the inactive status Standby Reserve will not be considered a source of pretrained manpower for full mobilization effective immediately.[38]

This guidance appears clear, if somewhat redundant. It is difficult to see how the active status Standby Reservists could be considered mobilization assets. In any event, the viable source of Standby Reserve manpower—the inactive Standby—was declared a "non-asset," effective immediately.[39] Nevertheless, since mid–1980 the Office of the Secretary of Defense has continued to include the Standby Reserve in its mobilization manpower planning process. In fact there are plans to update the DOD directive regarding the Standby Reserve and to issue policies that, in effect, reverse those delineated in 1979.

Regardless of the clarity of OSD policies concerning the Standby Reserve,[40] it should be noted that at least two of the Services continue to pursue Standby Reserve policies that are clearly contrary to OSD guidance. For example, the Marine Corps continues to transfer Ready Reservists to the Standby Reserve who fail to accrue a minimum of twenty-seven retirement points a year. The Air Force continues to transfer certain officers with critical skills to the active status list of the Standby Reserve even though they are not designated key civilian employees and do not have temporary hardships or disabilities. The rationale for this Air Force deviation is that it permits the officers, as active Standby Reservists, the opportunity to remain eligible for promotion and to earn retirement points. It is alleged that attempting to encourage these officers to join the Ready Reserve would cause many of them, because of the increased risk of mobilization, to elect discharge instead and thereby be unavailable as potential sources of manpower in critical skills.[41]

Notwithstanding such speculation, it is apparent that, just as with pretrained individual manpower assets, the Standby Reserve program must retain a degree of flexibility to the individual needs and traditions of the various Services. Since the Standby Reserve program remains a factor in mobilization planning, it appears that such flexibility is being maintained.

Regular and Reserve Retirees

The largest single source of experienced mobilization manpower includes all active force retirees and Retired Reservists, representing about one and one-half million people.[42] The Retiree Mobilization Management Program is also one of the most successfully implemented PIM programs ever developed. Although the program includes retirees from active force components, that is, regular retirees, the Retiree Mobilization Program is solely the responsibility of the Reserve function at OSD level.

Each of the Services maintains appropriate information on its retirees and has plans for using them in the event of a mobilization.[43] Although the Army is the only Service to have implemented an extensive retiree preassignment program—having preassigned over 126,000 retirees as of October 1983—all of the Services have preassigned retirees to some extent. For example, the Joint Augmentation Unit Program includes over 5,000 retired administrative and health professional personnel from all the Services who have been issued preassignment orders to report for duty at Military Entrance Processing Stations throughout the country in the event of mobilization. The Navy's Convoy Commodore Program (see note 43) has approximately 300 retired captains participating. Finally, the Marine Corps has preassigned approximately 500 retirees and Fleet Marine Corps Reservists to mobilization stations and to casualty notification and family assistance teams.

The mobilization potential of military retirees is, in large part, a function of the statutes pertaining to their liability for involuntary recall to active duty. This liability, in turn, depends upon whether the individual is a Regular or Reserve retiree, or a member of the Fleet Reserve or Fleet Marine Corps Reserve (see note 42). For example, the Secretary of the Military Department concerned may order *any* Regular retiree of that Service to active duty at any time.[44] A member of the Retired Reserve, Fleet Reserve, or the Fleet Marine Corps Reserve with at least twenty years of active federal service may be ordered to active duty at any time.[45] There need be no declaration of war or national emergency.

The liability for potential recall to active duty is somewhat less for Reserve retirees with less than twenty years active federal service but with at least twenty qualifying years of Reserve service. A primary rationale for this is that eligible Retired Reservists cannot draw retirement pay until age sixty.[46] Further, not all members of the Retired Reserve have earned twenty creditable years for retirement based on Reserve retirement points earned. In fact, some members of the Retired Reserve will *never* be eligible to draw a retirement annuity! [47] In any event, the Secretary of a Military Department may order a Retired Reservist to active duty only if two conditions are met. First, Congress must have declared war or a national emergency. Second, the Secretary of the Military Department, with the approval of the Secretary of Defense, must determine there are not enough Ready Reservists available who possess the needed skills.[48]

Associated with the issues regarding the composition of the Retired Reserve is the matter of giving otherwise eligible Reservists the option of electing discharge from the Military Service rather than transfer to the Retired Reserve. There is no statutory provision for transferring mandatorily to the Retired Reserve an individual who desires to leave the Ready Reserve and who has twenty or more creditable years of Reserve retirement points.[49] Such a Reservist may elect discharge and, upon reaching age sixty, apply for full retirement pay and benefits. During the period of his or her discharge, the individual is not subject to being ordered to active duty for mobilization. In 1980, the Office of the Secretary of Defense estimated that about 2,000 Reservists each year elect discharge rather than transfer to the Retired Reserve. Clearly, the best interest of national defense is not served when highly trained and experienced personnel are potentially not available for mobilization.

The degree of support for the Retiree Mobilization Management Program varies widely among the Services. The Army has implemented the program aggressively and extensively. The Marine Corps has also made significant strides in identifying mobilization positions for retirees and has made some advances in preassigning retirees. The Navy is in the process of identifying mobilization positions suitable for retirees, but its progress has been slow. Except for retirees preassigned under the Joint Augmentation Unit and Convoy Commodore Programs, the Navy has no other preassigned retirees. The Air Force has offered some support in identifying mobilization positions suitable for filling by retirees. Other than the Joint Augmentation Unit program, however, the Air Force has no other retirees preassigned to mobilization positions.

Regardless of the job yet to be done in building a viable Retiree Mobilization Management Program, the advances already made are tremendous. Almost 130,000 mobilization positions now have retirees preassigned to them. This represents a significant accomplishment in the efficient use of total PIM resources. It would not be farfetched if, by the end of the decade of the 1980s, as many as one-half million military retirees from all the Services were preassigned to mobilization positions.

Mobilization Yield Rates

This separate section is devoted to PIM mobilization yield rates in regard to PIM resources because of the controversy surrounding this important subject. Few areas in the realm of mobilization planning and manpower management have been subjected to such diverse and intransigent opinion and speculation as the issue of yield rates. As with most such issues, particularly in a bureaucratic environment, it has even achieved a level of semantic pugilism.[50]

Pointedly stated, a PIM yield rate is a percentage of a particular PIM resource population that, upon being ordered to active duty for a mobilization, is expected to report for active duty. The controversy regarding yield rates has centered on the appropriate level of these rates for each PIM resource. The subject is a significant one because the requirements for PIM assets are only partially determined by the wartime demand for manpower. Another determinant is the expected numbers of PIM members who will actually report for active duty, that is, the yield rate. A brief history of this controversy will assist in an appreciation of it.

A 1974 DOD study used what was termed "nominal show rates" of 95 percent for the Selected Reserve, 70 percent for the Individual Ready Reserve, 50 percent for the Standby Reserve, and 10 percent for the Retired Reserve.[51] What these meant, for example, was that if military retirees were ordered to active duty for a mobilization, only about one out of ten would actually report for duty. The rates for the Selected Reserve and the Individual Ready Reserve were approximations based on experiences with limited mobilizations in 1961 and 1968, and on rates assumed in previous studies. The Standby Reserve and retiree rates were largely "guesstimates."

The Secretary of Defense's *Consolidated Guidance* [52] for fiscal years 1980 through 1984 used the above show rates as maximum planning rates through the first six months of a mobilization. For example, after six months of mobilization the maximum yield one could expect of the

Standby Reserve was 50 percent. The *Consolidated Guidance* for fiscal years 1981 through 1985 established *minimum* IRR yield goals of 80, 85, and 90 percent by the end of fiscal years 1981, 1983, and 1985 respectively. A supplement to the *Consolidated Guidance* for fiscal years 1982 through 1986 repeated the 90 percent yield goal for the Individual Ready Reserve by the end of fiscal year 1985 and directed that show or yield rates not be used for retirees. In the *Defense Guidance* for fiscal years 1983 through 1987, the only reference to yield rates was that the Services should "improve IRR yield rates." The *Defense Guidance* for fiscal years 1985 through 1989 makes no mention of PIM mobilization yield rates at all.

Because of congressional criticism and DOD concern, the Strategic Studies Institute of the Army War College conducted a study of yield rates in 1979.[53] It concluded there was no scientifically supportable procedure for developing a single show rate for any Reserve manpower pool and, therefore, such rates were not appropriate management tools for estimating mobilization manpower. The study recommended that the use of show rates as a management predictor of deployable and employable pretrained manpower be discontinued.

Nevertheless, in 1981 the Army developed a methodology for measuring the effects of alternative personnel policies on the supply of military manpower.[54] It included a procedure for determining a possible mobilization yield rate for the Individual Ready Reserve based on actual IRR data. The various personnel loss factors and their effects on mobilization yield are shown in table 8.4.

Table 8.4

IRR MOBILIZATION LOSS FACTORS AND RATES

Factor	Percent Loss Rate
Underage for Mobilization (War Zone)	0.42
Fulltime College Students	3.71
In Hospital	1.28
Pregnant	0.02
Temporary Hardship—Single with Dependents	2.76
Approved Discharge—Married with 4 + Dependents	4.63
Incorrect Addresses/Nonlocatable	7.46
Total Mobilization Loss Rate	18.36*
Mobilization Yield Rate	81.64

*The sum of the loss rates is 20.28 percent; however, an adjustment is made for members with more than one applicable loss factor.

The expected IRR mobilization yield rate of approximately 82 percent that was derived from the 1981 Army study includes factors over which the Army or the Department of Defense has some control from a policy standpoint.[55] In fact, except for the factors regarding hospitalization and pregnancy, all the other factors could, theoretically, be eliminated. This would result in an optimum expected IRR mobilization yield rate of about 98 percent!

But that which is optimum, or is even derived from systematic analysis, is often significantly different from that which is *realistic* to expect. As a result, there is little agreement within the Defense community concerning appropriate mobilization yield rates for the various PIM categories. What agreement does exist is reflected in the fact that the Services largely use, without any particular supporting rationale, the yield rates rather loosely adopted it the 1974 DOD Total-Force Study. The Office of the Secretary of Defense, on the other hand, continues to favor across-the-board IRR yield goals of 85 percent and 90 percent for fiscal years 1983 and 1985 respectively, regardless of individual Service-related structural or managerial differences.

The need to use PIM yield rates in mobilization planning would seem obvious. To ignore yield rates is to assume, by default, yield rates of 100 percent! Such an assumption is naive and would result in an overstatement of available mobilization manpower assets. For this reason, a policy of not using yield rates for all PIM resources, including Standby Reservists and retirees, in the planning process does not appear to be a productive one.

So the question is not whether there ought to be yield rates used in the PIM mobilization planning process, but rather, what ought to be the level of those rates. And while having yield goals that are applicable to all the Services would seem nice and tidy, it is probably an unrealistic expectation—at least, experience has shown this to be the case. Perhaps, the solution lies, first, in realizing that the prediction of uncertain, future events is a necessary management function and cannot be an arbitrary exercise. What also may be needed is an appreciation of the fact that the Services *are* different—in structure, procedure, history, and mission. Why, therefore, should not various criteria for evaluating the Services' mobilization manpower planning processes be different since the effectiveness of such planning is partly a function of the confidence in it held by the various Service planning staffs?

There is at least one approach for relegating the use of PIM yield rates to the routine, noncontroversial place it deserves in the mobilization planning process. Each Service, as the Army did in 1981, could establish its own yield rates for each PIM asset based on a pertinent combination of systematically developed objective and subjective factors. These factors would be subjects of discussion and sources of compromise within the Services and the Office of the Secretary of Defense. Through this process, yield rates would be established that reflect Service differences, including varying levels of resource allocation within competing demands and limited funds. Further, the Services would share techniques for improving yield rates through various management actions. Thus, yield rates would not be regarded as static, unchanging planning variables.

This approach is somewhat inconsistent with that recommended to the President in 1982 by the Military Manpower Task Force.[56] That group suggested the "availability rates" should be identical for all the Services for any particular PIM category. Regardless, referring specifically to the Individual Ready Reserve, the Task Force recommended the development of better availability projections and the actions necessary for improving the propensity of IRR members to report for active duty when ordered to do so in an emergency.

In the final analysis, an individual's propensity for reporting as ordered for active duty will be directly and positively related to his or her expectations, experiences, and perceptions *prior* to being so ordered. Improving personnel management practices can lead to higher yield rates. Examples of such practices are maintaining accurate data regarding addresses, military skills, and physical condition; providing opportunities for periodic military skill refresher training and orientation training, either in residence or through correspondence; reducing the uncertainties of the individual's probable mobilization assignment; and providing information on the care of and benefits for dependents during a mobilization. Individuals must be made aware, in a constructive and positive way, of their responsibility to respond to a mobilization order and the necessity to make at least minimal advance preparations to assist themselves and their families in the mobilization process. A sense of comradery and belonging, even at a very basic level, is as important to Reservists as it is to their active force counterparts.[57]

The Continuing Process

In this chapter we have been discussing a trained military manpower force of nearly two million people! This force represents the largest portion of the total military manpower assets of this country. Even with the most pessimistic estimates of mobilization yield rates and of the usefulness of various PIM assets, the effective strength of this mobilization manpower resource is still at least one million trained individuals.

Even this impressive number cannot erase some of the shortcomings of such a formidable military force. It is true that a large number of these individuals are not as well trained as their active force and Selected Reserve counterparts. In fact, most of them train infrequently, if at all. And it is also true that the management emphasis regarding the PIM asset is oriented toward individuals rather than units. But it is also true that units are made up of individuals, and training opportunities are limited less by funds than by levels of creative leadership and managerial imaginativeness.

The essential thrust of this chapter has been to discuss objectively the strengths and shortcomings of the various categories of pretrained individual manpower as mobilization assets. Our nation can ill afford to waste the billions of dollars invested in this source of trained manpower, or fail to take advantage of the boundless patriotic motivation and energy these resources represent. The evidence is clear: The phoenix must be permitted to continue its flight from the ashes of benign neglect.

Part 4

Equipment and Logistics

9
Combat Readiness Suffers
W.D. McGlasson

Nothing detracts more from the combat readiness and rapid deployability of the nation's Reserve forces than equipment shortages and obsolescence. Those deficiencies seriously weaken US conventional war capabilities. Although the Reagan administration has proposed substantial increases in military procurement, the record does not give assurance that any of it will reach the equipment-poor Reserve forces. Therefore, high priority should be given to procuring enough equipment to satisfy the war-fighting needs of the total force—National Guard and Reserves as well as active forces.

That is the proposition Guard and Reserve leaders have been advancing, and there are strong arguments to buttress their case.

Because of the total-force development, it would be difficult for the active armed forces even to launch a major military operation without Guard and Reserve support, much less carry on sustained combat. Today, the National Guard and Reserves provide one-half of the combat power and two-thirds of the logistics support capability for the armed forces, the Department of Defense reports. Moreover, many units are expected to mobilize, deploy overseas, and enter combat on almost as tight a timetable as that prescribed for the active forces. There are even scores

Originally published in *National Defense* 65 (May-June 1981): 32–37. Reprinted by permission and with minor changes. —ED.

of Guard and Reserve units earmarked for the much-touted Rapid Deployment Force.

The US armed forces today must carry out their functions in an age of long industrial leadtimes and "come-as-you-are-war." Short-notice war is an ever-present possibility; short-notice acceleration of industrial output for defense is not. Therefore, if the nation becomes embroiled in another war, US armed forces will have to fight a year or longer with whatever equipment they have on hand on the day war starts. Thus, the "come-as-you-are" label.

Finally, there is not now any sizeable stock of equipment, or "war reserve," from which Guard and Reserve units can be outfitted on some future M-Day. They have given up sizeable quantities of equipment already to help build up pre-positioned stocks in Western Europe, yet they have not even been given assurance that they will inherit any of the residual equipment left behind by earlier-deploying active forces. The defense budget of the Carter administration called for increased procurement of major weapons and equipment, and of the less costly, common-place "readiness" items. The Reagan supplement boosted those amounts substantially. But here we go back to an earlier reference—leadtime. President Reagan will have completed his first term before much of the add-on reaches military units in the form of new equipment.

Louis J. Conti, Chairman of the Reserve Forces Policy Board (RFPB), which advises the Secretary of Defense on Reserve matters, recently told a congressional committee that the Board feels "equipment and resources issues are of over-riding concern and require immediate attention."

Emphasizing that he was speaking only for the Board, not for the Secretary of Defense, Conti went on:

> The sea and ground forces of the Guard and Reserve are not receiving the level of attention essential to readiness. Ship and helicopter squadrons are being retired with few or no equipment replacements. The Army Guard and Reserve have only 69 percent and 43 percent respectively of wartime equipment inventory in dollar value, with huge shortfalls in trucks, armored personnel carriers, and artillery pieces. Many units, if mobilized, would deploy with inadequate or incompatible equipment—including some [units] committed to support the Rapid Deployment Force.

Only if the total-force doctrine and its underlying assumptions are understood can one begin to comprehend the vital importance of the Guard and Reserve in US security and the extent to which their lack of adequate equipment could endanger the nation.

Total-Force Approach

The total-force idea was launched a decade ago, in the aftermath of Vietnam, under the aegis of Defense Secretary Melvin R. Laird. It was conceived as a way to cut back on high-cost active military structure by shifting more of the defense burden to upgraded National Guard and Reserve forces. Concurrent consideration would be given by the Services to the needs of the total force—active, National Guard, and Reserve—with the goal of increasing "the readiness, reliability, and timely responsiveness" of the Reserve components.

The total-force approach has been emphasized by every succeeding Secretary of Defense. This has projected the Reserve forces into an environment vastly different from their low-key operations of an earlier era. They are expected to reach and maintain readiness levels not far below those expected of fulltime military organizations. They are assigned early-deployment missions in contingency plans that once were considered the exclusive province of the "regulars."

There was a clear stipulation right from the start that ample quantities of modern equipment would go along with the expanded role under total force. Laird's initial memorandum called on the Services to "provide and maintain combat standard for Guard and Reserve units in the necessary quantities." Unfortunately, that highly desirable condition has never been achieved although ten years have passed since the total-force concept was adopted. The needs of the full-time forces had to be met first, and there was never enough to provide adequately for the Reserves' forces as well.

As matters developed, substantial quantities of new equipment became available after the phase-down of US military operations in Southeast Asia, and for a while, much of it was funnelled to the Guard and Reserve. It appeared that the promises implicit in the total-force planning directives soon would be realized. But after two or three red-letter years, someone turned off the spigot. The flow was reduced, in some cases even reversed, long before the requirements were met, due to several new developments.

One of those was the heavy drain placed on Army and Air Force equipment by foreign military sales, epitomized by the resupply of Israel after the destructive Six-Day War in 1973. Hundreds of tanks, trucks, jet fighters, and other items destined for the Guard went to Israel instead. That was only one of many such diversions to other nations of military equipment the Guard and Reserve badly needed.

Other developments that delayed modernization of US Reserve forces included administration and congressional budget-cutting during the years of antimilitary pressures, and a tactical innovation called POMCUS, meaning the "pre-positioning of materiel, configured in unit sets." POMCUS is the US Army's effort to build up stocks of war-fighting equipment in Western Europe. In an emergency, only the trained combat troops will have to be flown from the United States to reinforce NATO; the heavy war-fighting equipment will already be there, cutting weeks off deployment times. The original POMCUS objective was equipment for three combat divisions. Two years ago, that goal was raised to six divisions. Consequently, the Guard and Reserve not only lost equipment they had expected to receive in the future, but had to dip into their own meager stocks and hand thousands of items back to the Army.

The Reserve Forces Policy Board recently raised strenuous objections to continuing the withdrawals to fill POMCUS sets five and six. Pointing out that the withdrawals were originally considered acceptable because of severe Guard and Reserve understrengths, Chairman Conti told a House committee that continuing the drawdown makes the earlier assumption of continuing under-strength a "self-fulfilling prophecy." With strength on the upswing, Conti said that continued equipment withdrawals will reduce both readiness and morale, hamper US ability to project military force to other parts of the world, and threaten our ability to train new Service members in an emergency.

Obsolescence Problem

Another significant factor tended to nullify much of the progress toward modernization. It was the surge of technological improvement that struck the military establishment, most notably the ground forces, during the 1970s. Even while the Guard and Reserve were receiving quantities of Vietnam leftovers, new advances in technology were pushing much of that "new" equipment to the borderline of obsolescence. A good example is offered by the Army Guard and its helicopter fleet.

The Army Guard is authorized about 2,400 helicopters, of various types. That amounts to approximately one-third of the entire Army fleet. It actually has the required number of helicopters, but at least 900 of those in its possession are outmoded. The Guard operates approximately 370 attack helicopters, for example, which would be badly needed in a NATO conflict to destroy the large numbers of Warsaw Pact tanks. But the Army Guard fleet is made up almost entirely of old Vietnam war gunships, already out-dated for high-technology warfare, and not even deployable to Europe because they are not equipped with TOW antitank weapons systems.

The Army says it will supply seven TOW-equipped AH–1S Cobra attack helicopters to the Guard each year. In addition, Congress has approved the purchase of another thirty-one in the past two years, at the Guard's own urging. That averages twenty-two aircraft per year, at which rate modernization of just that one segment of the Guard fleet would require seventeen years!

Similarly, approximately 392 of the Guard's 884 observation helicopters are not deployable, the RFPB chairman told Congress in his March testimony. Numerous other items issued to the Guard and Reserves out of post-Vietnam stocks fit the same pattern. Modern then, outmoded today, only ten years later.

The Guard offers an appropriate case study because its two elements make up the largest segment of the Reserve components. At their desired peacetime strength, the Army National Guard and Air National Guard would have manning levels of 420,000 and 98,300 respectively. That totals well over one-half of the entire Selected Reserve, which has a strength target of about 950,000. At present, the Air Guard is at its authorized level. The Army Guard, with 371,000 members, is well below its prescribed level, but is moving steadily upward from the 345,000 to which it dropped during the 1970s.

The Army Guard provides 46 percent of the Army's combat power, with a structure that includes eight of the total Army's twenty-four combat divisions, twenty-one combat brigades, and four armored cavalry regiments. Its structure totals nearly 3,500 company-size units.

The Air Guard currently operates more than 1,500 aircraft, or 17 percent of the total Air Force fleet, and that figure will increase substantially over the next three years. Its structure includes 91 flying units, and more than 900 support units, including 75 communications units that comprise 70 percent of the Air Force communications capability.

The total force got off to a banner start. Massive quantities of first-line equipment commenced to reach the Guard and Reserves as the United States phased down its operations in Southeast Asia. In one red-letter year, the Army Guard alone received some $900 million in new issues. Then, the flow was sharply reduced under the pressure of events previously cited. The flow of equipment never again returned to a level that would permit 100 percent fill.

Inventories Below Combat Levels

Statistics help illustrate what has occurred. When the total force was launched in the early 1970s, the Army Guard inventory, for example, stood at $1.3 billion (budget value), or 33 percent of the total mobilization requirement. Since then, the M-Day requirement has been pushed up by a number of factors (such as inflation, increasingly complex technology, and structural reorganizations), to a goal of approximately $11 billion. The Army Guard inventory presently stands at about $7.4 billion, or 69 percent of that requirement. Thus, the Army Guard inventory has increased from 33 percent to 69 percent of what it would require if all its units were mobilized in an emergency. That appears to be an improvement to take pride in—until one looks at it from the opposite viewpoint, from the aspect of how much is lacking. It still is 31 percent below what is considered desirable for combat, and that is not a condition in which military leaders can take much comfort.

Equally significant, there has not been any appreciable gain for the past three years, not for the Army's backup forces, anyway. As Lieutenant General LaVern E. Weber, former National Guard Bureau Chief, told a congressional subcommittee in March 1981, in reference to the Army Guard: "Despite issues of nearly $1 billion of equipment during the past three years to replace obsolete items, the status of equipment fill in the Army Guard has remained at 69 percent of the wartime requirement."

Thus, the modernization process has moved so slowly for the Guard that obsolescence is catching up with and creeping ahead of modernization. Concurrently, the proportion of older materiel, defined by the Army as nondeployable, has dropped dramatically, from 27 percent to 2 percent. The latter figure is somewhat misleading, however, because "deployable" as defined by the Army does not necessarily denote current state-of-the-art. Neither does it imply full compatibility with the new materiel now considered standard in the active Army.

In all, the Army Guard today is short some 3,000 trucks, 570 artillery pieces, 400 antiaircraft weapons, 3,600 tracked carriers of various types, and hundreds of complete up-to-date radio communications systems, to name only the most prominent big-ticket shortages. (See table 9.1) It also is more than $200 million below required operational levels in organizational clothing and equipment. As Major General Francis J. Higgins of New York described the situation: "We're the greatest summer soldiers in the country—we couldn't fight in the winter because we don't have field jacket liners, cold-weather sleeping bags, or other gear for cold-weather soldiering."

Posing another serious problem for the Army Guard is the lack of modern automatic data processing (ADP) systems that are compatible with those the active Army currently uses. It would be difficult even to mobilize most Army Guard units because of that deficiency, as two large-scale mobilization exercises demonstrated—NIFTY NUGGET in 1978 and PROUD SPIRIT In 1980. The National Guard Bureau is urging the Army to let it account for Guard personnel, completely separate from the Army system, in any future mobilization until new ADP equipment has been provided to the Guard.

As 1980 ended, the best estimate of the cost to bring the Army Guard up to its authorized peacetime level of major equipment items was $2.6 billion. At least another $2 billion would have to be added to that amount to cover spares, repair parts, organizational clothing and equipment, and boost the total inventory to its M-Day requirement.

Table 9.1
ARMY NATIONAL GUARD
MODERNIZATION PROGRAM REQUIREMENT

Item	Quantity Short	Total Cost ($ M)
Aircraft	934	757.3
Tactical ADPE	74	111.0
Tanks	386	266.7
Trucks	2,960	144.4
Artillery	570	177.4
Radars	143	8.2
Air Defense	384	297.6
Carriers	3,574	295.9
Communications Multiple Configurations		594.0
*Total Shortage		$2,652.5

General Weber used the Guard's eight combat divisions to dramatize the effect of equipment shortages on the Guard when he testified before a House committee in March 1981. One-third of the Army's divisions are in the Guard, he said. "The overall readiness of those divisions is low and has not changed significantly in the last three years [because] equipment shortages prevent improvements in overall readiness."

Air Guard Deficiencies

The Air Guard has been cited regularly as the readiest of the Reserve components. It can respond in mere hours to emergency call-ups, as it demonstrated during the 1968 *Pueblo* crisis and on many later occasions. Many units maintain planes and alert crews on duty twenty-four hours a day, to perform air-defense missions and to refuel SAC bombers en route to a distant target. Its people and planes habitually fly to all corners of the world, training even as they perform live missions for the Air Force. Yet:

- Its 1,500 aircraft now have an average age of 14.8 years, and a substantial portion are twenty years old or more.

- Its flying tankers are powered by engines that the airlines got rid of years ago as fuel-hungry, noisy, and not powerful enough for takeoffs with heavy loads from many airfields.

- Its communications personnel are among the most experienced and skilled anywhere in the armed forces, but the equipment they must use can only be described as Late Marconi.

Virtually every one of its ninety-one flying squadrons has undergone one or more conversions to newer aircraft since the advent of the total force. Because modern aircraft are so costly, however, those that reach the Reserve forces customarily are in the twilight years of their useful lifetime by the time they "fall out" of the active force, which means they quickly become a doubtful asset for the high-intensity, high-technology combat environment that would exist in NATO Europe. By the time the 1980s end, therefore, the obsolescence problem will arise for much of the Air Guard's equipment that now is considered "new." It's only new to the Guard! (See table 9.2.)

Table 9.2
AIR NATIONAL GUARD
MODERNIZATION PROGRAM REQUIREMENT

Item	Needed	Total Cost ($ M)
F–15 Interceptor	100	1,847.9
F–16 Tactical Fighter	104	993.2
A–10 Tactical Fighter	76	600.4
A–7K Tactical Fighter	12	153.0
C–130 Tactical Airlift	53	536.8
HHX Rescue/Recovery Helicopter	14	103.6
KC–135 Re-engining	104	2,410.2
Tactical Communications—RDF Units		4.4
Tri-service Tactical Communications		125.5
Miscellaneous Telecommunications		219.1
Total Shortage		$6,994.1

The F–4 fighter, for example, will only be considered an effective fighter aircraft for a few more years. The Air Guard fleet of F–4s will continue to expand as F–15s and F–16s replace it in the active Air Force. But the Guard's F–4s *average* sixteen years in age—almost antiques in the world of fighter aircraft. In a few short years, they will assume the role played so long in the Air Guard by F–100 Sabrejets—they will be relics of a bygone age.

Similar comparisons can be applied to much, or most, of the telecommunications equipment in use in, or currently being issued to, both the Army Guard and Air Guard. What they currently are receiving is light years ahead of what they've been using, but well behind current state-of-the-art equipment issued to active units.

In the communications area, compatibility is the major problem, followed closely by the lesser capabilities of older equipment. The equipment now used by the Army Guard and Air Guard is of Korean war, or immediate post-Korean, vintage. It is, as an Air Guard communicator recently described it, "just a step above two cans and a string." It can be meshed into the systems used today by the Air Force only by awkward, jerry-built linkages. Moreover, it can handle nowhere near the radio traffic that the newer equipment does.

Communications Contrasts

The active forces moved into the microwave field years ago. The Guard is only now commencing to receive a trickle of that kind of equipment. Now, the Services all are moving into a still newer configuration—Tri-Tac, standing for tri-service tactical communications—a quantum jump ahead of all that's gone before. At current funding rates it will be years, perhaps decades, before Tri-Tac starts to reach Guard and Reserve units.

Another Air Guard communicator dramatized the problem very clearly during an interview at his Roslyn, Long Island, Air Guard work place when he pulled one unit out of a ceiling-high system and said: "Look! Vacuum tubes!" In an age of solid-state circuitry, the tubes were a dead giveaway.

A high-priority Army Guard signal battalion is in a similar situation. With a Table of Organization and Equipment requirement for fourteen TRC–138 microwave radio relay systems, it possesses none. Of five complex technical control centers—none! Of sixty-two pulse restorers—none! Of forty-six specialized distribution boxes—none! Of numerous out-dated, marginally effective substitutes—plenty!

Cost has been a major factor inhibiting procurement of modern communications equipment for the Reserve components. For just the two branches of the Guard family, Army and Air, it recently was estimated that almost $1 billion would be required to fund full modernization of their telecommunications—$594 million for the Army Guard, $350 million for the Air Guard.

If ten years of total force have proved anything, it is that National Guard and Reserve units can attain a very high state of deployability and combat readiness if—and it's a very large *if*—they are provided resources consistent with the readiness goals demanded of them. Reasons aplenty can be found for past failures to provide the armed forces with enough modern equipment to modernize both full-time and Reserve-type elements. Strained budgets, ever-growing social outlays, antimilitary sentiment, and others all played a part. The House Armed Services Committee offered its own assessment when it said in its 1980 report on procurement authorization: "Over the years, the political requirements of budget-making have overruled the real needs of the military."

A special investigative panel of that committee was even more pointed in describing the state to which the armed forces have been brought by underfunding. Said the panel in its 1980 report:

We are not buying the required ammunition, equipment, and weapons systems to fight even a short war. Even a cursory look at the equipment currently in the hands of our troops, at our war reserve materiel stockpiles, and at our five-year defense program, is proof positive of this claim. Our troops are outmanned and out-gunned at almost every turn. Plainly and simply, we are not prepared.

For the National Guard and Reserve, lowest on the procurement totem pole, you can say that over and over, in spades!

10
Reserve Component Logistics Units in the Total Force

Edward D. Simms, Jr.
Chris C. Demchak
Joseph R. Wilk

Total Force Policy and Logistics

During the final years of the Vietnam war, the United States sought to significantly and permanently reduce defense expenditures, while at the same time retain the capability to fulfill national security obligations. As one approach to obtaining the desired economies, the Department of Defense reduced the strengths and capabilities of the active force and increased its reliance on the Guard and Reserve. In 1970, Secretary of Defense Melvin Laird announced the "total-force concept" which emphasized the concurrent consideration of active and Reserve components in developing military capability to support national strategy. Secretary Laird stated: "Selected Reserves will be prepared to be the initial and primary source for augmentation of the active forces in any future emergency." He also directed that the total-force concept be applied to all aspects of Defense resource planning and programming.

Originally published in October 1982, by the Logistics Management Institute under contract to the Assistant Secretary of Defense (Manpower, Reserve Affairs and Logistics). Reprinted by permission. —ED.

In 1973, Secretary of Defense James Schlesinger added his support for the total- orce concept by stating, "total force is no longer a 'concept.' It is now the total-force policy." Since then, each succeeding administration has reaffirmed its commitment to the total-force policy.

The military services' implementation of the total-force policy in the 1970s was influenced by continued pressures to reduce active end strengths. Each Service selected a different approach to integrating its active and Reserve forces based on peacetime operating environments and wartime requirements.

While the total-force policy affected most aspects of military operations, its greatest impact was on the logistic support structure. The peacetime operating tempo of many combat elements generates relatively low demands on the military logistic system, especially when contrasted with those expected during war. These low demands allowed many logistics units to be identified as excess and transferred to the Reserve forces with no apparent effect on combat readiness. In addition, numerous peacetime logistics tasks were found to be more efficiently accomplished by the private sector.

The overall effect of the total-force policy, combined with related budget-cutting measures, is an active logistic structure that is sized to meet peacetime, not wartime, workloads. To accomplish the immediate surge in support requirements associated with any military response and to sustain a deployed fighting force require a rapid and large expansion of the current active logistic structure. Critical portions of this expansion must come from the Reserve components. This chapter describes the DOD's dependence on Guard and Reserve supply, maintenance, and transportation units after a decade of total-force policy evolution.

Dependence on Reserve Component Logistics Units

This section describes the military services' dependence on Reserve-component logistics units as portrayed in the current force structure. It focuses on the traditional logistics functions—supply, maintenance, and transportation—which are outside the responsibility of combat divisions and wings or beyond the organic capability of combatant ships. Particular attention is provided those functions in which the Reserve component has a critical support role.[1]

Army

The Army logistics units of interest are those which provide support in nondivisional areas, that is, the corps rear and the communications zone. Their support responsibilities include all aspects of the surface lines of communication from the sea and aerial ports of debarkation forward to the combat areas. They also store and distribute such commodities as ammunition, petroleum, and repair parts in the corps rear, as well as repair all theater and corps equipment.

The provision of these critical nondivisional logistic services is primarily the responsibility of the Army National Guard (ARNG) and the US Army Reserve (USAR). Together, they are assigned 78 percent of the supply companies, 73 percent of the maintenance companies, and 67 percent of the transportation companies (table 10.1).

Table 10.1

FY 1982 TOTAL ARMY PROGRAM

Type of Logistics Units	Total Units	Percent ARNG	Percent USAR
Supply	229	19	59
Ammunition Company (Conventional)	50	22	50
POL (Petroleum, Oil & Lubricants) Company	31	7	74
End Items & Repair Parts Company	42	10	79
Other Field & General Supply Company	106	25	51
Maintenance	218	50	23
Vehicle Maintenance Company	183	52	21
Watercraft Maintenance Company	3	33	33
Rail, Locomotive, Car, & Equipment Company	4	0	100
Aircraft Intermediate Maintenance Company (Nondivisional)	20	35	25
Special Functions Company (Calibration, Collection, & Classification)	8	63	37
Transportation	223	33	34
Vehicle (Cargo, POL Truck) Company	170	38	29
Terminal Service or Transfer Company	26	4	61
Watercraft (Boat, Amphibian) Company	13	8	54
Air (Helicopter) Company	14	57	14

Supply. While nondivisional supply companies provide most classes of supply to theater forces, they have particular significance in three crucial commodities of war: ammunition, fuel, and repair parts.

Over 70 percent of the Army's conventional ammunition companies are in its Reserve component. These companies operate all ammunition storage and transfer points in the theater; they also deliver ammunition to storage sites immediately behind the division as well as inside division boundaries.

Of the eighty-two petroleum distribution companies in the Army's force structure (including other supply companies with POL responsibilities), almost 75 percent are in the Army National Guard and US Army Reserve. These companies operate petroleum terminals and pipelines, pumping stations, and loading and storage facilities. They also issue and distribute petroleum products to units in the corps areas and communication zone.

The Army National Guard and US Army Reserve also dominate the Army's capability to stock and issue repair parts, especially those that are highly specialized or slow moving. Almost 85 percent of the Army's repair parts supply companies are in its Reserve component. When the Army's nondivisional maintenance companies are included (they stock their own repair parts), the Army Guard and Army Reserve still provide over 75 percent of the Army's capability to stock and issue repair parts outside divisional boundaries.

Maintenance. The nondivisional maintenance companies in the Army force structure support a wide range of equipment, from tactical and combat vehicles to locomotives and aircraft. Most of these companies are in the Guard and Reserve.

Almost 75 percent of the Army's nondivisional maintenance capability to support tactical and combat vehicles is in its Reserve component. The direct support maintenance companies repair end items and modules; they also adjust, align, troubleshoot, and calibrate designated items in support of equipment in the corps rear area and along the theater lines of communication. The general support companies repair major assemblies, evacuate materiel to CONUS for overhaul, and operate cannibalization and disposal activities. They also are the primary source of backup support to the maintenance assets in the combat divisions.

Sixty percent of the Army's capability to provide aircraft intermediate maintenance outside the divisional boundaries is in the Guard and Reserve. In addition to the aircraft-repair function, these companies recover and evacuate aircraft, and calibrate test, measurement, and diagnostic equipment (TMDE).

Even the Army's capability to repair harbor and landing craft is dependent upon assets from its Reserve component. That capability is split evenly among the active Army, Army National Guard and Army Reserve—each has about one-third of the units.

In some maintenance areas, the Army is totally dependent on the Guard and Reserve. These include collection and classification companies (that perform equipment triage by designating which equipments are to be repaired, cannibalized, or disposed of), calibration companies (that calibrate and provide repair parts for all general purpose TMDE), and rail companies (that repair locomotives and rail cars).

Transportation. The nondivisional transportation assets in the Army force structure are primarily assigned to the Guard and Reserve. These include truck and helicopter companies, terminal service and transfer companies, and watercraft companies.

Approximately two-thirds of the Army's truck companies are in its Reserve component. These companies transport materiel from the ocean terminals and aerial ports to direct and general support supply companies and user units within the corps rear area. The helicopter companies provide much of the same support as the truck companies except they primarily move higher priority materiel. They also offload cargo from ships to eliminate shoreline rehandling. More than 70 percent of these companies are in the Guard and Reserve.

Sixty-five percent of the Army's terminal service and transfer companies is in the Guard and Reserve. The terminal service companies offload both break-bulk and container ships; they also operate ocean terminals. The terminal transfer companies, while generally operating inland, load and offload cargo at air, rail, and river terminals.

The watercraft companies operate between the cargo ships and the ocean terminal to augment the offload capability of the terminal companies. They also operate on rivers and lakes. Almost two-thirds of these companies are in the Reserve components.

Air Force

Assets from the Air National Guard (ANG) and the US Air Force Reserve (USAFR) constitute over 50 percent of several key logistic services outside the tactical and strategic combat aviation wings. The Reserve component is integral to the Air Force capability to provide strategic and tactical airlift; rapid, aircraft battle-damage repair, and aerial refueling. Of the 230 squadron-equivalents providing these services in the total Air Force structure, 126 are in the Reserve components (table 10.2).

Table 10.2

FY 1982 TOTAL AIR FORCE PROGRAM

(In squadron-equivalents)

Type of Units	Total Units	Percent ANG	Percent USAFR
Supply Air Refueling (KC-135, KC-10 aircraft)	38	18	5
Maintenance Combat Logistics Support	11	0	55
Transportation	181	12	49
Strategic Airlift (C-5, C-141 aircraft)	34	0	50
Tactical Airlift (C-7, C-130 aircraft)	31	35	29
Aerial port (includes mobile sqdns)	116	10	54

Supply. Few supply funtions exist outside the wing/base or depot structure. Air wings deploy with a thirty-day supply of essential parts and other materiel, and merge their supply personnel with those of the receiving base. The number of supply personnel who deploy with the Guard or Reserve combat wing is tailored to offset only the increased supply burden at the wartime base, not to support active combat assets.

The major exception to this active/Reserve component alignment is in aerial refueling. The Air National Guard and the Air Force Reserve provide 23 percent of the Air Force's aerial refueling capability. Aerial refueling supports bomber operations and deployment operations of CONUS-based forces by reducing the need for additional enroute bases for strategic airlift and fighter aircraft.

Maintenance. During the early stages of any war, the rapid repair of aircraft is crucial to gain air superiority and, thereby, stabilize the theater of operations. Studies have shown that adequate maintenance capability, particularly the repair of battle damage, will not be available from the committed assets organic to the air wing. To improve the aircraft battle-damage repair capability, the Air Force Logistics Command established Combat Logistics Support Squadrons (CLSS), composed of highly skilled technicians specifically trained in expedient repair techniques. Six of the eleven CLSSs in the total Air Force structure are in the US Air Force Reserve.

In wartime, the CLSSs quickly deploy into the theater and send mobile repair teams forward to operating bases. Repair teams from the Air Reserve dominate the rapid, battle-damage repair operation for many weapons systems, including the most sophisticated aircraft in the Air Force (table 10.3).

Table 10.3
CLSS REPAIR TEAMS

Equipment	Total Repair Teams	Percent in USAFR
A–10	11	36
F–15	7	71
F–16	5	60
F–4	18	55
C–130	10	90
C–141	2	50
KC–135	2	50
B–52	4	50
Engines	74	54

Tranportation. As the single manager for airlift, the Air Force provides airlift transportation for all DOD components. Overall, the Air

Guard and Air Reserve provide 62 percent of the units that operate and support the DOD's air lines of communication.

Of the thirty-four Air Force squadrons dedicated to the strategic airlift mission, seventeen are in the Air Reserve. These USAFR units are organized as associate squadrons, providing air crews (50 percent of the Air Force's total) and maintenance personnel (35 percent of the total) but share the aircraft with collocated active units.

Two-thirds of the Air Force tactical airlift capability is in the Guard and Reserve. This capability is key to the rapid repositioning of troops or materiel within theater. The aerial port capability, which supports both strategic and tactical movements, is primarily assigned to the Air Force Reserve (65 percent of the aerial port units). These critical material handling, offloading, and routing functions cannot be accomplished effectively without Reserve aerial port assets.

Navy

The primary mission of the Naval Reserve is to augment active logistics units to enlarge their capacity to accommodate increased wartime workload. In a few cases, the Reserve provides entire units which operate independently in support of the fleet. The Navy's major dependency upon the Reserve occurs in transportation, with some significant dependencies also occurring in a few supply and maintenance organizations.

This assessment of the Navy's dependence on the Reserve is based on the mobilization billets of selected logistics support organizations. The specific types of organizations, by logistics function, are shown in table 10.4.

Supply. Reserve augmentation in the supply area ranges from 9 to 28 percent and averages 18 percent. The greatest augmentation occurs at the naval weapons stations. The Navy's five weapons stations, all in the continental United States, overhaul, rework, produce, store, transship, and distribute ordnance and weapons. Although predominantly staffed by civil service personnel, approximately 28 percent of 10,000 mobilization positions in the five weapons stations are for Reservists (not counting civilian workforce increases during mobilization). At two of the stations—the ammunition outload ports at Earle, New Jersey, and Concord, California—the dependency exceeds 40 percent.

Reserves are also critical to establishing advance supply bases, which do not exist in the active Navy. Examples of these bases include supply storage facilities, material handling facilities, and tank farms. The advance supply bases needed to support operational plans require slightly more than 800 positions. All are programmed to be filled by Reservists.

Table 10.4

PRIMARY NAVY LOGISTICS ORGANIZATIONS

Function/Type of Organization	Reserve % of Total Positions
Supply	
Underway Replenishment Ship	9
Supply Center and Depot	16
Air Station Supply Department	14
Weapons Station*	28
Advance Supply Base	100
Maintenance	
Destroyer Tender/Repair Ship	19
Shore Intermediate Maintenance Activity	46
Submarine Tender	16
Submarine Support Facility	34
Aircraft Intermediate Maintenance Department (Aircraft Carrier)	2
Aircraft Intermediate Maintenance Department (Air Station)	23
Naval Station (Aircraft Support)	19
Transportation	
Underway Replenishment Ship	9
Fleet Logistics Support Squadron	86
Carrier On-Board Delivery Squadron	7
Military Sealift Command Office*	62
Naval Control of Shipping Office*	100
Cargo Handling Battalion	86

*Includes current civilian positions but not civilian mobilization increases.

Maintenance. Most Navy maintenance organizations depend upon Reserve augmentation for less than 20 percent of their strength. A few are significantly higher—shore-based intermediate maintenance activities for surface ships, submarines, and aircraft.

The Navy's seven shore intermediate maintenance activities (SIMAs) for surface ships accomplish those ship repairs that do not require the use of a drydock or heavy industrial facilities. Operating in fixed facilities, SIMAs maintain electronics, hull, mechanical, and electrical equipment; they fabricate some parts and fixtures, and perform some underwater repairs. Their wartime staffing is approximately 46 percent dependent upon augmentation from the Selected Reserve, with individual SIMAs varying from 42 to 57 percent.

The Navy's two shore facilities for submarine intermediate maintenance are located at New London, Connecticut, and at Pearl Harbor, Hawaii. Although they provide a wide variety of submarine support services, their repair mission is analogous to that of a SIMA for surface ships. Overall, the New London facility is 20 percent dependent upon Reserve augmentation and Pearl Harbor is 31 percent dependent.

Aircraft intermediate maintenance is performed by specifically designated aircraft intermediate-maintenance departments (AIMDs). Their missions include calibration, repair, modification, and check of components, assemblies, and related support equipment. Thirty-nine AIMDs support tactical and patrol fleet aircraft: fourteen aboard aircraft carriers, twelve in CONUS and thirteen overseas.[2] Those aboard aircraft carriers are minimally dependent on Reservists (2 percent) while those at shore-based activities are significantly more dependent (averaging 23 percent, with a high of 31 percent).

Transportation. The Navy's primary organic transportation assets are the underway replenishment ships, naval aircraft in transport squadrons supporting intratheater fleet operations, and carrier onboard delivery aircraft. They are supported by specialized organizations for cargo handling and for management, coordination, and control of cargo.

The underway replenishment ships are minimally dependent on the Reserve (that is, less than 10 percent) while most of the remaining transportation organizations are heavily dependent. Fleet logistics support squadrons provide a rapid transportation link between the theater aerial and sea ports of debarkation and shore-based air facilities in close proximity to the operating fleet. Ten of the eleven fleet logistics support squadrons are in the Reserve. Approximately 85 percent of the total billets in these squadrons are assigned to the Reserve (2,621 of 2,708). In contrast, the three carrier onboard delivery squadrons are augmented by Reservists at a level of only 7 percent.

The Navy, as the single manager for sealift, requires several specialized organizations to support the sea lines of communication. Over 60 percent of the billets in Military Sealift Command (MSC) offices, which assist in coordinating the movement of ship cargo, are filled by Reservists. Worldwide Naval Control of Shipping Offices, which primarily route ocean traffic, are staffed exclusively with Reservists. The Reserve also provides six of seven cargo handling battalions, covering 1,700 of 1,980 positions or 86 percent of the Navy's deployable capability.

Marine Corps

The primary sources of logistics support for a deployed Marine Force is the Force Service Support Group (FSSG). The FSSG units provide extensive supply, maintenance, and transportation support which is not available from organic elements of the combat units. In peacetime, logistics units in the Marine Corps Reserve are organized into an FSSG that is associated with the Marine Reserve's 4th Division-Wing Team

(DWT). The Reserve FSSG provides slightly more than one-fourth of the total FSSG logistics capability of the Marine Corps (table 10.5).

Table 10.5
MARINE CORPS FSSG LOGISTICS UNITS

Type of Logistics Unit	Total Units	Percent Marine Reserve
SUPPLY	17	29
Supply Company	4	
Ration Company	4	
Ammunition Company	4	
Bulk Fuel Company	5	
MAINTENANCE	16	25
Motor Transportation Maintenance Company	4	
Engineer Maintenance Company	4	
Electronics Maintenance Company	4	
General Support Maintenance Company	4	
TRANSPORTATION	23	26
Landing Support Company	11	
Beach & Port Operations Company	4	
Truck Company	4	
Transport Company	4	
Marginal Terrain Vehicle Company (cadre)	0	

The need for Reserve logistics units is greater than the current force structure suggests. The primary wartime mission of many Reserve FSSG units is to augment (that is, fill unit-sized gaps in) or reinforce (that is, provide additional capability to) the logistics element of a deploying active Marine Air-Ground Task Force. Some active logistics units are currently understaffed (especially those providing bulk fuel, ration, and ammunition services) and require immediate augmentation by Reserve units at mobilization.

Supply. Of the seventeen supply companies in the FSSG structure of the total Marine Corps, five (29 percent of the total capability) are in the Reserve FSSG. These supply companies provide all classes of materiel to a deployed force. They manage and store materiel in the beach or port area and then distribute it, via truck companies, to combat battalions.

Maintenance. Maintenance units in the FSSG perform intermediate-level maintenance in support of deployed ground forces.[3] With the exception of the general support (GS) maintenance company, they are deployed in two sections, one near the port in fixed facilities, the other as forward contact teams giving direct assistance to combat units. Operating out of fixed facilities near the port area, the GS maintenance company provides the most comprehensive level of repair available in theater. The fiscal year 1982 Marine Corps structure authorized sixteen FSSG maintenance companies; four are in the Reserve.

Transportation. Marine Corps doctrine requires that each FSSG has three landing support companies and one each of the following companies: beach and port operations, truck, transport, and marginal terrain vehicle. These companies support initial landing assaults and sustain logistics operations in the established landing area. In conjunction with Navy cargo handling battalions (predominantly Naval Reservists) they link the Marine combatants with afloat source of supply. Currently, one active landing support company is at zero staffing, as are all marginal terrain vehicle companies. Of the twenty-three FSSG transportation companies, six (26 percent) are in the Reserve.

Wartime Implications

The wartime logistic structure is dominated by units and personnel from the Reserve components. While the Guard and Reserves have historically played a major role in the logistic support of any war, the magnitude, urgency, and hence significance of their current logistics responsibilities have never been so great. Today, the United States cannot mount a significant land combat operation without calling immediately upon a large number of Guard and Reserve logistics units to project forces by air and to flesh out and establish effective surface lines of communication.

Developed Theater

Scenarios involving operations in a developed theater are normally associated with large-scale military operations—a general war. Plans in support of the forward deployed US forces in Europe require Reserve component logistics units to be among the earliest CONUS-based units into theater. Although total mobilization of the Selected Reserve is envisaged under this scenario, logistics units (especially transportation) are among the most urgently needed.

Nearly one-half of the total Army's nondivisional support capability will deploy into theater within the first sixty days with three-fourths of those units being Guard and Reserve. This massive expansion of the theater logistics structure is indicative of the limited capability available to forward-deployed active units during peacetime. Within the first few weeks, one-half of the nondivisional capability of each forward deployed corps will be provided by Guard and Reserve units. Additional corps deployed into theater will be almost exclusively supported by Reserve component units. The operation and support for movement of supplies along the surface lines of communication from the ports of debarkation to the corps areas will be the responsibility of Reserve-component units in conjunction with prearranged support provided by several host nations.

Initially, the primary means of moving combat units forward into wartime locations will be airlift—strategic and tactical. The planned rapid infusion of forces into the European theater requires maximum use of all strategic airlift assets. The Air Force Reserve associate squadrons will provide the personnel to support the increased usage of the C–5 and C–141 fleets. Plans call for these units to be fully integrated with their active counterparts within seventy-two hours. The tactical airlift units will reposition combat assets within the theater, especially fighter units and priority munitions. The C–130 squadrons from the Guard and Reserve, which are critical to this repositioning, must be in theater within seventy-two hours.

This dramatic increase in airlift traffic will require a substantial increase in air terminal capability to ship, receive, and manage cargo. Many active aerial port squadrons will move forward in theater to open reception ports and manage the offloading of troops and supplies during the initial surge. Guard and Reserve squadrons will assume the strategic aerial port of debarkation (APOD) tasks vacated by active units and open new ports; others will deploy forward to support tactical airlift operations. The staffing of a typical APOD is 80 percent dependent on the Reserve-component. Many Guard and Reserve aerial port units will deploy within thirty-six hours of mobilization to complete the air lines of communication.

Most Naval Reserve logistics units will deploy quickly after mobilization to augment active units. Fleet logistics support squadrons will be needed immediately to link the deployed fleet with the ports of debarkation for the movement of high priority cargo.

Marine Corps Reserve logistics units will be required quickly to support the operations of the 4th Division-Wing Team (also in the Reserve). Additionally, some units will augment active logistic organizations to compensate for their lack of capability.

Undeveloped Theater

Operations in an undeveloped theater are characterized by a projection of a lesser combat force into a region with little or no available national logistic infrastructure. Consequently, that force must be self-sufficient. Since the active force does not contain enough logistics assets to support limited operations in one theater as well as peacetime requirements in other theaters, heavy reliance on Guard and Reserve logistics units is inevitable.

The ability to rapidly move a significant land combat force depends on the immediate availability of Air Force Reserve associate squadrons to increase the utilization of the strategic airlift assets. While the forces required to be moved will be fewer than in support of a general war, the distances will be greater resulting in extended sortie times. The active Air Force does not have the crews and maintenance capability to meet these requirements.

Establishing a logistic system to support land operations in an undeveloped theater will require significant Army Guard and Reserve logistics assets. Those assets will provide many of the same services available from commercial sources in a more developed theater. Deployment plans for a high-priority undeveloped theater indicate the Guard and Reserve will provide 80 percent of the truck companies and 45 percent of the ammunition companies.

To support operations in an undeveloped theater, the Navy will require several fleet logistics support squadrons and cargo handling battalions. The squadrons will tie the deployed fleet with the theater logistics system, while the battalions will support Marine Corps operations in the landing area. Most of these squadrons and battalions will be from the Naval Reserve.

Although the Marine Corps will primarily use active combat units in the undeveloped theater, several company-sized logistics units from the Reserve will be mobilized to round out the Force Service Support Group of the deploying force. Staffing deficiencies and other contingency requirements do not allow deployment of a complete Force Service Support Group from the active structure to support these operations.

Assessment

To successfully carry out their critical wartime responsibilities, Reserve component logistics units must be fully staffed, trained, and equipped before mobilization. They also must be fully interoperable with all equipment, systems, and procedures of the active force. If they are not, then the total force will not be effective—we will be unable to quickly project and sustain any significant military force.

11
Equipping the Total Force: The Continuing Dialog

Bennie J. Wilson III
Wilfred L. Ebel

In the early months of his Presidency, Ronald Reagan personally endorsed the total-force policy in the following pronouncement to the national security community:

> My administration is determined that these vital Reserve forces will be manned, equipped, and trained to meet their full responsibility as a combat-ready element of the total force.

This statement, together with additional prodding from the White House and a Reserve Forces Policy Board Report, *FY 1981 Readiness Assessment of the Reserve Components,* led to issuance on 21 June 1982 of a document that could become the "Magna Charta" on equipping the Reserve forces. The document, a memorandum from the Secretary of Defense to the Service Secretaries and to the Chairman of the Joint Chiefs of Staff, contains several policy statements mandating attention to the equipping of the National Guard and Reserve:

> The long-range planning goal of the Department of Defense is to equip all active, Guard, and Reserve units to full wartime requirements. . . .

This is an original article written especially for this book. —ED.

. . . units that fight first shall be equipped first regardless of component.

You must ensure equipment compatibility among Guard, Reserve, and active units which will serve together on the battlefield. . .

Equipment inventories adequate for effective training are also essential.

The President's Military Manpower Task Force, composed of the Secretary of Defense (chairman) and other top officials of the administration, addressed the Reserve equipment issue in its November 1982 final report to the President:

> With the improvement in the manpower situation, the time has come to focus on serious readiness deficiencies in training and equipment. Improving the state of training of Reserve units and raising their holdings of modern weapons and equipment will be difficult and costly. However, it will be far less expensive than it would be to expand the active force to assume wartime missions that are now assigned to the Selected Reserve.

In September 1982, shortly after being named Chief of Staff of the US Air Force, General Charles A. Gabriel told a National Guard conference: "We're committed, of course, to modernizing the Guard as fast as we can. Guard modernization will include the newest, most capable aircraft in the world."

The following month the Army Deputy Chief of Staff for Operations (and nominee to become Commander, TRADOC) Lieutenant General William R. Richardson stated: "Fully equipping the Reserve components is a high priority this year."

But will the visions of today become the facts of tomorrow? If one is sanguine about Reserve-component materiel readiness being achieved next year—or ten years hence—one might be wise to look back ten years and more. In 1971, Admiral Thomas Moorer, then Chairman of the Joint Chiefs of Staff, informed the Senate Armed Services Committee that "a major effort is now being made to provide combat serviceable equipment for the Army Reserve forces." Good intentions aside, the only certainty is the uncertainty of whether the existing equipment deficiencies in the National Guard and Reserve will *ever* be eliminated.

Why do we find ourselves in this dilemma? A historical awareness will provide a proper perspective from which we can reduce the discrepancy between expectation and reality. For example, in 1947 the first Secretary of Defense, James Forrestal, established a committee known as the Gray Board. The Board was to undertake what he called "a brutally realistic consideration of what Reserve units, or persons drawn from Reserve units, would in fact be able to do at the outbreak of a war," and, subsequently, to give "due regard to probable state of training, possible state of equipment, and time factors in mobilization."

The Gray Board discovered that during World War II nearly three years had elapsed before we were able to equip the Reserves for offensive operations, although troops to use the equipment were available at an earlier date. Not unexpectedly, the Board concluded that "initial issues of necessary equipment should be speeded up." To better equip the Reserve forces, the Gray Board's final report recommended:

> As the present status of supplies and equipment is inadequate for planned or required strengths, additional procurement should be initiated . . . [and] the Supply and Equipment program for the Reserve forces should be made more realistic and adapted to their mobilization status, their training, and the facilities available.

Shortly thereafter, the Department of Defense set a "get well" date for National Guard and Reserve units—a date when the units would have sufficient combat-serviceable equipment to "go to war." Unfortunately, that "get well" date and subsequent "get well" dates were generally in the out-years of the budget. Furthermore, whenever the Department of Defense seemed to make progress in improving the Reserve forces' equipment posture, there seemed to be setbacks as well, often because of intervening, unprogrammed higher priority items. For over three decades, there have been "ailing" Guard and Reserve units, as equipment "get well" dates have edged ever forward.

Problems in equipping the Reserve forces are not a post-World War II phenomenon. Historic precedents abound. When the regulars carried the breech-loading Springfield rifle, for example, their counterparts in the militia made do with the percussion-ignition musket. During the Spanish-American War, the regular Army fought with Krag-Jorgensen rifles, equipped with five-round box magazines and smokeless cartridges, while the mobilized National Guard troops had to rely on the single-shot, black-powdered Springfield. During a major mobilization exercise in the 1920s, the Reserve forces were found greatly dependent on horses and mules, and even these animals represented an "aging equipment" problem—many of them had been purchased during World War I. More recently, mobilization exercises found the Air Force Reserve flying piston-powered C–123 and C–7 aircraft.

The Reserve Force Policy Board (RFPB) in the Office of the Secretary of Defense began highlighting the seriousness of Guard and Reserve equipment deficiencies in 1980. In reports to the President, the Congress, and the Secretary of Defense, the Board offered indisputable proof that the equipment problem was the most serious factor limiting readiness of the Reserve forces. The Board shied away from the highly emotional, un-supported, and overelaborate rhetoric that much of the Reserve com-munity had been prone to use in the past. Instead, it carefully and methodically examined the major system acquisition cycle, starting with the determination of mission need and continuing through to the produc-tion and deployment phases. From this solid groundwork, the Reserve Forces Policy Board was able to draw several valid conclusions in its No-vember 1981 report, *The Reserve Forces in the 1990s:*

- Sufficient equipment to properly equip the total force does not exist.

- With the exception of Air Reserve forces, equipment shortages are greater in the Guard and Reserve than in the active forces.

- Equipment shortages are currently the major cause of Guard and Reserve unit-readiness deficiencies.

As shown in table 11.1, the RFPB's *Annual Report for FY 1982* con-firmed the continuing equipment shortfall in the Reserve forces.

As the Department of Defense attempts to formulate coherent and rational programs for effectively equipping the Guard and Reserve in the 1980s, it is important to recognize the inadequacy of measuring one year's equipment status against another. The correct measurement is made by observing and evaluating the quality and quantity of equipment in the hands of a potential aggressor. As long as the Soviets receive state-of-the-art weaponry with increased range, accuracy, reliability, and killing power, our defense planners must ensure that US forces receive improved weapons.

The United States should heed the Soviet adage "you can't chop wood with a penknife." In keeping with this maxim, the Soviet's historic quantitative advantage in deployed weapons is being buttressed by the technological superiority found in much of the fielded equipment of the Soviet forces. The United States has ground forces that suffer not only qualitative inferiority, but quantitative inferiority as well.

Five years ago it was popular to say that the Reserve forces must be prepared for a "come as you are" war. The implicit meaning in this phrase was that Reserve units—even if undermanned and under-equipped—would be promptly mobilized and deployed in a future crisis. In other words, a unit could be committed to battle with less than 100 percent of its personnel and equipment, and as a result, its staying power in combat could be severely limited. At best, it would be risky to consid-er deploying a unit that did not meet at least minimal combat readiness; at worst, it would certainly place an additional burden on the theater commander receiving the unready unit.

The "come as you are" philosophy was never intended to justify equipment shortages in the Reserve forces; instead, it was meant to con-

Table 11.1

CRITICAL FACTORS LIMITING OVERALL
READINESS OF THE RESERVE COMPONENTS,
FY 1982

Component	Most Critical Limitation	Second Most Critical Limitation
Army National Guard	Equipment on Hand	Personnel
Combat Units	Equipment on Hand	Personnel
Combat Support Units	Equipment on Hand	Personnel
Combat Service Support	Equipment on Hand	Personnel
Army Reserve	Skill Qualification	Equipment on Hand
Combat Units	Equipment on Hand	Training*
Combat Support Units	Skill Qualification	Equipment on Hand
Combat Service Support	Skill Qualification	Equipment on Hand
Naval Reserve	Training	Personnel
Commissioned Units	Personnel	Equipment Readiness
Reinforcing Units	Training	Personnel
Marine Corps Reserve	Skill Qualification	Equipment Readiness
4th Marine Division	Skill Qualification	Equipment Readiness
4th Marine Air Wing	Equipment on Hand	Training
Air National Guard	Equipment on Hand	Personnel
Combat Units	Personnel	Training
Combat Support Units	Equipment on Hand	Personnel
Combat Service Support	Equipment Readiness	Equipment on Hand
Air Force Reserve	Equipment on Hand	Equipment Readiness
Combat Units	Equipment on Hand	Personnel/Training
Combat Support Units	Equipment on Hand	Equipment Readiness
Coast Guard Reserve	Logistics Readiness	Training
Combat Units	Personnel	Logistics Readiness
Combat Support Units	Training	Logistics Readiness
Overall DOD	Equipment on Hand	Personnel

*Personnel and training categories reflect a lack of MOS skill qualification. Personnel limitation indicates that a high percentage of personnel are not skill qualified. Training limitations indicate that training is necessary to increase personnel skill qualification.

vey the importance of restoring Reserve units to a high state of peacetime readiness. The intended definition of "come as you are" can be seen in a 1981 statement by General David C. Jones when he was Chairman of the Joint Chiefs of Staff:

> We must view readiness . . . through bifocals—attentive to long-term fixes but concentrating on maximizing our capacity to fight with what we have today.

One of the long-term fixes implied in the total-force policy is that Reserve forces must be provided the equipment to enable them to complement and fight alongside regular US forces in the earliest stages of any conflict.

Some fixes are already under way. As obsolescent equipment is phased out of the Air National Guard and the Air Force Reserve, it is being replaced with new systems superior to or competitive with the best Soviet products. Air Force initiatives for modernizing the Air National Guard and the Air Force Reserve include introduction of the A-10 Thunderbolt II (replacing A-37s) and increases in F-106 Delta Darts. C-130H transports are replacing some C-7s while other Air Reserve units will convert from C-7s to C-130Es.

The Secretary of the Navy, John Lehman, a Naval Reservist, has provided the impetus for modernizing both the Air and Surface programs of the Naval Reserve. Present plans include a minimum of 19 Fast Frigates and Guided Missile Frigates to be in place by fiscal year 1987. Congress and the Navy differ regarding control of the ships—Congress believes peacetime control should be vested in the Chief of Naval Reserve; the Navy hierarchy believes control should remain with the fleet commanders.

Secretary Lehman has instigated a program to upgrade the Naval Air Reserve by what he calls horizontal integration. This plan introduces the F/A-18 Hornet into Reserve units at the same time active-force units receive the new aircraft. Also included in the Naval Air Modernization Package are the A-6E and A-7E attack aircraft, the E-2C Hawkeye early-warning planes, and an upgrading of the Reserve P-3A/B Maritime Patrol aircraft. Further, Congress, the Office of the Secretary of Defense, and the Navy seem to agree that considerable strength increases are needed in the Naval Reserve over the next four years.

The most difficult challenge in the equipment area is increasing the quantity of equipment available to the US Reserve ground forces. The seriousness of the equipment shortages plaguing the ground forces was vividly illustrated when the Marine Corps Commandant proposed a reduction in the active-troop strength as a solution to obtaining funds to equip the remaining force. Also, in calling for increased buys of weapons and equipment for the Army, Secretary of the Army John Marsh noted in testimony before the Congress in 1981:

> Many of our Reserve component units have significant shortages in essential types of equipment or are armed with older, less capable weapons. As we move to equip our Army with modern systems, we cannot forget that our Reserve soldiers, once mobilized and deployed, also must be prepared to face an enemy with modern, sophisticated weapons.

In recent years, Congress has sometimes mandated Reserve-equipment buys as "add-ons" to administration budget requests. Reserve-oriented associations have been known to lobby vigorously for equipment buys beyond those requested by the Services, the Defense Departments, and the administration. Some add-ons never survive beyond the committee level; others survive the entire authorization process only to fail the appropriations hurdle. The whole House (or Senate) is often quick to drop add-ons when it determines to trim the defense budget. And even when the House or Senate endorses add-ons, they often fail to survive the final hurdle, the Joint Conference.

Some Guard and Reserve lobbying for add-ons for equipment buys have been successful in recent years but this strategy may be unwise. If such add-ons become habit or, eventually, tradition, they could present problems for the Reserve forces. Budget planners at all levels are always seeking ways to pare budget requests. Should a budget planner perceive that Congress will direct the buying of Reserve-component equipment not requested in the Annual Authorization Bill, the temptation rises to cut the budget request by eliminating Reserve-component equipment buys from the Service (DOD/OMB) budget proposal. The budget planner then is able to present a smaller budget, having deliberately cut needed Reserve-component equipment items in anticipation that Congress will direct the buy of the Reserve-component equipment through the add-on process. But Congress is also under pressure to pare the defense budget, and add-ons for the Reserves might never materialize. This process is not a sound way to fund national defense.

The advantages of providing the Reserve forces equipment identical to that provided the active forces are obvious: commonality facilitates training of personnel, simplifies maintenance, maximizes utilization, and ensures effective combat integration of the Reserve forces with the active forces. Reserve units did not need their full allotments of equipment in an era when planning envisioned several months elapsing from the time of mobilization to the time of commitment to combat. These units simply required sufficient equipment for realistic training. Today's Reserve forces, however, are expected to deploy in days, not months. This means that early-deploying units must have on hand a complete set of wartime equipment to avoid having to draw additional equipment after mobilization.

Until one considers the costs involved, it appears the problem of equipping the Reserve components is open to a reasonably prompt solution. But estimates of the cost of completely filling shortages in Reserve equipment range from $11 billion to over $17 billion! At the end of fiscal year 1973, combat-capable equipment on hand for the Army National Guard and the Army Reserve totaled approximately $3.7 billion, or about half of the mobilization requirement. Today, the Army Reserve components have $10.2 billion worth of major equipment items on hand, but the wartime-requirement levels have increased to $18 billion. The Army Reserve achieved an illusory gain in fiscal year 1982 by decreasing its wartime-requirement levels. Even so, the on hand versus required percentage of major equipment items advanced from only 26 percent to a still totally inadequate 35 percent.

Although equipment-sharing and equipment-redistribution policies will help alleviate Reserve-component training needs, Reserve forces planners must also expedite procurement of the additional equipment needed to achieve the readiness requirements imposed by the total-force policy.

A subsidiary problem associated with equipment shortfalls is the spare-parts shortage that plagues both the active and the Reserve forces. Any commander discussing operational readiness can undoubtedly relate a particular horror story about a major piece of equipment that is deadlined for want of a part that costs only a few dollars. Almost everyone remembers the opening line of one of Ben Franklin's homilies: "For want of a nail, the shoe was lost"; some even recall the penultimate line: "For want of a horse the rider was lost." But too often we forget—or fail to heed—the concluding line: "For want of a rider *the battle was lost* [emphasis added]."

Regrettably, some budget planners do not fully perceive or appreciate the importance of spare parts to overall readiness. When underprocurement of spare parts becomes an established policy that results from dollar constraints, the supply system dries up. This often translates into a six-month or longer waiting period to get a relatively uncomplicated part off the production line.

Spare-parts shortages can also contribute to the temptation to cannibalize any deadlined piece of equipment. Once the cannibalization process begins on a given piece of equipment, that equipment is likely to become what is known in runway parlance as a "hanger queen"—a plane that is never flown because it is continually stripped of parts needed to keep other planes in the air. The most sophisticated weapon system in the world is of no value if it is out of commission because of a spare-parts shortage. Admittedly, better distribution and inventory management of spare parts can provide more efficient allocation. Over the long term, however, an increase in the procurement of spare parts is critical if any increase in readiness is to be achieved.

Concurrently, life-cycle management of equipment must be improved. Maintenance concepts and policies must adhere to the total-force policy a particular type of equipment cannot be forgotten just because it is found exclusively in the National Guard or Reserve. If an item is in the Army Guard or Reserve, it should be viewed as being in the

Army inventory, with the appropriate operator training and mechanical maintenance training provided. Manuals and spare parts also must be kept current and made available.

The cost of a jeep, a hand grenade, an M–16, or a bullet for an M–16 has tripled in the last decade. Nonetheless, this nation has little choice in affording what is necessary for national security. Neither the Congress nor the public will permit Warsaw Pact modernization to constantly outpace NATO modernization. In order to develop policies that are responsive to lessons learned and appropriate to the perceived challenges of the 1980s, the combat capabilities of our Reserve forces must not be constrained by programmed equipment deficiencies. Planning efforts must be geared to bring all Guard and Reserve units to the state of equipment readiness necessary to meet planned force deployment and employment schedules.

Part 5

Mobilization Readiness

12
Mobilizing Guard and Reserve Forces

Bennie J. Wilson III
James L. Gould

> The country is now mobilized. All men and boys able to carry a spear will report immediately to Addis Ababa for active duty. Married men will bring their wives to do the cooking. Women with babies, the very old, and the very young need not report for active service. Men that are not married will bring any women they can find. Anyone else found at home after the issuance of this order will be hanged.—Emperor Haile Selassie, 1936.

This order, issued almost fifty years ago, is a classic example of the mobilization of a small country to meet an external threat to its national security. In this rather direct statement, Haile Selassie assembled his country's greatest and most precious resource, its people. Although the weaponry of Ethiopia was primitive compared to the tanks, artillery, and aircraft of Italy, its people were organized quickly to fight the invader, and they did so for six months before falling to the superior Italian forces. This example, however, is an anachronism compared to the mobilization plans and technologies of today's nations who must rapidly assemble and deploy large, well-trained armies from Reserve forces. But the dependency on human resources for defense is the same now as it was in the Ethiopia of 1936.

Within modern industrialized nations, including the United States, the *nature* of the dependency on human resources for defense, however,

---

This is an original article written especially for this book.—ED.

has changed dramatically. Prior to the 1960s, Americans found it convenient to rely primarily on active military forces in maintaining national security. When those forces proved insufficient, members of the Guard and Reserve—largely "dormant" during peacetime—were called to active duty, given extensive training, and deployed to the war zone to augment the "regulars." The nature of war during these times relative to weapons capabilities, geographic locations, and the like, permitted an almost casual atmosphere in which to mobilize Reserve military forces.

Even during the 1960s, it was evident that other factors, primarily those that were political in nature, affected our nation's propensity to mobilize Guard and Reserve forces. National resolve, or the lack thereof, regarding the Vietnam conflict contributed to the decision not to call a significant number of Guardsmen and Reservists to active duty. At the same time, however, the huge monetary cost of the Vietnam conflict, budget cuts, and subsequent reductions in the armed forces at the end of that conflict, signaled the death knell for "mobilization as usual."

The total force policy, implemented in the early 1970s, was the result of these changes. It was recognition of the fact that we could no longer afford—in a political, economic, and psychosocial sense—to maintain a regular armed forces sufficient to serve as a creditable deterrent in peacetime and to fight even relatively small conflicts during times of crisis. In short, the Guard and Reserve could no longer lie "dormant" as a distant relative, available after considerable preparation to augment our nation's armed forces. They became a viable part of our total *deterrent* forces, available immediately to resist aggression. As a result, the entire mobilization process had to be altered. It is with this legacy that the present day system of mobilizing Guard and Reserve forces was developed.

Mobilization Defined

Mobilization, in its broadest sense, is the assembling of resources for the purpose of preparing for, or actually implementing, essentially industrial preparations and military operations that are taken either in response to an emergency such as war or the threat of war, or to accomplish certain national goals. Analytically, mobilization can be regarded as the *process* whereby a nation makes the transition from a normal state of peacetime preparedness to a war-fighting posture, both within the military and industrial context. For the purposes of this chapter, however, the term "mobilization" is defined in a relatively narrow sense—as the process whereby Guard and Reserve units and individuals are brought from an inactive duty status, in which they perform training and routine support missions, to an active duty status, in which they participate in contingency or wartime operations.

Before discussing this aspect of mobilization, it is worthwhile to address briefly another element of mobilization often overlooked by military strategists, its political dimension. Various levels of mobilization may have purposes that are primarily political, rather than military, in nature. For example, preliminary mobilization actions of a "low threat" nature may be undertaken to "show national resolve" over a specific international issue. The primary purpose of such "mobilizations" is not to engage in direct military action, although this ultimately could ocur, but to send a message to a potential adversary, or even to the American public in an attempt to gain public support.

Regardless of the motivation behind a mobilization, the process involves the assembly, organization, and application of all, or a portion of, the nation's resources for national defense, especially those related to industry, the economy, communications, and manpower. Insofar as military manpower is concerned, mobilization almost always involves the ordering to active duty of a nation's Reserve forces. Such mobilized forces augment the regular active component and, if military operations occur, they are conducted by a total-force team of full-time regular forces and Reservists in an active duty status.

This chapter addresses five major topics, the first being a brief discussion of the contributions the Guard and Reserve make to our nation's total military capability. The second is what can be termed the "mobilization structure"; namely, the principal agencies involved in mobilization. The third topic is mobilization planning and its underlying principles. The fourth is a description of the mobilization process. Finally, the chapter concludes with a discussion of several current and important issues pertaining to Guard and Reserve mobilization.

The Guard and Reserve and Total Military Power

Most of the factors that contribute to a nation's overall military power are well recognized. They include a strong industrial base supported by a vibrant economy, superior technological and innovative capabilities, reliable allies who share in maintaining military forces for deterrence or war-fighting if deterrence fails, and a strong military force composed of both active and Reserve components. However, one facet of military power has only recently begun to receive the attention it deserves. That facet is the combination of a strong, combat-ready Reserve and effective, reliable procedures for mobilizing that Reserve. When combined, these two factors constitute a genuine and essential component of military power and, therefore, of deterrence. By the same token, the absence of one or both detracts from a nation's military might, often to the extent of creating military weaknesses which potentially hostile nations may seek to exploit.

There should be no doubt that the US Guard and Reserve are a formidable military force. The 1.4 million members of America's Reserve components provide nearly 40 percent of the nation's overall military manpower resources. This contribution is so vital that units and individuals of the Guard and Reserve must be employed whenever the United States is called upon to mount and sustain significant military operations. It is the nation's capacity to perform these missions, with a combination of active and mobilized Reserve forces, that has become a fundamental part of America's military might in recent years.

The Mobilization Structure

Two entities outside the Department of Defense play key roles in mobilization planning and execution: the National Security Council (NSC) and the Federal Emergency Management Agency (FEMA). The National Security Council, whose statutory members are the President, Vice President, and the Secretaries of State and Defense, stands at the apex of the national mobilization structure. The Council advises the President with respect to the integration of domestic, foreign, and military policies relating to the national security. During an emergency involving actual or possible mobilization, the National Security Council would play a significant role in advising the President regarding options for the use of the nation's military forces.

The Assistant to the President for National Security Affairs, the Director of Central Intelligence, and the Chairman of the Joint Chiefs of Staff serve as advisors to the National Security Council and attend virtually all of its meetings. The Chairman would almost certainly be in attendance whenever the Council is considering military options which include mobilization of the Guard and Reserve. Nevertheless, it is significant to note that the President need not consult the National Security Council in order to make decisions regarding a mobilization.

The Federal Emergency Management Agency (FEMA) oversees those activities in the Government's civilian departments and agencies which would support the Defense Department in executing a mobilization. For example, working with the Department of Energy, FEMA has responsibility for ensuring that plans exist for providing the Defense Department the fuel and lubricants required by tanks, ships, and aircraft. And, in coordination with the Department of Labor, FEMA works with private industry to ensure that factories producing weapons have sufficient skilled manpower. FEMA also plays a vital role in coordinating the acquisition of the resources and war materiel required to support mobilization and sustain military forces after they are deployed. Finally, FEMA ensures that federal entities have plans and procedures for executing their responsibilities to support the Defense Department during a mobilization.

Within the Department of Defense, all agencies and staff elements have some responsibility for mobilization planning and execution. The general responsibilities include developing and coordinating mobilization policies and plans; developing procedures and authorizations, to include laws and standby legislation needed to execute mobilization decisions; identifying management information requirements for mobilization planning, decisionmaking, and execution; regularly evaluating the adequacy of mobilization plans and programs; and developing and exercising the crisis management procedures that would be employed during a national emergency.

Within the Office of the Secretary of Defense (OSD), the Under Secretary of Defense for Policy provides national defense policy guidance for the development of military operation and mobilization plans, ensures that the Department regularly exercises and evaluates its ability to carry out major mobilization and deployment plans, and serves as chairperson of the Department of Defense Mobilization and Deployment Steering Group. The Steering Group includes representatives from the Office of the Secretary of Defense, the Joint Staff, and the Military Departments. The Group has the broad mission of ensuring that there exists a credible, responsive, and flexible capability for the Department to meet requirements for mobilization and force deployment at any level of national military emergency, be it a relatively minor contingency-response operation or full-scale war. The Steering Group has numerous policy development, oversight, and information exchange responsibilities, three of which are particularly important insofar as Guard and Reserve mobilization is concerned: identifying needs for new or modified mobilization authorities, plans, and procedures; eliminating barriers to rapid mobilization and responsive deployment; and developing and implementing effective mobilization management information, communications, and command-and-control capabilities.

The Assistant Secretary of Defense for Manpower, Installations, and Logistics (MI&L)* also plays a key role in mobilization planning. This individual provides oversight to the mobilization planning and execution process so that, if necessary, manpower and logistic resources can be adequately and quickly marshalled. Within MI&L, the Deputy Assistant Secretary for Mobilization Requirements develops wartime manpower planning systems to meet mobilization requirements and ensures that the DOD maintains adequate plans for, and a readiness posture which supports, military mobilization. The ASD (MI&L) is also responsible for the Department's single most important document pertaining to mobilization, the Master Mobilization Plan. In a comprehensive, integrated fashion, the Master Mobilization Plan describes *what*

---

*Pending division into ASD(M) and ASD(I&L).

specific planning and execution actions must be taken to prepare for and implement mobilization, and *who* must take those actions.

Still another key OSD official in the mobilization structure is the Assistant Secretary of Defense, Reserve Affairs. This individual provides overall supervision of Guard and Reserve issues within the Department of Defense and ensures adequate plans and resources exist for the mission and mobilization readiness of Guard and Reserve forces.

The Organization of the Joint Chiefs of Staff (OJCS) also has major responsibilities for mobilization planning and execution. The Logistics Directorate, J–4, is the focal point for mobilization planning. It provides guidance for the coordination of Service mobilization plans, and establishes guidelines for coordinating mobilization planning with deployment planning. The J–4 also evaluates the capabilities of Service and Defense Department Agency mobilization plans to support a full mobilization, the most demanding augmentation requirement which the total force must be able to meet.

The Operations Directorate, J–3, maintains information on the readiness of military units, and, of critical importance to maintaining that readiness, conducts mobilization exercises involving the active, Guard, and Reserve components of all the Services. These exercises provide a vehicle for evaluating mobilization plans and procedures and for training key civilian and military leaders in mobilization execution. In conjunction with the Plans and Policy Directorate, J–5, the J–3 develops the procedures for submitting to the Secretary of Defense recommendations concerning the degree of mobilization (partial or full) which would be required in response to a military emergency.

During such an emergency, the Organization of the Joint Chiefs of Staff coordinates the nation's military response through the Crisis Action System, or CAS. CAS procedures provide the Joint Chiefs, the Services, and the Unified and Specified Commands information with which to develop recommendations to support the Secretary of Defense, and the President, in making decisions involving the use of US forces, including active, Guard, and Reserve. The Crisis Action System also identifies and describes the responsibilities of each agency involved in developing military responses from the onset of a military emergency through mobilization, deployment, and commitment of forces, or to the juncture where use of military forces is no longer necessary, and they are returned to normal peacetime operations and alert postures. It is during the execution of CAS procedures that the Organization of the Joint Chiefs of Staff would make the recommendation to mobilize all or part of the Guard and Reserve.

Of course, the Military Services are at the very heart of the mobilization structure. They execute mobilization and provide the forces that are deployed and employed in responding to crises. A brief explanation of how military forces are directed and provided to field commanders provides a useful framework for the subsequent discussion of mobilization planning and execution.

The employment of military forces is directed through a chain-of-command running from the President, as Commander-in-Chief, to the Secretary of Defense, through the Joint Chiefs of Staff, to the commanders of the Unified and Specified Commands. These field commanders are frequently referred to as CINCs, an acronym for Commander-in-Chief. European Command or EUCOM is an example of a Unified Command and the Strategic Air Command, or SAC, is an example of a Specified Command. Unified and Specified Commands are formed from major commands of the various Services. After a mobilization has occurred, those organizations comprise regular active component personnel and Guard and Reserve personnel who have been ordered to extended active duty.

The forces assigned to field commanders are provided by the Services. The chain-of-command by which those forces are employed runs from the President and the Secretary of Defense, through the Joint Chiefs of Staff, to the CINCs, and from thence to units in the field via Service components of Unified or Specified Commands. Therefore, from a mobilization perspective, the Services' primary role is a peacetime one of organizing, training, and equipping combat-ready forces that are assigned to Unified and Specified Commands for employment. To these ends, the Services establish requirements for their respective forces; prepare and execute budgets; develop doctrine and training standards; develop and acquire weapons systems; furnish administrative and logistics support; and recruit, train, and manage people.

Insofar as the Guard and Reserve in the mobilization process are concerned, the Services are responsible for acquiring, equipping, and training Reserve-component forces that are adequate to meet wartime augmentation requirements, and for developing the policies and procedures required for effective mobilization planning and execution. Each of the Services is responsible for maintaining the mobilization and combat readiness of its Reserve-component forces. That includes the total force integration and management of active, Guard, and Reserve forces so that they are mutually supportive in training for and meeting wartime operational requirements. From a planning perspective, such integration must harmonize the plans for Guard and Reserve mobilization with the operations plans whose execution is dependent upon augmentation of active forces.

The relationships described above are complex because they involve a great variety of organizations and individuals possessing diverse mobilization planning and execution responsibilities, and because mobilization itself involves a great number of decisions and actions.

Mobilization Planning

Mobilization planning is based ultimately on the requirement to support US military objectives. Three explicit objectives must be met: (1) deter attacks against the United States and its allies and against vital US interests, including sources of essential resources; (2) prevent political coercion of the United States and its allies; and (3) if deterrence fails, conduct successful military operations against an enemy. A fourth objective is implicit in these first three: maintain that mix of combat-ready active and Reserve forces that will provide the required military capability to ensure deterrence, or that will vanquish an enemy if American forces must be committed to battle.

These objectives serve as actual foundations for mobilization planning, and are embodied in policy guidance from the Office of the Secretary of Defense, the Organization of the Joint Chiefs of Staff, and the Services. That is accomplished in a variety of official memoranda and publications the most important of which is the annual Defense Guidance.

The Defense Guidance is the authoritative policy statement of the DOD's fundamental strategy for meeting national security objectives and needs, and of the force planning, resource planning, and fiscal guidelines by which that policy is executed. The Defense Guidance and other official statements of national defense policy form the basis for mobilization planning guidance which the Office of the Secretary of Defense issues to the Joint Chiefs of Staff and to the Services. The Services, in turn, determine the mix of active, Guard, and Reserve forces required to satisfy that guidance and establish, train, and support those forces.

The Joint Chiefs of Staff develop the Joint Strategic Capabilities Plan (JSCP). The JSCP provides the Unified and Specified Commands, the Services, and other Defense organizations the annual taskings and guidance for accomplishing the military objectives which derive from the Defense Guidance. The Services develop or modify mobilization plans consistent with the JSCP. These mobilization plans provide for the time-phased mobilization and deployment of forces needed to support execution of operational plans (OPLANs). They also provide for generating the nondeploying forces which support the military infrastructure that remains in the United States after combat forces deploy to overseas theaters of operation. The Joint Chiefs of Staff review Service mobilization plans to ensure that the Services can generate the forces that Unified and Specified commanders must possess to accomplish the missions which the JSCP directs them to perform. The Services adjust their mobilization plans whenever those missions are changed. As a result, the mobilization planning process is designed to ensure that the total force, including Guard and Reserve forces, is constantly postured to support CINC and OPLAN requirements.

Mobilization Planning Principles

During the course of many years of mobilization planning, a number of principles have emerged which, when adhered to, result in effective and reliable mobilization plans. Six of these principles are especially important and deserve discussion since they are particularly pertinent to the mobilization of the total force.

The first principle is summarized in the word *flexibility*. Mobilization plans must include phased, incremental execution options which are responsive to relatively minor contingencies as well as major conflicts. The mobilization process supporting those plans must be capable of gradual or rapid implementations and must permit Guard and Reserve mobilization along a spectrum ranging from partial to full, in phases or all at once, and at rates ranging from slow to rapid. It must provide a range of possible force structures from which to select the one appropriate to the specific contingency at hand. The process must provide mechanisms for varying the pace of mobilization when it is desirable to allow a pause in mobilization execution. The process must, in short, provide sufficient flexibility in the character, sequencing, and continuity of mobilization events to accommodate changing military and political requirements.

The second principle of effective mobilization planning is that it must integrate mobilization execution actions with overall crisis management operations. Mobilization of Guard and Reserve forces is one of many actions that can be taken in response to a military emergency or a political crisis. Generically, the decision to take any of those actions, and the process by which that decision is executed, is termed crisis management. Crisis management does not always entail mobilization, but since Guard and Reserve forces are essential to mount and sustain any but minor, short-term military operations, it is essential that crisis management procedures provide for evaluating the need for mobilization at key decision points in the crisis management process.

Another mobilization planning principle is that indices of enhanced readiness levels must include the Guard and Reserve. During a military emergency, active component forces can be brought to higher states of readiness by changes in Defense Readiness Conditions (DEFCONs). DEFCONs, which range from five to one, provide a system for progressively increasing alert postures to match the gravity of an evolving crisis. A complementary system must be used in the Reserve components that will augment the active forces which, through a change in DEFCONs, increase their readiness. Such a system would ensure that, in a crisis,

Guard and Reserve elements of the total force are brought to an enhanced readiness posture consistent with that of the active forces they are
designated to augment.

Consistent with this principle, a variety of flexible means must be
available for enhancing the readiness of mobilization forces. For example, *emergency assemblies* can be conducted at the home station in an
inactive duty status. The assembly could involve only the Reserve unit
commander and his immediate staff, or it could include the entire unit.
Additional training can be scheduled to increase the pace of training, or
review mobilization plans and procedures, when mobilization appears
imminent. *Extended assemblies* permit Reservists to maintain an increased state of readiness for a prolonged duration. For example, units
could conduct assemblies evenings and on weekends to accomplish premobilization administrative actions. Members would be free to engage in
civilian pursuits during the day. These readiness improvement measures
would continue during periods of rising tension until the necessary readiness levels had been achieved. This would help ensure that Guard and
Reserve units attain the same state of enhanced readiness as the active
units they are designated to augment.

A fourth principle of mobilization planning is that reliable methods
must exist to notify Guardsmen and Reservists of the requirement to report for active duty when mobilization occurs. Guardsmen and
Reservists must have their personal and civilian career affairs in order at
all times so that when they are ordered to report to active duty, they can
do so expeditiously. No member of the Ready Reserve should be exempt
from the requirement to report for active duty because of personal,
career, or other reasons. In cases where a Guardsmen or Reservist is prevented medically from reporting to duty, a delay can be authorized
providing a new reporting date is established in the orders granting the
delay. Delays can be authorized for other legitimate reasons *after* the
individual has reported, as ordered, to his or her initial duty station, just
as is done for members of the active force.

Peacetime Reserve training activities must support the acquisition
and maintenance of skills Guardsmen and Reservists require to satisfy
post-mobilization wartime mission requirements. As a fifth principle of
mobilization planning, then, units and individuals of the Selected Reserve must be informed of the operational plans they have been tasked to
support, and they must be kept abreast of changes in projected mobilization roles. This makes it possible to orient training to meet specific wartime duties in the planned deployment and employment phases of
mobilization.

Mobilization is an infrequent occurrence, but is a possibility for
which the nation must be prepared at all times. Mobilization plans and
execution procedures are the means by which an organization ultimately accomplishes its mobilization tasks. Therefore, it is a principle of

mobilization planning that periodic mobilization exercises and regular evaluations of plans and execution procedures be conducted as realistically as possible. This enables active and Reserve forces to validate the effectiveness of their mobilization preparations while identifying problems that must be solved if an actual mobilization is to be executed effectively. Exercises are useful tools in demonstrating that the total force, including the Guard and Reserve, can mobilize in the required time, at the right place, and in a state of readiness necessary to meet military requirements.

Initiating the Mobilization Process

It should be evident that the process of mobilization is not one that is self-initiated as the result of a specified chain of events. In fact, this process is activated by actions of either the President or the Congress, or both, as authorized by public law. It would be worthwhile at this point to discuss, in a general way, the statutory bases for initiating mobilizations and the various levels of mobilization that may be initiated. This will be followed by a discussion of the phases through which mobilizations take place.

The Guard and Reserve forces of the United States can be mobilized at any of a number of crisis levels and under legal authorities contained, generally, in Title 10 of the United States Code. These authorities vary with regard to whether a mobilization takes place in peacetime, after a presidential or congressional declaration of national emergency, or after a congressional declaration of war.

For example, the "presidential 100,000 call-up authority" may be exercised whenever the President determines that a crisis situation requires a limited expansion of the active military force for a relatively short period. Under this authority, the President may augment the active force with up to 100,000 Selected Reservists for any operational mission. A national emergency need not be declared and the Reservists may be retained on active duty involuntarily for up to ninety days.

Another level of mobilization, the partial mobilization, expands the active armed forces through action by the Congress or the President. A partial mobilization is intended to meet the requirements of a particular military contingency or requirements incident to hostilities. When the President declares a national emergency, members of the Ready Reserve may be ordered to active duty for not more than twenty-four months. However, no more than one million members of the Ready Reserve of all the Services may be on involuntary active duty without the consent of Congress. When declaration of a national emergency would be inappropriate, the President may ask Congress to provide special legislation authorizing partial mobilization of both units and individuals of the Ready Reserve within specified parameters.

A full mobilization can only be authorized by the Congress after declaration of war or national emergency. It may include augmenting of the active force through the mobilization of all units and individual Reservists of the Guard and Reserve components, including the equipment and logistical resources needed to support such a force.

The final level of mobilization is often referred to as "total mobilization." It involves expanding the active military force not only through the call-up of all Guardsmen and Reservists, but also through organizing additional units and personnel over and above the existing total-force structure. It includes marshalling all of the nation's resources needed to create and sustain such forces. A total mobilization takes place as a result of decisions by the President and the Congress to defend the country against a major military threat.

Mobilization execution is a process guided by operations planning and carried out through a sequence of events that relate to the Joint Operation Planning System (JOPS) and the Joint Deployment System (JDS). These two systems consolidate policies and procedures for developing, coordinating, and approving joint operational plans and the planning and execution procedures governing deployment of forces. The actions taken during the implementation phase of mobilization include requesting the President or Congress for authority to mobilize, alerting Reserve component forces, and mobilizing those forces. Figure 12.1 summarizes this process.

Generally each component of the Guard and Reserve forces has its unique procedures for mobilizing its personnel. For the Army and Air National Guards, unit mobilization consists of alert and notification from the appropriate Service, through the National Guard Bureau, to State governors and adjutants general. The Army Reserve accomplishes this from US Army Headquarters, through the Commander, Forces Command, to the Continental US Armies and their subordinate Reserve units. Similarly, US Air Force Headquarters mobilizes its Reserve units through instructions sent to major commands and field organizations that support these Reserve units.

The Chief of Naval Operations directs the Chief of Naval Reserve to issue mobilization orders to affected units and individuals. The Commandant of the Marine Corps directs the commanding generals of the 4th Marine Division and the 4th Marine Aircraft Wing to issue mobilization orders to affected units and, in the case of individual Reservists not assigned to units, directs the Director of the Marine Corps Reserve Support Center to issue appropriate orders. Finally, upon direction of the President of the United States, operational control of the Coast Guard is

Figure 12.1
THE MOBILIZATION IMPLEMENTATION PROCESS

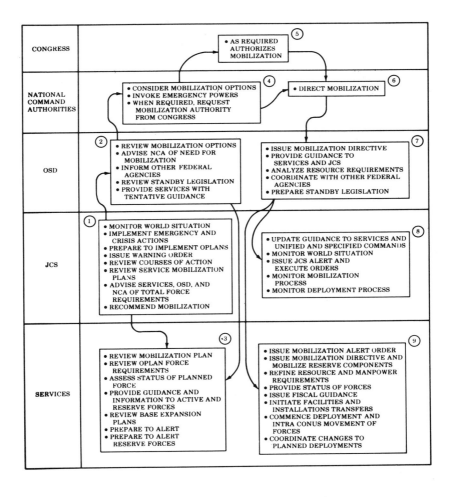

transferred from the Department of Transportation to the Department of the Navy. Once mobilization is directed, Coast Guard Reservists are called to active duty by the Commandant of the Coast Guard through the Chief, Office of the Reserve, by activating preassignment orders for individual Reservists.

For all Guard and Reserve components, mobilization takes place in five phases. Phase I, Preparation for Mobilization, includes all premobilization actions which contribute to readiness for the conduct of wartime operations. It includes the training of units and individuals, the care and maintenance of equipment and supplies, administration, and planning for mobilization. Peacetime Reserve training activities must relate to wartime mobilization missions.

Phase II, Warning/Alert, consists of the Office of the Secretary of Defense, the Joint Chiefs of Staff, and the Military Departments advising the civilian and military leadership and gaining commands that the necessity for mobilization may be imminent. *Warnings* are issued to Guard and Reserve units to take preparatory actions necessary for conversion to military and possibly combat status. Warning of impending mobilization is transmitted broadly to ensure all affected organizations, units, and individuals are informed.

An *alert* officially informs Reservists that mobilization is, or is likely to become, imminent. Alerted units accomplish those preparatory actions essential to the rapid and orderly execution of the mobilization. Individual Reservists recognize, on being alerted, that they are likely to be called to active duty involuntarily. Appropriate "stop-loss" actions are initiated for the entire Ready Reserve to avoid personnel losses through pending retirements, transfers, and the like. Increased readiness measures may be instituted within the Ready Reserve in response to a warning or an alert without having to place units or individuals on active duty.

Phase III of the mobilization process as it affects Guardsmen and Reservists begins with entry on active federal duty and ends with departure to the mobilization station, port of embarkation, or area of deployment. At the home station, the unit performs all necessary administration and training possible to become a fully operational *active* unit. For individual Reservists not assigned to specific Reserve units this phase begins with entry on active duty and ends with arrival at the initial operation station. Upon entry on active duty, Reservists become active duty military members of their respective Service. Assembly of units at home stations and reporting of individuals to their preassigned units or other initial active duty stations occur automatically.

Mobilization Phase IV, Movement to Mobilization Station, begins with the unit's departure from the home station and ends with its arrival at the mobilization station. The process of bringing active, Guard, and Reserve units to full wartime strength in people, equipment, and supplies

will normally be accomplished at such stations. Post-mobilization training may be coordinated here, as well as preparations and processing for
deployment and movement to ports for overseas deployment. Additionally, a mobilization station may be the home station, initial active duty
station, or initial operational station for a particular Selected Reserve
unit, depending on the unit's deployment classification. The five deployment categories are direct deploying units, early deploying units, later
deploying units, nondeploying units, and special mission units. A brief
discussion of each of these categories would be appropriate at this point.

Direct deploying units move from the home station to a port of embarkation and to their overseas operational station without processing
through an initial active duty station. A direct deploying unit does not
receive additional personnel, equipment, or supplies, or accomplish additional training after entry on active duty. These units must be able to
be at an air or sea port within a few days after entry on active duty in
condition to load on planes or ships and move overseas. Upon arrival
overseas, they commence wartime operations with minimum in-theater
processing. Direct deployment is useful for headquarters, some communications units, and service support units which are not equipment intensive and that can transport all or most of the unit equipment on organic
transportation.

Early deploying units move from home station to an initial active
duty station and subsequently to a port of embarkation for movement
overseas. While at the initial active duty station, early deploying units
engage primarily in preparations for overseas movement. Only a minimum amount of time is available for post-mobilization training. An
early deploying unit must be able to be at a port of embarkation ready to
load onto planes or ships from one to thirty days after entry on active
duty.

Later deploying units, like early deploying units, move from the
home station to an initial active duty station and subsequently to a port
of embarkation for movement overseas. While at the initial active duty
station, however, these units receive and assimilate additional personnel,
equipment, and supplies, and accomplish unit training. After the unit is
combat ready, it prepares for movement overseas.

Nondeploying units move from their home stations to initial operation stations within the Continental United States (CONUS). Nondeploying units are generally service and support units capable of starting
wartime operations immediately upon arrival at their operational stations. Postmobilization training is not conducted by these units. While
some personnel, equipment, and supplies may be received, they are as-
similated into the unit concurrently with the conduct of wartime
operations.

Finally, special mission units move directly from their home stations
to ports of embarkation and then to their initial operational stations.

However, these units may accomplish capability generation after arrival at initial operational stations. Special mission units are required to occupy certain key tactical areas in the event of a mobilization. It is very important that these units arrive at their intended areas of operations quickly. Since they are not expected to engage in combat operations immediately upon arrival, they can receive personnel, equipment, and supplies and engage in training after they have taken up assigned positions.

The final mobilization phase, Operational Readiness Determination, begins upon the mobilized unit's arrival at its mobilization station and ends with the unit's completion of any required additional training and is declared operationally ready. Mobilized units are assisted by all the administrative, training, and logistical assets of the mobilization station to obtain the required state of readiness as rapidly as possible. Mobilization Validation Teams evaluate each unit's level of readiness. Units are then deployed, based on their obtaining an appropriate match between readiness and expected mission requirements.

Current Guard and Reserve Mobilization Issues

A combat-ready Guard and Reserve structure, supported by an effective mobilization system, is critical to our nation's strategy of deterrence. Precisely because of this importance, the Guard and Reserve are subject to intense scrutiny when needed refinements and improvements are identified. Any discussion of the mobilization structure and process, therefore, must include comments regarding issues and initiatives that address these refinements.

One of the most significant issues regarding the viability of the Guard and Reserve is that of equipment shortages. These shortages adversely affect the Reserve component's ability to mobilize and meet its wartime mission requirements. Further complicating this issue is the fact that some of the equipment in Guard and Reserve units is incompatible with equipment in the active force and, therefore, cannot be employed effectively in combat. Despite 1982 guidance issued to the Joint Chiefs of Staff by the Secretary of Defense designed to correct these deficiencies, many Reserve component units continue to suffer low combat readiness because of equipment problems.

Another mobilization issue of considerable concern to members of the total force is the degree to which Reserve component units participate in annual exercises conducted by the Joint Chiefs of Staff. Although these exercises provide effective means for testing mobilization plans and procedures, some aspects of these plans and procedures are often excluded. For example, testing such mobilization events as transportation from home station to a port of embarkation would be valuable in evaluating the capability to link Reserve forces with equipment maintained at locations other than the home station. Exercises could also be enhanced if the training they provided were largely combat-mission oriented rather than primarily devoted to administrative activities.

The political dimension of the mobilization process was briefly addressed earlier. In discussing current Guard and Reserve mobilization issues it is worth noting that the political dimension, including its economic and social aspects, becomes even more important than it is when discussing mobilization in general. The reason is quite simple—when mobilizing a Reservist you convert a citizen who is primarily a civilian into a citizen who is solely a "soldier." While the political ramifications of this action are not as severe as drafting a "pure" civilian, they are much more sensitive than merely alerting a member of the active force to prepare for possible combat. It is precisely because of these political sensitivities that the process of mobilizing Guardsmen and Reservists could prove less than optimum from the standpoint of efficiency.

This issue is raised here not to suggest that politics be removed from the mobilization process. Even if possible, it would be undesirable given the nature of our democracy and the tenet of civilian control of the military establishment. Rather, the subject is broached in the belief that an awareness of such real-world, practical considerations may help mitigate their possible negative effects during times of crisis.

This review of current Guard and Reserve mobilization issues is far from complete. On the contrary, other issues continue to be addressed in an effort to improve the mobilization process. These include increasing the level of participation of Reservists in the mobilization planning process, and enhancing mobilization procedures through a more integrated management information system throughout the Department of Defense. This brief review should, however, provide some appreciation of the status of the mobilization process, and where certain refinements might improve that process.

While the mobilization process in a highly industrialized democracy might be somewhat more sophisticated than having married men "bring their wives to do the cooking" and requiring bachelors to "bring any women they can find," the goal of that process remains unchanged since the Ethiopia of 1936. If the mobilization process cannot efficiently and decisively bring a nation's manpower and other resources to bear on a wide range of threats to national security, it is useless. Issues such as sustainability, timeliness, and flexibility must remain key considerations for mobilization planners and decisionmakers. Only in this way can the total force approach to military preparedness succeed as an instrument of national security.

13
Defending Europe Against a Conventional Attack: The Increasing Gap Between the Army's Capabilities and NATO Commitments and What To Do About it

Kenneth J. Coffey

The inability of the US Army to meet its manpower mobilization needs for the conventional defense of Central Europe has been a progressively worsening problem during the all-volunteer force (AVF) years. In the draft era, there were large active forces and Selected Reserve units (Reserve and National Guard); large surpluses of trained, unassigned Reservists; and a functioning Selective Service System. By the end of 1982, however, strength reductions in both the active and Reserve forces, massive declines in the strength levels of the individual Reserve pools, and a conscription system in "deep standby" portended gravely on the ability of the Army to meet the requirements of the "worst case" contingency.

Originally published in *Air University Review* 31 (January–February 1980): 47–50. Reprinted by permission. Article has been edited to reflect more recent data on manpower strengths, mobilization plans, strategic airlift programs, sealift capabilities, and ammunition supplies. Manpower data are drawn primarily from Office, Deputy Assistant Secretary of Defense (Reserve Affairs), *Official Guard and Reserve Manpower Strengths and Statistics: FY 82 Summary*, Report RCS:DD:M(M)1147/1148, September 1982.—ED.

A Warsaw Pact attack on NATO forces in Central Europe would put a premium on the well-trained US forces already in Europe and on those units in the United States that could be rapidly moved overseas. There could also be a requirement for later-deploying reinforcements and a sustained war capability, and it is in this area that the greatest uncertainties remain.

If the Army is to have the resources to wage an extended NATO-Pact conventional conflict, the American people will have to strengthen their support, either by increased military service or higher tax payments. Whether such actions are desirable or necessary is still open to question.

Thus, this chapter analyzes the significance of the changes that have occurred during the AVF years, particularly regarding the Army's ability to provide massive reinforcements on a continuing basis in the event of a major land war in Europe.

Manpower Problems

The extent of the manpower-related problems that have developed in the AVF years can perhaps best be indicated by comparing the strengths and capabilities of the Army at the end of fiscal year 1964 with those at the end of fiscal year 1982. As 1964 was the last year of stable peacetime force levels before the buildup for Vietnam, its use as a benchmark for comparisons can be justified. During the eighteen years from 1964 to 1982, the strength of the active Army, Army National Guard, and Army Reserve was reduced by about 11 percent, while the primary pool of filler personnel and replacements, the Individual Ready Reserve (IRR), was reduced by 52 percent. As table 13.1 illustrates, the Army total force of almost 2.3 million in 1964 had been reduced by almost 630,000 personnel by 1982.

Table 13.1

FORCE LEVEL CONTRASTS: FY 1964–FY 1982—ARMY TOTAL FORCE

(Numbers rounded to nearest thousand)

Component	End FY 1964 Force Level	End FY 1982 Force Level	Size of Change	Percentage of Change
Active Army	972,000	780,000	−192,000	−20
National Guard	382,000	408,000	+26,000	+7
Reserve	269,000	257,000	−12,000	−5
IRR	461,000	219,000	−242,000	−52
Standby Reserve	208,000	400	−207,600	−99
Total	2,292,000	1,664,400	−627,600	−27

At mobilization, not all members of the National Guard, Reserve, Individual Ready Reserve, and Standby Reserve would be expected to report owing to personal or family problems, employment in critical occupations, and, for the IRR and Standby Reserve members, determinations that their skills would not be of value in the mobilization effort. Accordingly, the Department of Defense has developed "yield" rates for each category of manpower resource.[1] When these rates are applied, the manpower resources available on mobilization become clearer. As table 13.2 shows, the Army total force on mobilization would have been some 453,000 fewer in 1982 than in 1964.

Table 13.2

MOBILIZATION CONTRASTS: FY 1964–FY 1982—ARMY TOTAL FORCE.

(Numbers rounded to nearest thousand)

Component	End FY 1964 Mobilization Force Level	End FY 1982 Mobilization Force Level	Size of Change	Percentage of Change
Active Army (100 percent)	972,000	780,000	−192,000	−20
National Guard (95 percent)	363,000	388,000	+25,000	+7
Reserve (95 percent)	256,000	244,000	−12,000	−5
IRR (70 percent)	323,000	153,000	−170,000	−53
Standby Reserve (50 percent)	104,000	200	−103,800	−99
Total	2,018,000	1,565,200	−452,800	−22

On mobilization, the Army's need for pretrained manpower would increase to 1.570 million. This is the number of personnel necessary to bring all units of the active Army, National Guard, and Reserve to combat readiness and to provide casualty replacements for the three or four months after mobilization before an increased flow of newly trained recruits could begin.[2] Yet, as table 13.3 illustrates, the capability the Army possessed in 1964 to meet these requirements has seriously eroded.[3] Had a mobilization occurred in late 1982, there would have been many units with unfilled medical billets, there would have been grave shortages of combat engineers and other skilled personnel, and most important, there would have been a significant shortage of trained combat-arms personnel.

In addition to the 1.570 million trained personnel needed shortly after mobilization, Army war plans also identify a need for new recruits to

Table 13.3

MOBILIZATION MANPOWER REQUIREMENTS/ RESOURCES: 1964–1982 CONTRASTS

(Numbers rounded to nearest thousand)

	End FY 1964	End FY 1980	End FY 1982 [a]
Requirements	1,725,000	1,725,000	1,570,000
Resources [b]	2,018,000	1,572,000	1,565,200
Surplus/Shortfall (+ / −)	+293,000	−153,000	−4,800

Note: Components are Active Army, Mobilized National Guard, Reserve, Individual Ready Reserve, and Standby Reserve.

[a] See Editor's comment in note 3 to chapter 13.

[b] Assumes that the Army at M-day has stopped all losses of trained personnel and that the various Reserve elements would respond in accordance with the "yield factors" used in Army planning.

enter training within thirty days of the decision to mobilize.[4] Because of training delays, these recuits would not be available for assignment to operating units for at least three to four months after their entry on active duty. Thereafter, however, they would be available for use as casualty replacements, for the formation of new units, and, if the shortage of trained Reservists continues, for filling units of the existing force structure.

During the years of peace before the Vietnam War, the functioning Selective Service System guaranteed that such large numbers of new recruits could be provided. During the AVF years, however, the conscription agency has been allowed to stop all activities except contingency planning, a move prompted in large measure by the judgment of Pentagon officials in 1975 and 1976 that any possible conflict would more than likely be terminated before newly trained personnel could be deployed.[5] Consequently, by the end of 1979, the capability of the Selective Service for meeting sudden emergency demands for conscripts had fallen to a negligible level.

There also are a myriad of other manpower issues and problems. Foremost among these is the uncertainty of the yield rates used by the Army to predict mobilization gains. Whereas the loss of 5 percent from the Selected Reserve can be supported by both historical experience and various mobilization exercises in the late 1970s, the loss factors for the other manpower groups are less certain. In fact, the true availability of these mobilization resources cannot be determined. On the one hand, in total, there are enough pretrained personnel in the various personnel categories to meet the Army's needs, if the resources of the Retired Reserve are included. On the other hand, if estimated losses from these sources on mobilization are understated, the Army's problem would be even greater than 1982 projections.

Many factors influence the validity of the Army's "yield" rates. For example, the willingness of Americans to serve would vary considerably between a politically inspired mobilization in response to an insurgency in a third world, oil-producing country and a call-up in response to a major Warsaw Pact attack. In addition, there would certainly be a different response rate from personnel in terms of grades, skills, ages, and obligations for recall. Yet the Army is expecting the same responses from non-obligated, noncombat arms field-grade officers as from young, obligated combat arms enlistees.

Another major problem is matching the Army's specific needs with the available mobilization personnel. The Army estimates that some 70 percent of IRR personnel would report on mobilization, but has devoted little attention to whether these Reservists could perform useful functions. For example, approximately 75 percent of the Army's filler and replacement needs would be in combat arms or medical, combat engineer, and direct support fields; but only about 25 percent of IRR personnel possess these skills. An overabundance of officers in the Individual Ready Reserve compounds this problem.

A serious question also arises whether the manpower available on mobilization would be ready in time to play a useful role in the critical early weeks of a conflict. The Army has concentrated on developing new programs aimed at increasing the strength levels of the National Guard, Selected Reserve, and the Individual Ready Reserve, but it has generally ignored deployment-related problems. Yet the Army's manpower requirements at mobilization do not increase steadily; most of the personnel needed to boost the force to peak level are needed in the first few weeks. During this period, units of the active and Reserve forces would be filled to their wartime quotas. Thereafter, replacements would be needed, but their numbers would be smaller than those required during the initial weeks.

Nor would personnel from supplementary pools be immediately available for deployment. Initial ordering, administrative processing, and prereporting leave would take time. Many Reservists would need refresher training before they were able to resume old specialties; those assigned to new specialties would require even longer periods of training. Thus, although supplementary sources of manpower might eliminate peak manpower shortfalls, they would probably not satisfy needs immediately after mobilization, when trained personnel would be needed to fill deploying units.

Finally, even if the Army manages to resolve its projected shortfall problems, the deployed forces would be far less combat ready than the forces of the pre-Vietnam years. This conclusion is based on the fact that active Army personnel are readier than those of the Selected Reserve and that men and women in both these groups are readier than members of the individual Reserve pools or retirees or veterans. Although the Army possibly could field a mobilized force as large as that of 1964, it would not have as many trained active and Selected Reserve personnel.

Army Reinforcement Plans

The US military strategic goals for a conventional conflict in Central Europe between NATO and Warsaw Pact forces have not changed since the advent of the all-volunteer force. By maintaining a strong on-site force and a rapid, though limited, immediate reinforcement capability in concert with the forces of European NATO members, the United States hopes to deter aggressive action. Failing this, the readily available active force units, together with available forces of other NATO members, would be expected to contain any Pact advances within West German territory long enough to equalize the balance of forces through reinforcement and to prevent the conflict from escalating into a tactical or general nuclear exchange.

In a military emergency, American forces would be rapidly augmented by dual-based units serving in both Europe and the United States, and by other units having stockpiles of equipment and supplies in West Germany. In 1980, such stockpiles were sufficient for an augmented force of about four divisions, the personnel of which would be airlifted to Europe in case of potential or actual conflict. These initial reinforcements would be supplemented by other airlifted or sealifted divisions and support troops, including active Army units (augmented by Reserve fillers), and Army National Guard and Army Reserve combat and support units. The Secretary of Defense noted in 1975 that twelve or thirteen divisions would be deployed. But indications since then, such as the planned conversion of the Second Infantry Division to a NATO-oriented mechanized infantry division, are that even more divisions would be committed to the conflict.[6]

Because the deployment schedule would allow little time to send crucial reinforcements, most of the early transported units would be from the active Army, with National Guard and Army Reserve forces serving as a first echelon of reinforcements and as replacements for active Army units involved in initial combat. No doubt, however, most of the Army National Guard units, as well as the vast majority of combat support units in the Army Reserve, would be deployed to Europe for an extended conflict. Under current planning decisions, the first Reserve units to deploy would be those maneuver battalions needed to round out the active Army divisions. Such units would depart within thirty days of the mobilization decision. At the same time, certain support elements needed to augment supply and maintenance functions in Europe also would be deployed. Shortly thereafter, additional Reserve combat units and support elements would embark. Finally, the eight National Guard divisions would be committed. In total, planners expect that the full deployment of designated active Army, Army National Guard, and Army Reserve units could be completed in somewhat more than 100 days, though the Pentagon has established a deployment goal for all of the Reserve forces of 90 days or less.[7]

Strategic Mobility Limitations

The availability of trained reinforcements in the United States is but one of several conditions that must be met before US forces can fulfill their strategic commitments in the defense of Central Europe. Another key factor is the availability of adequate airlift and sealift resources. If we cannot get the troops to Europe quickly, their availability will add little to NATO defensive efforts.

In 1979, the US military air fleet was the world's best.[8] Although government policies have supported its development since the early 1960s, US strategic air transport still has shortcomings. The aircraft in the US military air fleet plus the resources of the Civil Reserve Air Fleet (CRAF) constitute an imposing resource. But at any given moment, many aircraft may be grounded for maintenance and service, and the combined capacity of all available aircraft would be sufficient to transport only a small portion of the massive reinforcements needed for a conventional conflict in Europe. For example, estimates are that it would take about ten days to transport the first reinforcing division, if most of the unit's heavy equipment were already stockpiled in West Germany.[9] Transporting the four-division equivalents that have stockpiled equipment waiting for them would therefore take three to four weeks.

If the Pentagon has its way, improvements in strategic airlift in the 1980s will double the capacity of the fleet. This program includes modifying C–5s, buying new midair refueling tankers/cargo aircraft (the KC–10) and a new airlift aircraft (the C–X); and modifying civilian airliners to improve handling of military cargo.[10] In total, the program would cost tens of billions of dollars. For this reason, and because of congressional opposition to providing funds to civilian airlines, the full amount of funds requested for the program has not been appropriated. Consequently, unless there is a major change in attitude in Congress, a vastly increased strategic airlift capacity cannot be expected.

If all of the total-force elements designated for transport to Europe are to be delivered on schedule, a major share of the burden must be assumed by sealift resources. Yet the US sealift capability is seriously deficient. For example, the Military Sealift Command (MSC) has available from the MSC-controlled fleet, the National Defense Reserve fleet, and the US Merchant Marine fleet only 432 dry cargo ships, as compared to 2,422 available during the Korean war and 1,200 during the Vietnam conflict. Of these 432 ships, 129 were built during World War II and are approaching obsolescence. Although almost 400 NATO ships have been identified for use in a NATO reinforcing effort, these ships and the US flag dry-cargo ships would be poorly suited for military use or not readily available.[11]

The success of limited US transport resources also would depend on preserving reception facilities in Europe. Many of these facilities are quite close to the East German border and militarily vulnerable. Indeed, if Pact forces should manage to penetrate West German territory to any significant degree and certainly if they should reach the Rhine in two to seven days, as some observers predict, airfields in West Germany that receive and unload the large American jet transports would be in enemy hands or under hostile fire.[12] The seaports where ships unload US reinforcements and supplies (such as those in Belgium and the Netherlands, as well as the main port, Bremerhaven, in northern Germany) also would be vulnerable, as would the 250-mile line of communication between the ports and Seventh Army units in southern Germany, although the line of communication to the US brigade in northern Germany would be more secure.

Equipment Stockpiles and War Reserve Limitations

The size and comprehensiveness of equipment stockpiles and war reserves in Europe also would affect US capabilities. If well-trained units of the total force can be transported to Europe but cannot be fully equipped on arrival or sustained with ammunition, food, fuel, and other supplies, their availability on the battlefront would add little to NATO defense.

The usefulness of early reinforcements in Germany following mobilization would depend on the status of the prepositioned equipment stockpiles. (The Army's phrase for this equipment is POMCUS, an acronym for "prepositioning of materiel configured to unit sets.")[13] As noted earlier, some four divisional sets of equipment are maintained.

In the Army's view, the limitations inherent in a reinforcement plan requiring the quick movement of men and material to Europe are such that European stockpiles should be enlarged; and in a major departure from previous policy, the Pentagon decided in 1977 to support a short-term goal of stockpiling equipment for three additional divisions by fiscal year 1983.

The NATO ministers endorsed the short-term goal at their spring 1978 meeting. Plans drawn up at that meeting called for placement of the first additional set by the end of fiscal year 1980; that goal was met in early 1981. Construction of a fifth POMCUS storage site began in October 1981, and construction of a sixth started in January 1982. These sites must be equipped, however (at an average cost of $1.5 billion for each division equipment set), and the POMCUS program has always been underfunded. To equip the existing POMCUS sites in Europe, the Army has had to resort to withdrawals from war reserve stocks and the inventories of active, Guard, and Reserve units, thus degrading those units' combat readiness and training capabilities.

To alleviate these equipment shortages, the Department of Defense requested that Congress authorize almost $1 billion in fiscal years 1983 and 1984 for the Army land-based prepositioning program. But even with increased funds for POMCUS, shortages of commonplace items of equipment will exist for some years to come because of the reduced capacity of the US defense industry, which now requires a long lead time to accelerate production of military equipment. Such improvements in equipping airlifted US reinforcements with POMCUS would be of little value, however, unless war reserve stocks also were improved. These stocks are combat-essential items stockpiled for use as replacements for losses.[14]

In the mid-1970s, the United States, alone among NATO allies, doubled its requirements for war reserve stocks.[15] This decision was based primarily on the very early but heavy losses of ammunition and other materiel in the 1973 Middle East war as well as on the increasing weight of opinion that a war in Europe would be fought largely with the materiel on hand.

Ammunition supplies are among the critical shortfall items, and this problem is compounded by a shortage of ammunition storage areas, port facilities with ammunition handling capabilities, and US production limits. The shortage of ammunition reserves is so severe that it has been suggested "the Army in Europe would have to curtail firing rates in the midst of battle unless the situation is corrected."[16] Increasing war reserve stocks of ammunition, therefore, has high priority, and approximately $50 billion has been programmed for fiscal years 1983–1987 to improve war reserve stocks of munitions and secondary items of equipment.[17]

European NATO members also have made some increases in their reserves, and have directed their efforts toward bringing their depleted stocks up to programmed levels. Indeed, much of the additional monies pledged for NATO improvements in 1977 and 1978 were used for this purpose. Despite these gains, however, the capabilities of European NATO members will remain well below the capabilities of US forces. This was confirmed by a special subcommittee of the Committee on

Armed Services of the House of Representatives, which concluded in early 1979 that the European nations would begin to run out of equipment and ammunition in a matter of days rather than weeks or months.[18] If this assessment is correct, the building of larger US war reserve stocks becomes an even more critical issue, for the United States would most likely provide support to its NATO allies in the event their reserves become exhausted in a protracted conflict.

The Army's Long-War Strategy

The Army has not publicly stated its planning goals; but indications—such as stockpiling targets for equipment and ammunition—are that Army plans are based on preparedness to fight for ninety days or more.[19] Obviously, such planning goals contain a hedge against uncertainty as well as a warning to the Soviets that the United States is serious about defending Central Europe for an extended period. This assumption, which is key to US strategy for the defense of Central Europe, has been maintained regardless of the fact that the European NATO forces appear to be oriented toward a much shorter war. While exact figures are classified, various observers have estimated that the European NATO members are not planning for a conventional ground war of much more than thirty days.[20] These nations' commitments for greater defense expenditures during the 1980s and beyond are likely to result in an extension of the thirty-day planning goal. But it is doubtful the European NATO members will match the US commitment.

The European NATO forces would not withdraw from combat when their equipment and manpower resources were depleted; nevertheless, despite the provision of equipment and ammunition from US sources, their full involvement in an extended NATO defensive effort would by necessity be limited. It therefore seems likely that a conventional conflict extending much beyond the supply limits of the European NATO members would become a struggle primarily between US and Warsaw Pact forces. In this case, the disparity between NATO and Pact forces would be so great that the conventional phase of the conflict would probably not last long—a view supported by many observers who believe, regardless of the capabilities of the two forces, that the conflict would be settled either by negotiation within thirty days or escalate into a nuclear exchange.[21]

Among all the estimates, official and unofficial, of the probable length of a NATO and Warsaw Pact conventional conflict in Central Europe, only the United States appears to believe in the possibility of a long war, and makes it the basis for strategic planning. In fact, the weight of evidence supports the likelihood of a short war. Thus, there appears to be a reasonable basis for questioning the validity of the

Army's long-war strategy and asking whether national security would be better served by abandoning the current strategy in favor of a short-war concept.

The potential benefits to be gained from adopting a short-war strategy would be great. For in terms of strategic capabilities, a formal short-war strategy would make available added resources to develop and equip a more effective short-war force. Furthermore, it would avoid the societal disruptions and additional costs that might be caused by the need to forge a national consensus on restoring the Army's strategic capabilities to their former levels. Nevertheless, there can be no certainty that a conventional conflict in Central Europe would end in a few weeks, for as Neville Brown has pointed out, military planning is not a mechanical science that lends itself to exact quantification.[22] Thus, if the United States were to endorse a short-war strategy, it might also run the risk of increasing the probability of aggression, though the US nuclear inventory would continue to make such aggression a remote possibility.

Despite such assurances, the relationship between force structures and capabilities and the deterrence of aggression is highly uncertain. Military and civilian leaders repeatedly assess this relationship, but, as Morton H. Halperin notes, NATO does not know exactly what the Soviet evaluation of forces on the central front is or how it would be affected by possible changes in NATO's war-sustaining capabilities.[23] Thus, the effect on the deterrent value of the armed forces of adopting a short-war strategy cannot be predicted with any certainty.

The Total-Force Concept

During the Vietnam War years, just prior to the adoption of the total-force policy, Army Reserve forces were treated as a second-rate military resource while the active forces received most of the attention and funding. In addition, since the President was unwilling to call major units to active service, the role of the Guard and Reserve was ill-defined. Their effectiveness was marginal to poor because most of their modern equipment had been sent to Vietnam and their units were staffed with many young men who had enlisted in order to avoid the draft and Vietnam combat assignments.

Since adoption of the total-force policy, however, noticeable improvements have been made in National Guard and Army Reserve units. The policy has reinstituted a clear sense of mission among Reservists, equipment inventories are being replenished and modernized, training is being intensified, and the draft-motivated enlistees of the Vietnam era are being replaced by volunteers. Nonetheless, because adoption of the total-force policy shifted a major portion of the Army's war-fighting responsibilities to the Reserve, the problems that emerged during the

AVF years have compounded what was an initial weakening of the Army's combat capabilities. This questionable ability to sustain extended combat operations in Europe has several implications.

First, the on-site units of the Seventh Army, and other units of the active Army that could be quickly flown to Europe, together with the forces of the European NATO allies, may not be strong enough to deter aggression by Soviet and other Pact forces or to avoid military defeat in the critical early weeks of a war. Second, a conventional conflict would be much more likely to escalate into a nuclear exchange or to end through negotiation. Third, if negotiations were to occur between NATO and Pact leaders before the outbreak of hostilities, during the initial stages of a conflict, or later, the absence of a strong US war-sustaining capability would greatly reduce NATO's bargaining power.

These conclusions are based, of course, on the assumptions that it would not be in NATO's interest to initiate a tactical or general nuclear war or to end a conflict through negotiation and that it would be in the Pact's interest to pursue an extended conflict with NATO forces. If NATO leaders are willing to use nuclear weapons, particularly tactical attacks on troops, staging areas, and supply depots, the availability of an extended war capability becomes somewhat of a moot point. Indeed, if the Pact perceives that NATO would rely on nuclear weapons, its forces would be unlikely to initiate any attack, save one for limited objectives which could be achieved quickly before the exhaustion of on-site NATO forces or a decision by NATO to use nuclear weapons.

In all likelihood, in a conflict between the forces of NATO and the Warsaw Pact, reinforcing units from the United States would be required. While one cannot guarantee this situation, the Army's ability to provide reinforcements would provide a major bargaining asset in negotiations during times of crisis, an added deterrence value to those forces already in Europe, and an actual military capability in times of armed aggression. Yet, as noted earlier, the US Army's capability to meet its reinforcing commitments diminished during the 1970s. The arguments for corrective action, therefore, are strong.

Nonetheless, before a less-than-popular action is taken, several decisions affecting the seriousness of manpower-related problems deserve critical scrutiny. One such decision meriting examination and validation concerns the judgment of wartime requirements.

Determinations of wartime needs are far from objective decisions: rather, they are subjective judgments which reflect a myriad of assumptions and value judgments. In addition, requirements have frequently changed, reflecting the judgment of military planners at a given time and current assessments of a multitude of related factors. Though a mobilization shortfall in training individuals and new recruits may have occurred at the end of fiscal year 1982, future adjustments in the requirements will either reduce the shortfalls or make them worse.

In evaluating the seriousness of the problem, it should be remembered that requirements are determined on a "worst case" basis and the chances of such a case occurring are considerably less than 100 percent. Because such a scenario, of course, could occur, the "worst case" planning process is a valid tool. Conversely, such emphasis on the most remote possibility creates an exaggerated sense of the magnitude of the problem. It is not the purpose of this chapter, however, to question the use of the "worst case" planning process. Suffice to say that most or all of the mobilization manpower shortfalls and other problems would be eliminated if the United States adopted a "more likely" scenario as the basis for determining needs.

Another uncertain requirement concerns the Army's need to fill completely all of its units prior to the availability of newly trained volunteers or conscripts. Particularly in light of the limitations noted earlier in strategic mobility, equipment, and supply resources, the Army should be made to justify its stated manpower-fill requirements. For if the Army can trade off some or all of its requirements for filler personnel and casualty replacements, many of its mobilization problems could be resolved by restoring the emergency induction capability of Selective Service.

It is doubtful, however, that a revalidation of the Army's force structure and manpower requirements would completely eliminate mobilization problems. Accordingly, the nation may be left with several less-than-satisfactory choices. For example, it could be agreed that we will accept the shortages. If the need for reinforcements does not materialize or occurs early enough before the outbreak of hostilities, the effect of the Reserve force shortfalls would be minimal. Also, if there is little or no warning of the outbreak of war, the Reserves would have little effect on the critical first weeks of fighting in Europe. However, if combat continued, a serious shortfall would jeopardize the Army's capabilities for sustained conventional combat and lower the nuclear threshold accordingly, but US strategic nuclear forces would not be affected.

It also could be agreed that a war in Europe would develop only after a period of warning longer than that now anticipated by Pentagon planners. If this decision were made and proved to be valid, it would allow a longer period for Reserve retraining, the reconstruction of Selective Service induction machinery, and the training of greater numbers of new conscripts and volunteers.

Finally, and most sensibly, the nation could agree that US strategic policy for the defense of Western Europe must be reconciled with the changed capabilities of the all-volunteer force. For within the context of a continuing commitment to a long war-sustaining capability, it is an unfortunate paradox that the all-volunteer force has fostered both the total-force policy and the progressively worsening ability of the Army to meet the obligations of that policy.

Perhaps, then, the total-force policy and the commitment to maintain a long war-sustaining capability are an anachronism of a past era when a large mass Army was the order of the day. In any event, in an era of volunteerism, the willingness of the American people to support the armed forces and participate therein should determine the level of strategic commitments.

Such compromising actions should not be taken lightly. Certain risks would accrue. Yet when there are inadequate personnel and funding resources to support both a short-war and a long-war capability, the continuation of such commitments will only perpetuate the inability of the Army to perform either mission fully—a condition that could contribute to a breakdown in detente or a change in the world order.

14
Mobilization for a European War: The Impact of Habeas Corpus

Jon P. Bruinooge

The little girl saw her first troop parade and asked,
"What are those?"
"Soldiers."
"What are soldiers?"
"They are for war. They fight and each tries to kill as many of the other side as he can."
The little girl held still and studied.
"Do you know . . . I know something?"
"Someday they'll give a war and nobody will come."
—Sandburg, *The People, Yes*

In August 1979, the author participated in a pretrial conference in the chambers of a United States district judge in Houston, Texas. The case at hand was a habeas corpus action filed by an Air Force Reserve physician seeking exemption from active duty. The petitioner proposed a compromise. If the Air Force would forgive his two-year active duty commitment, then the petitioner would agree to serve out his military obligation

This article is an abridgment of one that appeared in *The Air Force Law Review* 22 (1980–1981): 205–281. Reprinted by permission. Endnotes herein are also abridged, but retain their original numbers to assist readers who wish to refer to the original article. As a result, missing endnotes are those omitted in the preparation of this abridged version.—ED.

in the Selected Reserve. In the event of war, he promised, he would be immediately available. There was a touch of irony in his proposal that made one think of Carl Sandburg's poem. At the time, the Air Force had been trying for three years to call this officer to active duty—three years of continuous litigation. The petitioner won again that day. And although the United States Court of Appeals for the Fifth Circuit ultimately reversed the district court and vacated the writ of habeas corpus, the Supreme Court did not finally put the matter to rest until March 1981.[2]

This incident gives one pause to think about reliance on the "total force" and about the prospect that Air National Guard fighter pilots may well find themselves in combat within seventy-two hours after mobilization.[3] In a war where reserves and reinforcement will be crucial, what will happen if only one side decides that "nobody will come?" What role, we might ask, should the federal courts play in the midst of mobilization for a European war? Professor James B. Jacobs of Cornell University has suggested that the Supreme Court's decision in Parker v. Levy [4] "made it clear that judicial activism would not penetrate the armed forces." [5] The purpose of this chapter is to suggest a contrary view and to argue that the intervention of the federal judiciary could seriously obstruct mobilization efforts in the event of a conventional conflict with the Warsaw Pact in Europe.

The American legal system has changed markedly since 1962, and so has the US military posture in the world. In 1962, the United States had nuclear superiority, and President Kennedy consequently had the means at his disposal to force the Soviets to remove their intermediate range ballistic missiles from Cuba.[6] Today the military balance is altogether different. One analyst has likened NATO's posture in Europe to that of France and Britain on the eve of World War II.[7] General Sir John Hackett's widely read fictional account of a Third World War in Europe circa 1985 has a disconcerting air of authenticity about it.[8] The outcome of such a conflict, should fiction actually presage reality, will depend in large measure on US ability to quickly reinforce its NATO allies.

The burden of that effort will, in large part, fall upon the Reserve forces. Driven by the total force concept, we plan to commit these "weekend warriors" to battle with unprecedented haste and little time for preparation. "Come as you are" will be the order of the day. During the last major Reserve callup in 1968, however, some Reservists proved reluctant to answer the call. They sought habeas corpus relief or sued to enjoin their deployment to Vietnam. Although their efforts were generally unsuccessful, these cases suggest the possibility that litigation could be a factor to be reckoned with in any future mobilization. Since 1968, moreover, judicial review of military personnel decisions has become more widely accepted and more intensive. This fact underlines the need to explore in peacetime those legal impediments that might, in this litigious society, thwart mobilization efforts and diminish US war-fighting capability in any future conflict.

The potential for such disruption is illustrated by the events associated with *Miller v. Sloan*,[9] another habeas corpus action tried in the United States District Court for the Southern District of Mississippi during December of 1979 and January of 1980. The petitioner was an Air Force physician stationed at the US Air Force medical center, Keesler Air Force Base, Mississippi. Captain Miller had attended medical school on active duty at government expense. Once having completed his internship at Keesler, however, Captain Miller concluded that the Air Force had fraudulently induced him to enter the medical education program in the first place. From a mobilization standpoint, the complicated contractual issues raised in Captain Miller's petition for habeas corpus are largely irrelevant. What is significant is the delay and disruption wrought by the proceedings—confusion which, although perhaps acceptable in peacetime, the nation could ill afford at the onset of a "come as you are" war in Europe.

In addition to separation, Captain Miller sought the issuance of a temporary restraining order preventing the Air Force from either requiring him to see patients or transferring him outside the Southern District. The Air Force, he contended, by refusing to discharge him prior to the active duty service commitment specified in his contract, had induced such a degree of emotional and psychological stress that he was incapable of seeing patients. He refused to conduct even routine physical examinations without the constant presence and direct supervision of a senior medical officer.

The court ultimately held that it would not substitute its judgment for that of the hospital commander, himself a physician, that Captain Miller was competent to conduct routine physicals.[10] This decision, however, was not forthcoming until after a hearing requiring the presence of the Keesler hospital commander, his deputy, the chairman of the Department of Mental Health (a board-certified psychiatrist), and a clinical psychologist. Only Dr. Sloan, the hospital commander, had the opportunity to testify. The others spent the day waiting in the hallway. At the time of his initial hearing, Captain Miller was absent without leave. This incident suggests that even the threshold question of amenability to judicial review frequently cannot be resolved without a full-fledged hearing and the submission of briefs by the parties.

In *Miller*, moreover, a further hearing was required to address the contractual issues and fully explore petitioner's mental status. Captain Miller maintained that his emotional state rendered performance of his contractual obligations to the Air Force impossible. All the medical personnel mentioned above were again present. In addition, petitioner subpoenaed another Air Force psychiatrist from Texas, while the government required the testimony of a medical administrator from the Air Force Manpower and Personnel Center in San Antonio. After testifying on the first day of the hearing, the hospital's deputy commander, a full colonel, had to rush from Jackson back to Keesler so that someone from management could be present when the regional hospital accreditation commission completed its inspection of the medical center. Throughout subsequent proceedings, day-to-day hospital routine was hampered by the fact that Dr. Miller would not speak to his commander without his civilian attorney being present.[11] Ultimately, the district court ruled against Captain Miller and dismissed his petition. The Fifth Circuit affirmed on the basis of the district court's opinion.[12]

This brief account suggests the reality that can encumber judicial review at the district court level. It is important to a perspective of the mobilization problem for two reasons. First, if logistics constraints dictate an early end to the fighting—and exercise Nifty Nugget suggested that US forces would run out of ammunition within thirty days [13]—there would be little prospect of litigation beyond the district court level having any significant effect on the outcome. Second, *Miller* illustrates the way that even a few lawsuits, especially of the class action variety, could undercut combat readiness in units preparing to deploy overseas. Nifty Nugget indicated, for example, that medical personnel will be in critically short supply once the fighting starts. Even with the immediate dispatch of understrength Reserve medical units to Europe, soldiers will die on the battlefield for want of medical attention.[14] Yet physicians probably account for more litigation, on a per capita basis, than any other group of military personnel. Thus, the prospects for a swift and uneventful callup of Reserve medical units are dubious indeed.

It is from this vantage point, the view from the trenches, that the author will examine potential legal impediments to mobilization. The focus will be on the worst-case scenario—a short-notice, all-out Soviet conventional attack on NATO. Such an attack, however unlikely, would sorely test US ability to mobilize and deploy America's total force. The penalty for a failed mobilization would almost certainly be either a negotiated settlement on Soviet terms or a fateful decision to cross the nuclear threshold. The attention here will be primarily on the problem of getting Reservists "on board," an issue centering for the most part on the willingness of federal courts to intervene in military personnel matters in the midst of crisis. The author will largely ignore the Selective Service System on the premise that the draft is unlikely to produce significant numbers of trained personnel in time to alter the outcome of a "come as you are war." [15] Legislation imposing environmental, safety, and manpower allocation constraints will also be beyond the scope of this article, even though such considerations would clearly affect US ability to mobilize with the necessary speed.

The inquiry begins with a brief look at America's strategic posture in the world and at the total-force concept that has brought readiness and mobilization to the forefront of controversy in recent years. The focus then moves to some of the recent cases decided in the lower federal courts that increase the likelihood of Reservists being able to delay their deployment until the brunt of the attack has passed. Finally, some possible steps are suggested to increase the prospects that America's total force will actually be there when the balloon goes up.

Mandate for Mobilization

The United States is committed to the defense of Western Europe. This obligation goes beyond US legal obligations under the North Atlantic Treaty [16] and reflects, in the last analysis, a moral, cultural, and economic imperative.[17] President Carter symbolically reaffirmed this commitment in his 10 May 1977 address to the NATO Summit Conference in London.[18] The concrete manifestations of this commitment, however, are the US military personnel arrayed on the continent and the 7,000 tactical nuclear weapons in their armory.[19]

The Consequences of Nuclear Parity

The nature of the US commitment has changed markedly over the years. When American conventional forces were deployed to Europe in the early 1950s, "American strategic superiority was so great that we could defend Europe by the threat of general nuclear war." [20] The advent of a significant Soviet nuclear strike capability, however, ultimately rendered the doctrine of "massive retaliation" untenable. America's current countervailing strategy, nevertheless, contemplates that strategic and theater nuclear weapons will continue to "contribute to the deterrence of conventional aggression as well." [21] In the context of essential nuclear equivalence,[22] however, there are increasing doubts as to NATO's willingness to make good on its threat to make "first use" of tactical nuclear weapons to counter an overwhelming Soviet conventional attack.

Within the Alliance, the political constraints associated with obtaining nuclear release authority are such that the Soviets might readily conclude that "by the time the decision [to escalate] is made by NATO, [Warsaw] Pact forces will have advanced so far into Western Europe that NATO use of nuclear weapons would be ineffective, senseless, or both." [23] In a concerted attack, Soviet forces might well be astride the Rhine within forty-eight hours after crossing the German frontier.[24] Such reluctance to employ tactical nuclear weapons would obviously carry over to plans for employing strategic nuclear assets. The harsh reality is that "NATO can no longer improve war outcome by escalation or threatening to escalate the level of conflict. . . . [W]e are no longer able to reverse war outcome through escalation either to the use of theater nuclear weapons or to use of US strategic forces." [25] As a result, "the importance of a capacity to wage war successfully below the nuclear threshold has mushroomed because of the declining credibility of nuclear response to non-nuclear aggression." [28]

The Soviet Threat to NATO

In regard to US conventional war capability, however, there is increasing concern that "the Soviet Union and its Eastern European allies are rapidly moving toward a decisive conventional military superiority over NATO." [29] The massive nature of this Soviet buildup has been documented by John M. Collins of the Library of Congress in his book, *US-Soviet Military Balance: Concepts and Capabilities 1960–1980* (1980). It extends across the entire spectrum of military activity. As President Carter suggested in 1977, the resulting Warsaw Pact deployments are "much stronger than needed for any defens[ive] purpose." [30]

To offset the Soviets' numerical advantage, the United States has traditionally relied on technology as a force multiplier. Yet, as Dr. Steven L. Canby has suggested, "[t]echnological superiority is not a substitute for numbers when the opponent is using similar if less advanced equipment; it is an offset only when qualitatively different technologies are involved." [32] Moreover, as the Soviets continue to evolve and deploy large quantities of increasingly complex and capable equipment, America's search for technical sophistication has driven costs up and production runs down.[33] This trend means that the enemy's numerical advantage increases even as the US technological lead becomes more fragile.

As of 1 January 1980, NATO had some 999,000 troops arrayed in the central region opposite approximately 1,384,000 of their Warsaw Pact counterparts. These Pact forces are equipped with about 25,000 medium tanks and are organized into fifty-eight divisions. NATO can field some 8,970 tanks and twenty-three divisions. Warsaw Pact tactical aircraft number 3,330 in contrast to 1,550 for the Western alliance. Reinforcement with available active force units would temporarily give NATO some respite although the Soviets would still retain a sixty-seven to forty-six lead in divisions. Once the Soviets completed mobilization and deployed their Category III divisions garrisoned in the western military district of European USSR, however, the balance would shift further in their favor, ninety divisions to fifty-seven, notwithstanding the arrival of virtually all organized US Reserves.[34]

Pact forces are also positioned to take advantage of NATO troop dispositions which are the "legacy of World War II logistics arrangements and of postwar occupation agreements" rather than current day tactical considerations.[36] This maldeployment of NATO forces is complicated by a lack of theater reserves and a political commitment to forward defense at the inter-German frontier. There is, moreover, little room for maneuver in a theater only 130 miles deep at West Germany's narrowest point.[37] Consequently, "(a) successful forward defense would depend heavily on the timely arrival of reinforcing units from the United States, Canada, and the United Kingdom." [38]

Mobilization and the "Total Force"

The Defense Department's Rapid Reinforcement Program, if fully implemented, contemplates doubling the number of US ground forces deployed in Europe during peacetime and tripling the number of tactical air assets—all within fourteen days of mobilization.[39] Implementation of the total-force policy has, in addition, shifted "a major portion of the army's war-fighting responsibilities to the Reserves." [40] The magnitude of this shift is apparent from the fact that "[s]elected reserve units . . . [currently] provide about one-half the combat power and two-thirds of the logistical support in the total force." [41]

Air Force Reserve augmentation to the Military Airlift Command would be required immediately to sustain the airlift of reinforcements to Europe.[43] Air National Guard and Air Force Reserve tactical fighter units would, in many instances, be expected to mobilize and deploy to Europe within seventy-two hours.[44] Four of the Army's sixteen regular divisions would need to gain a National Guard "roundout brigade" before being ready for combat.[45] In addition, the Army expects to sustain between 130,000 and 200,000 casualties during the first few weeks of a European conflagration. Many of the pretrained fillers who would be needed immediately to replace these losses would come from the Individual Ready Reserves.[46] This heavy reliance on Reserve forces makes it essential that they be able to mobilize quickly and efficiently in the event of crisis.

Factors Inhibiting Mobilization

Time Constraints

NATO planners have assumed that the Soviets would launch an attack in Europe only after partial mobilization and extensive preparation. On the assumption that NATO intelligence services would detect such preparations soon after they commenced, this scenario contemplates that the West would have up to twenty-three days to mobilize before the enemy attack actually materialized.[47] This warning time has now dropped to an estimated eight to fourteen days.[48] There are, however, NATO officials who believe that the Soviet Union could initiate operations from a "standing start" and reach preplanned NATO positions before their defenders could arrive on the scene.[49]

This decreased warning time has far-reaching consequences. First, it greatly compresses the time frame for NATO's political leaders to make the crucial decisions necessary for mobilization to begin.[50] Second, it allows virtually no time for consensus formation among the citizenry of the Western democracies. This is crucial because mobilization is unlikely to be truly effective without the peer pressure generated by widespread public support.[51] Third, it places a tremendous premium on speed. If reinforcements do not arrive in theater before hostilities actually commence, they may never arrive at all. Finite US airlift and sealift assets are incapable of absorbing the attrition that would result from reinforcing under fire.[52] Any significant delay, moreover, could cause key airfields and port facilities to be in enemy hands. Rhein Main Air Base, for example, the focal point for strategic airlift on the continent, is only 178 miles from the East German border.[53] The value of prepositioned equipment for the Army is also diminished if the storage sites are in enemy hands when US reinforcements arrive.[54]

In addition, there are serious logistic shortfalls in Europe. Mobilization exercises such as Nifty Nugget (1978) and Proud Spirit (1980) have demonstrated that US forces will run out of ammunition before the conflict is thirty days old.[55] Adequate supplies of chemical protective equipment are not available.[56] Because of the long lead times involved, defense production, at least for major weapons systems, could not be expanded rapidly enough in a short war to have any significant effect on the outcome.[57] These considerations all dictate that the mobilization effort proceed posthaste. If NATO is unable to reinforce quickly and stabilize the situation, then the Alliance will be faced with the dubious choice between nuclear escalation and negotiated settlement on Soviet terms.[58]

Personnel Readiness

All these factors lead to the conclusion that there will be no time for many Reserve units to "shake down" before deploying overseas. Some Air Reserve tactical fighter units may find themselves in combat in less than seventy-two hours.[59] In the event of a Warsaw Pact attack on NATO, "[t]he US response . . . must be 'come as you are' employment of active and Reserve forces. There will be little or no time available for post-mobilization manning, equipping, and training of the Reserve forces." [60] The simulated deployments in exercise Nifty Nugget confirmed that, given an enormous shortage of trained individuals, Reserve personnel will be deployed overseas ready or not. During the month-long exercise, upwards of 400,000 men were dispatched to Germany, including most members of the Individual Ready Reserve.[61]

There is, moreover, a historical precedent for this sort of overnight deployment. Marine Reservists called up during the Korean War—many of whom had not completed even basic training—found themselves embarked for the Inchon landings only two weeks after being activated.[62] The risks inherent in such an endeavor are obvious, however, from the fate of two National Guard divisions also deployed in Korea. Both had seven months of training before embarkation. On arrival, however, they were deemed to be only 40 to 45 percent combat effective and required another seven to eight months of training before being committed to combat.[63] The time for such training will be an unaffordable luxury in any future European conflict, and casualty rates will no doubt reflect that fact.

Because of inadequate in-theater medical care, many of the 130,000 to 200,000 anticipated casualties will die.[64] American forces have become accustomed to operating with air superiority. Given the likelihood of chemical attack and repeated enemy bombing raids, a senior Air Force medical officer has suggested that Air Force personnel will suffer casualties on a par with those normally encountered by infantry units in close contact with the enemy.[65] Fighter pilots facing odds of five or six to one [66] will discover that the intensity of the battle and the magnitude of losses on both sides will preclude the reassuring search and rescue missions mounted during Vietnam.[67] Rear echelon units will have to be prepared to fend for themselves in the event of armored breakthroughs or airborne assault.[68]

The likelihood of becoming a casualty in this hostile environment will depend largely on a service member's physical condition, training, and equipment. Serious doubts have been raised on all three counts both in the active force [69] and the Reserves.[70] Physical conditioning is a particular problem for Reservists. In addition, recent studies have suggested that US troops are lacking in the sort of unit cohesion that makes for success in combat.[71] Some authors suggest that this situation reflects a state of anomie which characterizes many of today's recruits.[72] Others suggest it may be the result of personnel turbulence or the animosity prevailing between "dopers" and "juicers" in some units.[73]

In any event, this lack of cohesiveness, especially when coupled with inadequate training and poor physical conditioning, bodes ill for the combat performance of many units. It stands to reason that Reserve personnel who doubt their own personal state of readiness for immediate deployment, and that of their unit as well, may respond to a call-up with considerably less enthusiasm than reflected in DOD's projection of a 95 percent show rate for members of the Ready Reserve.[74] Even in peacetime, absenteeism remains a critical problem. Focusing on New York's 77th Army Reserve Command, the *Wall Street Journal* recently noted:

> On a recent training weekend, 149 of 815 men assigned to the command's 99th Signal Battalion were absent without an excuse. Another 90 were missing because they are chronic absentees who

already were in the process of being drummed out. "We still have the problem of recruits assigned to this unit whom we've never seen," says Maj. William Shepherd, commander of the 99th.[75]

Two additional factors may have some effect on the show rate in the event of mobilization. One is the way the Reserve program is sold to prospective enlistees. Recruiting literature stresses the benefits Reservists can derive from their participation—the opportunity for additional training and a supplementary source of income in economically troubled times.[76] When surveyed by the General Accounting Office, 86 percent of Reservists responding indicated that additional income was their primary motivation for remaining in the program.[77] One suspects that a certain number of such individuals have remained in the Reserves largely because they perceive little likelihood of being recalled in the event of an emergency. Such an attitude is consistent with the recollection that, except for the *Pueblo* crisis, Guard and Reserve units were not mobilized during the Vietnam War. A second factor is the increasing number of women and sole parents in the Reserves. How many of these individuals have seriously considered the possibility of being called up in the event of mobilization is unclear.[78] To the extent, however, that such individuals are inclined to subordinate their military duties to their family responsibilities, the anticipated number of hardship discharge applications could be expected to increase. Doubts, real or imaginary, as to the ability of women to perform in a combat environment could further disrupt unit cohesion.[79]

The foregoing observations are intended to suggest that motivation is an important variable in predicting the success of mobilization. If Reserve personnel are motivated by a sense of duty and a tinge of patriotism, then they will respond in the nation's hour of crisis. If, however, they are motivated primarily by selfish or mercenary considerations, then the risks associated with a major European conflict will be very disconcerting indeed. The total-force concept has made success in battle dependent on the capabilities and responsiveness of the Reserve forces. There must be some assurance that the total force will be there when the need arises.

Developments in the Law Affecting Mobilization

It is risky to speculate on how readily Americans would answer the call to arms in the event of mobilization. Senior military leaders, wedded by necessity to the total-force concept, respond to questions regarding the reliability of US Reserve components with allusions to the deep, undying patriotism of the American people. The lessons of Vietnam suggest, however, that noncompliance with a call-up order cannot be totally discounted and that widespread resistance, should it develop, could seriously impair the nation's ability to wage a conventional war in Europe.

Dr. Kenneth J. Coffey notes, for example, that of the 10 million plus men inducted during World War II, an estimated 72,000 claimed conscientous objector status. In contrast, "only 153,000 men were inducted [from 1971 to 1972], yet more than 121,000 men applied for CO status—a rate more than 100 times the rate of application during World War II." Where such applications were rejected during 1971 to 1972, 33 percent of the inductees appealed.[80] The New York Civil Liberties Union "claimed a 50 percent success rate for cases tried by their attorneys." [81]

Appeals from classification decisions generally reached the 67 percent level during 1968 when 136,256 appeals were forthcoming from the 203,707 men inducted. June of 1970 found the Selective Service System frantically struggling to cope with a backlog of 55,000 individuals who had requested personal appearances before their local draft boards.[82] Some individuals became draft evaders and simply went underground. During 1971, the Justice Department had a backlog of 27,000 draft evasion cases awaiting investigation or review. Some 4,006 young men were brought to trial during 1972 as the Justice Department sought to expedite these draft evasion cases.[83]

The outrage aroused in many Americans by the Vietnam War renders this war unique in US military history. It seems unlikely that such protests would arise in the event of a Soviet invasion of Western Europe. Nevertheless, at least some of the Vietnam draft evaders seem to have been more interested in their own safety than in matters of principle. In this regard, it is worth noting that American casualties in Vietnam were rather low except for small units engaged in direct contact with the enemy. Only 46,397 Americans were killed by hostile fire from January 1961 to March 1975.[84] Prompt aeromedical evacuation and surgical intervention meant that 81.3 percent of those wounded between 1965 and 1971 survived.[85] Moreover, rear echelon troops were relatively safe from enemy attack.[86] Today, the Army anticipates between 130,000 and 200,000 casualties during the opening weeks of a conventional NATO conflict.[87] Rear echelon air bases, depots, and command centers would be prime targets for enemy air interdiction. American medical facilities lack the capability to undertake surgical procedures in a chemically contaminated environment.[88]

Despite doubts as to their readiness, current plans call for Reservists to enter any future European conflict during the first days of combat. Logistical considerations dictate a short-war scenario, at least for the present. Under these circumstances, some Reservists, whose motivation, training, physical condition, and equipment are below par, may conclude that discretion is the better part of valor. In this context, the chronic absentees of the 99th Signal Battalion may simply vote with their feet. In urban areas, the task of locating them would be long and arduous. Middle-class Reservists have more to lose, however. They cannot simply disappear without sacrificing careers and harming loved ones. Such individuals may well find delaying actions in the courts preferable to outright disobedience. Their objective may not, in fact, be to avoid recall entirely but rather to delay their deployment until such time as the situation on the battlefield has stabilized, refresher training and proper equipment become available, a less demanding assignment comes along, or family problems are resolved.

At this juncture in a high-intensity European conflict, a delay of sixty days in going overseas could spell the difference between survival and an unmarked grave, and the likelihood of obtaining such a delay through the courts has increased markedly in recent years. Indeed, a willingness to review military decisions on their merits has become a deeply ingrained part of the judicial system. At critical moments in the nation's history, the executive branch of government has simply chosen to ignore such judicial intrusions in the name of military necessity.[89] But the pervasive influence of the judiciary in today's American society—and our inherent respect for the rule of law—make it unlikely that such a course of action will ever be repeated. This realization underlines the necessity of sorting out in peacetime the nature of wartime interaction between military and judicial authority. This discussion examines developments in the law that could severely affect rapid mobilization.

Military Service as a Restraint on Liberty

To the contemporary observer, schooled in the lessons of Vietnam, it seems perfectly natural to equate military service with the sort of custody required to invoke habeas corpus relief under 28 U.S.C. sec. 2241 (1976). As Justice Rehnquist has pointed out, however, this has not always been the case.[90] Indeed, from a legal perspective, this country's changed "notions of custody" will make mobilization for any future conventional war in Europe quite different from that preceding World War II.

The Supreme Court decisively upheld the constitutionality of conscription during World War I.[91] Local draft board decisions "within the scope of their jurisdiction [were] final and not subject to judicial review when the investigation [was] fair and the finding supported by substantial evidence." [92] However, because "[t]he induction of a civilian into military service is a grave step, fraught with grave consequences," [93] draftees in both World Wars were able to seek habeas relief based on proof that "the investigation had not been fair, or that the board [had] abused its discretion by a finding contrary to all substantial evidence." [94]

The rules of the game were different, however, for individuals who had voluntarily enlisted or accepted a commission in the armed forces. As recently as 1965, the United States Court of Appeals for the Second

Circuit denied habeas corpus relief to a seaman because "the normal restraint upon an individual's free movement incident to service in the armed forces is not such a restraint that one may predicate a petition for habeas corpus relief thereon." [99] In an earlier case, *Miller v. Commanding Officer, Camp Bowie, Tex.,*[100] the United States District Court for the Northern District of Texas dismissed a petition for habeas corpus on the theory that the applicant, though drafted, had acquiesced in his military status by failing to challenge his induction for a period of three years.

By this time, however, developments in the civilian community clearly pointed to the early demise of *Wales v. Whitney* [103] and its requirement that there be physical restraint. In 1963, for example, the Supreme Court held that habeas corpus was available to a parolee subsequent to release from prison.[104] This decision helped push the lower courts toward "recognition of the fact that restraints on liberty short of physical confinement can be of such magnitude as to warrant the protection of the writ." [105] At the height of the Vietnam War, the Second Circuit confronted this custody question directly in *Hammond v. Lenfest.*[106] Hammond, a Naval Reservist whose claim for conscientious objector status had been denied, was faced with orders to report for active duty predicated on his refusal to participate in scheduled training. Without any mention of *Wales,* the Court of Appeals concluded that "the better reasoned and modern view is that a petitioner in Hammond's predicament is under sufficient restraint of his liberty to make appropriate habeas corpus jurisdiction. Any other view would make the ends to be served by the great writ wooden indeed." [107] The United States District Court for the District of Maryland followed suit with a well-reasoned decision in *Donigian v. Laird.*[108]

Meanwhile, the Supreme Court still had not finally resolved the custody question with respect to active duty personnel serving voluntary enlistments. *Eagles v. Samuels* [109] remained subject to a narrow reading whereby the right to habeas corpus relief extended only to those individuals inducted into the armed forces over their objections. However, Justice Douglas, writing for the Court in 1971, firmly rejected this construction in *Schlanger v. Seamans.*[110] For the purposes of 28 U.S.C. sec. 2241 (c), he noted, the term prisoner "has been liberally construed to include members of the armed forces who have been unlawfully detained, restrained, or confined." [111] Justice Stewart reiterated this point even more forcefully the following year in *Parisi v. Davidson.*[112]

These cases made it clear that anyone "on active duty with the armed forces is sufficiently 'in custody' to invoke habeas corpus." [113] The status of Reservists, however, remained uncertain. In May of 1972, the Court articulated a similar standard with respect to Reservists in *Strait v. Laird.*[114] Although Strait's conscientious objector request had been denied by the Army, the petitioner was still free to go about his normal civilian routine. Notwithstanding the fact that his custodian for habeas corpus purposes was situated in Indiana, the Court held that Strait and other unattached Reservists could seek the writ in the district where they resided and had routine contacts with the military.[115] Implicit in this holding, however, was the Court's acceptance of the theory that potential liability for active duty would suffice to establish custody for Reserve personnel even in the absence of any physical restraint. *Wales* and its progeny had breathed their last.

The practical effect of this new concept of custody is to inhibit summary disposition of applications for the writ of habeas corpus by members of the armed forces and their Reserve components. Under 28 U.S.C. sec. 2243 (1976), a district judge is required to "forthwith award the writ or issue an order directing the respondent to show cause why the writ should not be granted, unless it appears from the application that the applicant or person detained is not entitled thereto." During World War II and the Korean War, a judge entertaining an application for the writ could frequently ascertain from the pleadings whether the petitioner had been inducted into the armed forces or had voluntarily enlisted. Where the petitioner had enlisted, the application could legitimately be denied absent some degree of physical restraint not normally inherent in military service. In *McCord v. Page*,[116] the Fifth Circuit Court of Appeals expressly sanctioned this practice.

The utility of this approach during a period of mobilization in anticipation of or subsequent to the outbreak of hostilities is, from a military standpoint, self-evident. As Justice Harlan suggested in *Oestereich v. Selective Service Board No. 11*,[118] "even though the scope of judicial review is narrow, . . . this [review of the documentary evidence] cannot be done quickly." Lengthy hearings of the sort described in the foregoing discussion of *Miller v. Sloan* [119] frequently could be avoided, and with them, the necessity for military commanders and senior staff officers to abandon their units for the courtroom for days at a time in the midst of mobilization and deployment. Yet the Supreme Court has essentially foreclosed such summary dispositions by abandoning the concept of physical restraint as a prerequisite for relief in habeas corpus actions brought by members of the armed forces.[120] Compelled to look at each petition on its merits, the conscientious judge has little alternative, given the complex issues frequently raised, but to set the case for a hearing. Since the petitioner may be entitled, with leave of the court, to at least some modicum of discovery,[121] these proceedings may develop into a highly complex affair at a time when the government's legal and administrative resources are least able to cope with the overload. These considerations suggest that a case-by-case approach to military personnel litigation may prove disastrous in the opening stages of a major European conflict.

Disposition of In-Service Conscientious Objectors

Exemption from conscription on the grounds of conscientious objection is a matter of legislative grace.[122] Individuals whose beliefs as to conscientious objection crystalized subsequent to their voluntary enlistment in the armed forces have no inherent right to be discharged.[123] Rather, as a matter of national policy, the Department of Defense has promulgated 32 C.F.R. sec. 75 (1980) which authorizes in-service conscientious objectors to apply for discharge or noncombatant status.

During the Vietnam War, the United States Supreme Court substantially expanded the scope of the conscientious objector exemption to encompass "all those whose consciences, spurred by deeply held moral, ethical, or religious beliefs, would give them no rest or peace if they allowed themselves to become part of an instrument of war." [124] The test as to whether moral and ethical beliefs will sustain a conscientious objector application is, according to *United States v. Seeger*,[125] "essentially an objective one, namely, does the claimed belief occupy the same place in the life of the objector as an orthodox belief in God holds in the life of one clearly qualified for exemption?" The net effect of this construction was, according to the dissenters in *Welsh v. United States*,[126] to extend the "draft exemption to those who disclaim religious objections to war and whose views about war represent a personal code arising not from religious training and belief as the statute requires but from readings in philosophy, history, and sociology." [127]

Notwithstanding such reservations, *Seeger* and *Welsh* have won general acceptance. The requirements for conscientious objector status have since been summarized by the Supreme Court in *Clay v. United States*: [128]

> In order to qualify for classification as a conscientious objector, a registrant must satisfy three basic tests. He must show that he is conscientiously opposed to war in any form. . . . He must show that this opposition is based upon religious training and belief, as this term has been construed in our decisions. . . . And he must show this objection is sincere. . . . In applying these tests, the Selective Service System must be concerned with the registrant as an individual, not with its own interpretations of the dogma of the religious sect, if any, to which he may belong.[129]

The Department of Defense has adopted the substance of this test in 32 C.F.R. sec. 75.3 (1980) as the criteria for in-service conscientious objector applications as well.[130]

Dr. Kenneth J. Coffey has argued that *Seeger* and its progeny "so complicated the criteria for granting C.O. claims that the submission of lengthy dissertations based on college philosophy courses or readings became common practice. As a result, most local draft board members had great difficulty comprehending the requests, let alone deciding on them." [131] The military has not fared much better with in-service applicants. Investigating officers appointed to conduct the hearing required by 32 C.F.R. sec. 75.6(d)(2) (1980) are frequently ill-prepared to cope with petitioner's counsel and experience great difficulty in gauging the applicant's sincerity.

Unlike the Department of Justice hearing officer in pre-1967 Selective Service cases, the military investigating officer lacks anything analogous to an FBI "inquiry" into the applicant's background and beliefs.[132] Although the regulations encourage him to "ascertain and assemble all relevant facts" and "create a comprehensive record," [133] the investigating officer, left to his own devices, will seldom interview anyone other than witnesses produced by the applicant. The applicant's proof will frequently include affidavits attesting to his sincerity and beliefs. Only infrequently will an investigating officer contact these references for clarification or elaboration. Applicants themselves are likely to be well-coached prior to the hearing—the more dubious the claim, the more extensive the preparation.

Only occasionally, as in the recent case of *Michael D. Werner v. Lt. Col. Cleo McWilliams*,[134] will an applicant admit that "[m]y views as a conscientious objector became crystallized when I talked to my lawyer" about getting out of the Air National Guard.[135] In this particular case, the airman was prompted to seek counsel by receipt of extended active duty orders issued as a result of his protracted failure to attend unit training assemblies. The attorney referred petitioner to a draft counselor who, over the course of twelve meetings, "helped [petitioner] to verbalize and crystallize his views." [136] In gauging the sincerity of such applicants, however, the military cannot rely exlusively on the correlation between applicants' receipt of active duty orders and the crystallisation of their views.[137] Often, however, there is little other evidence available.

Physicians have, in recent years, accounted for a disproportionate number of conscientious objector cases. By the very nature of their profession, they are engaged in noncombatant activities. Some, like pediatricians, are unlikely even to be providing medical care for the troops. Yet noncombatant status is not factor that can be considered in evaluating conscientious objector applications. As the Ninth Circuit Court of Appeals pointed out in *LaFranchi v. Seamans*,[138] "[t]he fact that appellant's assignment would not involve him directly in combat operations is irrelevant to appellant's professed conscientious objection to any form of military service under the governing test. . . . It was therefore improper to deny appellant a discharge on that ground." [139] The rationale for this view was articulated by the Fifth Circuit in *Helwick v. Laird* [140] when it granted habeas corpus relief to any Army corpsman who had come to realize after basic training "that the purpose of the medical corps—like that of other noncombatant elements—is to support the partisan efforts of the combat forces." [141]

The extraneous motives that sometimes prompt conscientious objector applications are illustrated by a recent Army case, *Cywinski v. Binney*. [142] The petitioner was serving on her second enlistment when she found herself confronted with an unwelcome assignment in Korea and the impending breakup of her marriage. After unsuccessfully seeking a medical discharge for being underweight, she discovered that her beliefs as to conscientious objection had crystallized. Of particular concern to the investigating officer was the fact that petitioner's "opposition to war was 'eloquently and convincingly stated *in word*; however it does not manifest itself clearly *in deed.'* " [143] The noncombatant nature of many combat service support jobs offers little opportunity for the rear echelon soldiers to demonstrate their beliefs by way of deeds. Thus, courts have taken the position that "a conscientious objector applicant's alleged failure 'to manifest his newfound convictions in a changed life-style, . . . seems of minor significance at best. [His] medical career was of a nature commonly supposed to be oriented toward public service, and there was no evidence, before or after crystallisation, of habits of life-style incompatible with sincerely held conscientious objector beliefs.' " [144]

Whatever their motivations, the fact is that many officers and enlisted men are capable, with proper counselling and guidance, of putting together a conscientious objector application that will pass muster under *Clay*. [145] From an administrative standpoint, the processing of in-service conscientious objector applications is a time-consuming and often frustrating business. During the initial phase of the total mobilization accompanying a Warsaw Pact attack against NATO, it is doubtful that the manpower and resources would be available to investigate and process large numbers of conscientious objector applications. Although applicants "on orders for reassignment" may be required to file at their new duty stations and are "expected to conform to the normal requirements of military service," [146] federal district court judges are commonly reluctant to permit a petitioner to be reassigned outside the district during the pendency of the action. [147] Should a substantial number of conscientious objector applications be forthcoming from Reserve personnel in the event of general mobilization, processing delays could thus keep numerous individuals from deploying with their units. In a short-war scenario, such individuals might even succeed in avoiding the worst of the fighting.

Remedies for Breach of the Enlistment Contract

One scholar has identified "[a] reemphasis on the legal and contractual nature of military service" as one of three dominant trends in military law since World War II.[148] The unique nature of the enlistment contract was first recognized by the Supreme Court in *United States v. Grimley*.[149] In *Grimley*, a soldier serving time for desertion sought his release by habeas corpus on the theory that his enlistment was void—and the court-martial which convicted him consequently lacked jurisdiction—by virtue of the fact that he was over the maximum statutory age at the time of his enlistment. The Supreme Court rejected this theory, holding that petitioner was precluded from pleading facts that he had previously concealed to avoid his status as a soldier.[150]

Grimley thus gave rise to the "view [that] regulations placing restrictions or qualifications on enlistments were for the benefit of the military, not the serviceman. Enlistments which did not conform to regulations were voidable by the government but not by the enlistee." [152] Traditionally then, the unique aspect of the enlistment contract has been its lack of mutuality.[153] Although the enlistment agreement remains, in many respects, a contract of adhesion,[154] there has been movement toward greater mutuality of obligation in recent years. The armed services have undertaken to provide various enlistment options and to guarantee them in writing prior to entry. The courts have ordered rescission and released members from their military obligations where such agreements have not been honored.[155] Other courts have, in effect, granted specific performance [156] or forced the government to choose between honoring its commitments or seeing the writ issue.[157]

In *Ex parte Blackington*,[158] a 1917 habeas corpus action, the United States District Court for the District of Massachusetts held that the question of whether an enlistment "contract is valid is determined by the principles of law applicable to contracts generally. Duress, fraud, misrepresentation void a contract of enlistment as they would any other contract." [159] *Peavy v. Warner* [160] and a number of other modern cases support this premise. Although contractual issues can readily arise in suits seeking damages or specific performance,[161] the primary concern here is with actions seeking rescission by way of habeas corpus. In this regard, there seems to be general agreement that rescission is not an appropriate remedy in purely monetary disputes.

Although habeas corpus is thus inappropriate in a case involving a service member's pay and entitlements, it remains a legitimate vehicle for resolving questions as to an individual's military status. A particularly thorny problem centers on the consequences of alleged oral misrepresentations by recruiting personnel. This issue may be of largely historical interest since current enlistment contracts contain an express disclaimer as to promises not set down in writing on the face of the enlistment contract.[166] Nevertheless, there has been some erosion of the traditional view that, absent actual authority, such representations are not binding on the government.

This movement is illustrated by the Eighth Circuit's decision in *Pence v. Brown*,[174] a recruiter misrepresentation case where the District Court had granted the writ. The Court of Appeals noted:

> This case is quite different from a suit against the government for misrepresentations in contracting in which the complaint seeks money damages or specific performance. The proposition that the government cannot be held responsible for the misstatement of its agents does not extend to representations which induce a contract when the remedy sought is rescission.[176]

This decision, if it meets widespread acceptance, will substantially complicate the government's task in defending such cases, especially where the recruiter is no longer available or cannot remember the specific conversation in question.*

All these recent cases arise in a peacetime environment. Their relevance in the event of actual hostilities is difficult to assess, primarily because application of the "War Powers" clause could render all such contractual questions moot. Notwithstanding contracts providing for fixed terms of enlistment, legislation already on the books permits the Secretary of Defense to extend "the period of active service of any member of an armed force . . . for the duration of any war and for six months thereafter." [206] Under 10 U.S.C. sec. 671b (1976), similar authority exists to extend enlistments for a period of six months when Congress is not in session and "the President determines that the national interest so requires."

The authority of the Congress to abrogate the terms of enlistment contracts in furtherance of its "War Powers" was extensively litigated subsequent to passage of the Department of Defense Appropriations Act, 1967.[207] That legislation substantially increased the vulnerability of Ready Reserve personnel to call-up. Prior to this enactment, 10 U.S.C. sec. 673 had permitted the recall of Ready Reservists only "in time of national emergency declared by the President after 1 January 1952, or when otherwise authorized by law."

The 1967 Appropriations Act, however, provided for the call-up of Ready Reservists falling within three broad categories. The first two involved individual Reservists who had not fulfilled their statutory Reserve obligations and who were either not assigned to or not participating sat-

---

*Omitted at this point is a lengthy discussion of recent cases involving rescission as a remedy for recruiter misrepresentations, detrimental reliance, and equitable estoppel. —ED.

isfactorily in a Selected Reserve unit or had not served on active duty or active duty for training for at least 120 days.[208] With respect to the third category, the statute provided that, "[n]otwithstanding any other provision of law, until 30 June 1968, the President may, *when he deems it necessary,* order to active duty any unit of the Ready Reserve of an armed force for a period not to exceed twenty-four months." [209]

Litigation commenced as nonparticipating Reservists began receiving orders directing them to report for active duty for up to twenty-four months. The pace quickened when President Johnson ordered the mobilization of twenty-eight Air Force and Navy units following North Korea's seizure of the USS *Pueblo* and her crew.[210] Common to all these suits was the Reservists' contention that their liability for recall was determined solely by the law in effect at the time of their enlistment—not by the more sweeping provisions of the Appropriations Act. The provisions of 10 U.S.C. sec. 673 were, they argued, part of their enlistment agreement. The subsequent call-up, the Reservists maintained, initiated without a declaration of national emergency, effectively breached their enlistment contracts.[211]

The courts responded to this challenge in two ways. The majority of them held that the phrase "when otherwise authorized by law" in 10 U.S.C. sec. 673(a) was prospective in nature and contemplated recall in accordance with such legislation as Congress might subsequently enact. This same gloss was given to similar language in the enlistment contracts themselves. As Judge Dooling explained in *Winters v. United States,*[212]

> Both the enlistment contract and the Statement of Understanding contemplate that the obligations which the enlisted man undertakes include not only an additional active duty imposed in a national emergency or in time of war but also additional active duty "otherwise prescribed by law" or "as the law may require." Neither the enlistment contract nor the Statement of Understanding says in so many words that it means duty prescribed by law whether already enacted or hereafter passed, but that is the evident and necessary meaning of any language so used in such instruments. Were such instruments construed otherwise they would in effect fetter and embarrass the power of the President and the Secretary of Defense to adopt uniform and practical regulations for the administration of the armed forces and the Ready Reserves, and could indeed operate indirectly as a fetter on the Congress itself.[213]

Although *Winters* involved the recall of a single individual, the language was given the same construction when whole units were called up.[214] Judge Kaufman put the point succinctly in *Morse v. Boswell* [215] when he wrote that, "[t]o this Court, the word 'when' clearly looks to the future." [216] Both *Winters* and *Morse* were subsequently affirmed, and the Supreme Court denied certiorari. Although the Supreme Court never addressed these issues directly, it did suggest its reluctance to get involved in the call-up process by repeatedly declining to stay the departure of Reserve units for Vietnam and other overseas stations.[217]

Not all courts, however, addressed the issues raised by the 1968 call-up in terms of statutory construction. In *Ali v. United States*,[218] the district court initially issued a temporary restraining order on 20 June 1968, barring plaintiff's recall. On 2 July 1968, however, the court lifted this restraint in an order grounded squarely on the War Powers clause. Judge Stephens elaborated, noting that,

> a military enlistment contract is not an insulating document which legally prevents the government of the United States from recalling to active duty an enlistee pursuant to an act of Congress which was passed after the date of enlistment although such recall is not expressly provided for in the terms of his enlistment contract; and that in this case, the recall of the plaintiffs was not tied to their contracts but was predicated upon Congress' right to raise an Army as well as Public Law 89–687 and 10 U.S.C. sec. 673a.[219]

Likewise, in *Pfile v. Corcoran*,[220] the court determined that Public Law 89–687 falls "within the 'wide discretion' which Congress possesses in the exercise of its [war] powers. . . . [Thus] the statute appears validly applicable to petitioner, even if it contravenes his enlistment contract." [221]

The petitioner in *Antonuk v. United States*,[222] however, argued that the provisions of what is now 10 U.S.C. sec. 673a did not actually involve the invocation of the War Powers. Antonuk maintained that the authority to activate unsatisfactory participants was intended solely for the purpose of "assuring greater discipline in Reserve units. Such a lesser purpose," he argued, "cannot justify the overriding of a contractual obligation which should bind the government as well as the enlistee, except in a national emergency." [223] The United States Court of Appeals for the Sixth Circuit was unimpressed with this approach. Even if the sole purpose of sec. 673a was to preserve discipline, the court opined, that "is simply the war power at one remove, and the nexus between Reserve discipline and the power of the Congress to raise armies is not so attenuated that it can be considered nonexistent." [224]

This discussion should suggest that the War Powers are likely to play a significant role in the litigation arising out of any future mobilization. Nevertheless, this authority is unlikely to provide a panacea for the contractual problems set out above. The primary factor involved is simply a matter of time. *Ali v. United States* [228] illustrates the nature of the problem. Even though the district court ultimately rendered a decisive opinion based on the War Powers clause, twelve days elapsed between the issuance of a temporary restraining order and judicial sanction for deployment of the Reservists. In a major European conflict, especially an attack preceded by little or no warning, a twelve-day delay in deploying US reinforcements could well find Soviet troops west of the Rhine and within striking distance of the Channel ports. The reinforcement process itself cannot be sustained without extensive Air Force Reserve augmentation to the Military Airlift Command. Early deploying National Guard and Reserve units are essential to provide logistics support and fill out regular Army formations earmarked for the battle. Selected Air National Guard and Air Force Reserve combat units must be enroute to the theater of operations within seventy-two hours if the lives of the 200,000 or so US troops already stationed in Europe are not to be endangered. The surge of battle, regretfully, will not await due process.

The Reality of Judicial Review

Struggling to cope with a flood of increasingly complex litigation, military lawyers cling desperately to the Supreme Court's 1953 admonition that "judges are not given the task of running the Army." [229] *Orloff* notwithstanding, however, the overwhelming reality today is that, outside the scope of "core military activity," [230] the courts are turning aside technical defenses in military cases and addressing the issues on their merits. The fundamental nature of military personnel litigation has thus changed. Standardized briefs stressing nonreviewability, lack of jurisdiction, and the defense of sovereign immunity were once often dispositive in military personnel cases. Where such arguments are raised today, it is often almost as an afterthought—a matter of form. In their place have come hearings replete with live witnesses and the extensive preparation that their involvement requires. Furthermore, the complex factual questions arising in such proceedings often necessitate the preparation of proposed findings of fact and conclusions of law or post-trial briefs. Such elaborate procedures, although unobjectionable and often helpful in a peacetime environment, are fundamentally at variance with the time constraints of a general mobilization.

Recent cases (discussion omitted) strongly suggest that courts will find jurisdiction under 28 U.S.C. sec. 1331 (1976), to review the type of nonmonetary claims likely to arise in the event of challenges to the recall of specific individuals during the course of a general mobilization. Assuming jurisdiction, the question next arises whether the court should, in fact, assert that jurisdiction in the realm of military affairs. In *Orloff v. Willoughby* [243] the Supreme Court counselled against such judicial involvement:

> Orderly government requires that the judiciary be as scrupulous not to interfere with legitimate Army matters as the Army must be scrupulous not to intervene in judicial matters. While the courts have found occasion to determine whether one has been lawfully inducted and is therefore within the jurisdiction of the Army and

subject to its orders, we have found no case where this Court has assumed to revise duty orders as to one lawfully in the service.[244]

Again, in *Gilligan v. Morgan*,[245] the Supreme Court rejected "a broad call on judicial power to assume continuing regulatory jurisdiction over the activities of the Ohio National Guard." The United States Court of Appeals for the Sixth Circuit had, in the wake of the Kent State shootings, remanded the case with instructions which, in the Supreme Court's view, would have required "that the District Court establish standards for the training, kind of weapons and scope and kind of orders to control the actions of the [Ohio] National Guard." [246] Concluding that such matters were "committed expressly to the political branches of government," the Supreme Court reversed, holding that the issues presented were nonjusticiable. In so doing, the Court warned:

> It would be difficult to think of a clearer example of the type of governmental action that was intended by the Constitution to be left to the political branches, directly responsible—as the Judicial Branch is not—to the elective process. Moreover, it is difficult to conceive of governmental activity in which the courts have less competence. The complex, subtle, and professional decisions as to the composition, training, equipping, and control of a military force are essentially professional military judgments, subject *always* to civilian control of the Legislative and Executive Branches.[247]

These cases have been construed as holding that "[c]ore military activity, such as the deployment of troops, is committed entirely to the judgment of military authorities and is reviewable, if at all, only for gross abuse of discretion." [248] Yet it would be a mistake to assume that the doctrine of nonreviewability espoused in *Orloff* will effectively thwart judicial review of military decisions in the event of mobilization for a major conventional war in Europe. Such an assumption would ignore the fact that it will be federal district judges, not members of the Supreme Court, who will have the crucial say during the first, critical days of mobilization. As the Fifth Circuit has observed, *Orloff* "has not proved to be an absolute bar to the review of military personnel decisions." [249]

One would think, for example, that the physical fitness standards for active Air Force personnel would fall within the "professional military judgments" which the Supreme Court held were nonjusticiable in *Gilligan v. Morgan*.[250] Yet the United States District Court for the Northern District of Texas, perceiving an equal protection issue in the Air Force weight control program, held otherwise in *Vance v. United States*.[251] Judge Hill dispensed with the reviewability question thusly:

> Although it is often said that matters within military discretion are not reviewable by the courts, this formulation is of little use in

> determining general principles for judicial review of consitutional
> challenges to military actions. . . . Most contemporary case law ex-
> hibits the . . . tendency to pay lip service to the idea of a non-re-
> viewable zone of military discretion while simultaneously analyzing
> the constitutional claim on its merits. . . . For this reason, the Court
> is not overly impressed with the Air Force's attempt to drape itself in
> bunting and dust off *Orloff v. Willoughby*. . . . The desire of the ju-
> diciary to avoid entanglement in military administration is strong,
> but no court today can avoid reasoned analysis of a serious constitu-
> tional claim under the catchphrase that judges do not run the
> army.[252]

Likewise, in *Cushing v. Tetter*,[253] the United States District Court
for the District of Rhode Island deflected a claim of nonreviewability
with the observation that "recent cases have made clear that, at least outside the context of the court martial, some degree of judicial review is
available for constitutional challenges to military actions." [254] *Cushing*
illustrates, moreover, how far some courts will extend the scope of their
inquiry into alleged constitutional violations. The plaintiff, a sailor, ab-
sented himself without leave when the aircraft carrier USS *America* de-
parted for a Mediterranean cruise. He subsequently was admitted to the
psychiatric ward of a Boston hospital. After spending some two weeks as
an inpatient, he reported in to the Naval Education and Training Center
at Newport, Rhode Island.

The court construed plaintiff's fifth amendment claim as an assertion that a "return to his former unit would deprive him of life and liberty without due process." [258] This would follow if he killed himself (life)
or murdered someone else (liberty). Chief Judge Pettine entered a preliminary injunction forbidding the Navy from returning Cushing to the
America. The Navy remained free, however, to reassign plaintiff else-
where and to take disciplinary action as required in light of his unauthor-
ized absence.[260]

The holding in *Cushing v. Tetter* is somewhat unusual because it involves two areas traditionally reserved as the exclusive realm of the military authorities.[261] Thus the case runs contrary to *Orloff's* counsel that
"it is not within the power of this court to determine . . . [the propriety
of] specific assignments to duty." [262] Nevertheless, the court's willingness
to enter this particular judicial thicket seems typical, in the author's experience, of a desire on the part of many courts to go to the merits. Thus,
even though Judge Cox ultimately ruled in *Miller v. Sloan* [263] "that the
plaintiff's [mental] competency to perform military services is a matter to
be resolved solely by the military and not by the Court," [264] he did not
come to this conclusion until hearing the testimony of expert psychia-
trists for both sides.

Absent some strong statement of policy to the contrary from the Supreme Court, the emerging view at the district court level seems to be that summarized by Judge Becker in *Neal v. Secretary of the Navy*:

> Developments since *Orloff v. Willoughby, supra,* the high-water mark of judicial non-intervention in military matters, demonstrate that while civilian courts are not insensitive to the unique problems of the military, there is no broad barrier to judicial review of military affairs. Although the decisions are not uniform, there is a trend toward at least limited exercise of [judicial] power to control abuses by military officials. Thus, traditional judicial trepidation over interfering with the military establishment has not prevented review to determine if a military official has acted outside the scope of his powers or in violation of regulations, . . . to determine the constitutionality of military statutes, executive orders and regulations, . . . and cases cited therein at 515; or to determine if an action was arbitrary, capricious, or an unlawful exercise of discretion.[265]

In asserting this jurisdiction, Judge Becker noted, however, that "we may not simply substitute our own judgment for that of the military in such matters of discretion." [266] As the Fifth Circuit has pointed out, "the conclusion of reviewability does not entail judicial second-guessing of military personnel decisions. Such decisions are reviewable only for arbitrariness." [267] Nevertheless, in actual practice, that boundary between judicial review and "judicial second guessing" is ill-defined and easily transgressed.[268]

Many military determinations currently subject to judicial review impact only peripherally on the nation's actual combat capabilities. Thus judicial review of administrative discharges,[278] promotion passovers,[279] or disability retirement cases [280] is unlikely to have any substantial adverse effect on the mobilization process. Also, the appeals process under the Uniform Code of Military Justice is so time consuming that collateral attacks on courts-martial [281] or other disciplinary proceedings [282] will come long after the decisive battle is over. The same can be said for suits seeking monetary damages from alleged deprivations of individual rights.[283]

Instead, our concern should focus on two areas. The first involves actions for declaratory or injunctive relief that seek to raise broad constitutional challenges to fundamental national or military policy. *Owens v. Brown* [284] is one such recent case.

In *Owens*, female sailors brought suit to challenge the constitutionality of the law that precluded women from serving in any capacity aboard any ship in today's Navy. Judge John Sirica ultimately held the statute unconstitutional as a denial of equal protection under the fifth amendment. *Owens'* immediate impact on operational capabilities, however, is minimal. Two recent cases, however, suggest the potential of such suits for disrupting the mobilization effort. In *Wolman v. United States of America, Selective Service System*,[285] the United States District Court for the District of Columbia enjoined the government from requiring Selective Service registrants to disclose their social security numbers. The court noted that no statute expressly authorized the Selective Service System to collect social security numbers and therefore concluded that the requirement contravened the Privacy Act.[286] "Citizens have a duty to serve in the Armed Forces," Judge Gesell wrote, "and a correlative right to register unimpeded by invasion of their privacy unless statutorily authorized."[287] Although such a legislative oversight can be readily corrected during peacetime, it is apparent that such a holding at the onset of mobilization would sow disorder and confusion at the most inopportune of moments.

Nevertheless, *Wolman* went only to the most superficial aspects of the draft. In *Goldberg v. Rostker*,[288] however, a three-judge court went to the heart of the program and declared the Military Selective Service Act[289] unconstitutional insofar as it excluded women from the requirement to register and potential liability for induction. Based on this denial of equal protection, the court enjoined the government from enforcing the Act's registration requirement. The court's 18 July 1980 order, however, was stayed the following day by Mr. Justice Brennan. The government promptly appealed, and the Supreme Court heard argument in the case on 24 March 1981. Some three months later, on 25 June 1981, the high court reversed.[291]

Had it been rendered during wartime, the lower court decision would have done grave injury to the nation's military effort. This very fact, however, suggests that such a decision would never have been forthcoming during a period of actual or impending hostilities. The history of *Goldberg v. Rostker* supports this conclusion. When plaintiffs filed their class action challenge to the Military Selective Service Act in 1972, the United States was still engaged in actual combat in Vietnam. Judge Gorbey, declining to convene a three-judge court, held that the issues raised were nonjusticiable political questions.[297] Although the Third Circuit ultimately reversed the district court on plaintiff's sex discrimination complaint and remanded the case for further proceedings, it did so only after the last US troops had actually been withdrawn from Vietnam.[298] Thus no actual impact on pending military operations was involved. This analysis suggests that the judicial system is capable of dealing with this type of challenge during a period of actual or imminent hostilities. From a practical standpoint, government legal resources would be adequate to focus on the relatively few cases likely to raise issues of such magnitude.

The real problem would arise instead if large numbers of Reservists petitioned for habeas corpus or injuctive relief based on statutory or regulatory claims of the sort commonly held subject to judicial review in recent years. Conscientious objection, a topic discussed at some length previously, is one such vehicle. Requests for delay or discharge on the basis of hardship are another. In this regard, 10 U.S.C. sec. 673(b) (1976), requires that the Department of Defense take "family responsibilities" and "employment necessary to maintain the national health, safety, or interest" into account in determining which members of the Ready Reserve shall be recalled to duty without their consent. To implement this policy, the Department of Defense has promulgated regulations authorizing delays of up to sixty days for "[R]eservists whose involuntary order to active duty would result in temporary, extreme personal or community hardship." [299] Similarly, they provide for the total exemption of "[R]eservists whose involuntary order to active duty would result in prolonged, extreme personal or community hardship." [300] In addition, Reservists who are attending college on a full-time basis may request a delay until completion of the semester or quarter for which they are currently enrolled. [301]

Notwithstanding some disagreement as to the standard of review to be employed, the federal courts have consistently reviewed the denial of requests for discharge based on extreme personal or community hardship. In the Second Circuit, hardship cases are reviewed for procedural compliance with mandatory regulations but not on their merits absent a denial "so arbitrary and irrational that it cannot stand." [302] Thus, in *United States ex rel. Schonbrun v. Commanding Officer*,[303] the court declined to review the hardship claim of an Army Reservist whose unit had been activated in the 1968 call-up. Schonbrun claimed both a personal and community hardship. His wife was suffering from a psychiatric disorder, and he was teaching severely disturbed children at a special school located in a high-poverty area. Petitioner failed, however, to identify any breach of regulations in the processing of his discharge application. In declining review, the court of appeals pointed out that:

> The very purpose of a "ready reserve" is that the reserve should be ready. Under the regulations, delay or exemption from active duty in hardship cases is authorized but not required. The hardship must be "extreme," and while the regulations wisely give more specific content to this criterion, a good deal is necessarily left to the judgment of the commanding officer. . . . While no one could reasonably assert that the country would perish if Schonbrun did not serve with his company, *delay in the call-up of a reservist, even during the period necessary for judicial consideration of his claim to discretionary exemption, inevitably means either a gap in the unit or the call of another reservist who otherwise might not have been reached.* . . . [T]he courts must have regard to the flood of unmeri-

torious applications that might be loosed by such interference with the military's exercise of discretion and the effect of the delays caused by these in the efficient administration of personnel who have voluntarily become part of the armed forces. We conclude that this is a subject on which civil review of discretionary action by the military should be declined.[304]

Other circuits, however, have been inclined to review the merits of such discretionary decisions for arbitrariness. These cases have generally involved claims by physicians that they were essential to the community in which they practiced.[305] At the district court level, however, there are a number of cases dealing with personal hardship claims asserted by junior enlisted personnel. The broad tenor of these cases was recently outlined by the United States District Court for the Eastern District of Pennsylvania in *Bandoy v. Commandant of Fourth Naval District*.[306] The court noted that such determinations were reviewable for arbitrariness or capriciousness. In addition, however, the court held that once an applicant had established a prima facie case of hardship, it was incumbent on the military to articulate specific reasons for rejecting the applicant's claim.[307] Although the objective criteria involved in hardship determinations make this task easier than that of evaluating a conscientious objector claim, it is apparent that the factual questions involved here may require a hearing.

Another area of possible concern may be training. At least two attempts were made during the 1968 Reserve call-up to enjoin overseas deployments on the grounds that the personnel involved were not adequately trained. In *McAbee v. Martinez*,[308] the plaintiffs were members of a Reserve maintenance unit earmarked for imminent deployment to Vietnam. Plaintiffs claimed that Army training records had been falsified and that they either lacked adequate training in their military occupational specialties (MOS) or else they had not received certain refresher combat training required by regulation prior to overseas duty. They sought injunctive relief to correct their training records and forbid their deployment until the requisite training was provided. The district court concluded that it lacked jurisdiction to grant the relief sought since "[t]he law does not require nor indeed permit this court to review the Army's conclusion whether or not a man is qualified to perform duties in his MOS." [309]

A similar claim was rejected in *Drifka v. Brainard*,[310] where 355 members of the 18th Cavalry sought to enjoin their call-up. These cases would undoubtedly be highly persuasive in any future conflict, especially in light of the Supreme Court's pointed comments as to the nonjusticiability of military training requirements in *Gilligan v. Morgan*.[312]

Unfortunately, however, there is another question as to the adequacy of training that is not quite so clear-cut. In *McAbee* and *Drifka*, the question was compliance with the Army's own training requirements—a subjective matter where judicial deference to military expertise is especially appropriate. Such deference might not be forthcoming, however, where clear-cut statutory training requirements exist. The problem arises from the restriction set out in 10 U.S.C. sec. 671 that "[n]o member of an armed force may be assigned to active duty on land outside the United States and its territories and possessions, until he has had twelve weeks of basic training or its equivalent." Although this provision will impact primarily on new inductees in the event of any future conflict, it also has application to Reserve personnel. This point became clear when the plaintiff in *Nicholson v. Brown*,[313] an Air Force Reserve physician, finally received active duty orders following the Fifth Circuit's rejection of his community essentiality claim.

Air Force doctors traditionally receive only a brief two- or three-week indoctrination course when they initially report for active duty. In this instance, Dr. Nicholson was displeased with orders assigning him to a base in Turkey. His attorney promptly telegrammed Air Force personnel officials, advised them that Nicholson's assignment was illegal because he had received less than three months of training, and threatened to file a second law suit to halt the transfer. After consulting with counsel, personnel officials determined that they had only two options available. They could either assign Nicholson to a stateside hospital for ten weeks of temporary duty, on-the-job training prior to his departure for Turkey or they could cancel the assignment. Because the overseas facility could not afford to wait ten weeks for a replacement, Nicholson was permanently reassigned to a stateside hospital and another doctor sent overseas in his stead.[314]

Since many Reservists without prior service may return to their units directly after basic training—as opposed to continuing on through technical school—the possibility exists that this provision could preclude their deployment overseas. If the requirement was for twelve weeks of continuous training, it is possible that some Reservists would never be available for immediate deployment with their units overseas. These individuals would have to be furnished additional training prior to rejoining their units. The DOD General Counsel's Office, however, has issued an opinion holding that the twelve weeks of training contemplated by 10 U.S.C. sec. 671 need not be continuous.[315] "The statute," Assistant General Counsel Robert L. Gilliat concluded, "requires only that the training must be twelve weeks in the aggregate and be equivalent to basic training." [316]

Although the two weeks of active duty for training which Reservists undergo annually would seem to meet these criteria, it is doubtful that weekend drills would qualify since they are hardly the equivalent of basic training. Assuming that a soldier has received only eight weeks of basic training, he would have to train with his unit for two full years before being eligible for immediate deployment overseas. This requirement might not be crucial in Army units scheduled to deploy only during the later stages of a conflict, but it could prove a cause for concern with early-deploying Air Force, logistics, and medical units. The issue could prove critical in those medical units staffed with a large proportion of doctors commissioned directly from civilian life. Where an individual could establish that he had not, in fact, received the twelve weeks of training required by 10 U.S.C. sec. 671 (1976), the courts would no longer be dealing with discretionary military decisions. In this context, injunctive relief, whether on an individual or a group basis, is not outside the realm of possibility.

Manning the Judicial System

Although unsupported by empirical data, the author's personal experience suggests that a substantial majority of Justice Department attorneys currently litigating military cases at the trial level have never served in the armed forces. Indeed, the residue of military experience in the judicial system would seem to be diminishing as federal judges with service in World War II near retirement. The dearth of military experience in the judicial system is, moreover, typical of American leadership structures generally.

During World War II, virtually the entire eighteen- to twenty-six-year-old population was mobilized to support the war effort. Among those individuals vulnerable to induction during the Korean conflict, approximately 70 percent actually served, regardless of whether they were high school dropouts, high school graduates, college dropouts, or college graduates. During the Vietnam era, however, manpower requirements were less pressing, and military service ceased to be a universal obligation.[318] Selectivity was possible because, even at their height in 1966, draft calls totaled only 382,010 out of an eligible population of something like two million young men.[319] Educational and occupational deferments served to channel better qualified young men into civilian technical fields while the war was "fought in the field by the less educated, the economically disadvantaged, and the poor."[320] As a result, the induction figures for Vietnam reflect "a sharp decline in service of those in college or with college degrees and from relatively high-income backgrounds."[321]

As illustrated by its recent decision in *Brown v. Glines*,[324] the Supreme Court's conservative majority is more inclined than their lower court brethren to accept the premise that "[t]he military is, by necessity, a specialized society separate from civilian society." Yet given the likely duration of any future European conflict, it will be district court judges who will have the greatest say as to the success or failure of mobilization.

And if lower court judges are less deferential toward the concept of military necessity, their approach may reflect a different view of the judiciary's role in society than that espoused by the Burger Court.

Although one is unlikely to encounter hostility toward the military on the federal bench,[327] the result of this influx is sometimes a diminished grasp of how military organizations actually work. The consequences of this void can be seen in the divergent analysis and contrary results forthcoming in two recent cases bearing on the discharge of homosexuals. In *Beller v. Middendorf*,[328] the United States Court of Appeals for the Ninth Circuit upheld the constitutionality of a Navy regulation requiring the discharge of individuals who had engaged in homosexual acts. Acknowledging that such concerns were not merely conjectural, the court concluded its opinion with the observation that "the constitutionality of the regulation stems from the needs of the military, the Navy in particular, and from the unique accommodation between military demands and what might be constitutionally protected activity in some other contexts."[331]

A much different attitude is evident on the part of newly appointed US District Judge Terence T. Evans in *benShalom v. Secretary of the Army*.[332] Here the court reviewed the honorable discharge of an Army Reservist and self-acknowledged homosexual for alleged homosexual tendencies.[333] While conceding that "the 'peculiar' nature of military life and the need for discipline gives the Army substantial leeway in exercising control over the sexual conduct of its soldiers, at least while on duty and at the barracks," the court nevertheless struck down the Army regulation as violative of the petitioner's constitutionally protected rights to privacy and freedom of association, expression, and speech.[334] Although some deference might ordinarily be accorded the Army's definition of what constitutes suitable duty performance for a soldier, Judge Evans perceived the Army's position as a throwback to the past. The court therefore issued the requested writ of mandamus ordering petitioner's reinstatement.

The foregoing examples are offered to suggest only that judicial officer's perception of the military, that is, as an instrument of social change or as a force geared "to fight or be ready to fight wars should the occasion arise,"[337] does have some bearing on the way they approach the issues before them. In terms of the result, however, military experience does not necessarily make judges more receptive to the government's position. Nevertheless, when a trial judge is unfamiliar with the military environment, there is an increased burden on government counsel to insure that all the facts are spread out on the record, that regulatory schemes are clear and understood. Of particular importance is the task of relating the issues at hand to the capability of a military unit to perform its mission. The effort is sometimes problematic because younger Justice

Department attorneys have seldom had military experience. By the same token, in most districts military cases arise infrequently in today's peacetime environment. There is thus little opportunity for assistant US Attorneys to develop expertise.[340] Moreover, military personnel cases tend to arise under emergent circumstances, often with little time for preparation before the assistant must make an appearance to oppose petitioner's request for a temporary restraining order. If the matter arises by way of habeas corpus, the government may have only three days to file a written return.[341]

The burden on the US Attorney is heightened by the fact that the petitioner's personnel records and other pertinent documents are frequently located at some considerable distance from the situs of the proceedings. Assembling them may take military lawyers in Washington most of the twenty-day extension authorized by 28 U.S.C. sec. 2243 (1976). The US Attorney's plight is hampered by two other factors. First, manning and workload constraints may limit the assistance available from the litigation staffs of the various military departments. Second, the demands of the US Attorney's own caseload often preclude adequate preparation time, especially on short notice. This is particularly true in smaller districts where assistants handle a mixed caseload of civil and criminal matters, because the requirements of the Speedy Trial Act [342] mandate priority for criminal matters.

Insofar as the military departments are concerned, the specialization required in the area of personnel litigation means that local judge advocates are often hard pressed to give assistance.[343] This fact, coupled with the heavy attrition rate experienced as seasoned litigators leave the military for civilian practice, deprives the services of any significant surge capability in the event of mobilization. Any major upsurge in personnel litigation associated with mobilization would thus severely tax, and probably overwhelm, the government's ability to muster the necessary evidence and formulate a defense. The result would almost certainly be a backlog of military cases much like the backlog of Selective Service cases that confronted the Justice Department in the waning days of the Vietnam War.[344] If this situation fostered an attitude among reserve personnel that mobilization orders could be readily thwarted or safely ignored, the consequences for those American troops in Europe awaiting reinforcements could be severe indeed.

A Systematic Response

The possibility, in Sandburg's words, that "nobody will come" is one which must haunt those charged with mobilization planning. There is an overwhelming temptation to ignore the problem. A conventional conflict in Europe is not, after all, really very likely, and Americans would surely answer the call. Yet a recent survey by the National Center for Educational Statistics reveals that 29 percent of all high school seniors in the United States would "try to avoid either military or civilian service if one or the other were required by law." [345] Are we, as one observer put it, "morally debilitated by an ethic that sneers at any semblance of individual duty to the nation?" [346]

Surely, however, those who join the reserves are driven by some higher motivation. In many instances, this is so. Still, there is reason to believe that the yield rates predicted by the Department of Defense are overly optimistic. A recent Air Force study of the members of the Individual Ready Reserves suggested that the likely show rate would be 49 percent between M-day and M + 60 days, 67 percent by M + 90 days, and 78 percent by M + 150 days. Such a response may be inadequate if, as suggested earlier, the United States is unable to sustain hostilities for more than thirty days because of chronic shortages of ammunition and war reserve materials. Air Force figures for the availability of Standby Reservists were even worse. Only 28 percent of these individuals would be available by M + 130 days and 33 percent by M + 210 days.[347]

A similar Army study, conducted during a 1976 mobilization exercise, had to be discarded because 65 percent of the Individual Ready Reserve and the Standby Reserve never responded to questionnaires seeking to establish their availability for recall in the event of mobilization.[348] Taking these results into account, the General Accounting Office has warned that "the attitude of people toward military service in the context of the World War II/Korean War time frame versus the antimilitary attitude of the Vietnam era may invalidate the predictions for 'yields' which are based on historical experience." [349] If there is some element of truth in this analysis, then military service becomes, once more, a matter of coercion.

As this article has sought to suggest, however, the US legal system may have evolved to the point where such coercion is no longer possible. Legitimate concern for individual rights has tended to overshadow the duties and responsibilities of citizenship. The problem, as Chief Justice Earl Warren described it, is that "[i]n times of peace, the factors leading to an extraordinary deference to claims of military necessity have naturally not been as weighty." [350] Yet in wartime, the national interest requires that "[m]ilitary personnel must be ready to perform their duty whenever the occasion arises." [351] And, in the era of the total force, this requirement extends with like urgency to members of the Reserve components. The question we must face then is whether, given the case law that has emerged over the past twenty years, the courts can change literally overnight from a peacetime view of military personnel issues to a role compatible with successful mobilization and survival on the battlefield.

Many readers may discount this threat as fanciful, as little more than paranoia. In terms of concrete numbers, one can readily argue that the likely volume of litigation could not possibly affect the success or failure of the mobilization effort. Even discounting the impact of class action suits, however, this argument misses the point. Actual numbers are not nearly so important as the perceptions such litigation may engender. Ominous news reports,[352] fear, and the demands of family will all weigh against the call of duty. If those facing call-up come to perceive that the legal system countenances, perhaps even aids, those who shirk their military duty, that perception could seriously erode the consensus necessary to sustain a successful mobilization.

Notwithstanding recent decisions by the Supreme Court reemphasizing the doctrine of military necessity,[353] this situation does not lend itself to solution on a case-by-case basis. Time will not permit it. Rather, the national interests at stake—and the survival of those already overseas who will die without reinforcement—demand a coherent, systematic response that will make clear to all concerned what the nation expects of its men in uniform, regular and Reserve alike, in time of peril. Two initiatives, both of them inherently controversial, are essential if we are to redefine the proper role of the judicial system during the initial phases of a general mobilization. First, the Department of Defense must rescind those regulatory provisions permitting the discharge of in-service conscientious objectors. Second, the Congress must authorize the President, under narrowly specified conditions and for a limited period of time, to suspend the writ of habeas corpus insofar as it pertains to members of the armed forces and their Reserve components.

As mentioned previously, in-service conscientious objector status is a matter of grace conferred by regulation.[354] The Department of Defense clearly has a moral duty to accommodate, to the greatest extent possible, those military personnel who have concluded that they cannot, as a matter of conscience, bear arms. This obligation can be fulfilled, however, by assigning such individuals to noncombatant status.[355] Because there is enough danger to go around for all, even noncombatants, liberal criteria can be employed to accord this status. Unfortunately, when danger is in the offing and discharge is the goal, the Supreme Court's expanded definition of conscientious objection makes this approach untenable. This is not to say that *Welsh* and *Seeger* are wrongly decided. It is to suggest, however, that the current criteria [356] for in-service applicants would prove totally unworkable in time of grave national peril.

At the onset, it is worth noting that these applicants are individuals who have voluntarily chosen to join the armed forces. Their status is thus appreciably different from that of persons who find themselves caught up at random in the draft. The current program is unworkable primarily because there are no clearcut and objective criteria for saying yea or nay to an applicant for conscientious objector status. When the military evaluates a hardship discharge application, there is explicit factual data available upon which to base a rational decision. In contrast, gauging the sincerity of a conscientious objector applicant requires a weighing of intangibles that is often beyond the capability of the Military Departments even in peacetime. During the initial stages of a conventional war in Europe—not the business-as-usual sort of conflict we fought in Vietnam—the complex evaluation process contemplated by 32 C.F.R. sec. 76.5 (1980) would turn to quicksand. It requires time, manpower, and expertise that simply would not be available. The system is, moreover, largely incapable of discerning truth from falsehood. Thus it lends itself to manipulation by the unscrupulous and works to the detriment of those service members who lack the background to wrap themselves in a mantle of philosophy.

Eliminating the discharge option for conscientious objectors would, it is hoped, provide some assurance that the applicant for noncombatant status was truly motivated by the pangs of conscience rather than avarice or selfishness or fear. This proposal has surfaced before within the Department of Defense and has always fallen by the wayside. There is a natural reluctance to circumscribe the options open to the true conscientious objector because of momentary pique at the success of some physicians in avoiding their military commitments. We are concerned, however, with a broader issue, and the present regulations provide an open door through which those inclined to shirk their duty can exit in the event of war. That possibility must be foreclosed. If this proposal misreads the will of the electorate, then the Congress will no doubt clarify the national mandate with legislation analogous to 50 U.S.C. App. sec. 456(j) (1976), which will expressly provide for the discharge of in-service conscientious objectors. Absent such a congressional judgment, the Department of Defense should put its house in order.

Although conscientious objectors have no constitutional guarantee that they will be exempted from military service, the Constitution provides very clearly that "[t]he Privilege of the Writ of Habeas Corpus shall not be suspended, unless when in Cases of Rebellion or Invasion the public safety may require it." [357] In this chapter the author has sought to demonstrate that the public safety may be endangered if the United States fails to mobilize effectively and make good on its treaty commitments in the event of a conventional war in Europe. At the very least, the lives of hundreds of thousands of servicemen and their dependents will be jeopardized if mobilization fails. At worst, an ineffective conventional response to Warsaw Pact aggression against NATO could precipitate a strategic nuclear exchange that would kill millions and spell the demise of American society as we now know it.

It is hoped that good sense would prevail in such a crisis, and the courts would refrain from interjecting themselves into the mobilization process. The foregoing analysis suggests, however, that such judicial restraint is by no means a certainty. Legislation authorizing a temporary suspension of the privilege of the writ of habeas corpus would provide a brief respite from litigation so as to avoid breaking the momentum of mobilization.* Both the purpose and the scope of such proposed legislation would be quite different from those that motivated Presidents Lincoln and Roosevelt to dispense with the writ during wartime. In those instances, suspension of the writ was intended to preclude judicial inquiry into the arrest and detention of individuals deemed potential security threats.[359] Generally speaking, those detained were civilians, and the suspension was effective with respect to everyone residing in a given geographic area.

In the present instance, our objective is to preclude judicial interference with the call-up of individuals who have voluntarily become members of the armed forces. The authority sought, moreover, would be exceptionally narrow. The proposed legislation would authorize the President to suspend the writ only as to members of the armed forces and their Reserve components and only for a period of ninety days. The authority could be invoked only where more than 50,000 members of the Selected Reserve had been involuntarily ordered to active duty and where the President determined that suspension of the writ was required in the interest of public safety because of rebellion or invasion or the imminent danger thereof. These criteria would insure that the authority was invoked only during a period of grave national peril. No civilians, including prospective draftees, would be affected, and the authority would expire of its own accord unless Congress extended it by legislation at the end of ninety days.

Because of the requirement that the danger of invasion be imminent, this proposal could not be employed in the event of peripheral conflicts in the third world. It contemplates only a direct attack against the United States or against US troops deployed in Europe under the provisions of the North Atlantic Treaty. Although the Constitution speaks only of invasion, this construction is consistent with Article 5 of the NATO Treaty which provides that "an armed attack against one or more of [the parties] in Europe or North America shall be considered an attack against them all." [360] It reflects, moreover, the reality that an attack on our troops and their dependents in Europe is, in fact, an attack upon the United States itself.

---

*In the unabridged version of this chapter, the author provides proposed legislative language for such authorizing legislation. —ED.

The proposed statute would also delineate, for purposes of habeas corpus jurisdiction, who is a member of the armed forces. The law might provide that a duly executed enlistment agreement or documents reflecting the acceptance of a commission shall be deemed conclusive proof that an individual is a member of the armed forces or the Reserve components thereof. This language is intended to preclude individuals from claiming recruiter misrepresentation, fraudulent inducement, or an alleged material breach of contract in order to negate their military status. There is no practical way to resolve such allegations except by a full-blown hearing. This language reflects a policy judgment that such representations, even if made, should have been raised prior to the receipt of mobilization orders.

Finally, the proposal would provide that during periods when the writ was suspended, the federal courts would lack jurisdiction over any claims for declaratory or injunctive relief by a member of the armed forces with respect to the terms or conditions of his or her military service. The obvious intent of this provision would be to insure that individuals are unable to circumvent suspension of the writ of habeas corpus by the resort to mandamus or other remedies.

Suspension of the writ of habeas corpus seems, or first impression, to be a draconian measure. Could it pass constitutional muster? As Justice Brennan has noted, "[m]ilitary (or national) security is a weighty interest, not least of all because national survival is an indispensible condition of national liberties." [362] As noted previously,[363] this issue would not have arisen during World War II, because a member of the armed forces who had voluntarily enlisted was not deemed to be in custody, absent some unusual restraint on his liberty not normally associated with military service. What is contemplated, therefore, is a temporary return to the legal status of military personnel vis-a-vis the federal courts that has prevailed throughout most of the nation's history.

At the onset, it seems clear that the President has no authority to suspend the writ without express congressional approval. While President Lincoln did purport to do so unilaterally, his actions were widely criticized and Congress ultimately passed enabling legislation expressly authorizing suspension of the writ.[364] More recently, this premise has been accepted as fact. Thus the district court in *Ex parte Stewart* [368] noted, almost as an aside, that "[a]bsent congressional action, the writ cannot be denied even in wartime."

The Supreme Court has considered suspension of the writ of habeas corpus in the context of both the Civil War and World War II. In *Ex parte Milligan*, [369] the Court ordered the release of an Indiana resident (a civilian) who had been convicted by a military commission of conspiracy, giving aid and comfort to the rebellion, and inciting insurrection, and was thereafter sentenced to death. The Court roundly condemned the martial law proceedings leading to Milligan's trial by a military commission. "Martial law," the Court explained, "cannot arise from a threatened invasion. The necessity must be actual and present; the invasion real, such as effectively closes the courts and deposes the civil administration." [370]

While condemning martial law proceedings as a denial of the civilian's constitutional right to a jury trial, the Court did not reject the judgment of Congress and the President that the privilege of the writ of habeas corpus should be suspended. Rather, the Court analyzed the language of the statute iself and concluded that Congress had "not contemplated that such a person should be detained in custody beyond a certain fixed period, unless certain judicial proceedings, known to the common law, were commenced against him." [372] In particular, the executive branch was required to apprise the federal courts as to the presence in a given judicial district of anyone not a prisoner of war being held under the President's authority. Thereafter, "if a gran[d] jury of the district convened and adjourned, and did not indict one of the persons thus named, he was entitled to his discharge." [373] Because the grand jury had, in fact, met and had not returned an indictment against Milligan, the Court held that he was entitled to his freedom.

Thus the Supreme Court's decision was based on the failure of the War Department to comply with the statutory requirements for suspension of the writ. As to the propriety of the legislation itself, the Court stated:

> It is essential to the safety of every government that, in a great crisis, like the one we have just passed through, there should be a power somewhere of suspending the writ of habeas corpus. In every war, there are men of previously good character, wicked enough to counsel their fellow citizens to resist the measures deemed necessary by a good government to sustain its just authority and overthrow its enemies; and their influence may lead to dangerous combinations. In the emergency of the times, an immediate public investigation according to law may not be possible; and yet the peril to the country may be too imminent to suffer such persons to go at large. Unquestionably, there is then an exigency which demands that the government, if it should see fit,, in the exercise of a proper discretion, to make arrests, should not be required to produce the person arrested in answer to a writ of habeas corpus.[374]

The factual situation was essentially similar when the Supreme Court reexamined this area of the law in *Duncan v. Kahanamoku* [375] at the end of World War II. On 7 December 1941, Governor Poindexter suspended the writ of habeas corpus by proclamation and placed Hawaii under martial law. His actions were based on an express provision in section 67 of the Hawaiian Organic Act,[376] and were ratified by the

President the following day. Military government continued in Hawaii, to a greater or lesser extent, until President Roosevelt restored the privilege of the writ of habeas corpus and terminated martial law on 24 October 1944.[377] In 1942, the United States Court of Appeals for the Ninth Circuit upheld suspension of the writ in *Ex parte Zimmerman*.[378]

The petitioners in *Duncan* were again civilians. Unlike Zimmerman, who was interned because of questions about his loyalty, they were tried by the military and subsequently imprisoned for essentially civil offenses. The district court granted the writ in each instance, and the government appealed. The Ninth Circuit thereafter reversed the order of the district court.[380]

Again, the Supreme Court did not focus on suspension of the writ but rather on the jurisdiction of the military authorities to try civilians. At the onset, the Court noted that the issue presented "does not involve the well-established power of the military to exercise jurisdiction over members of the armed forces." [381] It went on to conclude that the power to impose martial law conveyed by the Hawaiian Organic Act, "while intended to authorize the military to act vigorously for the maintenance of an orderly civil government and for the defense of the Islands against actual or threatened rebellion or invasion, was not intended to authorize the supplanting of courts by military tribunals." [382] The Court therefore ordered the petitioners released from custody.

Because the President had already terminated martial law, the Supreme Court "d[id] not pass upon the validity of the order suspending the privilege of habeas corpus or the power of the military to detain persons under other circumstances or conditions." [383] Had the Court reached these questions, Justice Murphy's concurring opinion suggests that concern would have focused on the duration of the suspension. Thus measures that would have been appropriate immediately after the Japanese attack on 7 December 1941, might well have become inappropriate two years hence if the immediate threat of attack or invasion had, in fact, subsided.[384]

Judged by these criteria, the limited authority proposed here for supending the writ seems to withstand scrutiny. The proposal does not extend to any civilians whatever. It is precisely limited in duration and applies only to individuals who have voluntarily submitted themselves to military jurisdiction. As Chief Justice Warren has pointed out, "there are some circumstances in which the [Supreme] Court will, in effect, conclude that it is simply not in a position to reject descriptions by the Executive of the degree of military necessity." [385] This is, the author would submit, one such question. Should the legislative and executive branches determine, as a matter of national policy, that the mobilization

process, once initiated, must proceed unimpeded by the threat of litigation, the doctrine of separation of powers renders that decision
nonjusticiable.[386]

Looking back at the bitter sedition trials that grew out of World War
I,[387] at the tragedy of the Japanese internment cases during World War
II,[388] it is clear that the demands of national survival can infringe on the
rights of individuals. As Chief Justice Warren observed:

> War is a pathological condition for our Nation. Military
> judgments sometimes breed action that, in more stable times, would
> be regarded as abhorrent. Judges cannot detach themselves from
> such judgments, although by hindsight, from the vantage of more
> tranquil times, they might conclude that some actions advanced in
> the name of national survival had in fact overridden the strictures of
> due process.[389]

The infringement of individual rights involved in suspending the right of
military personnel to challenge their status by way of habeas corpus in
the midst of mobilization is, in the author's judgment, a reasonable price
to pay for the assurance that our armed forces will "be ready to perform
their duty whenever the occasion arises."[390]

15
Toward Total-Force Mobilization Readiness

Wilfred L. Ebel

One of the promises of democracy is freedom from the burden of maintaining large standing armed forces. From pre-Revolutionary days to the present, a cross-section of American society has guaranteed the common defense by serving in the National Guard and Reserve forces. The modern-day Reserve components are integral to our stated total-force policy; it is therefore imperative that US Reserve forces be prepared to participate in the earliest phases of any future conflict.

When serving as Army Vice Chief of Staff, General John W. Vessey remarked, "the only true readiness is total-force readiness." The free world is fortunate that such a perceptive individual has become Chairman of the Joint Chiefs of Staff. Well-trained, fully manned Reserve forces reflect both national strength and national restraint. National strength is, in part, exhibited by the preparedness of the total force, including the Guard and Reserve forces, to defend successfully our vital interests should deterrence fail. National restraint is exhibited by the defensive nature of Reserve forces; they convey resolve and national will without threatening any nation whose intentions toward the United States are peaceful.

This is an original article written especially for this book. The author is widely respected throughout the Guard and Reserve community for his knowledge and insight regarding total force issues. —ED.

Reserve force readiness can be defined as the ability to achieve the training needed to perform wartime missions, to mobilize and deploy, and to assist in defeating the enemy. The ability to mobilize effectively depends on such diverse factors as presidential or congressional disposition to order a mobilization, and the willingness of the individual Guardsman or Reservist to respond promptly to a mobilization directive. Over the last two decades, progress has been made in improving the Reserve forces' readiness capabilities, and in particular, their ability to mobilize.

Twenty years ago, the United States responded to the Soviet threat to West Berlin by increasing the size of conventional forces through a partial mobilization of nearly 150,000 Guardsmen and Reservists, by expanding draft calls, and by involuntarily extending active-duty enlistment periods. In August 1961, Congress, at the President's request, authorized the mobilization of up to 250,000 Reservists. Within three months, two National Guard divisions and the Army Reserve's 100th Training Division were also mobilized. Those actions, coupled with other measures, permitted three active Army training divisions to be relieved of their training responsibilities and to prepare for their combat missions. By the end of 1961, these three divisions were declared combat ready. A few weeks later, the mobilized National Guard divisions completed their thirteen-intensified combat training program. It had taken about seven months to raise the number of combat-ready Army divisions from eleven to sixteen.

The Air Force mobilized twenty-five tactical Air Force squadrons and six transport squadrons of the Air National Guard in response to the Berlin crisis. Several tactical squadrons were deployed to Europe approximately six weeks after recall to active duty. The five troop carrier squadrons mobilized from the Air Force Reserve achieved operational capability within three months of recall. The Navy mobilized 8,000 Reservists in the antisubmarine warfare field. Although no Marine Corps Reservists were involuntarily recalled, significant numbers volunteered and were accepted for extended active duty when the Marine Corps' active-duty force was expanded to 190,000.

The 1961 mobilization marked the first time that Guardsmen and Reservists were mobilized to prevent rather than to wage a war. While this mobilization proved effective, the overall readiness of the Reserve components in 1961 was not entirely satisfactory and would be considered unacceptable in today's environment. In the 1960's, it took seven months to increase the number of combat-ready divisions. In the 1980s, the Department of Defense intends to have its principal combat units in-theater within the first ninety days.

As mentioned previously, the disposition of the President or the Congress to order a mobilization is significant. The 1961 mobilization of the Reserve components was delayed because President Kennedy had to seek legislative authority for the callup. Today, the President would not encounter such a delay. In 1976, Congress passed legislation authorizing the President to order to active duty 50,000 Selected Reservists for no longer than 90 days, without declaring a national emergency. This legislation provided the flexibility to deal with contingencies requiring a measured military response when a declaration of national emergency might be premature or have undesirable international or domestic consequences. Congress provided further flexibility in December 1980, when it increased to 100,000 the number of Reservists the President can order to active duty without declaring a national emergency. The Senate Armed Services Committee has proposed authorizing the President to keep personnel activated under this authority on duty for up to 180 days.

It should not be assumed, however, that these initiatives would preclude mobilization delays. Other factors such as political considerations, indecision, and level of congressional support play a part in the mobilization process. Statutory impediments to timely mobilization have, however, been largely eliminated.

Wartime planning and training for Army Guard and Reserve units have been enhanced under the CAPSTONE Program approved by the Chief of Staff in 1979. CAPSTONE designates for each unit the wartime chain of command, probable wartime mission, and probable area of employment. This enables the unit to focus training to meet a particular contingency; the training is frequently conducted overseas.

Today's international situation has necessitated abandoning the thirty-day alert period of the 1960s. Reservists are informed in unambiguous terms not to rely on having thirty days from the time of mobilization alert until they report for duty. They are now advised that instant mobilization may be a military necessity, and they may be ordered to report to their duty stations on a twenty-four hour notice. This has long been the case for Selected Reserve units; it is now being applied to the entire Ready Reserve.

It is a virtual certainty that any contingency operation requiring deployment of US Central Command (CENTCOM), formerly the Rapid Deployment Joint Task Force (RDJTF), will be accompanied by mobilization and deployment of Reserve-component units that are crucial to any CENTCOM deployment to Southwest Asia, East Africa, or the Persian Gulf. More than 12,000 Army Reserve personnel serve in units committed to CENTCOM.

The current plan is for many Reserve units to arrive in Europe during the first thirty days of a conflict. The NATO plans to place the European theater on a wartime footing include deploying some command headquarters to Europe from the United States within thirty days of mobilization. The goal is to have most, if not all, Reserve units scheduled to deploy to Europe in-theater within ninety days. Furthermore, a major segment of the Air National Guard and Air Force Reserve must be able to mobilize combat-ready units within twenty-four hours and to deploy them within seventy-two hours.

Reserve-component readiness goals are largely determined by the threat of the Warsaw Pact and the greatly increased level of Guard and Reserve contribution to the force necessary to meet that threat. The Pact's ability to mobilize its forces rapidly and to launch a no-warning or little-warning attack requires that the National Guard and the Reserves maintain a higher state of readiness than was demanded of most of the active units based in the United States during the active component oriented "total force" of the 1960s. It is likely that a NATO-Warsaw Pact confrontation would reach a critical phase in the first 180 days and the luxury of post-mobilization training for Guardsmen and Reservists is no longer a suitable option.

Another important reason for stringent readiness demands being placed on Reserve forces stems from the total-force policy. At the outset of the Berlin crisis, the active Army had eleven divisions and an authorized strength of 870,000 soldiers. Today's active Army has sixteen divisions, an apparent increase of nearly 50 percent; however, its authorized strength is below 800,000. This sixteen-division force can go to war only by calling on Reserve-component combat units as well as combat support and combat service support elements.

Initiated in 1974, the Army's Affiliation Program was designed to prepare Selected Reserve units to meet the challenge of prompt mobilization and deployment. Reserve-component units round out nine of the eleven CONUS- and Hawaii-based active-component divisions that currently do not have their full complement of units. A total of five brigades, eight separate battalions, and three company-size elements are an integral part of the nine divisions. The Guardsmen and Reservists assigned to these units must be prepared to deploy with the divisions. Affiliated units must be at a high state of readiness and prepared for early deployment to the combat theater. For this reason the 2d Battalion, 252d Armor, North Carolina National Guard is being equipped with the M-1 Abrams tank and the Bradley Infantry Fighting Vehicle. The battalion is a roundout unit for the 2d Armored Division.

Another outstanding example of the successful implementation of this concept is found in the 48th Infantry Brigade (Georgia Army National Guard), the roundout brigade for the 24th Infantry Division (Mechanized). The 48th has been issued M60A3 tanks and M901 anti-tank combat vehicles; almost any day of the year the officers, noncommissioned officers, and soldiers of the 48th are training with the 24th.

One important measure of total readiness is the ability to satisfy wartime manpower needs. The end of the draft in 1972 led to severe shortages of manpower in Selected Reserve units. Because of the unwillingness to offer needed incentives. The Reserve components were unable to enlist and retain sufficient numbers in the middle and late 1970s. These recruitment shortfalls necessitated setting Army Reserve-component recruitment levels at attainable figures that were considerably below peacetime force structure requirements.

Enlistment and reenlistment bonuses and educational benefits have increased Guard and Reserve strength in recent years; the Selected Reserve will soon be one million strong. Coincident with this turnaround, funding problems caused artificial personnel strength caps to be placed on the Guard and Reserve. Many manpower planners believe it would be wise to remove these caps and begin stockpiling personnel as a hedge against recruiting difficulties that loom in the future. Proponents of this approach point out that intensified and sustained recruiting and retention programs will be indispensable if Reserve-component manpower needs are to be met in the mid–1980s as the number of eighteen-year-olds declines and Reaganomics lessens reliance of individuals on a Reserve paycheck.

Incentives currently offered to increase Selected Reserve strength include an enlistment bonus of $1,500 or an education incentive of up to $4,000. Qualified individuals may receive reenlistment bonuses of up to $1,800. In addition, there are enlistment options that permit an individual to serve as few as three years in a Selected Reserve unit, and a split-training option that permits those agreeing to serve six years in a Selected Reserve unit to complete their basic training and advanced individual training at separate times, rather than consecutively. Steps have been taken to increase advertising funds, secure additional full-time recruiters, and improve the management of the recruiting force.

A Simultaneous Membership Program (SMP) now allows enlisted members of the Army Guard and Reserve to enroll in advanced Reserve Officer Training Corps (ROTC) while continuing to attend unit training assemblies in a pay status. A limited number of Army Guard and Reserve enlisted personnel attend college under a two year ROTC scholarship that guarantees them duty with the Guard or Reserve following graduation and commissioning.

A series of biennial mobilization exercises begun in 1976 have been instrumental in focusing attention on the critical shortages of pretrained individual Reservists. As the exercises identified manpower shortages in active units and in mobilized Guard and Reserve units, and as the computers highlighted casualty figures, the Army's Individual Ready Reserve (IRR) was found to be woefully shy of the numbers of trained manpower needed. Ten years ago the Individual Ready Reserve numbered over 1.2 milion persons; at the end of fiscal year 1982 it numbered about 385,000.

Unless the Individual Ready Reserve can immediately provide *individual* infantry, armor, and artillery troops as replacements for predicted front-line casualties, a Warsaw Pact attack against NATO could so weaken our European-based combat units as to threaten our ability to stay the enemy until reinforcing *units* from the States can enter the fray. Accordingly, attrition management has gained increased attention. A program has been established to employ cash bonuses of $600 to unobligated members agreeing to a three-year reenlistment in the Individual Ready Reserve. Additionally, the Army has preassigned over 100,000 retirees to appropriate wartime mobilization positions at installations and activities in the continental United States. Under full mobilization, these retirees would report to duty within seven days, thus freeing large numbers of younger soldiers for deployment to the battlefield.

The Defense Department has proposed legislation that would increase the military service obligation from the present six years to eight years. Also proposed is a $1,000 bonus for direct enlistment in the Individual Ready Reserve: such enlistees would undergo basic and advanced individual training in needed military skills, then be assigned to the Individual Ready Reserve for the remainder of their military service obligation.

These and other management initiatives are expected to bring the Individual Ready Reserve up to desired levels by the late 1980s. If they prove unsuccessful, the efficacy of a draft for the Individual Ready Reserve may have to be addressed again. An unpublished research paper written by several National War College students (Class of 1982) concluded: "Unless the strength of the *Selected* Reserve is increased enormously—to compensate for a substantial proportion of the IRR shortfall—it is probable that some form of conscription will be needed if IRR requirements are to be met. Such an option has political, social, and philosophical ramifications that extend far beyond the issue of pretrained individual manpower for the armed forces. The broader liabilities of conscription could indeed be judged to outweigh the military advantages—which has been the case since the advent of the all-volunteer force in 1973. Such a judgment, however, should not be allowed to color the analysis of purely military factors.

Readiness is dependent on well-trained troops skilled in the use of their equipment and weapons. On this account, considerable attention is being devoted to improving training and training management. For example, Reserve planners are increasing the number of full-time support-personnel assigned to the Reserves. The Army Reserve has undertaken a particularly rapid and tremendous expansion of full-time support personnel, with a projected strength of over 8,200 by the end of fiscal year

1983. Many full-time support personnel provide training assistance at the unit level; others are assigned to policy-making positions on high-level staffs. Some full-time personnel are assigned to administrative tasks that previously had to be accomplished by Reservists during scheduled training time; this frees the Reservists for training.

The Navy and Marine Corps rely heavily on active component personnel for full-time support assignments, while the Army and Air Force use large numbers of military technicians and Active Duty Guard and Reserve (AGR) personnel. Congress had directed that each Reserve component be free to determine the mix of military technicians and AGR personnel appropriate to its component; however, the continuing Resolution for fiscal year 1983, passed by the lame duck Congress, halted conversions of military technicians to Active Duty Guard and Reserve by establishing a floor for the strength of military technicians at the 30 September 1982 level.

Emphasis is given to hands-on skill training with the equipment a Guardsman or Reservist will use at mobilization. Additional funds also are being allocated to field training exercises and command post exercises. Many Reserve-component units are performing their two-week active duty deployment training outside the continental United States. Furthermore, an evaluation is being made of the advantages and disadvantages of expanding the two-week annual training period to three weeks for certain high-priority Army National Guard units. Guardsmen would be informed of the impending three-week tour one year in advance to minimize conflicts with civilian employers.

Although seeming somewhat contradictory, the changes in store for the National Guard and Ready Reserve in the 1980s will be more of the same—but with a quantitative and qualitative edge. Programs that have contributed to recent increases in the readiness posture will be continued and improved upon. And while no traumatic alterations to size or missions are forecast, some adjustments are inevitable. Pressure for changes will come from the Services, the Office of the Secretary of Defense, the Office of Management and Budget, the White House, and the Reserve community.

One new approach during this decade will permit a more realistic assessment of the personnel readiness of the Army Reserve components. By abandoning the previous policy of setting strength figures at attainable goals, Reserve forces planners intend to go beyond peacetime force-structure strength. Now the criterion for measuring personnel readiness will be the trained strength of a unit; personnel undergoing training will not be counted in the trained strength of a unit. At mobilization, these personnel will complete their training and probably will not deploy with their units. For this reason, units should strive to exceed their wartime structure by a figure equal to the number of training-pipeline personnel assigned to them.

Similarly, a continuous screening of the Ready Reserve has been mandated to remove Reservists whose civilian employment would preclude their mobilization. A rigid screening procedure is being applied to Reservists employed full-time by the federal government. Equally effective procedures will be used to screen Reservists employed by state and local governments and private industry. Renewed efforts will be made to increase public support for the National Guard and Ready Reserves through the Employer Support and Community Support Programs, and to foster a greater public awareness of the importance of an adequately sized, trained, and equipped Reserve force.

One of the most difficult and least understood tasks facing the Guard and Reserve is reorganizing units as new policies and plans are developed, and as doctrine and war scenarios change. If outdated units are kept in the Reserve structure, new units cannot be organized. Disconcertingly, such a restructuring may represent a more effective and efficient combination of the personnel and equipment required to accomplish a mission.

A decade ago the Army structure was reorganized abolishing two of the five Continental Armies and creating nine Army Readiness Regions, known today as Army Readiness and Mobilization Regions (ARMRs). Then in December 1982, the Army informed Congress that, as the result of an evaluation of the US Army Reserve command-and-control structure, the Army proposed to create two additional continental Armies and to abolish the nine ARM Regions. The Army Reserve needs long-term direction, but it also needs stability. Another reorganization is certain to provoke controversy in Congress. The command-and-control issue is particularly contentious; more than one Army Reservist has been heard to ask: "Where is it engraved in stone that the Army Reserve cannot be the master of its own fate?"

Another problem that has plagued both the active and Reserve forces has been the lack of a constituency for readiness. This lack of a constituency has made it difficult to overcome some of the routine inhibitors of readiness, such as insufficient funds for maintenance of equipment, spare-parts shortages, and inadequate supplies of training ammunition. Readers with a historical bent will recall that Hannibal, though a master tactician and a superb leader of men, was defeated in the Second Punic War because the merchant princes of Carthage would not provide him the wherewithal to overpower the Roman legions.

As this chapter was being written, the Reagan administration had just sent to the Congress a fiscal year 1984 defense appropriation request of \$273.4 billion. President Reagan's budget for fiscal year 1984 would continue the rapid defense buildup; he is seeking a defense budget nearly \$42 billion higher than Congress appropriated for fiscal year 1983. Congress is certain to attack the administration's military spending plan; it is hoped that the cuts imposed will be relatively slight. There will be real growth in defense spending, and it hopefully will be far greater than the 3 percent commitment made to NATO.

How will Congress reduce defense spending? Will weapons systems be eliminated? Will O&M (Operation and Maintenance) funds suffer? Will there be force reductions?

The media has enthusiastically promoted eliminating some "big tickets" weapons systems, such as the MX, the B-1 bomber, and additional nuclear aircraft carriers. Congress and the Pentagon are sometimes persuaded (intimidated, if you will) by the media and, therefore, one of the controversial weapons systems could be scratched. The uniformed leaders in the Pentagon may whisper in Congress's ear a willingness to absorb cuts in Operation and Maintenance. But cuts in O&M funds hurt near-term readiness, damage the logistical maintenance base, and dry up the supply system. Manpower reductions seem the most attractive approach because they can be implemented speedily. Besides, it is seen as more prudent to field a smaller force, properly trained and supplied with spare parts and ammunition, than to maintain a larger force, inadequately trained and supplied. It must be remembered, however, that, by the JCS's own admission, the "larger force" in being today is not large enough to execute the approved defense strategy.

A prominent Senator may have the most acceptable solution. He is studying the feasibility of lowering the number of active-duty personnel and increasing the number of Reserve-component personnel. If such a proposal can yield sufficient savings to fund a small increase in military pay *and* still lower the overall defense budget, his approach will find a plethora of supporters, not only in Congress but in the executive branch and among the general public.

There is no pretension of profundity in this chapter and the temptation to make the simple sound complicated has been avoided. Nevertheless, this chapter closes with a dictum that is, at once, both profound and simple: As long as the United States has neither the people nor the equipment to bring its Guard and Reserve units to full wartime capability, the total force cannot be fully ready. Faced with resource shortages, there is the great temptation to adjust readiness standards to make the Reserve components appear more ready than they are. Pro-Reserve rhetoric must be backed up by intensive efforts to improve and enhance the mobilization, deployment, and employment capability of our Guard and Reserve forces.

Appendix
Organizational Structure of the Guard and Reserve Components

Basic Management Structure

The President of the United States is Commander-in-Chief of all US Armed Forces. With the advice and consent of the US Senate, he appoints a Secretary to direct the Department of Defense. The President similarly appoints an Assistant Secretary of Defense (Reserve Affairs) whose duty is overall supervision of the National Guard and Reserve components of the total force. This official is appointed from civilian life by the President with the consent of the Senate. The Department of Defense Authorization Act for FY 1984 established the position of Assistant Secretary of Defense (Reserve Affairs), upgrading it from a Deputy Assistant Secretary position.

Each Reserve component is headed by a major general or rear admiral. In addition, the Directors of the Army and Air Guard, report to the Chief of the National Guard Bureau, currently a lieutenant general. Chiefs of the National Guard and Reserve components have ready access to top military and civilian leaders. They originate policy initiatives, participate in appropriate management decisions, and are responsible for the overall management of National Guard and Reserve programs. The Secretaries of the Army, Navy, and Air Force administer their respective Departments, each with its own Reserve manager, while the Secretary of Transportation administers the US Coast Guard and its Reserve component until it is transferred to become a separate service of the United States Navy in time of war.

The information in this appendix is drawn largely from US, Department of Defense, *Reserve Components of the United States Armed Forces, 1982.* —ED.

National Guard Bureau

The Army and Air National Guard are unique among the world's Reserve military forces, combining both federal and state functions. While its potential as a federal Reserve has been strengthened, the National Guard of each state remains constitutionally a state force under the command of the governor. The dual state and federal missions are set forth in National Guard regulations. The state mission is to provide units that are organized, equipped, and trained to function effectively in the protection of life and property and the preservation of peace, order, and public safety under competent orders of federal or state authorities. The Army and Air National Guards are administered on the federal side through the National Guard Bureau.

The National Guard Bureau formulates and administers a program for the development and maintenance of Army and Air National Guard units in each state, Puerto Rico, the Virgin Islands, the District of Columbia, and Guam in accordance with Departments of the Army and Air Force policy. Fiscal and administrative responsibility for Guard programs rests with the National Guard Bureau. The organization of the bureau is shown in figure A.1.

The National Guard Bureau is both a staff and an operating agency. It is a joint bureau of the Departments of the Army and Air Force. The Chief, National Guard Bureau, reports to the Secretaries of the Army and the Air Force through the respective Chiefs of Staff and is the principal staff advisor on National Guard matters. He is appointed for a four-year term by the President with the advice and consent of the US Senate from a list of National Guard officers recommended by state governors. The current Chief, National Guard Bureau, is a lieutenant general.

As an operating agency the National Guard Bureau is the channel for communications between the states and the Departments of the Army and the Air Forces.

Army National Guard

The Army National Guard is the largest of the nation's seven organized Reserve components and is composed of predominately combat units. It consists of over 3,400 company and detachment size units located in more than 2,600 communities in all states, Puerto Rico, the Virgin Islands, the District of Columbia, and Guam. In early 1982, the authorized peacetime strength of the Army Guard was 424,000. Wartime structure is more than 444,000.

The Army's worldwide commitments are characterized by large overseas garrisons and fighting forces already in place. All must be supported by additional forces available through rapid deployment from the United States. Selected Army National Guard (ARNG) units participate with the active Army through the Affiliation Program, which includes augmentation units, roundout units, and deployment capability improvement. These units train with designated active units to improve combat readiness. Augmentation units deploy as an additional element of their active Army organization. Roundout units deploy as an integral part of the active unit.

Figure A.1
THE NATIONAL GUARD BUREAU

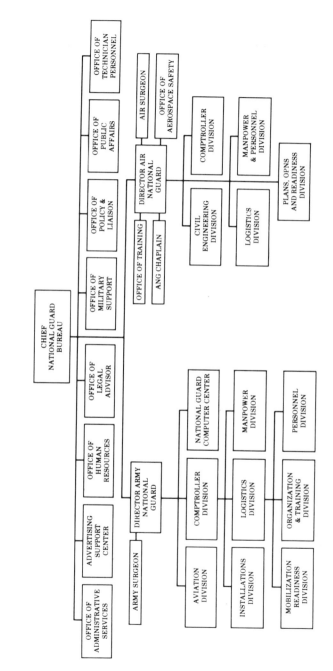

The Army National Guard operates 284 state training sites of various sizes and two semiactive Army installations. Increased emphasis on National Guard and Reserve readiness has resulted in additional requirements for maintenance, storage, and training facilities. In fiscal year 1982, Congress appropriated over $2.5 billion for the Army National Guard and the states appropriated additional monies directly for the National Guard. Substantial support was also provided by state, county, and municipal governments in land, policy, fire protection, and maintenance of roads. Direct county and municipal fiscal support was also provided to local units.

Direct supervision of the Army National Guard is the responsibility of each state adjutant general (AG), a state official who generally holds state cabinet rank and commands the Guard troops in his state when they are not under Federal control (see figure A.2). Most of the Army Guard's training is directed at the federal mission, but increasing emphasis is being placed on training for the state mission of assisting authorities during civil disturbances, emergencies, and disasters. Training is conducted primarily in tactical training areas during weekend training assemblies and annual training periods.

The Army National Guard provides 30 percent of the Army's entire organized structure and about 46 percent of its combat elements and 37 percent of its support forces. In the event of wartime mobilization, control of the Army National Guard is transferred to the active Army in accordance with existing plans.

Air National Guard

The Air National Guard (ANG) is a combat-ready force that is immediately available for mobilization to support active requirements. Air National Guard units train for air defense, tactical fighter, air refueling, tactical airlift, reconnaissance, communications, electronics, weather, and aeromedical missions. The over ninety Air National Guard flying units are equipped with fighters, interceptors, tankers, reconnaissance, airlift, and forward air control aircraft. They are continuously modernized with newer, more effective aircraft. The Air Guard also supports US Air Force missions in a nonmobilization status in Europe, the Middle East, and the Carribbean.

During peacetime, ANG units are in state status, commanded by state governors through their adjutants general. Peacetime management of the Air National Guard is shown in figure A.3. All ANG units are assigned for mobilization purposes to active Air Force major commands that advise units, establish training standards, and conduct inspections. Upon mobilization, they take their places in the organizational structure of their gaining commands. The gaining commands to which Air Guard units are assigned include the Military Airlift Command (MAC), Strategic Air Command (SAC), Tactical Air Command (TAC), Air Force Communications Command (AAC), Air Training Command (ATC), and Air Force Logistics Command (AFLC). More than 99,000 men and women are assigned to units in all fifty states, the District of Columbia, Puerto Rico, the Virgin Islands, and Guam.

The day-to-day management, training, and administration of Air Guard units is accomplished by 24,000 full-time military technicians and National Guard members on active duty.

Figure A.2
ARMY NATIONAL GUARD
PEACETIME MANAGEMENT STRUCTURE

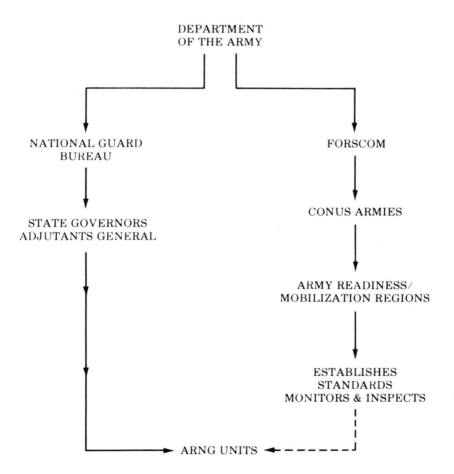

Figure A.3
AIR NATIONAL GUARD
PEACETIME MANAGEMENT STRUCTURE

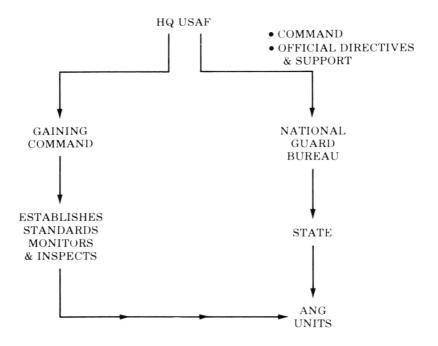

The Air Guard plays a vital role in the nation's air defense, providing the Air Force with combat-ready units immediately available for duty. Comprising 26 percent of the Air Force's Tactical Air Command strength and 66 percent of the interceptor fleet, the Air National Guard provides a major portion of the air defense capability for the Continental United States and provides the entire air defense capability for the Hawaiian Islands.

Army Reserve

The mission of the United States Army Reserve (USAR) is to provide trained units and individuals in support of Army mobilization plans. Units in a high state of readiness—strength, training and equipment—can be deployed with a minimum of post-mobilization training time. The Army Reserve is one of the primary sources of both units and individuals for initial expansion of the Army in the event of future emergencies. Although it shares the mission with the Army National Guard, the Army Reserve is a purely federal force having no responsibilities to state or territorial governments. The Office, Chief Army Reserve, provides direction for development, planning, training, and maintenance of the US Army Reserve.

The Chief of the Army Reserve is appointed by the President from the Army Reserve, confirmed by the US Senate, and serves in the grade of major general. Figure A.4 is an organizational chart of the Office, Chief Army Reserve (OCAR). The functions of the Chief, Army Reserve, include serving as principal advisor to the Army Chief of Staff on matters pertaining to the development, readiness, and maintenance of the Army Reserve; being appropriations director for USAR programs; and evaluating operational and readiness capabilities of the Army Reserve and the resources to accomplish these capabilities.

Army Reserve units are commanded by Forces Command (FORSCOM) through the Continental US Armies (CONUSA), or are commanded by an overseas major command in coordination with FORSCOM (see figure A.5) Training and Doctrine Command (TRADOC) supervises initial entry and service school training for individual Reservists. There are also nine Army Readiness/Mobilization Regions (ARMRs), each commanded by an active Army major general. The ARMR is the FORSCOM CONUSA executive agent for detailed mobilization planning assistance to the Army Guard and Army Reserve within its respective region.

All USAR units are assigned to a US Army Reserve Command (ARCOM) or to another general officer command (GOCOM). GOCOMs include all units authorized a general officer as commander except ARCOMs. An ARCOM, authorized a major general as commander, has command of USAR units located in a specific geographic area.

The Army's organization for the peacetime management and control of the Army Reserve has been a continuing issue since implementation of the total-force policy in 1973. The Senate Armed Services Committee has been particularly concerned regarding the relevant issues. They include the allegation that the active Army structure over the Army Reserve contains duplicative "layering" and inefficiencies. Additionally, there is the question of how much authority the Chief of the Army Reserve should have in the functional management of Army Reserve units and individuals.

Figure A.4
OFFICE, CHIEF ARMY RESERVE

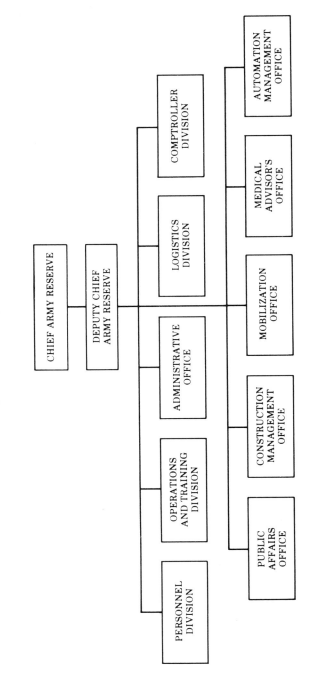

Figure A.5
ARMY RESERVE CHAIN OF COMMAND

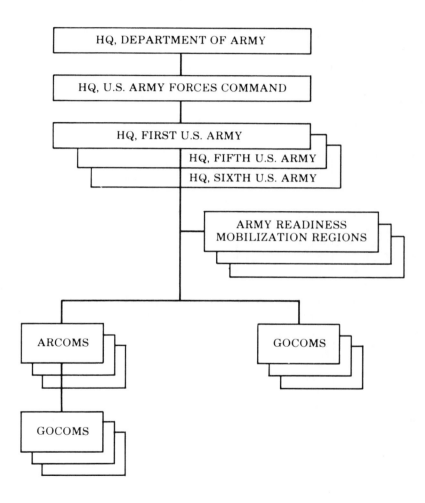

In response to these concerns, the Army has made tentative proposals to restructure the management of the Army Reserve by the active Army. These currently include eliminating all nine ARMRs, adding two CANUSAs, and consolidating or eliminating some ARCOMs. Enhancements to the responsibilities of the Chief, Army Reserve, have also been proposed. There is some concern, however, whether these latter proposals, in fact, enhance that position relative to Reserve units or, instead, merely expand the administrative responsibilities of the Chief, Army Reserve.

The Army Ready Reserve includes more than 200,000 men and women assigned to approximately 3,200 company and detachment sized units. Another 203,000 persons are assigned to the Army's Individual Ready Reserve.

About 70 percent of the combat support and combat service support units in the Army force structure are Army Reserve units. Nearly 50 percent of the Army's medical support is structured in the Army Reserve. USAR schools play a major peacetime role in the conduct of many of the enlisted individual skill proficiency courses and some senior school curricula for officers.

Air Force Reserve

The mission of the Air Force Reserve (USAFR) is to provide trained units and qualified individuals immediately for active duty in time of national emergency and as national security may require. To satisfy this mission, the Air Force Reserve follows programs of recruitment, training, and operational support having these objectives: to make possible the immediate augmentation of the active Air Force in time of selective, partial, or total mobilization; to replace losses through attrition or combat and provide for the deployment of new combat support forces; and to use Reservists productively in peacetime, in support of active force operations as a corollary to training. Two criteria must be met when assigning specific missions to the Air Force Reserve: (1) A requirement to augment the active force in wartime must be demonstrated, and (2) A cost savings must result from the use of Reserve rather than active forces. Because they are an integral part of the total force, all Reserve units must meet active duty training and combat readiness standards.

The Chief, Air Force Reserve, is a Reserve major general ordered to active duty to head the Office of Air Force Reserve, Headquarters, United States Air Force. He is principal advisor to the Air Force Chief of Staff on all Air Force Reserve matters. He develops overall policy for the Air Force Reserve and directs two separate field units within the Air Force Reserve: Headquarters Air Force Reserve (AFRES), Robins AFB, Georgia; and the Air Reserve Personnel Center (ARPC), Denver, Colorado. He also coordinates with and assists the other Air Staff agencies in the development of broad policies, plans, and programs pertaining to the Air Force Reserve. The AFRES management organization is shown in figure A.6.

Assisting the Chief, Air Force Reserve, in his duties are a Deputy Chief as well as a staff that provides functional support. In addition to his duties as a member of the Air Staff, the Chief of Air Force Reserve serves as Commander of AFRES, which oversees the daily operating activities of Air Force Reserve units. He also directs the Air Reserve Personnel Center which is responsible for all individual Reserve programs.

Figure A.6
MANAGEMENT ORGANIZATION
AIR FORCE RESERVE

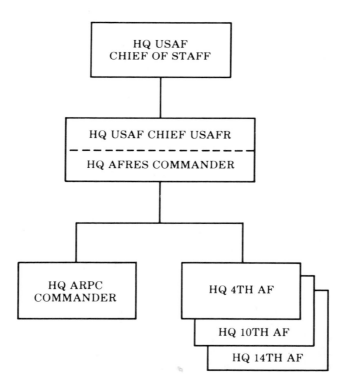

The Vice Commander and chief operating official of AFRES is also a Reserve major general ordered to extended active duty at the command's Georgia headquarters. Day-to-day operations of the command are managed through the three numbered air forces: the Fourth at McClellan AFB, California; the Tenth at Bergstron AFB, Texas; and the Fourteenth at Dobbins AFB, Georgia.

Each numbered Air Force is headed by a Reserve major general who is an Air Reserve technician, that is, a civilian employee of the US Government who is also an Air Force Reservist. Air Reserve technicians (ARTs) are employed by the Air Force Reserve to provide the daily support the units require to attain and maintain mobilization readiness. They are civil service employees full-time and Reservists part-time.

From its headquarters, AFRES administers 54 units flying combat-ready aircraft and 137 non-flying, combat-support units. The people responsible for the command's diverse missions include some 63,700 Air Force Reservists, including about 7,000 ARTs, and more than 3,000 non-ART civilians, and 400 active military personnel. These individuals insure that the Air Force Reserve is trained and ready to respond to any national emergency.

The primary mission of the Air Reserve Personnel Center (ARPC) is to mobilize the appropriate number of Reservists and retired regulars to meet a national emergency. Other major responsibilities are to provide personnel administration and management of assigned Reservists and to administer individual programs for Ready Reservists. The ARPC functions as the custodian of all master personnel records of personnel assigned to the Air Force Reserve and the Air National Guard. In matters affecting the Air National Guard, the Commander, ARPC, acts in coordination with the Director, Air National Guard.

The US Air Force Reserve provides the Military Airlift Command about 50 percent of the authorized aircrews and 35 percent of the maintenance force for its C–141, C–5, and C–9 aircraft. USAFR C–130s, along with the Air National Guard, have total responsibility for tactical airlift support of the US Southern Command. Over 70 percent of the nation's hurricane surveillance in the Caribbean and Atlantic is provided by the Air Force Reserve. USAFR C–123s conduct all USAF aerial spray missions requested by local, state, and federal agencies. Other USAFR missions include aerial refueling, tactical air operations, special air operations, close air support, fighter interception, civil engineering, aerial ports, and many others.

Naval Reserve

The mission of the Naval Reserve, as with the other Reserve components, is to provide trained units and qualified individuals for active duty in time of war or national emergency and at such other times as the national security may require.

The Chief of Naval Operations (CNO) is responsible for the organization, administration, training, and equipping of the Naval Reserve, and for mobilization planning to effectively reinforce and augment the active forces. The Naval Reserve command structure which supports the Chief of Naval Operations is headed by a rear admiral who holds the positions of Director of Naval Reserve

(DIRNAVRES) and Chief of Naval Reserve (CNAVRES). (See figure A.7) The position of DIRNAVRES is on the staff of the Chief of Naval Operations in Washington, DC and includes responsibility for all Naval Reserve affairs. The functions of the DIRNAVRES includes acting as principal advisor to the Chief of Naval Operations on all Naval Reserve matters, exercising (for the CNO) policy, direction, and control of the Naval Reserve, establishing plans, programs, organization, procedures, and standards for the Naval Reserve, and providing budgetary support for the Naval Reserve Commands, activities, and programs.

The Chief of Naval Reserve is responsible for administrating and managing Naval Research programs, managing assigned Reservists, and managing Naval Reserve activities. The Naval Reserve is supported by a unique combination of active duty military and civilian personnel. The active military portion includes regular Navy personnel who have one or more assignments in support of the Naval Reserve, a limited number of Reserve officers who are voluntarily recalled to active duty for a specific assignment, and approximately 10,000 Reservists in a special Naval active duty career program designed for Training and Administration of Reserves (TAR).

To perform its mission, the Naval Reserve is structured to provide a significant increase in the Navy's combat capability upon mobilization. This increase in capability rests primarily in Selected Reserve commissioned, reinforcing, and sustaining units. Commissioned units are those with organic equipment such as ships, aircraft squadrons, or construction battalions which are tasked to deliver a complete operational entity to the operating force. Reinforcing units augment active Navy commissioned units and operating staffs (and some Marine Corps combat commands) with trained personnel to provide a surge capability and sustain the high level of activity required to adequately support deployed forces.

As examples of the Naval Reserve contributions to the total force, it provides 100 percent of the CONUS logistics airlift, light attack helicopters, combat search and air rescue capability, and mobile inshore undersea warfare. In addition, the Naval Reserve provides within the Navy 14 percent of the carrier air capability, 86 percent of the minesweepers, and 35 percent of the maritime patrol squadrons.

Marine Corps Reserve

The mission of the Marine Corps Reserve is to provide trained units and qualified marines for active duty in time of war, national emergency, or such times as the national security requires. The Deputy Chief of Staff for Reserve Affairs, Headquarters, US Marine Corps, as a member of the staff of the Commandant of the Marine Corps, formulates and recommends plans and policies for the Marine Corps Reserve. Further, this individual is responsible for the organization, training, logistical support, and administration of the Marine Corps Reserve. Command relationships with the Marine Corps Reserve Support Center (MCRSC), 4th Marine Division, and the 4th Marine Aircraft Wing are shown in figure A.8.

The key element of the Marine Corps Reserve is the Selected Marine Corps Reserve (SMCR). The preponderance of the SMCR consists of a reinforced Marine division, a Marine division, a Marine aircraft wing (MAW), and a force

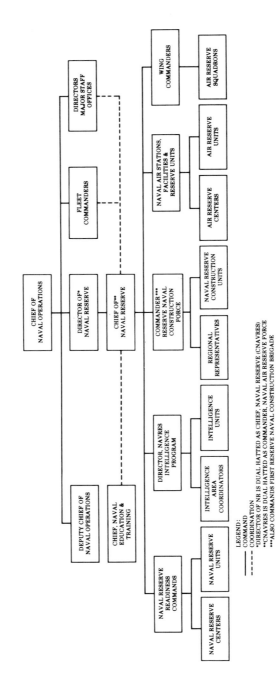

Figure A.7
NAVAL RESERVE ORGANIZATION

LEGEND:
——— COMMAND
- - - COORDINATION
*DIRECTOR OF NR IS DUAL HATTED AS CHIEF, NAVAL RESERVE (CNAVRES)
**CNAVRES IS DUAL HATTED AS COMMANDER, NAVAL AIR RESERVE FORCE
***ALSO COMMANDS FIRST RESERVE NAVAL CONSTRUCTION BRIGADE

Figure A.8
MARINE CORPS RESERVE ORGANIZATION

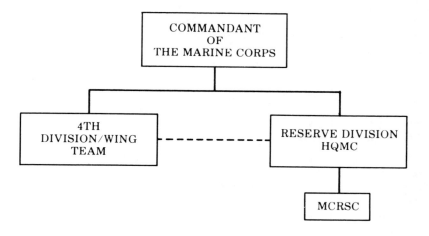

service support group (FSSG) as depicted in the organizational chart at figure A.8. The remaining element of the SMCR is composed of individual mobilization augmentees.

In the event of mobilization, the SMCR would be required to reinforce or augment active forces, and provide a Marine amphibious brigade or a 4th Division/Wing team. The Individual Ready Reserve, Standby Reserve, and Retired Reserve would provide individual Reservists to bring the Active Fleet Marine Force, SMCR units, and base support units to wartime strength.

Marine Corps Reserve training centers are at 177 locations in 45 states and the District of Columbia. The majority of units are collocated with the other Services' Reserve units to ensure maximum facility cost effectiveness.

In addition to the association with active marines during training, each SMCR unit is assigned a fulltime complement of active duty marines. Overall, the Marine Corps contributes 4,300 active officers and enlisted men to the Marine Corps Reserve. A continuous influx of marines from the active force, familiar with current Marine Corps training and equipment, produces a positive influence on unit training and provides the SMCR with a nucleus of active marines upon mobilization.

Within the total Marine Corps, the Marine Corps Reserve provides, for example, 29 percent of the observation aircraft, 34 percent of the light attack aircraft, and 33 percent of the antiaircraft missile battalions.

Coast Guard Reserve

The mission of the Coast Guard Reserve is to provide trained units and personnel for active duty in time of war or national emergencies to fill the needs of the parent Service whenever more units and personnel are needed than are in the regular component. Coast Guard mission assignments in the event of war or national emergency stem from two major sources. First, statutory missions are assigned to the Coast Guard by law. These missions include safety of the nation's ports and waterways, maritime law enforcement, search and rescue, commercial vessel safety, and polar and domestic icebreaking. Most of these activities would continue in wartime, some at increased and some at decreased levels. Some, such as port safety, would expand dramatically in wartime because of the need to protect the nation's ports and waterways. Second, war plan tasking is developed by the Joint Chiefs of Staff and assigned to the United States Navy. In turn, the Navy reassigns certain of these tasks or portions thereof to the Coast Guard. These include inshore undersea warfare, antisubmarine warfare, and coastal and high seas search and rescue.

Unlike the other US Armed Forces, which are components within the Department of Defense, the Coast Guard serves in peacetime as an agency within the Department of Transportation. In wartime or whenever the President directs, it serves in the Department of the Navy. The Coast Guard Reserve is directed by the Chief, Office of Reserve, US Coast Guard. The organization of the Coast Guard is shown at figure A.9.

The Coast Guard Reserve has a strength of approximately 22,000. Of this number over 12,300 are members of the Selected Reserve. They are assigned to

Figure A.9
ADMINISTRATIVE ORGANIZATION
OF THE COAST GUARD

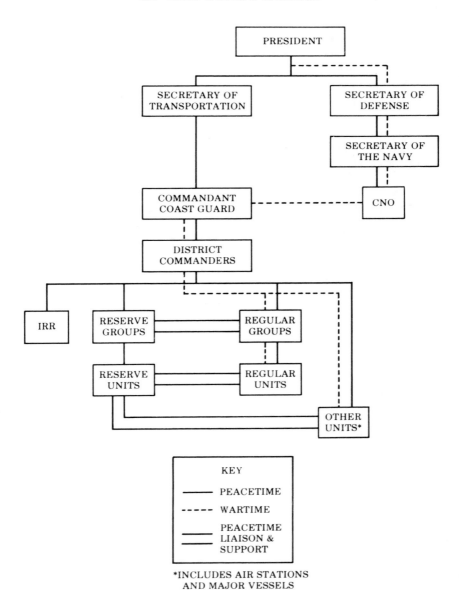

KEY

——— PEACETIME

----- WARTIME

PEACETIME
LIAISON &
SUPPORT

*INCLUDES AIR STATIONS
AND MAJOR VESSELS

over 320 Coast Guard Selected Reserve units in the United States, Puerto Rico, and Guam. These units are supervised by sixty-three Reserve group commanders who in turn report to the commanders of the twelve Coast Guard districts in which Reserve units are located.

Under the augmentation training program, particularly in major port areas, Reservists are fully integrated into the functions and responsibilities of Captain-of-the-Port operations, conducting waterfront pier inspections, safety and environmental protection patrols, and monitoring petroleum and hazardous material transfer and handling operations. At coastal search and rescue stations, Reservists are integrated into station operations, standing communication watches and participating as crew members of search and rescue boats. Many Reservists have qualified as boat coxswains and boat engineers and it is not unusual for a mixed regular/Reserve crew to have a Reserve coxswain.

Reservists who require afloat training for their mobilization billets perform augmentation training duty aboard Coast Guard cutters during their scheduled operations. Reserve training includes full integration of Reservists into the active crew at all times, both underway and in port. This training provides Reservists with practical hands-on training which simply would not be available otherwise. This kind of experience is essential to round out the formal training programs.

As an example of the contribution the Coast Guard Reserve is making to the total Coast Guard, it provides 75 percent of port safety and security, including 100 percent of explosive loading details. Of the remaining Coast Guard forces, 26 percent are Coast Guard Reservists.

Notes

Chapter 1 Notes

1. A description of this system in action can be found in Michael Prestwich, *War, Politics, and Finance under Edward I* (Totowa, NJ: Rowman and Littlefield, 1972), pp. 41–113.

2. Correlli Barnett, *Britain and Her Army, 1509–1970: A Military, Political, and Social Survey* (Bungay, Suffolk, Great Britain: Penguin Books, 1974), pp. 3–50; C.G. Cruickshank, *Elizabeth's Army*, 2nd ed. (New York: Oxford University Press, 1966), pp. 1–40; A.L. Rowse, *The Expansion of Elizabethan England* (London: Sphere Books, Ltd., 1973), pp. 373–86.

3. The principles of voluntarism and localism applied to freemen possessing full civil and political rights. If persons were excluded because of their inferior socioeconomic status, it merely limited the applicability of the principles, rather than their philosophical soundness as viewed by the mass of Englishmen.

It is also important to note that the two systems described here existed side by side for a long period of time, applying as they did to two different segments of society. In the late thirteenth century, for example, mounted knights under feudal or quasi-feudal obligation formed the majority of the cavalry, while most of the infantry were conscripts from local militia. Prestwich, *Edward I*, pp. 91, 99–105. In general, the decline of cavalry in the fifteenth and sixteenth centuries hastened the decline of the traditional royal summons of great feudal nobles and their personal retinues, as the nobility's advantage of being mounted became less important. The direct responsibility of the nobility to bring their own vassals and subjects into the military service of the Crown appears to have been shifted into a more diffuse responsibility to lead the popular mititia, resulting in a blending of the two military service traditions—that of nobles for service of the Crown and that of the people to defend the homeland. In particular, "The equation of military responsibility and socioeconomic status encouraged the belief that military talents were inherent in the well-to-do classes. Although the feudal array was in the early seventeenth century and before a military anachronism, romantic chivalric myths and hierarchical ideas about military responsibility remained." Lois G. Schwoerer, "No Standing Armies!" The Antiarmy ideology in Seventeenth Century England (Baltimore: Johns Hopkins University Press, 1947), p. 13. In the face of the obsolescence of the feudal system, therefore, leadership of the popular militia provided an outlet for the "romantic chivalric myths and hierarchical ideas about military responsibility" which still existed in the minds of the upper classes.

4. Rowse, Elizabethan England, pp. 374–75, 380–81, 384–86 makes this quite clear.

5. Barnett, Britain and Her Army, pp. 30, 36, 50.

6. Schwoerer, "No Standing Armies!" provides a detailed dissection of the roots of English antimilitary attitudes.

7. Barnett, Britain and Her Army, pp. 36–37.

8. Cyril Falls, Elizabeth's Irish Wars (London: Methuen & Co., Ltd., 1950), passim, but especially pp. 35–66.

9. Barnett, Britain and Her Army, pp. 71–76; C.V. Wedgood, The King's Peace, 1637–1641 (London: William Collins Sons & Co., Ltd., May 1972), pp. 297–326.

10. Barnett, Britain and Her Army, pp. 31–37.

11. Fully 25 percent of the white population of Virginia was killed during Opechancanough's Rebellion of 1622. Casualties were similar during the latter chief's second attack in 1644 and Kieft's War in the Hudson Valley in 1642–45. Douglas Edward Leach, Arms for Empire: A Military History of the British Colonies in North America, 1607–1763 (New York: Macmillan Co., 1973), pp. 42–77; Russel F. Weigley, History of the United States Army (New York: Macmillan Co., 1967), p. 9. Weigley's work, it should be noted, is most important for anyone examining any aspect of the history of US military manpower policy.

12. Weighley, History of the United States Army, p. 8; pp. 4–12 summarize these characteristics of the militia.

13. Leach, Arms for Empire, p. 65.

14. Ibid.

15. For example, in Arms for Empire, p. 69, Leach estimates that over 1,000 colonial soldiers and civilians died in King Philip's War. If the "worst Indian war of the seventeenth century" could result in the death of less than one percent of the estimated 1675 colonial population of 125,000, the population balance had clearly turned decisively against the Indians.

16. See Leach, Arms for Empire, pp. 80–510, passim, for a history of the wars of 1689–1763.

17. Don Higginbotham. The War of American Independence: Military Attitudes, Policies, and Practice, 1763–1789 (Bloomington, Ind.: Indiana University Press by arrangement with Macmillan Co., 1977), pp. 11–22, contains an

excellent discussion of the transmutation of European ideals of military service to the American context.

18. For Indian wars from the Revolution through the War of 1812, see Francis Paul Prucha, *The Sword of the Republic: The United States Army on the Frontier, 1783-1846* (Bloomington, Ind.: Indiana University Press by arrangement with Macmillan Co., 1977), pp. 1-118.

19. Weigley, *History of the United States Army*, pp. 86-87.

20. Ibid., pp. 93-94; Maurice Matloff, ed., *American Military History*, 1st ed., rev. (Washington, DC: Office of the Chief of Military History, United States Army, 1973), pp. 108-09.

21. An outstanding discussion of the militia—unorganized mass and organized volunteers—can be found in Marcus Cunliffe, *Soldiers and Civilians: The Martial Spirit in America, 1775-1865* (New York: The Free Press, 1973), pp. 179-254.

22. Weigley, *History of the United States Army*, p. 94.

23. R. Arthur Bowler, *Logistics and the Failure of the British Army in America, 1775-1783* (Princeton: Princeton University Press, 1975); Higginbotham, *War of American Independence*; Matloff, *American History*, pp. 58-60, provides a good short discussion of British logistical and administrative problems in waging transoceanic war in the eighteenth century.

24. John Shy, *Toward Lexington: The Role of the British Army in the Coming of the American Revolution* (Princeton: Princeton University Press, 1965), is an extraordinarily acute examination of the many reasons for growing colonial antimilitary sentiments resulting from the British Army's actions between the Seven Years War and the beginning of the Revolution.

25. Higginbotham, *War of American Independence*, pp. 392-93; and Weigley, *History of the United States Army*, pp. 41-42.

26. John Shy, in his "American Strategy: Charles Lee and the Radical Alternative," has argued that conscription of the militia amidst such a revolutionary situation was feared by the American political and military leadership, who had no desire to "change the war for independence into a genuine civil wear with all its grisly attendants—ambush, reprisal, counter-reprisal. It would tear the fabric of American life to pieces. It might even undermine the political process, and throw power to a junta." *A People Numerous and Armed: Reflections on the Military Struggle for American Independence* (New York: Oxford University Press, 1976), pp. 132-62. Higginbotham, *War for American Independence*, pp. 93-94, 432, also makes the same point.

27. Weigley, *History of the United States Army*, p. 126.

28. Richard H. Kohn, *Eagle and Sword: The Beginnings of the Military Establishment in America, 1783-1802* (New York, The Free Press, 1975), pp. 286-88.

29. Kohn, *Eagle and Sword*, pp. 277-303, has a good summary of the tensions and birth pangs of American military institutions during the twenty years immediately following the Revolution.

30. Prucha, *Sword of the Republic*, pp. 118-231, 249-318.

31. Ibid., pp. 139–92, 233–48, 339–95; Robert M. Utley, *Frontiersmen in Blue: The United States Army and the Indian, 1848–1865* (New York: Macmillan Co., 1967); Robert M. Utley, *Frontier Regulars: The United States Army and the Indian, 1866–1890* (New York: Macmillan Co., 1973).

32. There are concise descriptions of the post-War 1812 Army reforms in Matloff, *American Military History*, pp. 148–51; and Weigley, *History of the United States Army*, pp. 139–43. For the steady growth in Army Indian-fighting capability during the nineteenth century, despite numerous problems and chronic personnel shortages, see Prucha, *Sword of the Republic*, 169–92, 319–37; Utley, *Frontiersmen in Blue*, pp. 18–58, 341–59; and Utley, *Frontier Regulars*, pp. 10–92.

33. Kenneth Bourne, *Britain and the Balance of Power in North America* (London: Longsman, Green & Co., Ltd., 1967) is an authoritative discussion of this issue. A whole body of literature has grown up refuting the popular conventional wisdom that America-Canadian relations have always been good, of which the most notable is probably Charles P. Stacey's legendary "The Myth of the Unguarded Frontier, 1815–1871," *American Historical Review* 56 (1950–51): 1–18. As Bourne's study makes clear, however, contingency plans and occasional war scares do not mask the obvious if slow growth of mutual Canadian-American accommodation throughout the nineteenth century and the progressive relegation of serious plans for war to the backs of file drawers.

34. The reasons the Civil War had so little fundamental effect on American military institutions are explored in Cunliffe, *Soldiers and Civilians*, pp. 427–35; and Shy, *A People Numerous and Armed*, pp. 242–45.

35. This is exactly what happened with those militia volunteer units that were in existence before the Civil War.

36. These ideologies found more explicit expression in naval and maritime writings, led by those of Mahan, and seconded by those persons in and out of government pressing the late nineteenth and early twentieth century revitalization of US naval power. For an example of popular writing incorporating these concepts and demonstrating amazing predictive capacity for strategic and geopolitical analysis as well, see Homer Lea's two books: *The Valor of Ignorance* (New York: Harper and Brothers, 1909), and *The Day of the Saxon* (New York: Harper and Brothers, 1912).

37. Weigley, *History of the United States Army*, p. 309.

38. For a representative collection of such proposals, see Wakter Millis, ed., *American Military Thought* (Indianapolis: The Bobbs-Merrill Co., Inc., 1966), pp. 179–92, 240–61, 273–303, 342–49.

39. The Department of Defense has had occasion to prepare an official memorandum on the dual state-federal status of the National Guard, discussing both its history and current statutory basis. US, Congress, House, Committee on Armed Services, *Hearing on H.R. 871. . . S.3906. . . H.R. 1201. . . H.R. 5056. . . H.R. 12860* before Subcommittee No. 4 of the Committee on Armed Services, 93d Cong. 2d sess., 1974, pp. 9–13.

40. The militia/Reserve reforms of the 1898–1920 period are summarized in Weigley, *History of the United States Army*, pp. 320–22, 335–50, 396–400.

41. The Reserves of the Navy and Marine Corps are wholly federal in nature, as might be expected in a Service (with its land arm) whose very nature makes it a centralized institution from the moment of its inception, rather than one capable of being broken down into local subunits. That an Air National Guard exists at all is almost certainly due to the comparatively late date (1947) at which the Air Force became a separate Service; it is likely that the establishment of an independent Air Force in the infant days of military aviation (as happened with the Royal Air Force) would have precluded the Air National Guard from ever coming into existence and would have ensured a wholly federal Air Force Reserve component.

42. I have discussed the distinction between this system and more traditional conscription-based Reserve systems in two official publications. "The Applicability of Selected Foreign Military Reserve Practices to the US Reserves: Proposals Based on the Reserve Forces of the United Kingdom, Federal Republic of Germany, Israel, and the U.S.S.R.," in US, Congress, House, Committee on Armed Services, *Military Posture and H.R. 5068 (H.R. 5970), Department of Defense Authorization for Appropriations for Fiscal Year 1979, Hearings,* 95th Congress, 2d sess., pt. 5 of 7 pts., "Military Personnel," 1978, pp. 1437–1604; and US, Library of Congress, Congressional Research Service, *Military Manpower Policy and the All-Volunteer Force,* Issue Brief 77032, 12 March 1979, pp. 11–12.

43. The main reason for this latter problem was the system itself, which sustained an independent Reserve structure staffed by Reserve officers with little if any recent active duty experience (rather than the Continental European systems of cadred active units, commanded and staffed by active-force officers, filled with prior-service Reservists upon mobilization). For a survey of the extent to which this situation still exists today, see Irving Heymont, *Demographic Characteristics of Selected Reserve Components and Active Army Commanders,* Report No. CR–187, prepared for Office of the Director for Planning and Evaluation, Department of Defense (McLean, Va.: General Research Corporation, May 1977).

A second reason for this problem was the lack of a ruthless up-or-out personnel management system which regularly pruned the ranks of both regular and Reserve forces of the professionally unfit, particularly those men lacking in mental and physical drive, stamina, and endurance (often through no lack of motivation on their part). For an illuminating discussion of the latter problem during the initial phases of the World War II mobilization, see Mark Skinner Watson, *Chief of Staff: Prewar Plans and Preparations, The War Department, United States Army in World War II* (Washington, DC: Historical Division, Department of the Army, 1950) pp. 241–69.

For an excellent general summary of US Army Reserve mobilization from World War II through Vietnam, see I. Heymont and E.W. McGregor, *Review and Analysis of Recent Mobilization and Deployments of US Army Reserve Components,* Report No. RAC–CR–67, prepared for the Department of the Army (McLean, Va.: Research Analysis Corporation, October 1972).

44. A comprehensive discussion of NATO and the Warsaw Pact is found in John M. Collins, *American and Soviet Military Trends Since the Cuban Missile Crisis*

(Washington, DC: Center for Strategic and International Studies, Georgetown University, 1978), *passim*, but especially pp. 321–79.

45. The most recent statements to this effect can be found in US Department of Defense, *Annual Report, Fiscal Year 1980, Secretary of Defense Harold Brown* (Washington, DC: 25 January 1979), pp. 100–04, 284–90.

46. For two studies of the continuing vitality of the independent politiical and social base of the Reserves, one academic and the other sulphurously popular, see William F. Levantrosser, *Congress and the Citizen-Soldier: Legislative Policy-Making for the Federal Armed Forces Reserve* (Columbus, Ohio: Ohio State University Press, 1967); and Jim Dan Hill, *The Minute Man in Peace and War: A History of the National Guard* (Harrisburg, Pa.: The Stackpole Company, 1964). See also Martha Derthick, *The National Guard in Politics* (Cambridge, Mass.: Harvard University Press, 1965).

47. A concise summary of many of these programs is in US, Department of Defense, Office of the Assistant Secretary of Defense (Manpower, Reserve Affairs, and Logistics), *Manpower Requirements Report for FY 1980* (Washington, DC: February 1979), pp. IX–8, IX–9.

48. In 1965, Secretary of Defense Robert S. McNamara proposed merging the Army Reserve into the Army National Guard. See US, Congress, Senate, Committee on Armed Services, *Proposals to Realine the Army National Guard and the Army Reserve Forces, pts. 1 and 2, Hearings,* 89th Cong., lst sess., 1965; in 1973, an amendment to the FY 1974 Department of Defense Appropriations Authorization Act (Public Law 93–155, sec. 810) required the department to study the possibility of merging the Air Force and Air National Guard. See US, Department of Defense, *A Report on the Merger of the Air Force Reserve and Air National Guard* (Washington, DC: January 1975). Nothing came of either proposal. The General Accounting Office is currently attempting yet another resuscitation of the concept. See Larry Carney, "NG, Reserve Merger Recommended Again," *Army Times,* 9 April 1979, p. 6.

49. For a discussion of such proposals, noting their desirability in purely technical military terms, see my study for the House Armed Services Committee. "The Applicability of Selected Foreign Military Reserve Practices to the US Reserves," pp. 1469–80.

50. I have expanded on this theme at slightly greater length in Office of the Director of Net Assessment, Office of the Secretary of Defense; Directorate of Concepts, Headquarters US Air Force, and Defense Studies Institute, University of Edinburgh, "Method and Mystique in Military Manpower Analysis," in *Final Report of the Seminar on Soviet Military Manpower: A Focus on the Soviet Military District,* seminar held at the University of Edinburgh, Scotland, 5–7 April 1978, app. C.

Chapter 2 Notes

1. Emory Upton, *The Military Policy of the United States* (Washington, DC: Government Printing Office, 1912).

2. US War Department, General Staff, *Report on the Organization of the Land Forces of the United States* (Washington, DC: Government Printing Office, 1912), Appendix III.

3. Jim Dan Hill, *The Minute Man in Peace and War: A History of the National Guard* (Harrisburg, Pa.: Stackpole, 1964), pp. 187–89, 203–05, 218.

4. Rusell F. Weigley, *History of the United States Army* (New York: Macmillan, 1967), p. 340.

5. John M. Palmer, *America in Arms: The Experience of the United States with Military Organization* (New Haven: Yale University Press, 1941), pp. 135–36.

6. *Report on the Organization of the Land Forces*, pp. 57–59.

7. Ibid., p. 12.

8. Ibid.

9. Ibid., pp. 60–61.

10. US War Department, General Staff, Army War College, *Statement of a Proper Military Policy for the United States* (Washington, DC: Government Printing Office, 1916), p. 128.

11. US Congress, *The National Defense Act Approved 3 June 1916, As Amended to 4 March 1929* (Washington, DC: Government Printing Office, 1929), sec. 70, 73, 109, 110; pp. 59–60, 72–73.

12. John M. Palmer, *An Army of the People: The Constitution of an Effective Force of Trained Citizens* (New York: G.P. Putnam's Sons, 1916), pp. 58–62, 126.

13. Introduction by Pershing to John M. Palmer, *Washington, Lincoln, Wilson: Three War Statesmen* (Garden City, NY: Doubleday, 1930), p. xiii.

14. Palmer, *America in Arms*, p. 165.

15. Edward M. Coffman, *The Hilt of the Sword: The Career of Peyton C. March* (Madison: University of Wisconsin Press, 1966), pp. 176–77.

16. Introduction by James W. Wadsworth, Jr., to John M. Palmer, *Statesmanship or War* (Garden City, NY: Doubleday, 1927), pp. xi–xvi. Palmer, *America in Arms*, pp. 167–69.

17. Quoted in US Congress, *The National Defense: Hearings Before the Committee on Military Affairs, House of Representatives, Sixty-Ninth Congress, Second Session* (Washington, DC: Government Printing Office, 1927), p. 307.

18. Palmer, *America in Arms*, p. 169.

19. *The National Defense: Hearings*, pp. 315–16.

20. *The National Defense Act Approved 3 June 1916, As Amended*, sec. 3 and 3a, p. 10.

21. Weigley, pp. 397–400. Palmer, *America in Arms*, p. 185.

22. *The National Defense Act Approved 3 June 1916, As Amended*, sec. 2, p. 9.

23. Larry L. Bland and Sharon R. Ritenour, eds., *The Papers of George Catlett Marshall*, vol. I: *The Soldierly Spirit, December 1880–June 1939* (Baltimore: Johns Hopkins University Press, 1981), pp. 208–10. On Palmer and the Harbord Board, see *The National Defense: Hearings*, pp. 568–83.

24. Palmer, *Statesmanship or War*, pp. 162–63.

25. Palmer, *Washington, Lincoln, Wilson*, pp. 19–27, 55–61. Richard H. Kohn, *Eagle and Sword: The Beginnings of the Military Establishment in America* (New York: Free Press/Macmillan, 1975), pp. 45–47.

26. Bland and Ritenour, vol. I, pp. 46–47, 338–39, and 346.

27. Ibid., p. 313.

28. US War Department Circular No. 347, 25 August 1944, sec. III; John M. Palmer, "General Marshall Wants a Citizen Army," *Saturday Evening Post*, 18 December 1944, pp. 9–10, 56–57. This article is perhaps the briefest expression of Palmer's historical arguments for the citizen-soldier.

29. US War Department, Office of the Chief of Staff, *War Department Basic Plan for the Post-War Military Establishment*, mimeographed, November 1945.

Chapter 4 Notes

1. As quoted in *Supplementary Military Forces: Reserves, Militias, Auxiliaries,* Louis A. Zurcher and Gwyn Harries-Jenkins, eds. (Beverly Hills: Sage Publications, 1978), p. 69.

2. *Managing the Air Force,* Air War College, Department of Executive Management Studies, Maxwell AFB, Al., 23 May 1979, p. 458.

3. G.H. Fisher, *The Air Reserve Forces Study, Volume II: A Discussion of Some Conceptual Issues,* RM-5327-PR (Santa Monica: The Rand Corporation, July 1967).

4. F.J. Morgan, et al., *The Air Reserve Forces in the Total Force: Volume I, Overview and Analytical Approach,* R-1977-1-1-AF (Santa Monica: The Rand Corporation, September 1977).

5. *Purpose, Policy and Responsibilities for Air Reserve Forces (ARF),* Air Force Regulation 45-1, Department of the Air Force, Washington, DC, 5 January 1979, p. 2.

6. Bonner Day, "Air Reserve Forces Face Increasing Difficulties," *Air Force Magazine,* August 1979, p. 82.

7. Major David E. Heistand, "Utilization of Air Reserve Forces—Concepts of Management and Applications for the Future," research study prepared at the Air Command and Staff College, Air University, Maxwell AFB, Al., May 1969, p. 24.

8. "Every Air Guardsman and Reservist Fits into One of These Programs," *The Air Reservist,* May–June 1978, p. 16.

9. *Managing the Air Force,* p. 458.

10. F. J. Morgan, et al., p. 18.

11. Ibid., p. 19.

12. Lt. Col. James L. Gould, "Reserve-Active Force Comparisons," USAF Office of the Deputy Assistant Secretary of Defense (Reserve Affairs), Washington, DC, 19 November 1979.

13. *The Guard and Reserve in the Total Force,* Department of Defense, Washington, DC, June 1975, p. 24.

14. *Can the Army and Air Force Reserves Support the Active Forces Effectively?* General Accounting Office, report to the Congress, LCD 79-404 (Washington, DC: Government Printing Office, 25 April 1979), p. 125.

15. F.J. Morgan, et al., p. 22.

Chapter 5 Notes

1. Subsection 403(a), P. L. 93-365, Department of Defense Appropriation Authorization Act for FY 1975, 5 August 1974; 88 Stat. 403.

2. See the discussion of the Naval Reserve in US, Congress, Senate, Committee on Armed Services. *Department of Defense Authorization for Appropriations for Fiscal Year 1981. Hearings*, 96th Cong. 2d sess., pt. 3, Manpower and Personnel (Washington, DC: US Government Printing Office, 1980), pp. 1573-1600.

3. See Ibid, 1581-82, for an enumeration of repeated Naval Reserve mission and strength requirement studies.

4. See Department of the Navy, Office of the Secretary, *Precept for Convening a Planning Group to Develop Plans for Implementing a New Personnel System for Naval Reserve Management,"* 7 February 1977.

5. US, Congress, House, *Department of Defense Appropriations Bill, 1982; Report on the Commitee on Appropriations*, Report 97-333, 16 November 1981, p. 172.

6. See Chief of Naval Operations, *CNO Objectives for 1980*, Series 00.10062 of 11 December 1979, p. 12.

7. See Chief of Naval Operations, *Responsibility of Active Navy Commanding Officers with Respect to Assigned Naval Reserve Reinforcement/Sustaining Units*, Series 09/300739, 21 May 1981.

8. Chief of Naval Reserve message 110850 December 1981, "NAVRES 1982 Goals and Objectives."

9. See Secretary Lehman's *Department of the Navy Posture* and Admiral Hayward's *Fiscal Year 1983 Military Posture and Fiscal Year 1983 Budget of the United States Navy*, given to the House Armed Services Committee, 8 February 1982.

10. Secretary Lehman's remarks given at the 18th annual San Diego Naval Reserve Officer's Ball on 20 March 1982. *Naval Reserve Association News* 29 (May 1982): 6.

11. US, Congress, House, Committee on Armed Services, *Department of Defense Authorization for Appropriations for FY 1982, Hearings*, 97th Cong. 1st sess., pt. 6 of 6 pts., Military Personnel and Civil Defense (Washington, DC: US Government Printing Office 1981), pp. 383-408.

12. OSD estimates that 400,000 Army IRR personnel (as contrasted with the current strength of approximately 200,000) will be on the rolls by the end of FY 1985, and that this number—plus improved availability rates due to "better management" of the IRR pool—will be sufficient to meet requirements. See Office of the Secretary of Defense, *An Evaluation Report of Mobilization and Deployment Capability Based on Exercises Nifty Nugget-78 and Rex-78*, 40 June

1980, p. 15; and US, Congress, House, Committee on Armed Services, *Department of Defense Authorization for Appropriations for Fiscal Year 1981*, pt. 5 of 6 pts., Military Personnel, *Hearings*, 96th Cong. 2d sess., (Washington DC: US Government Printing Office, 1980), pp. 177–78. On the other hand, if the "improved management" initiatives designed to result in a greater proportion of the IRR pool actually being available for mobilization do not work, then estimates based on testimony of the Chief of Army Reserve imply that the Army IRR requirement would be closer to 600,000 personnel. This testimony can be found in US, Congress, Senate, Committee on Armed Services, *Department of Defense Authorization for Appropriations for Fiscal Year 1981*, pt. 2, *Hearings*, 96th Cong., 2d sess., (Washington DC: US Government Printing Office, 1980), pp. 680–81. This assumes that 70 percent of IRR personnel would be actually usable in the event of mobilization, rather than the 90–95 percent that "improved management" would lead to if successful. How *any* such figures can be verified short of actual test mobilizations is not clear. See US, General Accounting Office, *Can the Individual Reserves Fill Mobilization Needs?* GAO Report Nos. FPCD–79–3 and B–148167 (Washington DC; 28 June 1979), pp. 11–14.

13. See the *Annual Report of the Reserve Forces Policy Board* since FY 1978 for repeated recommendations that an IRR draft be considered.

14. See Office of the Secretary of Defense, testimony of Louis J. Conti, Chairman, Reserve Forces Policy Board, before the Military Personnel and Compensation Subcommittee, House Armed Services Committee, 11 March 1981, pp. 7–13; and Office of the Secretary of Defense, Reserve Forces Policy Board, *The Reserve Forces in the 1990s*, vol. 3: "Equipment Allocation/Acquisition Policies and the Guard/Reserve" (Washington DC: October 1981).

15. See *Reserve Forces in the 1990s*, vol. 3: "Equipment Allocation/Acquisition Policies and the Guard/Reserve."

16. Robert L. Goldich, "Historical Continuity in the US Military Reserve System," *Armed Forces and Society* (Fall 1980): 88–112.

17. P. L. 94–286, 14 May 1976; 90 Stat. 517; amended by P. L. 96–584; sec. 2, 23 December 1980; 94 Stat. 3377.

Chapter 6 Notes

1. Defense Manpower Commission, *Defense Manpower: The Keystone of National Security* (Washington, DC: Government Printing Office, April 1976), p. 98 (cited hereafter as *Defense Manpower*).

2. US, Department of Defense, *Annual Report Fiscal Year 1982* (Washington DC: January 1981), pp. 99, 104, 288 (cited hereafter as DOD, *Annual Report FY 1982*).

3. US, Congress, Senate, Committee on Armed Services, *Department of Defense Authorizations for Appropriation for Fiscal Year 1979*, Hearings Before the Committee on Armed Services, 95th Cong., 2d sess., 1978, pp. (2005–2008, and US, Department of Defense, *United States Military Posture for FY 1982* (Washington, DC: 1981), pp. 57–58.

4. US, Department of Defense, *Annual Report Fiscal Year 1979*, Washington, DC: 1978), p. 324; and US, Department of Defense *Manpower Requirements Report for FY 1981* (Washington, DC: February 1980), p. XI-1 (cited hereafter) as DOD, *Annual Report Fiscal Year 1979*, and *Manpower Requirements, FY 1981*, respectively).

5. *Defense 81* (September 1981):20.

6. US, Department of Defense, *Manpower Requirements Report for FY 1982* (Washington, DC: 1981), p. II-2 (cited hereafter as *Manpower Requirements, FY 1982*).

7. US, Department of Defense, *Manpower Requirements Report for FY 1979* (Washington, DC: February 1978), p. II-14 (cited hereafter as *Manpower Requirements, FY 1979*).

8. US, Department of Defense, *United States Military Posture for FY 1983* (Washington, DC: 1982), p. 53.

9. *Manpower Requirements, FY 1982*, p. X-3.

10. US, Department of Defense, *Reserve Forces Manpower Requirements Report Fiscal Year 1976* (Washington, DC: April 1975), p. 3.

11. In 1978, the Army tested a mandatory mobilization preassignment system for members of the Individual Ready Reserve (see *Manpower Requirements, FY 1979*, p. IX-9).

12. *Defense Manpower*, p. 428.

13. Ibid, p. 420.

14. Kenneth J. Coffey, *Manpower for Military Mobilization* (Washington, DC: American Enterprise Institute for Public Policy Research, 1978), p. 44.

15. Richard V. L. Cooper, *Military Manpower and the All-Volunteer Force* (Santa Monica: Rand Corporation, 1977), p. 152.

16. Ibid.

17. DOD, *Annual Report FY 1982*, p. 288.

18. *Manpower Requirements, FY 1979*, p. XIV-14, and *Defense 81* (September 1981):29.

19. DOD, *Annual Report FY 1982*, p. 289.

20. US, Congress, Senate, Committee on Appropriations, *Department of Defense Appropriations Fiscal Year 1979, Hearings Before a Subcommittee of the Committee on Appropriations*, 95th Cong., 2d sess., 1978, p. 40 (cited hereafter as *Hearings Before a Subcommittee*); see also *Manpower Requirements, FY 1982*, sections III, IV, V, and VI.

21. Cooper, *Military Manpower*, p. 150.

22. US, Department of Defense, Deputy Assistant Secretary (Reserve Affairs), *Reserve Compensation System Study, Final Report* (Washington, DC: June 1978), p. III-19.

23. US, Congress, *Department of Defense Authorizations*, p. 2003; DOD, *Annual Report FY 1982*, pp. 290-291; and US, Department of Defense *Annual Report to the Congress, Fiscal Year 1983* (Washington, DC: 8 February 1982), p. III-186.

24. Coffey, *Manpower for Military Mobilization*, p. 44; and Cooper, *Military Manpower*, p. 150.

25. Major General W. Stanford Smith, AUS (Ret.), "Reserve Readiness in a Changing Environment," *Defense Management Journal* 17 (1981):25-26; and Association of the United States Army, *A Compilation of Data, Requirements for Manning the Armed Forces in the 1980's* (Arlington, Va.: n.d.), p. 12.

26. Cooper, *Military Manpower*, p. 153.

27. *Hearings Before a Subcommittee*, p. 15, and US, Department of Defense, Assistant Secretary (Public Affairs), "Secretary of Defense Weinberger Announces Year-End Results of Volunteer Force Accessions; Reenlistments Are Encouraging," Press release, 17 November 1981, Washington, DC.

28. DOD, *Annual Report FY 1979*, p. 334; DOD, *Annual Report FY 1982*, p. 288; and Colonel Wilfred L. Ebel, USAR, "Upgrading Reserve Readiness in the Eighties," Defense Management Journal 17 (1981):37-38.

29. Cooper, *Military Manpower*, p. 154.

30. US, Department of Defense, *Reserve Compensation System Study*, p. IV-77.

31. Cooper, *Military Manpower*, p. 153; *Manpower Requirements, FY 1982*, pp. VIII-1-VIII-4; DOD, *Annual Report FY 1982*, pp. 92-93; and "The Real Manpower Issues," *Defense 82* (January 1982):5.

32. *Hearings Before a Subcommittee*, p. 55; Wayne S. Sellman and Lonnie D. Valentine, Jr., "Aptitude Testing, Enlistment Standards, and Recruit Quality" (Paper presented at the Eighty-ninth Annual Convention of the American Psychological Association, Los Angeles, California, August 1981); and US, Department of Defense, *Reserve Forces Manpower* (Washington, DC: 31 March 1980), pp. III-8-III-10.

33. DOD, *Annual Report FY 1979*, p. 325; and DOD, *Annual Report FY 1982*, p. 92.

34. DOD, *Annual Report FY 1982*, p. 8.

35. DOD, *Annual Report FY 1979*, p. 326; and DOD, *Annual Report FY 1982*, p. 92.

36. US, Congressional Budget Office, *Budget Options for Fiscal Year 1978* (Washington, DC: Government Printing Office, February 1977), p. 62; and US, Department of Defense, *United States Military Posture for FY 1983*, pp. 56–61.

37. *Defense Manpower*, p. 412.

38. US, Congress, *Department of Defense Authorizations*, p. 2408.

39. Coopers, *Military Manpower*, pp. 390–394; US, Congressional Budget Office, *Budget Options for Fiscal Year 1978*, pp. 60–66; and DOD, *Annual Report FY 1979*, pp. 327–331.

40. DOD, *Annual Report FY 1982*, pp. 272–273.

41. Association of the United States Army, *Compilation of Data*, p. 13.

42. William R. King, "The All-Volunteer Armed Forces: Status, Prospects, and Alternatives," *Military Review* 57 (September 1977):12; and "Are USAR Volunteers Good Enough?" *Army Reserve Magazine* (Fall 1981):14–15.

43. In 1966, the Department of Defense announced it would lower mental standards and admit up to 100,000 men (Project 100,000) who had previously been disqualified for military service because of educational deficiencies. These men were considered functionally illiterate. In order for the men to become useful soldiers, the Army developed a highly successful remedial reading program—one of the largest literacy programs ever instituted in the United States. Project 100,000 was terminated in 1972, but the Army continues programs to improve soldiers' reading ability (See Agnes Lee Clawson, "Teaching the Soldier to Read," *Army* (December 1974):25–26.

44. US. Department of Defense, *Reserve Compensation System Study*, p. III–46; and US, Department of Defense, *Reserve Forces Manpower* (Washington, DC: 30 June 1980), pp. II–3, III–5.

45. See US, Department of Defense, *United States Military Posture for FY 1983*, pp. 52, 60; and "The Real Manpower Issues," p. 10.

46. *Manpower Requirements, FY 1982*, p. III–13.

47. US, Department of Defense, *United States Military Posture for FY 1983*, p. 60; and *Manpower Requirements, FY 1982*, pp. I-4–I-5.

48. Cooper, *Military Manpower*, p. 282.

49. US, Department of Defense, *Reserve Compensation System Study*, pp. III-3–III-5.

50. Ibid, p. II–6.

51. *Defense 81* (September 1981):28.

52. Clifford L. Alexander, Jr., Remarks at National Guard Association Conference, October 1978.

53. *Defense Manpower*, p. 20.

54. Coffey, *Manpower for Military Mobilization*, p. 44; and Cooper, *Military Manpower*, p. 150.

55. *Defense Manpower*, p. 421.

56. Bob Pratt, "Mobilization: We Forget History's Lessons," *Army Reserve Magazine* (Spring 1982):12–13.

57. Cooper, *Military Manpower*, p. 154.

Chapter 7 Notes

1. All manpower strength numbers were obtained from *Official Guard and Reserve Manpower Strengths and Statistics*, Report RCS: DDIM (M) 1147/1148, Office, Deputy Assistant Secretary of Defense (Reserve Affairs), 30 September 1982.

Chapter 8 Notes

1. This word is borrowed unabashedly from its inventor, Victor A. Thompson, as described in "Bureaucracy and Bureaupathology" and presented in his book, *Modern Organization*, 1961. As we have used the word, it implies an irresistible, organizationally induced behavioral dysfunction, e.g., gobbledygookitis.

2. Later we will discuss Individual Mobilization Augmentees as Reserve members of active force organizations, and retirees as preassigned to mobilization positions within units or installations. Even these, however, do not represent the traditionally accepted connotations of unit membership.

3. H. Rowland Ludden, "Strategic Assessment of National Military Mobilization in the 1980s—Manpower," in *U.S. Defense Mobilization Infrastructure: Problems and Priorities*, Robert L. Pfaltzgraff and Uri Ra'anan, eds. (Medford, Mass.: Urchon Books, 1983), pp. 66–79.

4. Note the qualification of the word "reality" in terms of time. Because only change is certain, it would be an error to imply that the current consensus regarding, say, a return to conscription is an unchanging one.

5. Military Manpower Task Force, *A Report to the President on the Status and Prospects on the All-Volunteer Force*, rev. ed., November 1982, p. VI–6.

6. Under tit. 10, US Code, sec. 673, up to one million members of the Ready Reserve may be ordered to activy duty for up to twenty-four months during a national emergency declared by the President.

7. Under tit. 10, US Code, sec. 651, persons who become members of an armed force shall serve for a total of six years, i.e., a six-year military service obligation (MSO). The period of active duty may be less than six years; however, if a person is released from active duty before fulfilling the MSO, the balance must be served in the Guard or Reserve. A person may not normally be discharged until he or she completes a total of at least six years of military service. In September 1983, Congress authorized a change in the MSO from six years to not more than eight years, to be prescribed by the Secretary of Defense. An eight-year MSO was implemented in June 1984.

8. The source for all strength figures used in this paper, unless otherwise noted, is *Official Guard and Reserve Manpower Strengths and Statistics*, RCS: DD: M (M) 1147/1148, Office of the Deputy Assistant Secretary of Defense (Reserve Affairs), September 1982.

9. US, Congress, House, 95th Cong. 2d sess., Committee on Armed Services, Report No. 95–1118, *Department of Defense Appropriation Authorization Act, 1979*, p. 106.

10. US, Department of Defense, OASD (MRA&L) letter, 15 November 1982, to the General Accounting Office, Federal Personnel and Compensation Division, and an 8 September 1982, memorandum from the Deputy Assistant Secretary of the Army (Reserve Affairs and Mobilization) to the Deputy Assistant Secretary of Defense (Reserve Affairs).

11. Ibid., *A Report to the President on the Status and Prospects on the All Volunteer Force*, pp. VI–8 to VI–9. Enacted in Public Law 98–94, 24 September 1983.

12. The MSO was eight years until the mid-1950s, when it was reduced to six years, partially because of a lack of a mobilization manpower shortfall problem in view of a large active force and Selected Reserve manpower structure. The early 1970s saw a resurgence of support for an eight-year MSO. As noted in the Task Force's report to the President, an eight-year MSO for the American military would keep the average enlisted person in the IRR until about age twenty-six. In contrast, the MSO termination age range for our NATO allies is from age thirty-two to age fifty. It should be noted, however, that these nations are under military draft systems and have histories of fighting invading armies on their home territories.

13. Aggregate figures merely combine shortage skills with overage skills and ignore the issue of substitutability.

14. It might be argued that, given the necessities of war, some skills can be performed by almost anyone with little or no training, e.g., truck drivers, ammunition bearers, etc. Since all Army recruits receive some basic combat training there are those who believe that, in a "crunch," shortages of infantrymen could be filled with soldiers having other skills. The Army, however, feels such soldiers would not be effective as combat troops because they would lack the unit-oriented experience of combat operations.

15. In its *Readiness Assessment of the Reserve Components for Fiscal Year 1980*, the Reserve Forces Policy Board recommended the institution of a draft as what it considered to be the only means of correcting serious manning problems in the IRR. This recommendation was reiterated in US, Congress, Senate, 97th Cong., 1st Sess., Committee on Armed Services, Report No. 97–58, *Department of Defense Authorization for Appropriations for Fiscal Year 1982*, p. 128.

16. Of course, to be cost effective and efficient these programs must be limited to truly *critical* mobilization skills, not just to merely shortage skills. To do otherwise is to allocate limited funds inefficiently and to ignore the basic universality of many task requirements across all individuals, no matter what their fields of occupational expertise. During the fiscal year 1981 test of the IRR reenlistment bonus, the only Army occupational specialty that was not eligible for the bonus was bandsman. Any new such program with limited resources should consider targeting higher priority specialties.

17. Tit. 32, US Code, sec. 303.

18. Air National Guard members who, for various reasons, can no longer train with their units are transferred to the IRR.

19. Under tit. 10, US Code, sec. 673b, when the President determines it is necessary to augment the active forces for any operational mission, he may authorize the call of up to 100,000 Selected Reservists for up to 90 days of active duty. He may do this without the necessity of a declaration of war or national emergency.

20. See tit. 10, US Code, secs. 267(b), 273(c), 1332(b)(3), 1334(a); tit. 32, US Code, sec 303(c); and tit. 37 US Code, sec. 206(c).

21. US, Department of the Army (OCLL) memorandum, 29 October 1981, to Director of OSD Legislative Reference Service, subj.: MISC 1788, Proposed Legislation, "To amend titles 10 and 32, USC, to revise the provisions of law relating to the inactive National Guard, to establish a National Guard Augmentation Force, to authorize pay, promotion, and retirement points for members of the National Guard Force, and for other purposes."

22. Selected Reserve training categories range from Category "A" (minimum of twelve days annual training and forty-eight training assemblies) to Category "D" (minimum of twelve days annual training). All members of Selected Reserve units are in Category "A." The training category of IMAs is determined by their active force organizations and is dependent upon the amount of peacetime training necessary to insure immediate and effective performance of duty upon mobilization.

23. This was accomplished through Executive Order 12148, 20 July 1979. Other existing functions transferred or reassigned to FEMA by that order included those of the Federal Disaster Assistance Administration of the Department of Housing and Urban Development, the severe weather-related emergency readiness planning functions of the Department of Commerce, the functions of the Federal Preparedness Agency of the General Services Administration, and those functions performed by the Office of Science and Technology Policy under the provisions of the Earthquake Hazards Reduction Act of 1977 (42 U.S.C. 7701 *et seq*).

24. Paragraph 2–205, Executive Order 12148, 20 July 1979.

25. J.R. Loome; R.E. Cottle; R.L. Beskin; and R.E. Walsh, *Pretrained Individual Manpower Mobilization Policies and Procedures*. General Research Corporation for Office of the Deputy Assistant Secretary of Defense (Reserve Affairs), February 1982, p. 5–14.

26. This has been authorized by the Judge Advocate General of the Army to insure sufficient numbers of lawyers fill IMA requirements for such officers.

27. Tit. 10, US Code, sec. 268(b).

28. In fact, this argument was presented by Dr. Edward Philbin, Deputy Assistant Secretary of Defense (Reserve Affairs), in a 29 June 1982, memorandum to the Assistant Secretary of the Army for Manpower and Reserve Affairs.

29. Specifically, the Navy asserted that the reference in tit. 10 US Code sec. 268(b) to tit. 10 US Code, sec. 270(a)(1) in delineating Selective Reserve training requirements as Category A, did not include the exception language contained in tit. 10 US Code, sec. 270(a), which gives the Secretary of Defense authority to deviate from the specific provisions of the law relating to the training of Ready Reservists—including Selected Reservists, according to the Office, Secretary of Defense.

30. J.R. Loome; R.E. Cottle; and J.J. McNiff, *Pretrained Individual Manpower Study*, General Research Corporation, February 1981, pp. 5–14 to 5–18.

31. Ibid, p. 5–18.

32. Tit. 10, US Code, sec. 267. The Selected Reserve is a subset of the Ready Reserve under tit. 10, US Code, sec. 268(b).

33. Tit. 10, US Code, sec. 273.

34. US Department of Defense, DOD Directive 1235.9, *Management and Mobilization of the Standby Reserve*, 28 August 1973.

35. Tit. 10, US Code, secs. 672 and 674. It should be noted that until September 1980, the law also required the Director of the Selective Service System to determine a Standby Reservist's availability before the Department of Defense could order that person to active duty during a mobilization. At the initiative of the Office of the Secretary of Defense, and with the support of the Selective Service System, Congress passed Public Law 96–357, which deleted this requirement.

36. Basically, key civilian employees are those in a federal, state, commonwealth, territory, or local government agency, or in a DOD supporting industry whose job position involves production, research requirements, or other required activities that are vital to national defense. The designation of a position as key is done jointly by the employer and the Department of Defense. The rationale for this program is that, during a mobilization, national defense would be better served if the individual remained in his or her civilian occupation rather than called to active duty in his or her Reserve capacity.

37. Remember, by law inactive Standby Reservists cannot receive retirement points or pay for participating in Reserve training—even if such training were provided by the Services, which it is not.

38. US, Department of Defense, *Consolidated Guidance*, OSD, 12 April 1979, sec. N, p. N–11.

39. In a 23 January 1980, memorandum to the Services, the Office, Secretary of Defense (OSD) affirmed its Standby Reserve policy and provided guidance and policy changes to assist the Services. These included instructions to discharge Standby Reservists who were determined to be of no mobilization use. Further, OSD reversed its policy of transferring IRR members without military service obligations to the Standby Reserve solely if they failed to earn at least twenty-seven points a year. In a 19 March 1980 memorandum, OSD permitted the Army and Air Force to continue temporarily the transfer to the Standby Reserve of certain officers who were in danger of being twice failed for promotion and therefore faced the possibility of mandatory discharge. Under tit. 10, US Code, the Navy could retain such officers on a selective basis.

40. It is argued, not without some validity, that OSD still regards the Standby Reserve a mobilization asset since it was at OSD's initiative that Congress deleted Selective Service System involvement in the Standby Reserve mobilization process (see note 33). Why would such an initiative be necessary if there were no plans to treat Standby Reservists as mobilization assets?

41. Loome et al, *Pretrained Individual Manpower Study*, p. 6–9.

42. Includes all retirees under tit. 10, US Code, chaps. 61, 63, 65, 67, 367, 571, 573, and 867. It includes US Coast Guard (USCG) retirees under tit. 14, US Code, chaps. 11 and 12; however, these will not be discussed here since they are not considered DOD resources until control of the USCG is turned over to the Navy during wartime. The Retiree Mobilization Management Program also includes those individuals in retiree-like status; that is, members of the Fleet Reserve and the Fleet Marine Corps Reserve under tit. 10, US Code, sec. 6330.

These are enlisted personnel of the regular or Reserve Navy and Marine Corps who have completed at least twenty years of active service and who draw retainer pay in an amount equal to retirement pay.

43. Two of the Services had retiree mobilization initiatives prior to OSD initiatives in this area. In 1976, the Army began its planning for the use of retirees in a mobilization. This planning was based on the idea that, during a mobilization, retirees could be utilized in Continental United States installations, thus freeing active duty personnel for combat overseas duty. This, in fact, became a primary rationale for implementing the DOD-wide Retiree Mobilization Management Program. In addition, the Navy had fully instituted its Convoy Commodores Program whereby a number of retired Navy captains are preassigned to assume command of convoy staffs during mobilization.

44. Tit. 10, US Code, sec. 688.

45. Ibid.

46. US, Department of Defense, DOD Directive 1352.1, *Management and Mobilization of Regular and Reserve Retired Members*, 28 July 1983, prohibits the recall of retired Reservists unless they are eligible for retired pay at age 60 or are receiving Reserve retirement pay.

47. This situation is, in large part, created by DOD policy under the provisions of para. II.C.2.a. (3) and (4) of DOD Directive 1200.15, 16 February 1973, *Assignment to and Transfer Between Reserve Categories, Discharge from Reserve Status, Transfer to the Retired Reserve and Notification of Eligibility for Retired Pay*. This directive permits a physically disabled Reservist with as little as one day's service, or any other Reservist with as little as ten year's active service, to transfer to the Retired Reserve. What are unofficially referred to as Honorary Retirees are also put into the Retired Reserve. The law contributes to the situation also. The provisions of tit. 10, US Code, sec. 274, are so flexible as to permit this casual manning of the Retired Reserve. Although DOD Directive 1352.1 precludes the recall of these individuals to active duty, their presence on the rolls of the Retired Reserve clearly distorts the viability of the Retired Reserve as a mobilization asset.

48. Tit. 10, US Code, sec. 672.

49. There are numerous sections of law that delineate or imply a Reservist's option to either discharge or transfer to the Retired Reserve, including tit. 10, US Code, secs. 269, 274, 1002, 3375, 3843, 3850, 6389, 6410, 8843, and 8851.

50. The term "yield rate" is also referred to in various DOD literature as "yield goals," "show rate," "show rate goals," etc. In 1980, the Office, Secretary of Defense (OSD) proclaimed that "yield goal," rather than "show rate," was the proper term because, in addition to recognizing the reality that some Reservists and retirees would not be available to report for active duty for various reasons, the term removes the passive implication that OSD will merely wait for its members to "show up" for a mobilization! There is, however a valid distinction between a "goal," which is a desired objective, and a "rate," which is an actual or a predicted achievement.

51. US, Department of Defense, *Guard and Reserve in the Total Force* ("The Total Force Study"), July 1974.

52. Over the past few years, the *Consolidated Guidance* has taken several forms. Sometimes it is merely a memorandum summarizing discussions and firm or tentative agreements between senior Defense officials and Service Secretaries. At other times it consists of a "final" draft document that is never put in final form. For fiscal years 1982–1986, a supplement to the *Consolidated Guidance* regarding logistics and manpower programs took the form of a memorandum from an Assistant Secretary of Defense. For fiscal years 1983–1987, the Secretary of Defense formally issued a classified memorandum on 10 June 1981, with the unclassified title: *FY 83–87 Defense Guidance*. Consolidated and Defense Guidances are classified; however, the data referred to in the text are unclassified.

53. Strategic Studies Institue, US Army War College, *Feasibility of Predicting Reserve Show Rate at Mobilization: A Proposed Model for Mobilization Manpower Management*, ACN 78067, Carlisle Barracks, Penn. 18 July 1979.

54. US Army Concepts Analysis Agency, *Mobilization Manpower Policy Analysis Study (U)*, (S), Study Report CAA–SR–81–13, Bethesda, Md., September 1981. All data used are unclassified.

55. The Army study states it is DOD policy that military persons under eighteen years old not be deployed to a combat zone. This is not necessarily a "loss" but could create assignment and mobilization turbulence. It is Army policy to permit members in mid-semester or mid-quarter college study on a fulltime basis, and single members with dependents who document that mobilization would cause an undue hardship, to delay entry on active duty. These latter individuals, however, should be in the active status of the Standby Reserve rather than in the Ready Reserve under the provisions of DOD Directive 1200.7, *Screening the Ready Reserve*, 28 November 1978, and DOD Directive 1235.9, *Management and Mobilization of the Standby Reserve*, 28 August 1973. It is also Army policy that if before a mobilization alert, a Reservist has an approved, but unconsummated, discharge by reason of having four or more dependents, the discharge will be consummated rather than rescinded. Reconsideration of such a policy might be appropriate.

56. Ibid., *A Report to the President on the Status and Prospects of the All-Volunteer Force*, p. VI-9.

57. The Air Force still does not issue Reserve identification cards to its IRR members, contrary to the provisions of DOD Directive 1000.13, *Identification Cards for Members of the Uniformed Services, their Dependents, and Other Eligible Personnel*, 16 July 1979. It's surprising that these individuals even appreciate their military status or that they have knowledge of their potential mobilization responsibilities!

Chapter 10 Notes

1. A detailed discussion of the dependency of each Military Service upon its Reserve component for wartime logistics functions is provided in four working notes under LMI Task ML206: "Army Reserve Components and Logistics Support Functions," April 1982; "Air Force Logistics and the Reserve Components," August 1982; "Navy Reserve and Logistic Support Functions," September 1982; and "Marine Corps Reserve and Logistic Support," October 1982.

2. Another twenty support training and specialized missions.

3. Aircraft intermediate maintenance capability is organic to the Air Wing.

Chapter 13 Notes

1. Planners within the Pentagon have estimated reporting percentages from the various Reserve categories. These were based on evaluations of the mobilizations of 1940, 1950, 1961, and 1968, with allowances for better management and control. Despite the fact that the Standby and Retired Reserves have never been activated and the United States has not fully mobilized since 1940, the Pentagon estimates that 95 percent of the Selected Reserve unit members, 70 percent of the IRR, and 50 percent of the Standby Reserve would respond to a mobilization call. Both the percentages for the Selected Reserve and the Individual Ready Reserve are higher than historical precedents. See US, Department of Defense, Secretary, *The Guard and Reserve in the Total Force* (Washington, DC: Department of Defense, 1975), p. 11; see also, Richard D. Crossland, "Suppose the Balloon Goes Up: Then What?" *Army Reserve Magazine* (Winter 1981): 24–27.

2. US, Department of Defense, Office of the Secretary, *A Report to Congress on US Conventional Reinforcements for NATO* (Washington, DC: Department of Defense, 1976), p. IX–3.

3. Although the requirements for the mobilized force structure have not changed significantly since 1964, estimated combat replacement needs have increased, primarily because of the high casualty rates of the 1973 Middle East war. Consequently, if a mobilization had occurred in 1964, the manpower surpluses would have been even greater than indicated. [Editor's Note: Coffey's assertion that the Army's capability to meet its mobilization requirements "has been seriously eroded" is based on his calculation of a 153,000 manpower shortfall at the end of fiscal year 1980. Using Coffey's methodology, the Army's mobilization shortfall at the end of fiscal year 1982 was "only" 4,800 personnel, still an erosion of mobilization capabilities from the fiscal year 1964 surplus. It should be noted that Coffey's methodology ignores the Army's resources under the retiree preassignment program and the Inactive National Guard. On the other hand, the reduced requirement in fiscal year 1982 is primarily a result of the DOD's redefinition of the proper full mobilization scenario, a situation that many in the Congress refer to as a convenient sleight of hand to reduce the manpower shortfall. Nevertheless, regardless of the level of the Army's projected mobilization shortfall, most experts within the Army, the rest of DOD, and the Congress agree that there would, indeed, be a shortfall.]

4. Statement of Dr. John P. White, Assistant Secretary of Defense (Manpower, Reserve Affairs, and Logistics), made before the House of Representatives, Budget Committee, *Hearings Before the Task Force on National Security*, 13 July 1977, Tab R–5, "Standby Draft."

5. Statement of William K. Brehm, Assistant Secretary of Defense (Manpower, Reserve Affairs, and Logistics), made before the House of Representatives, Committee on Armed Services, *Hearings on the Selective Service System*, 27–29 January and 2–3 February 1976.

6. US, Congress, House, Appropriations Committee, *Department of Defense Appropriations for 1976* (Washington, DC: Government Printing Office, 1975), pt. I, p. 105, and US, Department of Defense, *Annual Report Fiscal Year 1982* (Washington, DC: January 1981), p. 204.

7. US, Congress, Senate, Committee on Armed Services, *Fiscal Year 1978 Authorization for Military Procurement, Research, and Development, and Active Duty, Selected Reserve, and Civilian Personnel Strengths, Hearings,* March–April 1977, p. 2436.

8. US, Department of Defense, *United States Military Posture for FY 1983* (Washington, DC: 1982), p. 55.

9. Estimate by former Secretary of Defense Harold Brown, quoted in "US Ground Forces: Inappropriate Objectives, Unacceptable Costs," *Defense Monitor* (November 1978): 5. A more detailed analysis of the US airlift capability was provided by the US Army to the Library of Congress and is cited in Library of Congress, Congressional Reference Service, *United States/Soviet Military Balance: A Frame of Reference for Congress* (Washington, DC: 1976), p. 30. The Army estimate stated that the planned move of the Eighty-second Airborne Division to the Middle East in 1973 would have required one week if alert times had permitted prior preparation and longer if not. This move would have involved a somewhat smaller than normal US division (approximately 11,000 men), a basic load of ammunition, and five days' supply of rations and fuel.

10. US, Department of Defense, *Annual Report Fiscal Year 1982*, pp. 200–203.

11. Kent J. Carroll, Vice Admiral, USN, "Sealift. . . . The Achilles' Heel of American Mobility," *Defense 82* (August 1982): 9–13.

12. The main airfield reception area for C–5 transports in West Germany has been Frankfurt's Rhein/Main airport, which is only 178 miles from the East German border.

13. The POMCUS equipment and supplies are located east of the Rhine River and reasonably close to major airfields (and to the border with East Germany). Equipment is maintained in controlled humidity warehouses, covered storage facilities, and some open storage facilities (see Colonel W.D. Glasson, NGUS (Ret.), "POMCUS: The Most Affordable Alternative?" *National Defense* (December 1981): 28–30, and US, Department of Defense, *Annual Report to the Congress, Fiscal Year 1983* (Washington, DC: 8 February 1982), pp. III-96–III-98).

14. Prepositioned war reserve stocks are a separate category of equipment from POMCUS, though many of the same items are contained in each. POMCUS equips dual-based units; war reserve stocks replace items such as ammunition and tanks that are likely to be expended once a conflict begins.

15. Richard Burt reported in 1978 that the US five-year defense plan called for the provision of war reserve stocks for a ninety-day conflict (see "US Analysis Doubts There Can Be Victor in Major Atomic War," *New York Times*, 6 January 1978, pp. A–1 and A–4).

16. Eric C. Ludvigsen, "Huskier NATO Heads '79 Defense Priorities," *Army* (March 1978): 16; Bob Pratt, "Mobilization: We Forget History's Lessons,"

Army Reserve Magazine (Spring 1982): 12–13; and Roy A. Werner, "Our Logistics Lag: How Sharp the Teeth if Tail Won't Thrash?" *Army* (February 1982): 32.

17. US, Department of Defense, *Annual Report to the Congress, Fiscal Year 1983*, p. III–154.

18. US, Congress, House, Committee on Armed Services, Special Subcommittee on NATO Standardization, Interoperability, and Readiness, *NATO Standardization, Interoperability, and Readiness* (Washington, DC: Government Printing Office, 1979), p. 2, and Werner, "Our Logistics Lag," p. 32.

19. In 1976, a leading DOD official expressed a concern about the need for an even longer "sustaining" capability. Testifying before the Senate Armed Services Committee, the Assistant Secretary of Defense (Manpower and Reserve Affairs) spoke at length about the Army's manpower shortfall problems in Europe for the first seven months following a mobilization (see statement of William K. Brehm before the Subcommittee on Manpower and Personnel, Senate Committee on Armed Services, 6 February 1976).

20. A special congressional subcommittee determined in 1979 that the European NATO countries lack the capability to fight for thirty days and that plans did not provide for achieving such a capability until 1983 (see US, Congress, House, *NATO Standardization, Interoperability, and Readiness*, p. 2; also see Sloss, *NATO Reform*, p. 34).

21. See, for example, Sir Bernard Burrows and Christopher Irwin, *The Security of Western Europe* (London: Charles Knight, 1972), pp. 63–64, and Edward L. King, *The Death of an Army: A Pre-Mortem* (New York: Saturday Review Press, 1972), pp. 140–143.

22. Neville Brown, *Strategic Mobility* (New York: Praeger, 1964), p. 199.

23. Morton H. Halperin, *National Security Policy-Making* (Lexington, MA: D.C. Heath, 1975), p. 162.

Chapter 14 Notes

2. For the history of petitioner's first commmunity essentiality case, see *Karlin v. Reed*, 584 F. 2d 365 (10th cir. 1978).

3. Office of the Secretary of Defense, *Review of the Guard and Reserve: A Framework for Action* 5 (28 December 1979).

4. 417 US 733 (1974).

5. Jacobs, "Legal Changes Within the United States Armed Forces Since World War II," 4 *Armed Forces & Soc'y*, 391, 404 (1978).

6. Snow, "Current Nuclear Deterrence Thinking." 23 *Int'l Stud. Q.* 445, 458–59 (1979); J. Collins. *US-Soviet Military Balance: Concepts and Capabilities 1960–1980*, at 46–47 (1980). Collins offers a comprehensive sketch of the military balance between the superpowers at 25–38.

7. Record, "France 1940 and the NATO Center 1980: A Disquieting Comparison," *Strategic Rev.* 67, 73 (Summer 1980).

8. J. Hackett, *The Third World War: August 1985* (1978).

9. Civil No. S79-0437(C) (S.D. Miss., 13 February 1980), *aff'd mem.*, No. 80-3250 (5th Cir., 29 December 1980).

10. *Id.*, slip op. at 2.

11. These observations are based on the author's participation in the trial of this case and extensive interviews with Col. (Dr.) Alexander M. Sloan, the hospital commander, and other medical personnel both prior and subsequent to the hearing held in this matter on 24 January 1980.

12. *Miller v. Sloan*, No. 80-3250 (5th Cir., 29 December 1980).

13. Fialka, "The Grim Lessons of Nifty Nugget," *Army* 14, 17 (April 1980).

14. "United States Not Medically Ready for European War, Military MDs Assert," *Am. Med. News*, 5 December 1980, at 13.

15. K. Coffey, *Strategic Implications of the All-Volunteer Force*, 103–10 (1979).

16. *Opened for signature*, 4 April 1949, 63 Stat. 2241, T.I.A.S. No. 1964, 34 U.N.T.S. 243; Accession of the Federal Republic of Germany, *opened for signature*, 23 October 1954, 6 U.S.T. 5707, T.I.A.S. No. 2390, 126 U.N.T.S. 350.

17. D. Middleton, *Can America Win the Next War?* 15–16 (1975); Nunn & Bartlett, "NATO and the New Soviet Threat," 15 *Atlantic Community Q.* 18, 19 (Spring 1977).

18. Carter, "The Heart of Our Foreign Policy," 15 *Atlantic Community Q.* 133 (Summer 1977).

19. Wormer, "NATO Defenses and Tactical Nuclear Weapons, 16 *Atlantic Community Q.* 22 (Spring 1978).

20. Kissinger, "NATO—The Next Thirty Years," 17 *Atlantic Community Q.* 464, 470 (Winter 1979–80).

21. Address by former Secretary of Defense Harold Brown at the Naval War College, Newport, Rhode Island (20 August 1980) (OASD (Public Affairs)) News Release No. 344–80, at 6.

22. *Id.* at 5–9.

23. Vernon, "Soviet Options for War in Europe: Nuclear or Conventional?," *Strategic Rev.* 56, 60 (Winter 1979).

24. Worner, *supra* note 19, at 24.

25. Scowcroft, "A Military Report," 17 *Atlantic Community Q.* 411, 413–14 (Winter 1979–80).

28. Nunn & Bartlett, *supra* note 17, at 18.

29. *Id.*

30. Carter, *supra* note 18, at 135.

32. Canby, "General Purpose Forces," 5 *Int'l Security Rev.* 317, 330 (Fall 1980).

33. See generally, "The Defense Production Gap: Why the US Can't Rearm Fast," *Bus. Week,* 4 February 1980, at 80.

34. J. Collins, *supra* note 6, at 540–41, table 24.

36. Nunn & Bartlett, *supra* note 17, at 28.

37. J. Collins, *supra* note 6, at 316.

38. Joint Chiefs of Staff, *FY 1982 United States Military Posture* 11 (Supp. 1981).

39. Dep't of Defense, *supra* note 31, at 48–49.

40. Coffey, "Defending Europe Against a Conventional Attack," *Air U. Rev.* 47, 56 (January–February 1980).

41. Dep't of Defense, *DOD Annual Report: Fiscal Year 1982,* at 104 (1981).

43. G.A.O., Rep. No. LCD 79–404, *Can the Army and Air Force Reserves Support the Active Forces Effectively?* 131 (1979).

44. Office of the Secretary of Defense, *supra* note 3, at 5, 34.

45. J. Collins, *supra* note 6, at 92; see also, G.A.O., *supra* note 43, at 42–44.

46. The 130,000 projection was used in the Nifty Nugget scenario. Fialka, "The Grim Lessons of Nifty Nugget," *supra* note 13, at 17. Coffey suggests the 200,000 casualty figure over a somewhat longer period of 120 days. K. Coffey, *supra* note 5, at 79.

47. J. Collins, *supra* note 6, at 308–10.

48. *Id.* at 310.

49. Worner, *supra* note 19, at 24, 26; J. Collin, *supra* note 6, at 309.

50. See Nunn & Bartlett, *supra* note 17, at 24, 26–27.

51. See generally, O'Meara, "The Democratic Army and the Nation State," *Parameters* 35 (June 1978).

52. The Military Airlift Command estimates it would lose one-third of its strategic transport aircraft within the first 180 days of a full-scale European war. J. Collins, *supra* note 6, at 272 n. 22.

53. K. Coffey, *supra* note 15, at 124, 127, 133 n. 24; Coffey, *supra* note 40, at 52–53, 59 n. 12.

54. K. Coffey, *supra* note 15, at 127.

55. Fialka, "The Grim Lessons of Nifty Nugget," *supra* note 13, at 17.

56. See generally, Burton, "CB Winds of Change," *Mil. Rev.* 22 (December 1980); Dashiell, "A Realistic Look at Chemical Warfare," *Defense* 81, at 16 (January 1981).

57. See "The Defense Production Gap," *supra* note 33.

58. K. Coffey, *supra* note 15, at 139; Coffey, *supra* note 40, at 57.

59. Office of the Secretary of Defense, *supra* note 3, at 5, 34.

60. *Id.* at 4.

61. Fialka, "The Grim Lessons of Nifty Nugget," *supra* note 13, at 17.

62. Owen, "Chosin Reservoir Remembered," *Marine Corps Gazette* 52, 53 (December 1980).

63. Congressional Budget Office, *Improving the Readiness of the Army Reserve and National Guard: A Framework for Debate* 21 (1978).

64. Fialka, "The Grim Lessons of Nifty Nugget," *supra* note 13, at 17.

65. See *Am. Med. News, supra* note 14.

66. For an enlightening discussion of the impact of cost, complexity, and numbers in tactical air combat, see Fallows, "America's High-Tech Weaponry," *The Atlantic* 21 (May 1981).

67. See generally, McGrath, "Evasion and Escape: Still a Stepchild," *Air U. Rev.* 47 (September–October 1976).

68. See, e.g., Schoch, "Tactics of Desperation," *Army Logistican* 16 (May–June 1980).

69. See, e.g., Barlotta, "Basic Training: The Verge of Destruction," *Mil. Rev.* 47 (November 1980).

70. See, e.g., Congressional Budget Office, *supra* note 49, at 31.

71. R. Gabriel & P. Savage, *Crisis in Command* (1978).

72. Jacobowitz, "Alienation, Anomie, and Combat Effectiveness," *Air U. Rev.* 21 (September–October 1980).

73. Sorley, "Turbulence at the Top: Our Peripatetic Generals," *Army* 14 (March 1981).

74. See Coffey, *supra* note 40, at 49, Table II.

75. Seib, "Army Reserve Is Hurt by Shortages of Personnel and Sharp Drop in Enlistees' Educational Levels," *Wall Street Journal*, 23 April 1981, at 56.

76. Barlotta, *supra* note 69, at 55; Jacobowitz, *supra* note 72, at 28.

77. G.A.O., *supra* note 76, at 51.

78. See generally, Landrum, "The Changing Military Family: Impacts on Readiness," *Parameters* 78 (September 1980).

79. See generally, Adams, "Jane Crow in the Army: Obstacles to Sexual Integration," *Psychology Today* 50 (October 1980); Beck "Women as Warriors," *Army* 26 (February 1981); Cropsey, "The Military Manpower Crisis: Women in Combat?" *Public Interest 58* (Fall 1980).

80. K. Coffey, *supra* note 15, at 8.

81. Jacobs, *supra* note 5, at 404.

82. K. Coffey, *supra* note 15, at 12.

83. *Id.* at 14.

84. Casualty figures obtained from the US Army Center of Military History, Washington, DC.

85. J. Helmer, *Bringing the War Home* 27, n. 63 (1974).

86. R. Gabriel & P. Savage, *Crisis in Command* 11–12 (1978).

87. See note 46 and accompanying text *supra*.

88. *Am. Med. News, supra* note 14.

89. *Ex parte* Merryman, 17 F. Cas. 144 (Taney, Circuit Justice 1861), reprinted in *The Milligan Case* 459, 473 (S. Klaus ed. 1929). See J. Anthony, *Hawaii Under Army Rule* 69, 178–79 (1955).

90. *Strait v. Laird*, 406 US 231, 351 (1972).

91. *Arver v. United States*, 245 US 366 (1918).

92. *Arbitman v. Woodside*, 258 F. 441, 442 (4th Cir. 1918).

93. *Ex parte* Steward, 47 F. Supp. 410, 413 (S.D. Cal. 1942).

94. *Arbitman v. Woodside*, 248 F. at 442. Accord, *Ex parte* Thieret, 268 F. 472, 476 (6th Cir. 1920); *Napore v. Rowe*, 256 F. 832, 834 (9th Cir. 1919); *Franke v. Murray*, 248 F. 865, 869 (8th Cir. 1918); *Angelus v. Sullivan*, 246 F. 54, 64 (2d Cir. 1917).

99. United States *ex rel. McKiever v. Jack*, 351 F. 2nd 673 (2d Cir. 1965).

100. 57 F. Supp. 884 (N.D. Tex. 1944).

103. 114 US 564 (1885).

104. *Jones v. Cunningham*, 371 US 236 (1963).

105. *Donigian v. Laird*, 308 F. Supp. 449, 451 (D. Md. 1969).

106. 398 F. 2d 705 (2d Cir. 1968).

107. *Id.* at 711.

108. 308 F. Supp. 449 (D. Md. 1969).

109. 329 US 304 (1946).

110. 401 US 487 (1971).

111. Id. at 489.

112. 405 US 34 39 (1972).

113. *Strait v. Laird*, 406 US 341, 350 (1972).

114. 406 US 341 (1972).

115. *Id*. at 343–44. Active duty personnel, however, must still file in the district wherein their commander or custodian can be found. *Schlanger v. Seamans*, 401 US 487 (1971).

116. 124 F. 2d 68 (5th Cir. 1941).

118. 393 US 233, 241 (1968)

119. Civil No. S79–0437 (C) (S.D. Miss., 13 February 1980), *aff'd mem.*, 80–3250 (5th Cir., 29 December 1980).

120. *Strait v. Laird*, 406 US 241 (1972).

121. See *Harris v. Nelson*, 394 US 286 (1969).

122. *Hammond v. Lenfest*, 398 F. 2d 705, 708 (2d Cir. 1968); *Brown v. McNamara*, 263 F. Supp. 686, 691 (D.N.J. 1967), *aff'd*, 387 F. 2d 150 (3d Cir.), *cert. denied*, 390 US 1005 (1968).

123. *Sanger v. Seamans* 507 F. 2d 814 (9th Cir. 1974).

124. *Welsh v. United States*, 398 US 333, 344 (1970).

125. 380 US 163, 184 (1965).

126. 398 US 333 (1970).

127. *Id*. at 367.

128. 403 US 698.

129. *Id*. at 700.

130. See *Gillette v. United States*, 401 US 437 (1971).

131. K. Coffey, *supra* note 15, at 9.

132. Prior to its repeal in 1967, The Selective Service Act of 1948, c.625, title 1. sec. 6(j), 62 Stat. 613, required that conscientious objector claims be referred to the Department of Justice for "inquiry and hearing."

133. 32 C.F.R. sec. 75.6(d) (2) (1980).

134. Civil No. 79–903 (W.D.N.Y., filed 8 November 1979) (habeas corpus).

135. *Id*., Administrative Record at 102.

136. *Id*., Administrative Record at 18.

137. The timing of a C.O. application, although not in and of itself an adequate basis-in-fact for denying the claim, may be considered with other evidence on the question of sincerity. *Goldstein v. Middendorf*, 535 F. 2d 1339, 1344 (1st Cir. 1976).

138. 536 F. 2d 1259 (9th Cir. 1976).

139. *Id*. at 1260 (citations omitted).

140. 438 F. 2d 959 (5th Cir. 1971) (citations omitted).

141. *Id*. at 966.

142. 488 F. Supp. 674 (D. Md. 1980).

143. *Id*. at 679 (emphasis in original).

144. *Daly V. Claytor*, 472 F. Supp. 752, 755 (D. Mass. 1979) quoting *Lobis v. Secretary of the Air Force*, 519 F. 2d 304, 307 n.2 (lst Cir. 1975).

145. 403 US 698 (1971).

146. 32 C.F.R., sec. 75.6(h) (1980).

147. See, e.g., *Ansted v. Resor*, 437 F. 2d 1020, 1023 (7th Cir.), *cert. denied*, 404 US 827 (1971); *Hammond v. Lenfest*, 398 F. 2d 705, 709 (2d Cir. 1968).

148. Jacobs, *supra* note 5, at 399.

149. 137 US 147 (1890).

150. Id. at 152.

152. Jacobs, *supra* note 5, at 400.

153. Schleuter, "The Enlistment Contract: A Uniform Approach," *Mil. L. Rev.* 1, 43 (1977).

154. See *Shelton v. Brunson*, 454 F. 2d 737 (5th Cir. 1972).

155. *Novak v. Rumsfed*, 423 F. Supp. 971 (N.D. Cal. 1976); *Myers v. Parkinson*, 398 F. Supp. 727 (E.D. Wis. 1975).

156. *Larionoff v. United States*, 533 F. 2d 1167 (D.C. Cir. 1976), aff'd on other grounds, 431 US 864 (1977); *Caola v. United States*, 404 F. Supp. 1101 (D. Conn. 1975).

157. *Pence v. Brown*, 627 F. 2d 872, 875 (8th Cir. 1980); *Frentheway v. Bodenhamer*, 444 F. Supp. 275, 287 (D. Wyo. 1977).

158. 245 F. 801 (D. Mass. 1917).

159. *Id*. at 803.

160. 493 F. 2d 748, 750 (5th Cir. 1974). *Accord, Johnson v. Chafee*, 469 F. 2d 1216 (9th Cir. 1972); *Shelton v. Brunson*, 465 F. 2d 144 (5th Cir. 1972); *Chalfont v. Laird*, 420 F. 2d 945 (9th Cir. 1969); *Novak v. Rumsfeld*, 423 F. Supp. 971 (N.D. Cal. 1976).

161. See, e.g., *Jackson v. United States*, 573 F. 2d 1189 (Ct. Cl. 1978).

166. See Schlueter, "The Enlistment Contract: A Uniform Approach," 77 *Mil L. Rev*. 1, 42 n. 167 (1977).

174. 627 F. 2d 872 (8th Cir. 1980).

176. *Id*. at 874 (citations omitted).

206. 10 U.S.C. sec. 671a (1976).

207. Pub. L. No. 89–687, 80 Stat. 980 (1966).

208. Pub. L. No. 89–687, sec. 101(a), (b), 80 Stat. 981 (1966) (codified at 10 U.S.C. sec. 673a).

209. *Id.*, sec. 101(e) (emphasis added).

210. See *Linsalata v. Clifford*, 290 F. Supp. 338, 314 (S.D.N.Y. 1968); Exec.

Order No. 11, 392, 33 Fed. Reg. 951 (1968), *reprinted in* [1968] *US Code Cong. & Ad. News* 4685.

211. See, e.g. *Linsalata v. Clifford*, 290 F. Supp. at 341; *Pfile v. Corcoran*, 287 F. Supp. 554, 555 (D. Colo. 1968).

212. 281 F. Supp. 289 (E.D.N.Y. 1968), *aff'd mem.*, 390 F. 2d 879 (2d Cir.), *cert. denied*, 393 US 896 (1968).

213. *Id.* at 295–96.

214. See, for example, *Johnson v. Powell*, 414 F. 2d 1060, 1065 (5th Cir. 1969) (105 separate habeas corpus petitions from members of the 2nd Howitzer Battalion, 138th Artillery, Kentucky Army National Guard, enroute to Vietnam); *Driska v. Brainard*, 294 F. Supp. 425 (W.D. Wash. 1968) (class action habeas corpus proceeding involving 355 members of the 18th Cavalry, California Army National Guard, enroute to Vietnam); *Linsalata v. Clifford*, 290 F. Supp. 338 (S.D.N.Y. 1968) (class action habeas corpus proceeding involving 325 Air Force reservists, some of them on orders to Korea, from the 904th Military Airlift Group (AFRES) at Stewart AFB, New York).

215. 289 F. Supp. 812 (D. Md. 1968), *aff'd mem.*, 401 F. 2d 544 (4th Cir.), *cert. denied*, 393 US 1052 (1969) .

216. *Id.* at 817.

217. See *Morse v. Boswell*, 393 US 802.

218. 289 F. Supp. 530 (C.D. Cal. 1968).

219. *Id.* at 531.

220. 287 F. Supp. 554 (D. Colo. 1968); *accord, Schultz v. Clifford*, 303 F. Supp. 965, 970–71 (D. Minn. 1968), *aff'd*, 417 F. 2d 775 (8th Cir. 1969), *cert. denied*, 397 US 1007 (1970).

221. *Id.* at 561.

222. 445 F. 2d 592 (6th Cir. 1971).

223. *Id.* at 599.

224. *Id.* See also, *Karpinski v. Resor*, 419 F. 2d 531, 533 (3d Cir. 1969).

228. 289 F. Supp. 530 (C.D. Cal. 1968).

229. *Orloff v. Willoughby*, 345 US 83, 93 (1953).

230. *Santos v. Franklin*, 493 F. Supp. 847, 851 (E.D. Pa. 1980).

243. 345 US 83(1953).

244. *Id.* at 94–95.

245. 413 US 1 (1973).

246. *Id.* at 5.

247. *Id.* at 10.

248. *Santos v. Franklin*, 493 F. Supp. 847, 851 (E.D. Pa. 1980).

249. *Nicholson v. Brown*, 599 F. 2d 639, 645 (5th Cir. 1979).

250. 413 US 1 (1973).

251. 434 F. Supp. 826, (N.D. Tex. 1977), *aff'd mem.* 565 F. 2d 1214 (5th Cir. 1977).

252. *Id.*, 434 F. Supp. at 832–33.

253. 478 F. Supp. 960 (D.R.I. 1979).

254. *Id.* at 965.

258. *Id.* at 968.

260. *Id.* at 973.

261. *United States v. Sowul*, 447 F. 2d 1103, 1105 (9th Cir. 1971), *cert. denied*, 404 US 1023 (1972); *Byrne v. Resor*, 412 F. 2d 774, 775 (3d Cir. 1969).

262. 345 US at 93. *Accord, Schlanger v. United States*, 586 F. 2d 667 (9th Cir. 1978).

263. Civil No. S79–0437 (C) (S.D. Miss., 13 February 1980), *aff'd mem.*, No. 80–3250 (5th Cir., 29 December 1980).

264. *Id.*, slip op. at 2.

265. 472 F. Supp. 763, 776 (E.D. Pa. 1979), *rev'd on other grounds*, 639 F. 2d 1029 (3d Cir. 1981).

266. 472 F. Supp. at 776.

267. *Nicholson v. Brown*, 599 F. 2d 639, 646 (5th Cir. 1979).

268. See *Karlin v. Mark*, No. 79–3975, slip op. at 4 (5th Cir., 17 October 1980), *cert. denied*, No. 80–1048, 49 U.S.L.W. 3710 (23 March 1981).

278. See, e.g., *Harmon v. Brucker*, 355 US 579 (1958); *Beller v. Middendorf*, 632 F. 2d 788 (9th Cir. 1980), *cert. denied*, 69 L. Ed. 2d 405 (1981); *Giles v. Secretary of the Army*, 627 F. 2d 554 (D.C. Cir. 1980).

279. See, e.g., *Grieg v. United States*, 640 F. 2d 1261 (Ct. Cl. 1981); *Hary v. United States*, 618 F. 2d 704 (Ct. Cl. 1980).

280. See, e.g., *Craft v. United States*, 210 Ct. Cl. 170, 544 F. 2d 468 (1976); *Storey v. United States*, 209 Ct. Cl. 174, 531 F. 2d 985 (1976).

281. See, e.g., *Middendorf v. Henry*, 425 US 25 (1976); *Schlesinger v. Councilman*, 420 US 738 (1975).

282. As to collateral review of Article 15 proceedings, see *Campella v. United States*, 624 F. 2d 976 (Ct. Cl. 1980).

283. See, e.g., *Dynes v. Hoover*, 61 US (20 How.) 65 (1858); *Wilkes v. Dinsman*, 48 US (7 How.) 89 (1849).

284. 455 F. Supp. 291 (D.D.C. 1978).

285. 501 F. Supp. 310 (D.D.C. 1980).

286. *Id.*

287. *Id.*

288. 509 F. Supp. 586 (E.D. Pa. 1980); *rev'd*, 101 S. Ct. 2646 (1981).

289. 50 U.S.C. App. sec. 451, *et seq.* (1970).

291. See *Rostker v. Goldberg* 101 S. Ct. 2646, 2649–50 (1981).

297. *Rowland v. Tarr*, 341 F. Supp. 339, 342 (E.D. Pa. 1972).

298. *Rowland v. Tarr* 480 F. 2d 545, 547 (3d Cir. 1973).

299. 32 C.F.R. sec. 76.4(e)(6)(iii)(1980).

300. 32 C.F.R. sec. 76.4(e)(4)(ii)(1980).

301. 32 C.F.R. sec. 76.4(e)(6)(ii)(1980).

302. *Feliciano v. Laird*, 426 F. 2d 424, 427 (2d Cir. 1970).

303. 403 F. 2d 371 *cert. denied*, 394 US 929 (1971).

304. *Id.*, F. 2d at 374–75 (emphasis added).

305. See, e.g., *Nicholson v. Brown*, 599 F. 2d 639 (5th Cir. 1979); *Karlin v. Reed*, 584 F. 2d 365 (10th Cir. 1978).

306. 495 F. Supp. 1092 (E.D. Pa. 1980).

307. *Id.* at 1095, *citing Rickson v. Ward*, 359 F. Supp. 328 (S.D. Cal. 1973) and *Townley v. Resor*, 323 F. Supp. 567 (N.D. Cal. 1970); *contra, Nicholson v. Brown*, 599 F. 2d at 649.

308. 291 F. Supp. 77 (D. Md. 1968).

309. *Id.* at 79.

310. 294 F. Supp. 425 (W.D. Wash. 1968).

312. 413 U.S. 1, 10 (1973).

313. 599 F. 2d 639 (5th Cir. 1979).

314. Memorandum from the Chief, General Litigation Division, to the Judge Advocate General of the Air Force (27 November 1979), regarding "Overseas Deployment of Air Force Personnel."

315. Memorandum from Mr. Robert L. Gilliat to Mr. Raymond S. Webster (16 December 1977), reprinted in, *Reserve Readiness Legislation: Hearings on H.R. 5822, 2224, 7295, and 7294 Before the Military Personnel Subcomm. of the House Comm. on Armed Services*, 96th Cong., 2d sess. 21–22 (1980).

316. *Id.* at 22.

318. J. Helmer, *supra* note 85, at 5–7; see generally, Fligstein, "Who Served in the Military, 1940–73," 6 *Armed Forces & Soc'y* 297 (Winter 1980).

319. K. Coffey, *supra* note 15, at 32–33.

320. J. Helmer, *supra* note 85, at 6–7.

321. Fligstein, *supra* note 318, at 304–06.

324. 444 US 348, 354 (1980), quoting *Parker v. Levy*, 417 US 733, 743 (1974).

327. An unusual lack of objectivity was demonstrated in Baltimore recently by a newly elected city judge. Judge William H. Murphy, Jr., noting that he had had several deferments himself, was quoted as urging young people to use all lawful means at their disposal to resist the draft. "Judge Urges Draft Resistance," *N.Y. Times*, 8 December 1980, at 18.

328. 632 F. 2d 788 (9th Cir. 1980), *cert. denied*, 69 L. Ed. 2d 405 (1981).

331. *Id.* at 812.

332. 489 F. Supp. 964 (E.D. Wis. 1980).

333. *Id.* at 969.

334. 489 F. Supp. 976.

337. *Toth v. Quarles* 350 US 11, 17 (1955)

340. The heavy concentration of military cases in the United States Court of Claims and the United States District Court for the District of Columbia makes these forums an exception.

341. 28 U.S.C. sec. 2243 (1976).

342. 18 U.S.C. sec. 3161–3174 (1976).

343. Base-level personnel actions normally involve military justice and administrative matters. Judge Advocates at base level ordinarily lack ready access to the *Federal Reporter* system.

344. K. Coffey, *supra* note 15, at 14.

345. "New survey shows many seniors would attempt to avoid service," *Montgomery Advertiser,* 18 April 1981, at 3A.

346. This characterization of prevailing American values has been advanced by Dr. Jeffrey Record of the Institute for Policy Analysis in Washington, DC. See Record, "Is Our Military Incompetent?" *Newsweek,* 22 December 1980, at 9.

347. G.A.O., *Can The Individual Reserves Fill Mobilization Needs?, supra* note 70, at 12–13.

348. *Id.* at 13.

349. *Id.* at 14.

350. Warren, "The Bill of Rights and the Military," 37 *N.Y.U.L. Rev.* 181, 193 (1962).

351. *Brown v. Glines,* 444 US 348, 354 (1980).

352. For a discussion of the likely impact of news reports on popular opinion in the midst of a European confrontation, see Ikle, *supra* note 23, at 20.

353. See generally, Levine, "The Doctrine of Military Necessity in the Federal Court," 89 *Mil. L. Rev.* 3 (Summer 1980).

354. See notes 121–127 and accompanying text, *supra.*

355. See 32 C.F.R. sec. 75.4(a) (1980).

356. 32 C.F.R. sec. 75.5 (1980).

357. US Const., art. 1, sec. 9, cl. 2.

359. See *Ex parte Milligan,* 71 US (4 Wall) 2, 125 (1866); *Ex parte Zimmerman,* 132 F. 2d 442, 446 (9th Cir. 1942).

360. *Supra* note 16, at 63 Stat. 2244.

362. *Brown v. Glines,* 444 US 348, 369 (1980).

363. See notes 25–28 and accompanying text, *supra.*

364. *Ex parte Milligan,* 71 US (4 Wall) at 115.

368. 47 F. Supp. 410, 412–13 (S.D. Cal. 1942).

369. 71 US (4 Wall) 2 (1866).

370. *Id*. at 127.

372. *Id*. at 115.

373. *Id*. at 116.

374. *Id*. at 125–26.

375. 327 US 304 (1946).

376. 31 Stat. 304, 30 April 1900.

377. For a chronology of the events involved, see *Duncan v. Kahanamoku*, 327 US at 353–54 n.6.

378. 132 F. 2d 442 (9th Cir. 1942).

380. *Ex parte Duncan*, 146 F. 2d 576 (9th Cir. 1944), *rev'd* 327 US 304 (1946).

381. *Duncan v. Kahanamoku*, 327 US at 313.

382. *Id*. at 324.

383. *Id*. at 312, n.5.

384. *Id*. at 327–28.

385. Warren, *supra* note 350, at 192.

386. Cf. *Gilligan v. Morgan*, 413 US 1, 10–11 (1973).

387. E.g., *Schenk v. United States*, 249 US 47 (1919); *Frohwerk v. United States*, 249 US 204 (1919).

388. *Korematsu v. United States*, 323 US 214 (1944); *Hirabayashi v. United States*, 320 US 81 (1943).

389. Warren, *supra* note 350, at 191–92.

390. *Brown v. Glines*, 444 US 348, 354 (1980). As outlined above, this proposal does not reach either the civilian pilots who would man the Civil Reserve Air Fleet upon mobilization or the civilian mariners who would man the Ready Reserve Force of the National Defense Reserve Fleet. Two of the most essential links in the reinforcement chain are thus the province of civilians over whom, at least in the short run, the government can exercise little or no control even after mobilization gets underway. The failure of either group to respond fully could seriously impede the reinforcement process. To insure a more certain response, it may be appropriate to consider a special type of reserve status for those personnel identified to man CRAF and the Ready Reserve Force.

Selected References

Abert, J.G. "The Naval Reserve Should Work," *US Naval Institute Proceedings*, February 1980, pp. 49–53.

Brinkerhoff, J.R., and Lindsay, W.A. "A Comprehensive Model for a Total-Force Military Personnel System," *Defense Management Journal* 14 (July 1978): 4–11.

Canby S.L. "European Mobilization: US and NATO Reserves," *Armed Forces & Society* 4 (Winter 1978): 227–244.

Chase, H.W. "Guard & Reserve: Better But Not Good Enough," *Defense/80,* November 1980, pp. 12–17.

Coffee, K.J. *Manpower for Military Mobilization.* Washington, D.C.: American Enterprise Institute for Public Policy Research, 1978.

Cooper, R.V.L. *Military Manpower and the All-Volunteer Force.* Santa Monica, CA: Rand Corporation, 1977.

Derthick, M. *The National Guard in Politics.* Cambridge, Mass: Harvard University Press, 1965.

Heymont, I. "Can Reserve Support Units be Ready in Time? *Army* 32 (September 1982): 31–33, 36.

Heymont, I., and McGregor, E.W. *Review and Analysis of Recent Mobilizations and Deployments of US Army Reserve Components,* Report No. RAC–CR–67. McLean, Va.: Research Analysis Corporation, 1972.

Hill, J.D. *The Minute Man in Peace and War: A History of the National Guard.* Harrisburg, Pa.: The Stackpole Company, 1964.

Kohn, R.H. *Eagle and Sword: The Beginnings of the Military Establishment in America.* New York: Free Press/Macmillian, 1975.

Lane, J.M. "The Militia of the United States: An Analysis," *Military Review* 62 (March 1982): 12–18.

Levantrosser, W.F. *Congress and the Citizen-Soldier: Legislative Policy-Making for the Federal Armed Forces Reserve*. Columbus, Ohio: Ohio State University Press, 1967.

Lyons, R.W. "The Naval Reserve: Separate and Unequal," *US Naval Institute Proceedings*, July 1978, pp. 45–51.

Manning, L.C. "Sealift Readiness: You Don't Get What You Don't Pay For," *US Naval Institute Proceedings*, October 1981, pp. 34–43.

Palmer, J.M. *An Army of the People: The Constitution of An Effective Force of Trained Citizens*. New York: G.P. Putnam's Sons, 1916.

Reserve Forces Policy Board, *The Reserve Forces in the 1990's*. Vol. 1: *Executive Report*. Washington, DC: Office of the Secretary of Defense, 1980.

Reserve Forces Policy Board, *The Reserve Forces in the 1990's*. Vol. 3: *Equipment, Acquisition/Allocation Policies and the Guard/Reserve*. Washington, DC: Office of the Secretary of Defense, 1981.

Smith, P.E. "Challenge of the Eighties: Equipping the Guard and Reserve," *Defense Management Journal* 17 (Third Quarter 1981): 46–49.

Turley, J. "Mobilization Manpower: A Credible Force or an Empty Promise?" *Military Review* 61 (August 1981): 2–12.

US General Accounting Office, *Military Readiness, Mobilization Planning*, and *Civil Preparedness: Issues for Planning*, Report PLRD–81–6, 25 February 1981.

Weigley, R.F. *History of the United States Army*. New York: Macmillan Company, 1967.

Woller, R. *Warsaw Pact Reserve Systems: A White Paper*. Munich: Bernard & Graefe Verlag, 1978.

Editor and Contributors

Editor-Author

Bennie J. Wilson III, B.S., San Jose State College, 1965; M.B.A., University of Rochester, 1969; Ed.D., Auburn University, 1979. Colonel Wilson is a member of the US Air Force and is currently assigned as Director of Personnel, Edwards AFB, California. He recently completed a tour as a Senior Fellow, National Defense University, and he has served on the staffs of the Deputy Assistant Secretary of Defense (Reserve Affairs) and the Chief of Air Force Reserve. Colonel Wilson has also been assigned to the staff of the United States Representative to the NATO Military Committee, and as Command Education Services Director, Air University. He has been a visiting lecturer in graduate management and organizational behavior and a professor in management on the adjunct faculties of several colleges and universities. A graduate of the National War College, Colonel Wilson is the author or coauthor of numerous articles on military, education administration, and industrial relations issues.

Authors

Gerald D. Ball, B.S., United States Air Force Academy, 1969; M.A., University of California at Los Angeles, 1979; M.S. and Ph.D., Texas A&M University, 1978 and 1983. Dr. Ball is currently a Scientific Analyst, Studies and Analysis Directorate, Headquarters Air Training Command. He is also a major in the US Air Force Reserve, filling a Reserve position as Assistant Deputy Commander for Resource Management of a technical training wing. He has taught undergraduate courses in statistics and has served as undergraduate advisor within the Economics Department, Texas A&M University. Dr. Ball has contributed several articles on Reserve matters to professional military publications. He is a graduate of the Air Command and Staff College.

James W. Browning II, B.S., United States Naval Academy, 1964; M.A., Pepperdine University, 1976; M.B.A., National University, 1979; Ph.D., United States International University, 1981. Commander Browning is a member of the US Naval Reserve and currently is a member of the Senior Faculty, War Gaming and Simulation Center; National Defense University. He is a naval aviator and has served on the mobilization planning staff of the Commander of Naval Air Forces, US Pacific Fleet. He has written several articles on aviation safety for military publications. Commander Browning is a graduate of the National War College.

Jon P. Bruinooge, A.B., Tufts University, 1967; J.D., Vanderbilt University, 1970; LL.M., George Washington University, 1979. Lieutenant Colonel Bruinooge is a member of the US Air Force and is currently assigned as Civil Litigation Counsel, Office of the Judge Advocate General, Headquarters US Air Force. He is a member of the bar of the state of New Jersey and is admitted to practice before the Supreme Court of New Jersey, the US District Court for the District of New Jersey, the US Court of Military Appeals, the US Court of Claims, and the US Supreme Court. Colonel Bruinooge is a distinguished graduate of the Air Command and Staff College.

Frederick E. Bush, Jr., B.S., United States Naval Academy, 1967; M.S., George Washington University, 1971; Ed.D., University of Southern California, 1976. Lieutenant Colonel Bush is a member of the US Air Force and is currently assigned as Assistant Air Attache to the United Kingdom. He recently completed tours within Headquarters Air University, first as Assistant Chief, Officer Professional Military Education; and next as Executive Officer to the Director of Education. He formerly served as Executive Officer to the Director, Reserve Forces, Air Force Intelligence Service. Colonel Bush is a distinguished graduate of the Air Command and Staff College.

Kenneth C. Carlon, B.A., Oklahoma State University, 1968. Colonel Carlon is a member of the US Marine Corps and is currently assigned to the Operations Division, Allied Forces, Southern Europe, in Naples, Italy. He formerly served as an assignment officer, Headquarters, US Marine Corps. Colonel Carlson specializes in marine aviation and amphibious warfare and has served as the commander of a helicopter squadron. He is a graduate of the National War College.

Kenneth J. Coffey, B.S., Northwestern University, 1955; Ph.D.; University of London, 1979. Dr. Coffey currently holds the position of Associate Director for Military Personnel Studies, US General Accounting Office. Before assuming this position, he was a consultant in military manpower matters to the General Accounting Office; the Office of the Secretary of Defense; the Congressional Budget Office; and the National Security Council. Dr. Coffey has written numerous articles and books on the subject of military manpower, including *Strategic Implications of the All-Volunteer Force* and *Manpower for Military Mobilization*.

Chris C. Demchak, B.S., University of California at Riverside, 1975; M.P.A., Princeton University, 1977; M.A., University of California at Berkeley, 1980. Ms. Demchak is a Research Fellow, Logistics Management Institute (LMI), and is on temporary leave of absence from the University of California at Berkeley, where she is engaged in postgraduate study in political science and organization theory. She is also an officer in the US Army Reserve and holds a Reserve position as a war planner. She has experience in the analysis of national economic systems development and large-scale energy systems, having worked in these areas within the Organization for Economic Cooperation and Development in Paris, and at the International Institute for Applied Systems Analysis in Austria. Ms. Demchak's work with LMI currently focuses on military organizations and the application of highly technical systems.

Wilfred L. Ebel, B.A., Upper Iowa University, 1979. A member of the US Army Reserve, Colonel Ebel holds the civilian position of Assistant Director of the Selective Service System for Government and Public Affairs. He has served as the Assistant Executive Officer within President Reagan's Military Manpower Task Force, and was previously a member of the Presidential Clemency Board under President Ford. He has also served on the staff of the Defense Manpower Commission. A graduate of the Army War College, Colonel Ebel has been a frequent contributor to professional military journals on Guard and Reserve issues and on US and Soviet military history.

James R. Engelage, B.S., Southwest Missouri State University, 1965; M.S., Troy State University, 1968; M.A., Central Michigan University, 1978; Ph.D., Saint Louis University, 1977. Lieutenant Colonel Engelage is in the US Army Reserve and is currently assigned as Chief, Mobilization Manpower Team, Office of the Deputy Chief of Staff for Personnel, Department of the Army. His past assignments include service as Acting Director of Pretrained Individual Manpower, Office of the Secretary of Defense; and Assistant Executive Officer, Office of the Chief of Army Reserve. He is a member of the adjunct faculty of the Army Command and General Staff College, and has served as a professor of management on the adjunct faculty of several colleges. A graduate of the Industrial College of the Armed Forces nonresident program, Colonel Engelage has written many articles on the military and on financial and manpower management.

Robert L. Goldich, B.A., Claremont McKenna College, 1971; M.A., George Washington University, 1977. Mr. Goldich currently holds the position of Specialist in National Defense, Congressional Research Service, Library of Congress. A former Graduate Teaching Fellow in National Security Policy and International Affairs, George Washington University, he has written numerous articles for professional military journals, and has been the author or coauthor of several studies for Congress regarding defense manpower policy issues. Mr. Goldich is a graduate of the National War College.

James L. Gould, B.A., Santa Clara University, 1955; M.A., Indiana University, 1962. Colonel Gould is a US Air Force Reservist and formerly served as Director of Mobilization Planning and Operations, Office of the Deputy Assistant Secretary of Defense (Reserve Affairs). He served previously as the Reserve Forces Advisor to the Assistant Chief of Staff for Intelligence, Headquarters US Air Force. Prior to that assignment, he was Executive Associate in charge of the Ford Foundation's Foreign Area Fellowship Program. Colonel Gould is fluent in six foreign languages and is the recognized expert in the Office of the Secretary of Defense and within NATO regarding Reserve mobilization and other total-force issues. A graduate of the Air War College seminar program, Colonel Gould is a frequent contributor to articles and studies that address mobilization and other readiness concerns.

Neal F. Herbert, B.S., United States Coast Guard Academy, 1960; B.C.E., Rensselaer Polytechnic Institute, 1965; M.S.A., George Washington University, 1973. Captain Herbert is a member of the US Coast Guard and is currently assigned as Chief of the Bridge Administration Division, Headquarters US Coast Guard. He is a specialist in civil engineering and project management. Captain Herbert has served as Commanding Officer of the US Coast Guard Base, Honolulu. A graduate of the National War College, Captain Herbert is a frequent contributor to professional military journals.

Jonathan M. House, A.B., Hamilton College, 1971; M.A. and Ph.D., University of Michigan, 1972 and 1975. Captain House is a member of the United States Army and currently serves as Teaching Fellow, Combat Studies Institute, US Army Command and General Staff College. He has taught military history at the same institution, as well as at the University of Michigan, the US Army Armor School, and the US Army Intelligence Center and School. Captain House is widely respected, both in and outside of the Defense community, as an expert on the history of the US Army.

W.D. McGlasson, National Guard of the United States, retired. Currently a free-lance writer who has written several books, Colonel McGlasson is a frequent contributor to professional military journals. A former newspaper editor, he spent thirty-four years in the Army National Guard, including the Guards of Kansas, California, and the District of Columbia. He served twenty-three years on the staff of the National Guard Association of the United States, finally serving as its Deputy Executive Vice President. Colonel McGlasson is widely respected throughout the total-force community as an expert on military history and mobilization readiness.

Theodore R. Mosch, B.A., Ripon College, 1960; M.A., University of Wisconsin, 1967; M.A. and Ph.D., University of Oklahoma, 1970. A lieutenant colonel in the US Army Reserve, Dr. Mosch holds the civilian position of Professor of Political Science, University of Tennessee. His Reserve position is Individual Mobilization Augmentee within the Office of the Assistant Chief of Staff for Intelligence, Department of the Army. He has served on the faculties of the US Army Command and General Staff College and the US Army Intelligence School. Dr. Mosch has held a Ford Foundation Fellowship and a fellowship under the National Defense Education Act. He is a graduate of the National War College.

Arthur L. Moxon, (deceased), B.S., United States Air Force Academy, 1968. Major Moxon was a member of the US Air Force and, among other assignments, served for four years as Assistant Professor of Economics and Management at the Air Force Academy. He was a distinguished graduate of the Air Command and Staff College (ACSC) in 1979. After completing ACSC, Major Moxon was assigned to a tactical fighter squadron in the United Kingdom and, while on a mission, he lost his life.

Gordon R. Perkins, B.A., Columbia College, 1974; M.A., Webster College, 1974. Colonel Perkins is a member of the Army National Guard and currently serves as the National Guard Advisor to Army ROTC headquarters. He formerly held positions as Chief of the Officer's Branch within the Army Personnel Division of the National Guard Bureau, and as National Guard Advisor to the Commander, Reserve Components Personnel and Administration Center.

Colonel Perkins has also been an adjunct member of the faculty at Columbia College. He is a graduate of the National War College.

Edward J. Philbin, B.S., San Diego State University, 1957; J.D., University of San Diego, 1965. The Honorable Dr. Philbin served as Deputy Assistant Secretary of Defense (Reserve Affairs) and was the highest ranking Presidential appointee with specific staff responsibility for the management of the nation's Reserve components. He is also a colonel in the US Air Force Reserve, has served on active duty as a navigator and bombardier, and has served as a unit commander. As a Reservist he has also served as Director of Research for the Secretary of Defense Reserve Forces Policy Board. He is a tenured Professor of Law, University of San Diego School of Law, where he has also served as an Assistant Dean. He has written over two dozen articles and studies in the fields of engineering, physics, law, and military affairs. A distinguished graduate of the Air War College, Dr. Philbin was the first Reserve officer to be appointed to the Air War College faculty.

Edward D. Simms, Jr., B.S., United States Military Academy, 1969; M.S., Georgia Institute of Technology, 1975. Mr. Simms is a Research Fellow with the Logistics Management Institute (LMI) and has conducted studies involving the Reserve components and logistics war planning, the design of the total force, and the readiness of the Department of Defense logistics system. Before joining LMI he was an officer in the US Army and served in various infantry and operations research assignments. Mr. Simms has been a principal contributor to LMI studies on the training of US and Soviet tank crews, and the development of training concepts for the Reserve.

W. Stanford Smith, A.B., University of Georgia, 1941. Major General Smith is retired from the United States Army. Since his retirement, he has engaged in numerous independent research projects on behalf of the Assistant Secretary of Defense (Manpower, Reserve Affairs, and Logistics). He formerly held the position of Executive Officer, Reserve Forces Policy Board, Office of the Secretary of Defense. A graduate of the Army War College, General Smith is a frequent contributor to professional military journals on Guard and Reserve issues.

Gerald W. Swartzbaugh, B.S., Drake University, 1969; M.B.A., Auburn University, 1974. Colonel Swartzbaugh is Deputy Commander for Operations of an Iowa Air National Guard tactical fighter wing. He has served as an aircraft maintenance officer, a comptroller, and in several operational positions, including commander of a tactical fighter squadron. Colonel Swartzbaugh is a graduate of the National War College.

Joseph R. Wilk, B.S., American International College, 1959; M.S., George Washington University, 1971. Mr. Wilk is a Research Fellow at the Logistics Management Institute (LMI). Before joining the LMI staff, he served as an officer in the Supply Corps of the US Navy. Mr. Wilk has participated in LMI publications on topics that include Navy intermediate maintenance, host-nation support management, Army combat and tactical vehicle maintenance, ship operating and support costs, and transfer of tender and repair ships to the Military Sealift Command.

Index

THE GUARD AND RESERVE IN THE TOTAL FORCE
The First Decade 1973-1983

Test and display lines in Palatino
Design by *Evelyn Lakes*
Cover and title page art prepared by *Laszlo L. Bodrogi*
with display lines in University Roman
Figure illustrations by *James W. Price*

Special Credits
Editor: *Evelyn Lakes*
Editorial Clerks: *Pat Williams, Laura Hall, Carol Valentine*

☆U.S. GOVERNMENT PRINTING OFFICE: 1985-461-039:10014

NATIONAL DEFENSE UNIVERSITY PRESS
FORT LESLEY J. McNAIR
WASHINGTON, DC 20319-6000

THE NATIONAL DEFENSE UNIVERSITY

Lieutenant General Richard D. Lawrence, US Army
President

THE INSTITUTE FOR
NATIONAL STRATEGIC STUDIES

Colonel John E. Endicott, USAF
Acting Director

THE NATIONAL DEFENSE UNIVERSITY PRESS

Frederick Kiley, *Director*

Colonel Robert Kvederas, USA
Associate Director

Major Donald Anderson, USAF   Lieutenant Monica M. Cain, USN
Deputy Director for Production   *Deputy Director for Administration*

George C. Maerz, *Senior Editor*

Dora Alves, *Writer-Editor*   Janis Hietala, *Writer-Editor*
Thomas Gill, *Writer-Editor*   Edward H. Seneff II, *Writer-Editor*

L. J. Conk, *Office Supervisor*

Pat Williams, *Lead Editorial Clerk*   Laura W. Hall, *Director's Secretary*
Dorothy M. Mack, *Editorial Clerk*   Cecelia Giles, *Office Assistant*
Carol A. Valentine, *Editorial Clerk*